AFTER ONE HUNDRED WINTERS

AFTER ONE HUNDRED WINTERS

IN SEARCH OF RECONCILIATION ON AMERICA'S STOLEN LANDS

MARGARET D. JACOBS

PRINCETON UNIVERSITY PRESS

PRINCETON & OXFORD

Published by Princeton University Press
41 William Street, Princeton, New Jersey 08540
6 Oxford Street, Woodstock, Oxfordshire OX20 1TR

press.princeton.edu

All Rights Reserved
ISBN 9780691224336
ISBN (e-book) 9780691226644

British Library Cataloging-in-Publication Data is available

Editorial: Priya Nelson & Thalia Leaf
Production Editorial: Ali Parrington
Text Design: Karl Spurzem
Jacket Design: Amanda Weiss
Production: Danielle Amatucci
Publicity: Maria Whelan & Amy Stewart

Jacket illustration by Sarah Rowe

This book has been composed in Arno

Printed on acid-free paper. ∞

Printed in the United States of America

10 9 8 7 6 5 4 3 2 1

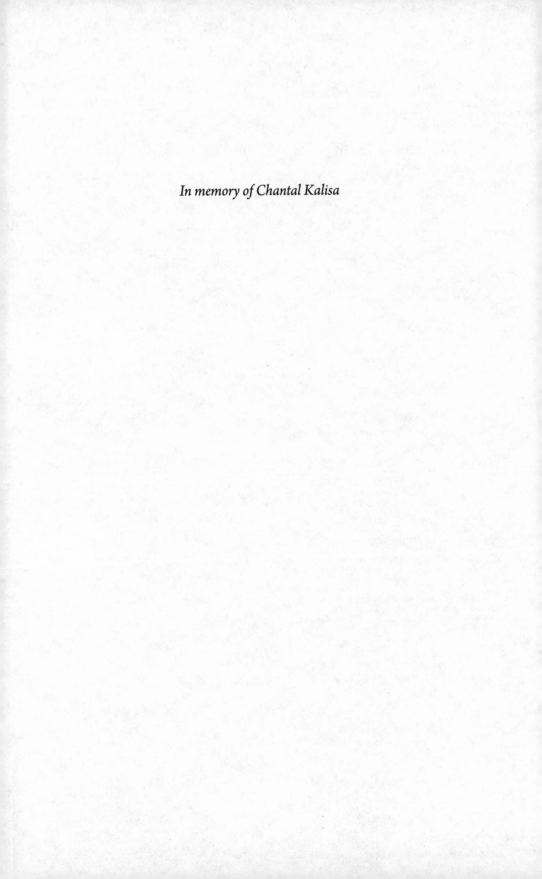

In memory of Chantal Kalisa

CONTENTS

Introduction   1

PART ONE   OUR FOUNDING CRIMES

Chapter 1   Blood   21

Chapter 2   Eyes   36

Chapter 3   Spirits   56

Chapter 4   Bellies   63

Chapter 5   Tongues   87

PART TWO   PROMOTING RECONCILIATION
         IN NINETEENTH-CENTURY AMERICA

Chapter 6   Rousing the Conscience of a Nation   109

Chapter 7   Friends of the Indian   126

Chapter 8   Indian Boarding Schools   148

PART THREE   SEARCHING FOR TRUTH AND
         RECONCILIATION IN THE TWENTY-FIRST CENTURY

Chapter 9   America's Stolen Generations   167

Chapter 10   The Hardest Word   192

Chapter 11   Where the Mouth Is   209

PART FOUR   A GROUNDSWELL FOR RECONCILIATION

Chapter 12   Skulls   233

Chapter 13   Bones   255

Chapter 14   Hands   266

Conclusion   Hearts   284

Acknowledgments   295

Notes   297

Further Reading   319

Index   329

AFTER ONE HUNDRED WINTERS

INTRODUCTION

June 10, 2018: It's a typical summer day in Nebraska—hot, humid, hazy. An insistent wind blows the heat around, like a convection oven. We are on a farm. Yes, there will be corn. The farmers Art and Helen Tanderup are white and in their sixties. Art is portly, a bit aloof and gruff. Helen exudes both stand-by-your-man farm wife and tough-as-nails take-no-crap rural woman.

This farm has been in Helen's family ever since the late nineteenth century, pioneering days. If you are imagining a two-story clapboard farmhouse, circa 1900, with a big porch, surrounded by a tangle of rose-bushes, dignified old shade trees, and a generous circle of grass, you'd be right. Art is preparing to plant corn in his field near Neligh (pronounced Neeley) in north-central Nebraska. Helen is working the kitchen.

But the tractor remains in the barn, and the big sacks of field corn—the kernels all the same size and the same weak yellow color—sit unopened in the utility shed. Art won't be planting those today. Instead, about one hundred people are slowly gathering to help Art sow something else on his land, by hand. They come bearing small beaded bags of seeds. Poured out in your palm, they are dusty blue, pomegranate red, with some cream and butter thrown in.

These sowers have also brought tubs of potato salad and coleslaw, hefty watermelons, and still-warm pies, and many are pitching in to help Helen serve the large crowd. Perhaps, you think, it's a neighborly barn raising, a return to the homesteading era. Maybe you feel a little nostalgic, just thinking about it, if you're from a farm family, or if your childhood diet of pop culture was filled with such scenes, as mine was.

But this isn't a reunion of pioneer families. Many of the visitors are members of the Ponca tribe—separated by federal fiat into northern (Nebraska) and southern (Oklahoma) branches for over 135 years. Indians from other nearby tribes—the Omahas, Winnebagos, and Santee Sioux in the northeastern corner of the state—also have come to the gathering. They ride up to the Tanderups' farm in fully decked-out pickups. They tumble out of their trucks, laughing, in shorts, jeans, and flip-flops. Some of the women dress in handmade calico skirts ringed with ribbons. Some sport hand-beaded accessories. Almost everyone is wearing a turquoise-blue T-shirt, made especially for this day, emblazoned with several ears of multicolored maize. There are non-Indians, too, in their baseball caps and cargo shorts, their Birkenstocks and sneakers. Kids turn cartwheels on the grass; their grandparents lounge in folding chairs near the big utility shed where the food will be served.

It's clear from the hugs and the smiles, the comfortable ease, that many of these people have known one another for a while. Indeed, these modern and these ancient corn planters had originally come together in 2013 to oppose a transnational oil pipeline—the Keystone XL—that would bisect the Tanderups' farm and the homelands of the Poncas. These strangers didn't know each other then, but they shared a common concern that a pipeline spill would contaminate the water, quietly flowing underground in the Ogallala Aquifer. They feared the poisoned water would disperse for hundreds of miles.

They worried, too, that the pipeline, which would transport sticky tar sands oil over 2,200 miles from Alberta, Canada, to the Gulf of Mexico, would just make climate change worse. Against the pipeline's champions who claimed it would create much-needed jobs in rural Nebraska in the immediate future, they said it would only bring environmental calamity in the long run. And they shared a common indignation that a foreign corporation, with the government's backing, could simply take the precious land for its own purpose without the consent of its owners. Slowly the strangers became political allies.

And then something else happened. Political alliances grew into personal friendships. In November 2013, the Tanderups hosted their first spirit camp, "where a group gather together and do a lot of prayers, ceremony, visiting, getting to know each other," as Art explains. The harvest was done. Winter was creeping in and starting to chill and darken the bright days of autumn. Everything grew quieter.

For four cold days, with about six inches of snow on the ground, forty to sixty people gathered each day at the spirit camp. Many of them hailed from seven or eight nearby tribes. Non-Indian farmers and environmental activists converged on the farm, too. They built fires to keep warm and raised a tepee. They joked that cowboys and Indians were finally uniting.

The Keystone XL protesters strategized politically, but they also became closer as they tended the fire, made and shared meals, prayed together, and told stories. Most attendees left at twilight as the temperature dropped and night set in. But a few hardy souls remained. "A bunch of us would stay and . . . we would go into the tepee, and we had a fire in there," Art recalls, "and we could take our coats off and . . . be nice and comfy, and we would sit around and talk about things."

Mekasi Horinek, from the Ponca tribe of Oklahoma, was one of those who stayed during the cozy evenings in the tepee. From him and other Poncas, the Tanderups learned the tribe's history. The Poncas had been a small tribal nation; by the 1870s, they numbered just about seven hundred. In the early 1800s they had lived for most of each year in a village where the Niobrara River greets the Missouri River, about fifty miles north of the Tanderups' farm.

There in the fertile river bottom the Poncas grew the "three sisters"—squash, beans, and corn—as well as tobacco. Each summer most tribal members journeyed out onto the vast surrounding grassy plains for the annual buffalo hunt. They returned to their home base each August or September to harvest and preserve their crops for the winter ahead.

The site of the Poncas' former village in Nebraska is now a state park. It attracts state residents and some out-of-state tourists, intent on canoeing, rafting, tubing, or tanking down the Niobrara River. This last endeavor consists of riding with a bunch of people in a big metal stock tank, usually with large quantities of beer. You hear tales of virtual traffic jams on the river on hot summer weekends. Since I'm a bit of a recluse, and sunburn easily, I always stayed away from the scene.

I had lived in Nebraska for fifteen years before I made it to the Poncas' homelands. I could not believe how stunning it was. From a high bluff in Niobrara State Park, the tall grass willowing all around in the early summer, you can turn to the north and track the Missouri River as it might have looked hundreds of years ago, before Lewis and Clark rowed up its waters. You can face to the south and see the sand bars forming little islands in the broad Niobrara River. At this spot there is no sign of the dams that plug the rivers. The water flows as if it were free.

Walking along the bluffs today, you can appreciate why it was a favorite spot for European and American traders, as well as artists, in the early 1800s. You can see why other tribes, the American government, and settlers coveted this land. You can understand why the Poncas loved this place so much and resisted attempts by all these other invaders to wrest it away from them.

To stay in their homelands, in 1858 the Poncas sent a delegation to Washington, D.C., to negotiate a treaty, their third, that secured for them a small reservation of about 58,000 acres on the Niobrara River in exchange for ceding the rest of their land—an estimated 2,334,000 acres—to the U.S. government. They thought that with this concession they could finally live undisturbed and in peace. But it was not to be.

On one of those tranquil nights in the spirit camp tepee, Mekasi told the Tanderups that in the mid-1870s the U.S. government decided to forcibly move his tiny tribe to Indian Territory, present-day Oklahoma. The Poncas could not fathom why they were to be uprooted. They were not at war with the United States, as many of the nearby Lakota nations were. The Poncas, in fact, impressed American government authorities as "friendly," "loyal," "peaceable," and "well-behaved."

The Poncas got along well with their settler neighbors and had their sympathy when the government suddenly ordered them into exile. Local white settlers sent telegrams to the secretary of the interior and the commissioner of Indian affairs to protest. Two local newspapers vociferously opposed the Poncas' removal.

But the Poncas' record of amiability and their support from local settlers did not matter. The U.S. government insisted on their removal. And it did so in the cruelest fashion. A federal inspector simply showed up out of the blue at the Ponca Agency in 1877 and informed the tribe that they were to be removed. Most of the tribal members refused to go. The inspector brought sixty members of the cavalry to force the Poncas to move. As Chief White Eagle described it, "The soldiers got on their horses, went to all the houses, broke open our doors, took our household utensils, put them in their wagons, and pointing their bayonets at our people, ordered them to move." Despite Ponca protests, the government marched the seven hundred Ponca men, women, and children six hundred miles to Indian Territory.

In the tepee, as the fire crackled and bathed each person in an amber light, Mekasi told the Tanderups the story of what happened on the Poncas' Trail of Tears. Their ancestors had trudged over this very spot 136 years earlier. Storms pummeled them almost every day of their journey. Many died on the long walk, including an eighteen-month-old child, White Buffalo Girl, who was buried nearby in Neligh.

When they finally arrived in Indian Territory after fifty-five days, the government had not made any provisions for their new home. The Poncas, who had been living in wooden frame houses in Nebraska, now had to huddle in makeshift tents. They had arrived too late to plant crops, so they faced starvation. About a quarter of the tribe succumbed to malaria and other diseases. That's right. The Poncas lost 25 *percent* of their members. Most of their livestock died as well.

What happened to the Poncas also happened to hundreds of other Indigenous groups in every territory and state of the United States. We could call what happened something benign, something euphemistic, and we often do. We could label it westward expansion. Winning of the west. Pioneering. Homesteading. Even in 2019 a *New York Times* writer dubbed it "opening the West." But what happened to the Poncas, and other American Indian nations, was theft.

The theft did not stop with the land. Settlers stole the primary food source from many tribes: buffalo. Settler livestock appropriated the grass of the Great Plains that Indian horses and buffalo had long grazed on. Travelers on the Overland Trail plundered Indian timber and destroyed habitats where Indian people grew food or hunted. Miners dug coal and extracted uranium from under the ground on which Indian people lived. Today the theft continues. Multinational companies are fracking oil and natural gas underneath and running pipelines on top of what remains of Indian land.

Settlers also stole what we might call—in a deceptively abstract way—*human resources*. European and American invaders, especially in New Mexico, Arizona, California, and Utah, stole the labor of children. Later, the U.S. government's agents stole Indian children outright, shipping them off to boarding schools—often without the consent of their families—for years of their young lives. There, too, the schools exploited the children for their labor. After World War II authorities removed thousands of Indigenous children from their families and communities to be raised in non-Indian families.

From the beginning of the European colonization of North America, many settlers sexually assaulted Native women, robbing them of sovereignty over their very bodies. This continues today with the disproportionate numbers of American Indian women who go missing, are murdered, or are sex-trafficked.

Then there is the pillage of Indigenous *cultural* resources. The boarding schools sought to eradicate Indigenous languages. Settlers stole Indian ceremonial items, sacred objects, and cultural artifacts and put them on the market or in museums. They even lifted Indian skeletons right out of their graves. Some settlers appropriated Indian spiritual traditions or artistic styles.

Most of this theft went unpunished. And most of it also went unrecorded, at least within settler society. The crimes involved elaborate cover-ups. Settlers sought to destroy the evidence: to erase the presence of Indigenous people from the land and to silence their voices and repress their histories. Settlers told and retold a heroic history of western expansion that denied that the crimes had ever occurred in the first place. This story—of intrepid European explorers, of colorful fur traders and plucky miners, of rugged cowboys, of brave pioneers and long-suffering homesteaders—remains our dominant popular narrative about the West.

Our national mythologies claim that the United States was founded on the principles of equality and freedom. The persistence of slavery over two and a half centuries has long belied that uplifting narrative. But the history of settler colonialism is another stark rejoinder. Our nation is built on the plunder of Indigenous people. In Australia, where settlers engaged in similar robbery against Aboriginal people, the Australian settler writer Xavier Herbert declared in the 1970s that his country was "not a nation, but a community of thieves." You could say the same for the United States.

For many settlers, it is tempting to stiffen into a defensive position when confronted with the disquieting truth of America's founding crimes. Maybe this is all true, and it might have been unfair or unfortunate, some settlers concede, but look at all the progress we've made: the railroads laid, the settlements founded, the crops grown, the cities built, the millions of people employed. It is common to tie the settling of the West with the growth of the American nation, to protest that it all turned out great in the end.

It can be deeply uncomfortable for many settlers to face the illegitimate foundations upon which our settlement is based, to consider that what might have been progress for settlers was devastation for the Poncas, and for other Indian nations. It's hard to acknowledge that we settlers are trespassers on Native land. It just doesn't square with the stirring heroic story we like to tell. We settlers have been taught through our formal education and countless informal messages to believe that we are entitled to be here. It can unsettle us—literally—to realize that our settler histories of triumph are inextricably intertwined with Indigenous histories of theft.

Many academics call this theft "settler colonialism," a phrase that sounds nearly as evasive as "westward expansion," until you learn what it means: a form of foreign intervention bent on transferring vast territories from Indigenous peoples to their colonizers. Settler colonialism sought to replace the Indigenous population with that of settlers, a process of subjugation meant ultimately to eliminate Indigenous people rather than merely exploit them as laborers, as is so common to other forms of colonialism.

We may be tempted to see "settler" as a simple stand-in for "white person." But the term "settler" homogenizes an enormously diverse group. There were newly freed African Americans who took up home-steads in the West, land that had only recently been expunged of Indig-enous people. There were immigrants from Asia and Mexico, who faced their own set of indignities, humiliations, and injustices when they came to America but who nevertheless occupied land once belonging to In-digenous people. Settlers encompass more than those who have been classified as white.

Nevertheless, it is clear that settler colonialism has worked in tandem with the American racial caste system to compound the privileges and magnify the benefits of white supremacy. Settler colonial dispossession of Indian people was intimately bound up with America's other found-ing crime: slavery. Slave owners imported 450,000 Africans to work the land from which they had removed Indigenous people. After the slave trade ended in 1808, slave owners gained ever more Indigenous land. Millions more African Americans, now born into bondage, labored on their new plantations. Native-born Protestant white settlers often guarded the perimeter of settlerdom, putting those immigrants they regarded as non-white on a provisional probationary status as settlers. Some immigrants, then as now, were good enough for labor but not for full-fledged citizenship. Thus, coming to terms with settler colonialism also entails reckoning with white supremacy.

The United States is not the only British settler colonial nation that sought to appropriate Indigenous lands. It shares this designation with a number of other countries around the world with similar histories: Australia, New Zealand, and Canada. In Australia, British authorities gained possession of nearly the entire continent, confining Australia's Indigenous people to a few tiny Aboriginal reserves or missions. In New Zealand, in just one generation, the British transferred over 95 percent of the land from Maori to settler hands.

British authorities negotiated dozens of treaties with Indigenous people in the North American lands that would eventually become Canada and the United States. U.S. officials brokered 374 treaties from 1778 to 1871. These treaties and other land acquisition schemes effec-tively redistributed 98 percent of Indian land to settlers in what became the United States.

The idea of negotiating treaties has the air of legitimacy, but authorities rarely compensated Indigenous peoples adequately for the land they ceded through treaty, and tribal leaders often signed many treaties under extreme duress. And as the Poncas found, settler authorities routinely violated the treaties' provisions. Treaties could not protect Indigenous people from further theft.

On a global scale, settler colonialism involved the appropriation of millions upon millions of acres worldwide from the hands of Indigenous people to those of European colonizers. In just a few generations, Indigenous people lost lands and waterways that they had possessed for centuries or millennia. New Zealand settler historian James Belich calls this the settler revolution. He notes that the spread of European migrants from their continent to settler colonies exploded in the nineteenth century, from one million migrants in the eighteenth century to fifty-six million in the next century. It was, indeed, a shockingly fast and nearly thorough change in landownership and the status of Indigenous people.

For the Indigenous families and communities that lived through this revolution, settler colonialism was not some abstract phenomenon that occurred far removed from their daily lives. Nor, as noted literary scholar and writer Beth Piatote pointed out to me, could her Nimiipuu (or Nez Perce) ancestors gain distance from or a bird's-eye view of it. It exerted a relentless and insidious force that intimately affected all those who endured it. As Larry Wright Jr., chairman of the Ponca tribe of Nebraska, puts it, "we became strangers in our own land."

What would it be like to lose so much, over so many generations? How would it feel to fear that there is no safe place, that one must always be on guard against violence and abuse? What must it be like to live with a constant threat to one's land, one's home, one's labor, and even one's children? Many Indigenous people speak of "intergenerational trauma," as well as a fierce resilience, that passes down through the generations. Black theologian and ethicist Katie Cannon wrote memorably, "Our bodies are the texts that carry the memories."

But it is not just Indigenous people who carry these embodied memories down through the generations. These histories became embedded within settler families, too. In this case, however, they conferred benefits, advantages, and privileges to settler descendants more than trauma, impoverishment, and hardship. This history is thus an intimate one for settlers, too. We need to engage in truth and reconciliation to heal from it.

Learning of and from our settler colonial past is part of the historical reckoning we are going through collectively as a nation. Many white Americans are finally willing to face up to our nation's history of slavery and its ongoing legacies of systemic racism. It is also crucial for Americans to reckon with our occupation of stolen land, and this is a task of particular import for *white* settlers.

I myself am a white settler, and I address this book primarily to other settlers. We have work to do to educate ourselves about our settler colonial past, to seek out and listen to Indigenous voices, past and present, and then to become accountable for what has been done in our names and from which we have long benefited. It can no longer be acceptable to reap the advantages of settler colonialism without facing up to the damage it inflicted, and still inflicts, on Indigenous people. It can be deeply uncomfortable to confront and take responsibility for this history, but it can also be liberating and lead in unexpected and rewarding directions. The Tanderups learned this as they deepened their friendships with the Poncas.

American Indian people like Mekasi want settlers like the Tanderups to know their histories, but they get weary of telling their tales of misery and despair. It's hard to talk and think about the atrocities your grandmothers and grandfathers had to endure. And what's more, Indian people don't want to be defined solely by what Dakota intellectual Vine Deloria Jr. identified as narratives of "plight." "Other groups have difficulties, predicaments, quandaries, problems, or troubles. Traditionally, we Indians have had a 'plight,'" Deloria wrote in his classic *Custer Died for Your Sins.*

To American Indians an equally significant story is this: We endured. We are still here. We survived. And even more than that, we are reviving our lifeways, and we will thrive. Survive, revive, thrive. So it was that

Mekasi and other Poncas shared their dreams for the future in the spirit camp tepee. Mekasi told the Tanderups, "Our people lost the sacred corn when we were removed to Oklahoma, and it would be great to bring that corn back to its homeland. This is where it grew; this is the area it used to grow in, and it would be great to revitalize that corn." Mekasi asked Art, "Would you mind if we plant it here?" Without hesitation Art said he wouldn't mind at all. "Absolutely. Absolutely, we can plant it here," he enthused.

But the last time the Poncas had planted corn in their homelands had been 137 years before. Had any of their seeds survived? Art explained that Mekasi "and another gentleman, Amos Hinton, started searching for the medicine bundle that had some of that corn crop, that the Lakota had harvested [in the] fall of 1877," when the Poncas had been removed. "They found that medicine bundle and were able to get that handful of red sacred corn." The Poncas worked with the Pawnees who had also resurrected some of their sacred corn in the Grand Island, Nebraska, area. They brought some of their seed varieties, too, to plant at the Tanderups' farm.

After more than one hundred winters, however, would the seed grow again? Art, who had been planting corn for decades, was concerned that the seed would not germinate. "We had planted about four acres of corn that year," Art recalls. "When we were planting the red [corn] first, I said to Amos and Mekasi, 'Did you save some, in case it doesn't grow?' And they said, 'It'll grow, have faith! It will grow. This corn is sacred, and it will grow.'"

Sure enough, the Poncas and Art were delighted a few weeks later when little corn seedlings pushed out of the spring soil and began to climb toward the sun. "We had a beautiful crop of corn that year," Art remembers. "We harvested the five different varieties. Mekasi hauled it all back to Oklahoma, and they planted eighty acres of corn next year." Ever since then, the Poncas have been converging on the Tanderups' family farm twice a year, first in the early summer to plant and then in the fall to harvest their corn.

This fifth year of Ponca corn-planting at the Tanderup farm is special. Before the planting begins, a ceremony is held. Four VIPs sit in front of a large table, covered with a bison robe. Art Tanderup sits on one end; Larry Wright Jr. is seated on the other. Helen nestles cozily between her husband and Casey Camp-Horinek, a councilwoman of the southern Ponca tribe of Oklahoma and Mekasi's mother.

Almost exactly 160 years ago, Ponca chiefs had signed over millions of acres of their homelands to the U.S. government, later to be redistributed as homesteads to people like Helen Tanderup's family. Today, on this topsy-turvy farm, instead of the Poncas giving up more of their land, Art and Helen Tanderup are signing a different kind of treaty, a deed that returns the Poncas' one-acre corn plot to them. Later the Tanderups will expand to ten acres the parcel of land that they are repatriating to the tribe.

During the ceremony, Art talks about how the Tanderups' return of the land grew out of facing the Poncas' history together at the spirit camp. This day on the farm "has been many years in the making," Art says. "We remember Mekasi talking about such an action several years ago when we sat in that tepee at the Ponca Trail of Tears camp. . . . We talked about bringing the corn back to its homeland. We talked about the homeland being taken away from the people. We talked about growing that corn again. And making all the relatives healthy. We talked about how it would be great to have some of the homeland back again."

Art acknowledges, too, that the Tanderups' return of ten acres to the Poncas is one modest step toward making amends for the history that dispossessed and divided the Poncas. "It's an honor for Helen and [me] to make this happen," he says, "and to give a small piece of what was theirs, and so terribly taken away. Such a tragedy in our American history and then to have to be driven away from this land that was taken from them. So, this is just a small gesture. . . . It can never make what went wrong right, but it can show how we feel about this and how we are honored to give this small piece of land back to the people that . . . were the stewards of this land. They took care of it. They knew how to take care of it."

After he speaks, Art signs the deed to transfer the land to the Poncas and then passes it to Helen, who quietly and decisively adds her signature. The onlookers clap their hands. Casey and Larry wipe tears from their eyes. Casey is to speak next, but she is overcome with emotion; she bows her head on Larry's shoulder. Helen comforts her. After a few moments, Casey composes herself and says, "This day our Mother the Earth sustained us, and gave us reason to live. This day the wind is blessing us . . . allowing us to become one in spirit."

It is clear Casey is thinking of her relatives and their painful experiences. She offers "my deepest sincerest prayers to the ancestors of my people," and breaks down again. Referring to those standing behind her, she says, "My children back here; they're all named for those who walked this very trail you're standing on. And when we call their names, we're calling those spirits. They're here with us." Casey then signs the deed to great applause. She hands it to Larry to sign.

Larry tells of how pleased he is to be "with our friends, our relatives . . . to be here as part of this historic [day]. For Art and Helen and their family to be willing to do this says a lot of them." He continues, "This means a lot. To be able to sit here as partners, to come together out of the goodness of your heart and undo what the federal government did. The federal government separated our Ponca people into two different governments but Art and his family . . . have brought our nations back together to unite us with this land." Larry adds that the Ponca Tribe of Nebraska is buying 1,800 acres of land near Niobrara. "One day we'll plant Ponca corn there," he says. The Poncas then honor Art and Helen by draping Pendleton blankets, woven with colorful geometric patterns, over their shoulders. The couple accept the gift gratefully, even as the sweat rolls down their faces on this summer day.

It is not often that settlers learn about the specific piece of land they occupy, of how Indigenous people were dispossessed and displaced from it. It is rare, too, that Indigenous people have the opportunity to meet and share their history with the descendants of the settlers who displaced them. The Tanderups came to know the truth of the place where they had settled. The Poncas gently offered this truth to them, as a kind of gift.

It is even more unusual for settlers to take some responsibility for this truth, and rarer still to take action to make amends for it. The Tanderups are uncommon settlers, indeed. They went from allying with the Poncas politically, to working with them to plant their sacred seeds, to repatriating some of their land to them in an act of accountability and personal atonement.

I don't tell you this story to lionize the Tanderups as white saviors who took pity on the Poncas and gave them a small donation of land. I am relating what the Tanderups did because they show us what can happen when settlers and Indigenous people face their painful truths together, plant new seeds of friendship, uncover paths to reconciliation and redress, and imagine new futures. They show us other possibilities of how we can hold unsettling knowledge within us and learn to live together on haunted land.

The ceremony that took place on the Tanderups' farm was reminiscent of much grander processes to reckon with and make amends for widespread human rights abuses that have occurred around the globe since World War II. These enterprises go by many names, including restorative justice, reparative justice, transitional justice, redress, and truth and reconciliation. They are big umbrella concepts that cover an array of measures: restitution, compensation, reparations, rehabilitation, apologies, and memorials.

Some atrocities have involved so many victims, have entangled such a web of perpetrators, and have been condoned by so many members of the larger society that conventional legal systems cannot adequately deal with them. Truth and reconciliation experts—whether survivors, activists, scholars, or lawmakers—have all struggled to figure out how to bring healing and justice to huge numbers of people who have suffered collective trauma. They have wrestled with how to hold perpetrators responsible for such heinous abuses and how to properly engage with the bystanders who stood silent in the face of these crimes or benefited from them.

Beginning in the 1980s, nations in Central and South America, the Caribbean, Africa, and Asia established truth (or truth and reconciliation) commissions to investigate and make redress for human rights abuses as they sought to transition from dictatorships to democratic societies. Nelson Mandela's government enacted the most high-profile

Truth and Reconciliation Commission (TRC) after the majority-black population finally toppled apartheid and gained power in South Africa in the 1990s. In the twenty-first century, other nations have continued to use TRCs to investigate past crimes and make amends.

Everyday citizens have also initiated truth and reconciliation processes to bring to light abuses and agitate for redress. In 2004, for example, the city of Greensboro, North Carolina, established a TRC to inquire into a 1979 confrontation between white supremacists and anti-racist demonstrators that left five protesters dead. Two criminal trials by all-white juries had failed to convict any of the white supremacists involved, although a civil trial had found the Ku Klux Klan and neo-Nazis jointly liable with the city's police department for the wrongful death of one victim. Many Greensboro residents believed that there was a larger systemic problem at the heart of the conflict and that Greensboro needed a truth and reconciliation process in order to address it.

Nearly all truth and reconciliation efforts, whether at the international, national, or local level, encompass at least three components: truth telling, bearing witness and acknowledgment, and redress. The humble ceremony at the Tanderups' farm followed this model. Ponca leaders told of the mistreatment their people had suffered. The Tanderups acknowledged these past harms while witnesses looked on. The Tanderups then made some recompense for past acts of dispossession.

This gesture of personal truth and reconciliation may seem like a quaint throwback to the early civil rights era or a naive dream of a utopian future. Many Americans may think the Tanderups and the Poncas are Kumbaya-singers hopelessly out of touch with the mainstream.

Yet, in a global context, the Tanderups and the Poncas are in step with a growing movement for reconciliation between settlers and Indigenous people. It is the United States that is the outlier. New Zealand created a tribunal to hear and respond to the grievances of its Indigenous people, the Maori, way back in 1975. In 2008 the Canadian and Australian governments both made official apologies for Indigenous child removal. Truth and reconciliation processes in these places have been far from perfect, but all of these nations are seriously confronting, in a very public manner, the damages their past policies inflicted on Indigenous peoples.

But in the United States, wide public dialogue about and awareness of American Indian experience is nearly nonexistent. Most settler Americans are willfully forgetting these histories. Sometimes an event, like the protest against the Dakota Access Pipeline at Standing Rock, flares up and briefly ignites a public conversation, but most Americans have little understanding of the broader context of Indigenous struggles. The fire of interest burns down and leaves only a faint whiff of smoke.

As a historian for more than two decades, I have written about and discussed how settler authorities forcibly removed Indigenous children in Australia, Canada, and the United States. Wherever I speak—whether on a college campus, in a church, or for a civic organization—I am invariably asked why the United States has not done what Canada and Australia have done. Why have we not held an investigation about and apologized for this heinous abuse?

Sadly, the United States is simply engaging in business as usual. As Canadian historian and politician Michael Ignatieff wrote in 1998, "All nations depend on forgetting: on forging myths of unity and identity that allow a society to forget its founding crimes, its hidden injuries and divisions, its unhealed wounds." Or as Roger Epp, another Canadian, puts it, for a liberal democratic society to operate, "some things ha[ve] to be forgotten."

This book explores what could be possible in the United States if we engaged in collective soul-searching and dared to remember and acknowledge. Histories of dispossession have shaped all of us on this stolen continent. And they will continue to do so. Witness the 2020 Supreme Court decision *McGirt v. Oklahoma*, which ruled that land that had been reserved for the Muscogee (Creek) nation in the nineteenth century—most of the eastern half of Oklahoma—remains Native American territory.

If you are a settler descendant, you didn't point the bayonet, shoot the gun, or sign the law that led to dispossession. You didn't squat on Indian land or take up a homestead. That was a long time ago, and something that maybe your ancestors, but certainly not you yourself, did.

What's more, many of you do not even have ancestors who took part in dispossession. They may have come here not as settlers but as slaves. Or they may have been recruited from Asia to build railroads in the Sierra Nevada or from Mexico to pick grapes in the Central Valley of California or harvest sugar beets in Colorado. Or maybe your ancestors immigrated directly to urban areas in the twentieth century, far removed from Indian lands. Maybe you and your family just recently arrived. You had nothing to do with America's founding crimes.

But unless you are an American Indian or Alaska Native, you are living on stolen land. The theft may have happened a long time ago and been carried out by others, but most of us are nevertheless still trespassers. And we are also ongoing beneficiaries of this theft. Even though we rarely admit it, Indian dispossession and removal opened up new possibilities and prospects for settlers, even as it foreclosed so many opportunities for Indigenous people.

We do not have to remain captive to this history, however. Many tribes, like the Poncas, and many settlers, such as the Tanderups, have made truth and reconciliation an intimate encounter and practice. They show us that confronting our painful histories can enrich and empower all of us. As Art puts it, "This whole pipeline thing is something we wish didn't happen. But, the other side of it has fulfilled our lives so much. . . . the experiences we've had, the relationships we have built. . . . it has been just phenomenal."

What would it mean to face our history of settler colonialism, as the Tanderups and the Poncas have done? How would it change us, in our everyday lives and in our relationships, to confront our past? How would it transform our society? Reckoning with the past is not to be feared or avoided. It is a path to living more fully and responsibly. Not just to survive, but to revive and thrive.

The first step, as I learned from the Tanderups and the Poncas, is for each of us settlers to become familiar with the history of our own families and the places where we have settled, to learn how this land passed from Indigenous to settler hands.

PART ONE

Our Founding Crimes

CHAPTER 1

Blood

When I was growing up in the mountains west of Colorado Springs, it didn't seem there was any history to be learned about this place where I lived. History, as I was taught in school, was something that happened in far-distant places. It was a parade of presidents, a litany of wars, a series of unconnected dots, all to memorize. If my teachers ever taught our local or state history, I don't remember it. Somehow, though, I absorbed a View-Master version of Colorado's history filled with stock characters: explorers, mountain men, miners, cowboys.

It was understood that Colorado's founders were white and male, although not all of them were (in fact, some of the earliest gold seekers in Colorado were Cherokees from Indian Territory, and James Beckwourth, a freed slave, helped to found Pueblo, Colorado). A few women gained the stage now and then. I remember hearing of Baby Doe Tabor—wife of a silver magnate who lost his fortune in 1893. She ended up as a notorious madwoman in a Leadville cabin.

American Indians did not figure much at all in my education. My grade school class took a field trip every year to a museum where we listlessly traipsed past glass cases of Indian relics—pottery shards, baskets, cradleboards, even skeletons. So, I vaguely knew that Indians had once lived in the area I now inhabited. Place-names gave a hint to their past presence: we lived up Ute Pass; Cheyenne Mountain loomed large over Colorado Springs; and I careened recklessly down the slopes at Arapaho Basin as a teenager.

But from grade school to high school none of my classes ever studied or talked about why the Utes no longer lived up Ute Pass, why the Arapahos and Cheyennes no longer occupied the Front Range: those sheltered foothills, bountiful river valleys, and grassy plains that unfurl eastward from the Rocky Mountains. Indians, firmly contained in the past, just provided a little local color to the region where I grew up, another potential draw for tourists. Like nearly all settler descendants, I lived in a state of ignorance, and innocence, about the true history of where my family had settled.

For many centuries before it became squared into a state, Colorado had been the homelands and hunting grounds of many different Indigenous groups, from the Ancestral Puebloans and their cliff dwellings in the southwest corner of the state to the Utes in the mountainous western part of the state. Several Plains tribes vied fiercely for control of the plains east of the Rockies. In the early 1800s the Apaches, Comanches, and Kiowas had become power players on the southern plains, and the Lakotas had gained dominance in the north. The Arapahos and Cheyennes were latecomers to the Front Range, having migrated from the area that became northern Minnesota. In 1840, these tribes negotiated a "Great Peace" and designated the vast central plains a common hunting and camping terrain of a "broad alliance of former enemies." Europeans had also set their sights on this land. Spanish conquistadors and missionaries, from their base in New Spain, and later New Mexico, had sought to colonize it. French fur traders and trappers had ventured into the region, eager to exploit its bountiful wildlife for profit.

But up until 1858, few Americans had been interested in Colorado. Most saw it as a mountainous hurdle or hostile crossroads on their way to California or Oregon Territory. Only a handful of Americans had lingered in the area, mainly working as fur traders or trappers. One of these was William Bent. William was born to an affluent family in St. Louis, Missouri, in 1809, one of eleven children of Silas Bent, who became a Missouri Supreme Court judge, and Martha Bent.

In 1824, when he was just fifteen, William and his older brother Charles left home to make their fortunes as fur trappers in the West. In 1833, the Bents gave up their traps and their wandering for a more lucrative and less grueling lifestyle. Together with a French trader named Ceran St. Vrain, they set up a trading fort—known as Bent's Fort—in southeastern Colorado, along the Santa Fe Trail, shuttling goods from St. Louis all the way to Mexico City and back. They exchanged pots, knives, axes, cloth, and other manufactured goods with the local Cheyennes for bison robes, horses, and mules.

When William came to the area that became Colorado, he did not seek to take over Indigenous land or to re-create American society in the West. Instead he became thoroughly enmeshed within Cheyenne society. In 1835, he married Owl Woman, daughter of an influential Cheyenne man named White Thunder, who was the tribe's Keeper of the Arrows, an esteemed religious and healing role. William became a member of the tribe, even a sub-chief. In 1844, he also married two of Owl Woman's sisters, Yellow Woman and Island. Polygamy was customary for high-status men in Cheyenne society.

Just a generation later, William Bent's model of becoming kin with Indigenous peoples was rare. Most white settlers who came to the West in the 1850s and 1860s sought not to integrate into the Indigenous groups that already lived there but to transplant their families to and re-create white settler communities in the West. Unlike Bent, they did not regard this as Indian country to be respected but as settler territory to be claimed.

The year 1858 was a pivotal one. As historian Elliott West tells it, the Cheyennes and Arapahos had been out on the plains for their annual bison hunt that summer and into the early autumn. When they moved back to the Front Range, as they did every winter, they found settler men building cabins and laying out streets in the tribes' usual haunts. They found miners setting up camps in the foothills and along the streams where the tribes relocated in the winter. A few prospectors had found veins of gold in 1858 in the creeks along the Front Range. Now a gush of miners—60,000 the first year—poured into the Cheyenne and Arapaho lands.

Settler horses were eating up the grass that the tribes' horses needed. The invaders were cutting down all the cottonwoods that provided shelter to Indian bands in the winter. And less visibly, the newcomers brought epidemics that would ravage the Cheyennes and Arapahos. The miners saw only the potential money they could make. They were heedless of the havoc they were wreaking on the Cheyenne and Arapaho people.

William Bent, with his long experience in the area, sought to inform the government about the injustice that was occurring against the people who had become his family. He wrote to the commissioner of Indian affairs that developers were gridding out and erecting new towns in the most coveted areas without compensating Native people. As thousands more miners and settlers poured into the area, he raised the alarm about the growing crisis:

> The prominent feature of this region is the recent discovery and development of *gold*. . . . I estimate the number of whites traversing the plains across the center belt to have exceeded 60,000 during the present season. The trains of vehicles and cattle are frequent and valuable in proportion; post lines and private expresses are in constant motion. The explorations of this season have established the existence of the precious metals in absolutely infinite abundance and convenience of position. The concourse of whites is therefore constantly swelling, and incapable of control or restraint by the government. . . . [The] numerous and warlike Indians, pressed upon all around by the Texans, by the settlers of the gold region, by the advancing people of Kansas and from the Platte, are already compressed into a small circle of territory, destitute of food, and bisected athwart by the constantly marching lines of emigrants. A desperate war of starvation and extinction is therefore imminent and inevitable, unless prompt measures shall prevent it.

In short, Bent was telling the government that many Indian people had been reduced to starvation during the Colorado Gold Rush.

This is not the story we usually tell about gold rushes. Our settler lore likes to recount fables of striking it rich, winning it big. We tell colorful tales of lucky miners and heart-of-gold saloon girls, a chapter in our larger progressive epic of "winning the West." But there is perhaps no better illustration of how settler opportunity and benefit was inversely connected to Indigenous disadvantage than the history of the Colorado Gold Rush.

And the government did not act as a neutral arbiter of competing interests. Instead it lent its hefty weight to the miners and the settlers. It had erected only four forts in the area before 1858. Six years later there were fifteen, even at a time when the government's resources were stretched thin by fighting the Civil War. The government also strung telegraph lines and built other settler infrastructure to make it possible for miners and settlers to flood into Colorado, to pursue new economic opportunities.

At the same time, the government failed utterly to meet its obligations under the 1851 Fort Laramie Treaty: to protect Cheyenne and Arapaho lands from encroachment and to provide rations to replace their traditional food supply. The Office of Indian Affairs was chronically late with the food and tools that were guaranteed by the treaty. Corrupt Indian agents also sometimes sold Indian rations to others to supplement their income. When foodstuffs finally arrived, they were often spoiled or inadequate. As a result, the Cheyennes and Arapahos were starving at the very time and in the very place that some miners were striking it rich.

The Cheyenne and Arapaho people faced an impossible bind. They wanted to maintain their lands and their way of life. Barring that, they wanted to at least survive this onslaught of settlers who had made them starving strangers in their own lands. They divided over the best course of action.

Some Cheyenne and Arapaho leaders insisted that they must fight against the settlers to defend what was theirs. They charged migrants tolls through their land, they raided settler livestock, they killed some settlers and took others captive, and they fought against soldiers. Bent could understand their response. He told the commissioner of Indian affairs that a "smothered passion for revenge agitates these Indians" because of "the failure of food, the encircling encroachment of the white population, and the exasperating sense of decay and impending extinction with which they are surrounded." Most other newcomers to Colorado were outraged. They failed to understand how the Cheyennes and Arapahos were simply trying to defend their land, homes, and families. They agitated for the government to protect them from what they called Indian "depredations."

Other leaders argued that war with the Americans would be disastrous, and they sought to make peace. Southern Cheyenne chief Black Kettle and a few other peace-seeking Southern Cheyenne and Arapaho chiefs signed a new treaty with the United States in 1860 at Fort Wise (which later became Fort Lyon). U.S. negotiators demanded that the tribes cede most of the rest of their land and agree to confine themselves to a small triangular reservation, Point of Rocks, between Sand Creek and the upper Arkansas River in southeastern Colorado. The tribes were to move to the new Point of Rocks Reserve in 1861 and to abandon their nomadic hunting life and adopt sedentary farming and ranching.

In return for their land, the federal government made many of the same promises it had made in the 1851 Fort Laramie Treaty. It pledged to protect the tribes, provide livestock and farming equipment, plow and fence fields, build a sawmill and mechanic shops, and provide dwellings for the tribes' members. Plus, it guaranteed fifteen years of annuities. Black Kettle and other peace leaders signed the treaty because they sought to avert a war, fearing they would most certainly lose and pay a heavy price.

Northern Cheyenne and most of the Arapaho leaders refused to sign the treaty. They were deeply disillusioned and did not trust the government to follow through on its promises. And they were right. The government violated the terms of the new treaty almost immediately, just as it had the prior one. Settlers still encroached on the new reservation. Rations were still late, inadequate, or inedible. Epidemics compounded the misery. To survive, small hunting groups struck out from the new reservation in the spring and summer to hunt bison. Officials accused them of becoming hostile, rather than simply trying to feed themselves.

If the Cheyenne and Arapaho people were divided over the best course of action, incoming settlers were almost completely united in their indignation at ongoing conflict with Indians. The crisis grew more intense in the summer of 1864. In June residents of Denver learned about the gruesome murder and mutilation of Ward Hungate, his wife, and two young daughters at a ranch along Running Creek, about twenty-five miles southeast of Denver. (The murders have remained unsolved, but Coloradoans assumed the perpetrators were Indians.)

Angry settlers brought the bodies of the Hungate family to Denver and put them on display, fueling calls among the local populace for vengeance against the Cheyennes and Arapahos. The *Weekly Commonwealth* opined, "Those that perpetrate such unnatural, brutal butchery as this ought to be hunted to the farthest bounds of these broad plains and burned at the stake alive."

Colorado newspapermen and leaders increasingly cast settlers as the defenseless victims of Indian aggressors. Governor John Evans, for example, issued a proclamation in August 1864, in which he declared, "The conflict is upon us, and all good citizens are called upon to do their duty for the defence of their homes and families." This enabled Evans and his supporters to justify an all-out attack on the Cheyenne and Arapaho people, at least those who were considered "hostile." Evans authorized "all citizens of Colorado, either individually or in such parties as they may organize, to go in pursuit of all hostile Indians on the plains, . . . also, to kill and destroy, as enemies of the country, wherever they may be found, all such hostile Indians." Thus, Evans deputized the entire adult male population of Colorado and made it legal for them to kill Indians.

Although Evans called for settlers to "scrupulously avoid" Indians who had obeyed his orders "to rendezvous at the points indicated," the governor must have known that few settlers would make such a distinction between peaceable and resistant Indians. In August, in fact, after some militant Cheyennes raided freight stations, cut off supplies to Denver, and took a few white women captive, the *Rocky Mountain News* reported that *all* the tribes "on the plains are combined in a war on the whites."

Violence and land appropriation went hand in hand. Evans gave settlers free rein to confiscate Indian property. He proclaimed, "As the only reward I am authorized to offer for such services, I hereby empower such citizens, or parties of citizens, to take captive, and hold to their own private use and benefit, all the property of said hostile Indians that they may capture, and to receive for all stolen property recovered from said Indians such reward as may be deemed proper and just therefor."

Evans also asked the federal government to send him ten thousand troops to defend Colorado's settlers. The War Department instead authorized Evans to recruit a formal regiment—the Colorado Third Volunteers. It stipulated that the regiment would have a limited mission: it was only to fight Indians and only for the next one hundred days.

Evans put the Third under the command of Colonel John Chivington, who had served as a major during the Union victory over Confederate forces at Glorieta Pass in 1862 in New Mexico and overseen the military district of Colorado since its creation in that year. Chivington was also a Methodist minister who organized Denver's first Sunday school. Now he was to oversee a group of untrained settlers in Colorado who longed to avenge the deaths of the Hungates and to subdue the Front Range tribes.

As the crisis escalated throughout the autumn, Black Kettle and other peace leaders sought a resolution. They convinced Major Edward Wynkoop of Fort Lyon to meet and negotiate with the Cheyennes at their camps on the Smoky Hill River, the headquarters of the more militant Dog Soldiers. Some progress was made. The Cheyenne leaders returned all captured white children. In return Wynkoop promised to organize an immediate conference with Governor Evans.

You might think the governor would have been relieved that Wynkoop's meeting had helped to ease tensions and had created a means to move toward a peaceful resolution of the conflict. But Evans was furious. According to Wynkoop, he repeatedly remarked, "What shall I do with the Third regiment if I make peace?" He was adamant that "they had been raised to kill Indians and they must kill Indians." It was clear that Evans preferred to use violence, and Wynkoop's diplomatic move undermined the governor's plans to order the Third Company to attack Colorado's Indians within the next hundred days.

Had the governor lost sight of the larger goal: peace in the new territory he governed? Did he truly believe that Indian people must be eliminated for Colorado to be settled and to become a new state? That was surely part of his motivation. But something more mundane may have also driven him. He had received funding for his hundred-day cavalry and didn't want to lose that money.

Evans eventually agreed to meet with Cheyenne leaders as well as Chivington, Wynkoop, two other officers, and some prominent Denverites at Camp Weld in Denver in late September. It looked at first as if a peaceful resolution was in sight. The Cheyenne leaders came to Denver and were escorted by members of Colorado's First Volunteer Regiment in a parade up Larimer Street. Several chiefs carried American flags, and according to Tom Bensing, "carriages of many of the leading citizens tagged along the rear of the formation." At the meetings, the Indians assured Evans they wanted peace. Many Denverites seemed willing to give peace a chance. But volunteers with the Third Regiment nearly mutinied when they learned that they might not get a chance to attack Indians. It was hard to stop the momentum.

Seeking refuge from the growing crisis, peaceful bands headed toward Fort Lyon. About 650 Arapahos under leaders Little Raven and Left Hand arrived at the fort in mid-October. Major Wynkoop issued the starving band emergency rations. For Wynkoop's valiant efforts to fulfill U.S. treaty obligations and to keep the peace, he was rewarded with a reprimand and a transfer. The government charged him with coddling the Indians with food and supplies and allowing them to loiter around the post and to leave the district without authority.

The Army replaced Wynkoop with Major Scott Anthony, who maintained a hard line at first but ultimately followed Wynkoop's model. Anthony demanded that all the Arapahos who came to Fort Lyon surrender their guns, and they complied. Recognizing their peaceable intent, Anthony continued to issue rations to the Arapahos, until he ran out. Anthony had to turn Black Kettle's band away from the fort, but he told them that if they went to Sand Creek, twenty-five miles to the northeast, "no war would be waged against them."

But Governor Evans and Colonel Chivington had other ideas. The one hundred days of the Third Regiment were about to end. Denverites had taken to ridiculing them as the "bloodless Third" because they had engaged in no true battles. These men did not take kindly to having their masculinity called into question.

Chivington ordered them into the field on November 14. He could have marched them toward the camps on the Smoky Hill River where the Cheyenne Dog Soldiers and other militant groups were based. These were the Indians who were at war with the United States. Instead, Chivington ordered his men to march to Fort Lyon and toward the bands that had renounced violence. The troops arrived on November 28.

At the fort, Chivington convened a group of military officers and local settlers to propose his plan of attack on the Cheyennes and Arapahos at Sand Creek. He must have known that not all military leaders would support his decision to strike the peaceable groups camped nearby. Upon his arrival, he immediately put a guard around the fort to prevent anyone leaving and alerting the Indians to an imminent assault.

Major Anthony told Chivington that now that there were enough troops, he favored attacking the Indians camped at Sand Creek. Several military officers were stunned and questioned Anthony's decision. Captain Silas Soule reminded Anthony that he had pledged to Black Kettle that "no war would be waged against them." A delegation of officers, local civilians, and the Indian agent tried to dissuade Chivington and Anthony from any attack. Undeterred, at 8:00 p.m. on November 28, Chivington and Anthony led their troops out of Fort Lyon and toward Sand Creek.

Warning: what follows is horrific. I do not share this history lightly. Some of my colleagues think we should no longer write about such violence, that in reproducing it we are potentially retraumatizing the descendants of those who suffered it while enabling gratuitous historical rubbernecking for everyone else.

Other colleagues think that only Indigenous people themselves should tell their own histories. A white settler historian like me should not be writing about this history. We have certainly read enough settler accounts of Indigenous defeat. Many of these narratives have either mythologized this history as the inevitable triumph of settlers or turned Indigenous people into the most abject victims.

I respect these objections. Yet I've decided to write about this atrocity because it is as much a part of settler history as it is the Cheyenne and Arapaho past. And I think as a settler scholar I have a responsibility to reach out to other settlers who have never learned this truth. We settlers need to own this truth, to "wear" it, as one Australian settler friend puts it.

My intent in retelling this atrocity is to grapple with *settler* experience and history, to reckon with what some of our settler ancestors did and to contemplate what we have therefore inherited. I want us to consider how this history lives within us today, whether we are direct descendants of settlers from this place and time or those who simply now live on this stolen land.

November 29, 1864. It was that quiet time of year in Colorado when the soft chill and occasional snow of late fall shifts to a deeper cold. There are many brilliant sunny days, but the light retreats early and then the cold descends. An estimated 700–1,100 Cheyenne and Arapaho Indians had lofted their tepees—about 120 in total—along a sharp bend of Sand Creek, far out on the plains of southeastern Colorado.

That day in the Cheyenne and Arapaho camp George Bent was just a teenager. He had grown up on the Front Range, the third son of Owl Woman and William Bent. On most such winter days George would have awakened to a peaceful scene. Perhaps he liked to linger in his bed of bison robes, encircled in the tepee by his family, sheltered in his camp by low sandy bluffs and groves of willows and cottonwoods that curved around the bend in the creek bed.

But on this day George awoke to a rumbling. He must have looked quizzically at his relatives in his lodge. What could that sound be? Some of them thought it might be a large herd of bison. After suffering from near starvation for over a year, maybe they smiled with anticipation of a successful hunt and full bellies.

Suddenly, though, shouts and the noise of people running about the camp pierced the quiet morning. George rushed from his lodge to see hundreds of American troops charging their horses up the creek bed. About 675 soldiers had ridden nearly fifty miles overnight from Fort Lyon to make this surprise attack on a peaceful camp. Think about that ratio: nearly one soldier for every Indian person in the camp. Consider, too, that this was a camp primarily of children, their mothers, and their grandparents. Many of the adult men were away hunting.

George Bent later described this scene of utter terror to George Hyde, a sympathetic settler Nebraskan who wrote early histories of Plains Indian tribes: "From down the creek a large body of troops was advancing at a rapid trot, . . . all was confusion and noise—men, women, and children rushing out of the lodges partly dressed; women and children screaming at the sight of the troops; men running back into the lodges for their arms, other men, already armed, or with lassos and bridles in their hands, running for the herds to attempt to get some of the ponies before the troops could reach the animals and drive them off."

Black Kettle tried to signal to the oncoming soldiers that the people there were friends of the United States, not enemies. George told Hyde, "I looked toward the chief's lodge and saw that Black Kettle had a large American flag tied to the end of a long lodgepole and was standing in front of his lodge, holding the pole, with a flag fluttering in the grey light of the winter dawn. I heard him call to the people not to be afraid, that the soldiers would not hurt them." But Black Kettle's gesture was futile. George recounted that soon after Black Kettle's announcement, "the troops opened fire from two sides of the camp."

Most of the people in camp were at the mercy of the soldiers. They tried to flee up the dry creek bed. But few made it. George told Hyde, "We ran up the creek with the cavalry following us, one company on each bank, keeping right after us and firing all the time. Many of the people had preceded us up the creek, and the dry bed of the stream was now a terrible sight: men, women, and children lying thickly scattered on the sand, some dead and the rest too badly wounded to move."

George ran for two miles up the creek—about the equivalent of a modern-day three-thousand-meter steeplechase race—in sand and all the while being chased by armed men on horses. Those who escaped the cavalry attack dug holes in the sides of the creekbanks, searching for protection. George joined two young girls and their parents to frantically dig a burrow into the high bank. They all must have been utterly exhausted, sweating, panting, trembling. Somehow, they mustered the energy to scoop out great handfuls of sand as fast as they could. Then they waited together for hours in their cramped pit, unable to mute the unrelenting gunfire or the desperate cries of their relatives.

The killing went on until the middle of the afternoon, perhaps seven to eight hours. Seven or eight hours: A day's work. A night's sleep. A flight from New York to London. A drive from Los Angeles to San Francisco. That's a long time to be under siege. That's also a very long time to *carry out* a siege, especially after having ridden eight to ten hours through a freezing Colorado night.

We don't know the exact number of Indian people that Chivington's troops killed. The National Park Service estimates that 230 people died. Black Kettle and his wife survived, but the Cheyenne leaders Ochinee and White Antelope were slaughtered. The Arapaho chief Left Hand died of his wounds several days after the massacre. The Arapaho people he had led suffered some of the heaviest casualties.

The wanton killing was bad enough, but the aftermath of the massacre compounded the trauma of those who had survived the attack. As it grew dark, and the soldiers withdrew down the creek, the survivors came out of their hiding places and surveyed the gruesome damage. George's friend Little Bear had also run up the creek bed as twenty cavalrymen chased him. "I passed many women and children, dead and dying, lying in the creek bed. . . . After the fight I came back down the creek and saw these dead bodies all cut up, and even the wounded scalped and slashed. I saw one old woman wandering about; her whole scalp had been taken off and the blood was running down into her eyes so that she could not see where to go."

Later that night, the Sand Creek survivors straggled out on to the "bleak, frozen plain, without any shelter whatever and not a stick of wood to build a fire with." George recalled that "most of us were wounded and half naked." Those who were not wounded built fires all night long with grass to try to keep the wounded alive. George told Hyde, "That was the worst night I ever went through." The next day the survivors headed on to the Smoky Hill camp, where other Cheyennes met and mourned with them and tended their injuries. Governor Evans and Colonel Chivington had literally driven a group of peace-seeking Indians into the arms of those the government deemed hostile and at war.

While the Cheyenne and Arapaho survivors mourned their dead, most of the soldiers rejoiced and made merry. They picked through the Indians' camp, pirating knives and pots and beaded moccasins before burning all the lodges to the ground. They collected other "mementos" from the day. They sheared scalps from heads. They severed beringed fingers from hands. They carved women's breasts from their chests and sliced men's and women's genitalia from their bodies. They even castrated the Cheyenne peace leader White Antelope and used his scrotum as a tobacco pouch. I can almost hear the laughter and bravado of the hundreds of men as they compared their gruesome trophies.

Nearly a month later, most of the soldiers were still reveling in their victory. They marched back to Denver a few days before Christmas. As a jubilant crowd cheered, the men paraded through the city streets, led by the First Regiment Band and Colonel Chivington. Many of them displayed the scalps and body parts they had retrieved after the massacre. The governor and other prominent citizens feted the volunteers. A Denver Theater troupe created a musical revue about Sand Creek that packed houses for days. One evening, the theater hosted a special display of the "trophies" that soldiers had taken at Sand Creek.

I ponder how these men could reconcile what they had done at Sand Creek with the hymns they sang in church on Sundays or the unofficial anthem, "My Country 'Tis of Thee, Sweet Land of Liberty" they crooned on the Fourth of July. I wonder, too, how the citizens of Colorado could sanction and celebrate such violence.

To live with what they had done, the soldiers and the settlers who supported them had to come up with a powerful justification for engaging in and supporting such violence. They needed to narrate a history that erased Indian people and their claims to the land and utterly denied their humanity. They needed a lore that authorized their right to take over the land. That is how our winning-the-West narratives developed and became so popular.

It was just over a hundred years after George Bent had awakened to pure terror on a cold November morning that my family moved to the Front Range. Every year as a child I treasured the gradual shift from fall to winter. When I woke up each morning, I would lie warm under the covers and gaze out my window, the sun rising over Rampart Range. On some days, a gentle snow would be falling, muffling the day's noises, coaxing me back to sleep if it weren't a school day. On most days the morning light would gradually flood the backyard, growing in intensity and brilliance. The cottonwoods down by the creek no longer had their leaves, but they stood as familiar sentinels, offering a comforting shelter around our 1960s ranch house.

It was Fountain Creek that streamed through my backyard and skittered down Ute Pass. It gurgled through Manitou Springs, then got channeled through concrete culverts in Colorado Springs. It turned south and eventually burst free from its industrial straits. It grew wider and muddier as it headed to Pueblo. There it rushed headlong into the Arkansas River, which came down from its mountain home and rolled out across the plains to the east. Other little creeks also met up with the Arkansas. One of these was Big Sandy Creek, or Sand Creek. It was often dry parts of the year. At other times its waters would mingle in the Arkansas with the water that had journeyed from my backyard.

I had so little idea of what had transpired in this place where I grew up, on this land that I loved so much. When I became a historian of the West, I learned to sift through accounts of the past, to gauge the credibility of a source, to weigh the eyewitness accounts against the media puff pieces. And the truth of settler crimes, at Sand Creek and at so many other sites of terror and trauma, became inescapable. It horrified me to learn, and it still never fails to appall me, that the place I grew up in was founded in such a way—through deceit and through the most brutal violence imaginable.

Few settlers want to believe that the creation of our nation depended on such cruelty. Many of us prefer the heroic version: the daring exploits of brave pioneers, hardy homesteaders, enterprising miners, and stalwart mountain men. And thus, the history of the American West and of events like Sand Creek becomes another kind of battleground, one where we wage war over historical meaning as much as the land.

CHAPTER 2

Eyes

It has taken a long time, but many settlers now agree that Sand Creek was an abomination. And we acknowledge that there were other such atrocities, like the 1890 Wounded Knee Massacre. But we settlers like to comfort ourselves that these were isolated incidents, rogue events, the exception, not the rule. But do you actually know how many massacres of Indigenous people in America took place?

As a historian who studies settler-Indigenous relations in the West, I should know. I should be able to give you a definitive number or at least a ballpark figure. And I should be able to list them. But most of these massacres have been thoroughly covered up. We are learning all the time of other Sand Creeks. As I was writing this book, I learned for the first time of the Bear River Massacre of Shoshone people, which occurred in 1863, just a little under two years before Sand Creek.

It was Darren Parry, chairman of the Northwestern Band of the Shoshone Nation, who taught me about it when I interviewed him at a Western History Association conference in Las Vegas in 2019. The only place we could find to do the interview was in a back room of the conference hotel where the air vents rattled as the air conditioner whirred. We had arranged with the manager ahead of time to use the room, but hotel employees pushed dollies in and out of the room, and piled supplies on pallets all around us, as we talked about an event every bit as gruesome as Sand Creek.

But Chairman Parry was unfazed. He told me that he was raised by his grandmother for the first six years of his life while his parents worked. She was a native speaker of his language and a tribal historian. She was frustrated, she told her grandson, that "I've been trying to tell our story for my whole life, and no one will listen." She told him, "One day you're going to have to tell our story." He in fact has made it his mission to convey the history of his tribe to settlers in Utah and beyond.

Parry estimates that he has told the story of the Bear River Massacre at least three hundred times, but he often still gets emotional when he recounts it. "I don't put it on autopilot and just start talking about it. Sometimes it's tough." He adds, "I talk about it all the time, but it's still new to me every day." And so, he recounts it again, for me.

Parry's people lived in the mountainous Cache Valley, where they had access to abundant fish and game as well as seeds and berries. Their horse herds fed on lush grasses. Mormon settlers migrated to the Salt Lake City area, eighty miles south of the Cache Valley, beginning in 1847. As their population swelled, they began to colonize land further and further afield.

The Mormons "sent four thousand head of cattle one summer" to the Cache Valley, "and now those cattle are eating the seeds and grasses that the Shoshone depended on. . . . The pioneers are hunting the same deer, elk, moose that we relied on. They were fishing out all of the streams to survive. And now you have a depletion of resources that frankly left our people in a tough spot."

It was an all-too-familiar settler colonial story. "So, now you have Mormon settlers who are putting up fences, building homes, they have their cattle out in their field and our people are starving now, their way of life is completely gone. . . . Now you have the California and Oregon trails cut right through the heart of it. . . . And it was just too much."

Conflict between settlers and the Shoshone ensued in northern Utah and southeastern Idaho just as it did in the eastern half of Colorado. "I'm sure there were Indian depredations that took place. I think our people—I say this all the time—had three options. Beg for food, starve, or steal. And I'm sure they did all three." The Mormon "saints that lived in that area were writing letters to Brigham Young, come take care of the Indian problem. They are stealing our cattle. You know, they're a nuisance to us and we need to get rid of them."

The response of the Army to the growing crisis was similar, too, to what happened in Colorado. Colonel Patrick Connor, at Camp Douglas in Salt Lake City, had been overseeing a regiment of soldiers, Chairman Parry explains, who were "men who had signed up in California years earlier to fight in the Civil War [but] found themselves babysitting the Mormons who weren't causing much of a problem." Then they "got word that there's an Indian problem less than eighty miles away." So, Connor and his bored soldiers "jumped at the chance to go take care of the problem."

It is as if the Bear River Massacre was a prototype for Sand Creek. The soldiers marched northward from Camp Douglas on January 27 and arrived early on the morning of January 29. They surveyed the peaceful Shoshone camp from the bluffs overlooking the Bear River. The Shoshone leader, Sagwitch, saw the troops above the camp and advised his people to gather their weapons. But, as he had done in the past, he expected to negotiate with the troops to prevent any conflict.

Instead, Connor and his men charged down the bluff, rode across the river, and then started firing as they got closer. "Indian men, women, and children were now being butchered like rabbits," Chairman Parry recounts. "They killed everybody they could find. One of the local Mormon saints who lived there . . . watched from the bluff, and he said that some of the men were taking the infants by their heels and bashing their heads out on rocks."

The conflict, Parry says, "started maybe as a battle for about the first ten minutes, . . . and then it really rapidly turned into a wholesale massacre over the next four hours." Later that day a local settler surveyed the scene and counted a little over four hundred dead, mostly women and children. Because the ground was frozen, neither the Army nor local soldiers made any attempt to bury the bodies. "Those bones were just left there, and they are still there today, they are just under the surface."

Parry explains that Sand Creek and many other massacres followed a similar script. "I think Chivington and [Connor] probably had a little correspondence. . . . Here's the playbook for Native Americans, you know, if we want to take care of them, here's the playbook. You don't attack them in the summer when they're out and about and scattered and can hide. The winters were always story time. They're always time of being with family. They never prepared for war and other tribes didn't attack other tribes in the winter. It was always a sacred time of the year. But once the Army figured that out, I think it became the playbook going forward for other massacres."

Parry talks about the massacre every chance he gets, because so few people know about it. He only found "a three-line blurb, a tiny little piece in the *San Francisco Chronicle* that said there was a massacre at Bear River, 250 Indians were killed. And that's about it." Even local settlers are unaware of the massacre. "Even as I go around Logan, which is fifteen miles away from this horrific massacre, it's crazy to me how many people don't know about it at all."

I asked him why more people in America are ignorant of the Bear River Massacre. "I think the shock and horror of seeing what had happened the next day for those [Mormon settlers] was really too much." They simply could not face up to what had happened. I asked him if any of the soldiers and settlers had spoken out against the atrocity. He said no, although many had written of it in their diaries. These are the very journals that Chairman Parry uses today to provide corroboration for the histories his grandmother relayed to him, written records that today's settlers are more likely to believe.

Bear River and Sand Creek are two of at least hundreds, if not thousands, of violent settler massacres of Indigenous people that occurred across the nation. My colleague Benjamin Madley has documented more than 370 massacres—of five or more Indigenous people—in California alone between 1846 and 1873 in his book *American Genocide*. Most likely, unless you are a California Indian, you have never heard of any of these. In September 1864, for example, just two months before Chivington's troops opened fire on the Arapahos and Cheyennes at Sand Creek, settlers killed 300 California Indians just north of Millville.

Our lack of knowledge of all this violence surely has something to do with Michael Ignatieff's insight that "all nations depend on forgetting." We have been calling this abject violence "westward expansion" for a very long time. For most of us, it is deeply uncomfortable to contemplate that what we have been celebrating as "winning the West" is really mass murder, committed in order to appropriate the land.

I never heard about Sand Creek as a child, but more and more settlers in Colorado and the nation have learned at least something about it in the last few decades. But why do we know about Sand Creek when we know little to nothing about countless other massacres?

What made the difference is that two settler soldiers, Captain Silas Soule and Lieutenant Joseph Cramer, broke ranks and reported the abominable violence they witnessed at Sand Creek. Soule and Cramer had opposed the action from the beginning, but they were forced to lead their men on the overnight march from Fort Lyon to Sand Creek. Once the massacre began, however, Soule and Cramer commanded their men to refrain from charging or firing.

Soule and Cramer witnessed the carnage and confirmed the accounts of George Bent and other survivors. Silas wrote to his mother a few weeks after the atrocities at Sand Creek, a week before Christmas. He began by apologizing for his tardy reply to her last letter. "The day you wrote," he told her, "I was present at a Massacre of three hundred Indians mostly women and children. It was a horrable [sic] scene and I would not let my Company fire. They were friendly and some of our soldiers were in their Camp at the time trading. It looked too hard for me to see little Children on their knees begging for their lives, have their brains beat out like dogs." Soule wrote again to his mother a few weeks later, telling her, "I spent New Year's day on the battle ground counting dead Indians. . . . most of them were women and children and all of them scalped."

Soule spared his mother the grisliest details. These he included in a letter to Major Edward Wynkoop. I include his words here as an act of witnessing, with a warning that they are more disturbing still than George Bent's account of the carnage. Soule described how Major Anthony had rushed with three companies of soldiers to within a hundred yards of the Cheyenne and Arapaho camp. By this time, he wrote, "hundreds of women and children were coming toward us and getting on their knees for mercy." The major shouted, "'kill the sons of bitches.'"

Soule described something of his horror to Wynkoop: "I tell you Ned it was hard to see little children on their knees have their brains beat out by men professing to be civilized."

Soule was deeply disturbed by the actions of his compatriots. In his letter he used a derogatory term for American Indian women, a term that stings bitterly today. But he demonstrated much empathy toward the Cheyenne and Arapaho women and utterly condemned the butchery that he saw:

> One squaw was wounded and a fellow took a hatchet to finish her, and he cut one arm off, and held the other with one hand and dashed the hatchet through her brain. One squaw with her two children, were on their knees, begging for their lives of a dozen soldiers, within ten feet of them all firing—when one succeeded in hitting the squaw in the thigh, when she took a knife and cut the throats of both children and then killed herself. One Old Squaw hung herself in the lodge— there was not enough room for her to hang and she held up her knees and choked herself to death. Some tried to escape on the Prairie, but most of them were run down by horsemen. I saw two Indians hold one of anothers hands, chased until they were exhausted, when they kneeled down, and clasped each other around the neck and both were shot together. They were all scalped, and as high as half a dozen taken from one head. They were all horribly mutilated. One woman was cut open and a child taken out of her, and scalped. White Antelope, War Bonnet, and a number of others had Ears and Privates cut off. Squaws snatches [vaginas] were cut out for trophies. You would think it impossible for white men to butcher and mutilate human beings as they did there, but every word I have told you is the truth, which they do not deny.

Lieutenant Cramer also wrote to Wynkoop to testify about the atrocities he had witnessed. "Bucks [Indian men], women, and children were scalped, fingers cut off to get the rings on them," Cramer wrote to Wynkoop, "and this as much with Officers as men, and one of those Officers a Major, and a Lt. Col. cut off Ears, of all he came across, a squaw ripped open and a child taken from her, little children shot, while begging for their lives and all the indignities shown their bodies that was ever heard of (women shot while on their knees, with their arms around soldiers begging for their lives). Things that Indians would be ashamed to do. To give you some little idea, squaws were known to kill their own children, and then themselves, rather than to have them taken prisoners. . . . But enough! For I know you are disgusted already." Cramer knew that even a seasoned military man like Wynkoop would be sickened by this report.

Cramer confirmed, too, what George Bent relayed: that the camp was led by chiefs seeking peace and who still held out hope—through the bullets—that the Americans would make good on their promises. "Black Kettle said when he saw us coming, that he was glad, for it was Major Wynkoop coming to make peace. Left Hand stood with his hands folded across his breast, until he was shot saying, 'Soldiers no hurt me—soldiers my friends.' One Eye [Ochinee] was killed; was in the employ of Gov't as spy; came into the Post a few days before, and reported about the Sioux, were going to break out at Learned, which proved true."

If Soule and Cramer had not relayed their eyewitness accounts to Wynkoop settlers might have little knowledge of this atrocity today. Sand Creek might have remained an obscure event, still embedded in the memories of its survivors and their descendants, but unknown to most settlers. Sadly, it seems that only when settlers spoke out against the atrocities they witnessed did settler authorities take the abuses seriously and record them for posterity. And sadly, few massacres gained national attention because most settlers averted their eyes from these crimes. So it may be that without Soule and Cramer coming forward, the Sand Creek Massacre would have remained a story that the Cheyennes and Arapahos told among themselves or to a few history buff settlers who were willing to listen.

I am not suggesting that we should credit Soule and Cramer with rescuing the Cheyennes and Arapahos, their truths, or their histories. This is not a book about white saviors. But it is a book about becoming accountable as settlers for the histories of injustice and abuse against Indigenous peoples. Many of us learn best by example, and Silas Soule and Joseph Cramer offer powerful models of how to bear witness to atrocities and to be accountable.

It would be easy to focus on the majority of settlers who witnessed injustice and atrocity but did not speak out. In the case of Sand Creek, only two men out of the 675 or so soldiers who attacked the camp decided to report on the atrocities. We could be deeply disappointed in the 673 men who took part in the killings and held their tongues.

But we could also marvel at the two men who refused to obey orders that they knew to be wrong, who had the moral courage to step forward and testify to what they saw. It only takes a few committed persons to turn the course of history. I ponder what qualities and experiences led Soule and Cramer to buck the trend of fear and hatred that were all around them in Colorado in 1864. And I wonder about how we can cultivate such qualities among settlers today to face injustice, past and present.

Perhaps Soule's abolitionist upbringing in New England had predisposed him to care not only about injustices against African Americans but also about those suffered by American Indians. His family had harbored escapees from slavery on the Underground Railroad. Like many ardent opponents of slavery, his family felt compelled to emigrate to Kansas shortly after Congress passed the Kansas-Nebraska Act, allowing the new territory of Kansas to decide through so-called popular sovereignty if it would be a free or a slave state. Soule's father and brother moved to Lawrence, Kansas—a town of Free Staters—in 1854. Soule was seventeen when he and the rest of his family joined them in 1855.

Through his family, Soule was caught up in the abolitionist politics of his time. But he was also susceptible to other trends; he and his brother ventured to Colorado in 1860 to prospect for gold. When that didn't pan out, Soule found work as a blacksmith and then joined the military. He was known among his fellow soldiers as a practical joker. He managed to get a lieutenant's commission in the new Company K of the Colorado First Infantry at the end of 1861, and he did his part during the Civil War by fighting against Confederate forces in New Mexico. After his service, he settled in Denver, where he became a recruiter for his unit, now converted from the First Infantry to the First Cavalry. He was also a Denver media darling. He was promoted to the rank of captain in the spring of 1864 and put in command of

Company D of the First Colorado Cavalry. Soule oversaw a company of 94 troopers at Fort Lyon beginning in June 1864. He was just twenty-six years old.

Much less is known about Lieutenant Joseph Cramer, Joe to his friends. He was born in New York in 1838, so he was the same age as Soule. We don't know if he was as steeped in the moral crusades of his time as Soule was. (This was the period in which a large number of Americans not only campaigned against slavery but crusaded for women's rights and joined utopian communities.) But Cramer did have at least two things in common with Soule: he had come to Colorado as a prospector, hoping to strike it rich, and he had grown tired of the mining life and joined the same regiment as Soule. He was likely to have participated in the Battle at Glorieta Pass against Confederate forces in New Mexico with Soule. He was promoted to second lieutenant in 1863.

Soule and Cramer were not pacifists, and they were not opposed to settler colonialism. They certainly did not resist all military action against Indians. Cramer had avidly participated in an attack on a band of Arapahos in 1864. But both men made careful distinctions between which Indians remained at war with the United States and which sought peace. They did not subscribe to the popular adage of the day: the only good Indian is a dead Indian. They also utterly opposed the wanton killing of women and children.

Soule's life had some eerie parallels with that of Colonel John Chivington, the mastermind behind the Sand Creek Massacre. Chivington was almost a generation older than Soule; he had been born in 1821 in Ohio. But like Soule, Chivington had been deeply influenced by the Second Great Awakening, an upsurge of religious revivalism, and the social justice movements of the early to mid-nineteenth century.

In 1842, at a religious revival meeting, Chivington converted to Methodism, a radical denomination at the time that outspokenly championed women's and black rights. He became an itinerant minister for the Methodist Episcopal Church in Illinois, Missouri, and Kansas. After the passage of the Kansas-Nebraska Act in 1854, Chivington became an ardent opponent of slavery. It took great courage on his part to preach as a Free State Methodist minister in slave-state Missouri in this period.

Chivington also seemed to have some sympathy for, or at least some nonviolent encounters with, Indians in the 1850s. Beginning in 1853, he served as a missionary to the Wyandot Indians in Kansas. The newly organized Kansas-Nebraska conference of the Methodist Episcopal Church recruited him to serve as pastor of the Methodist Episcopal Church in Omaha in 1856. In 1858, he became the presiding elder in Nebraska City.

Chivington impressed his followers, both by his physical stature and by his preaching. Journalists described him as having a "commanding presence" and a "herculean frame." According to historian Lori Cox-Paul, the *Nebraska Advertiser* in nearby Brownville reported that he was "making rapid advancement as a public speaker and sound theologian. We can but regard him as a man of extraordinary natural abilities, destined to make his mark in the religious world."

Soon Chivington moved to the new territory of Colorado, taking up the post of presiding elder of the Rocky Mountain District of the Methodist Episcopal Church in 1860. His parishioners were very sorry to see him go. The *Nebraska City News* expressed "regret . . . in the loss of so valuable and worthy a citizen." The *People's Press*, a rival newspaper in the same town, declared that the citizens of the area "have learned to respect and esteem him for his manly character in society, and his zeal and activity in his spiritual calling."

When the Civil War broke out, Colorado's new territorial governor offered the Methodist minister a post as regimental chaplain, but Chivington requested a military commission instead, asserting, "I feel compelled to strike a blow in person for the destruction of human slavery and to help in some measure to make this a truly free country."

In his post as major of the First Colorado Regiment in 1861, Chivington seemed to win the respect of his men but the enmity of his superior officer, Colonel John Slough, who labeled Chivington that "crazy preacher who thinks he is Napoleon Bonaparte" and called for his court-martial. But Slough grudgingly praised Chivington's actions at the 1862 Glorieta Pass battle. It is here that the lives of Chivington and Soule intersected. They, in fact, knew each other and had even been friends through their military service.

These two men had very similar backgrounds and were both ardent opponents of slavery. They were animated by the big moral questions of their time. So, it's puzzling that Soule and Chivington parted ways so dramatically over Sand Creek. Colorado's Indigenous people were starving, due to the pressure of incoming miners and settlers, and settlers were plundering their land. But Chivington had virtually no sympathy for the Cheyenne and Arapaho people who stole stock from settlers to try to alleviate their hunger. He agreed wholeheartedly with the sentiments of a Colorado official who declared "they are stealing large numbers of stock, and refusing to give them up, . . . there is but one course left for us to pursue, that is, to make them behave or kill them, which latter it now seems we shall have to do."

It's hard to fathom the motives of people in our own time—from our own sisters and brothers to the president of the United States. So it is even more difficult to comprehend what might have driven a man like Chivington—an abolitionist and Methodist minister—to become such a bloodthirsty Indian killer.

It's clear that Chivington developed grand ambitions and was frustrated when he was thwarted. He gained promotion to colonel and appointment as commander of the Military District of Colorado after the Battle at Glorieta Pass, but he hoped in vain to become a brigadier general. He ran for state representative for Colorado in 1864, should the territory be admitted to the Union as a state. He ran on a campaign of Indian killing, allegedly promising to "'kill and scalp all [Indians], little and big.'" But Colorado did not become a state in 1864 (it didn't until 1876), so Chivington didn't gain political power. Some of the citizens of Colorado had even complained that Chivington was failing in his role as commander of Colorado's Military District. One stagecoach owner asserted that Chivington was not doing enough to protect freight lines from Indian attack.

It may have been that Chivington saw Sand Creek as a means to save face, prove his valor, regain his honor, and position himself for future authority. Chivington's masculinity was under threat. Still, you probably could find a huge number of white settler men in Colorado whose manhood was dangerously fragile. Failed miners. Ne'er-do-wells. There had to be other conditions that made it possible for Chivington to unleash his vicious rage on the Cheyenne and Arapaho people at Sand Creek who had bent over backward to be peaceable and accommodating.

The conditions were this: Evans, Chivington, and some other military leaders, the press, and some settlers had utterly dehumanized the Cheyennes and Arapahos. The *Rocky Mountain News* referred to the Indigenous inhabitants of the area as "thieving and marauding bands of savages" and advised "a few months of active extermination against the red devils" in August 1864. They had created the environment that enabled a seemingly insecure and power-hungry man like Chivington to ignore his own Christian convictions and attack a peaceable camp of Indians with a vicious hatred. They had also transformed white settlers from aggressors into victims, often invoking white womanhood to do so.

Silas Soule and Joe Cramer, on the other hand, though just twenty-six, kept true to their moral compasses. When Chivington arrived at Fort Lyon on the morning of November 28, and Soule and Cramer learned of his plans, they tried to talk Major Anthony out of the attack. Soule also went to the room of Lt. James Cannon, where many officers were gathered. He "berated the assembled men and said that any man who would take part in the murders was a 'low lived cowardly son of a bitch.'"

Cramer approached Chivington and told him that his planned attack was not justified warfare but outright murder. He reminded him that Black Kettle had saved their lives and was in favor of peace. Chivington responded that he "believed it to be right or honorable to use any means necessary under God's heaven to kill Indians that would kill women and children, and damn any man that is in sympathy with Indians." Soule planned to make his case against the attack to Chivington, too, but Cramer warned him against it; he said some members of the Third wanted to hang Soule after some of the men in Cannon's room had reported Soule's comments to Chivington. Anthony also warned Soule that Chivington had made threats against him.

So it was that on the morning of November 29, although Soule and Cramer led their men to Sand Creek, both refused to allow their men to fire. And following the massacre, both men wrote to Major Wynkoop, who forwarded their letters up through the military command. Their decision to bear witness to the Sand Creek atrocities, rather than to participate in them, led to three comprehensive investigations, a process not unlike some of the truth and reconciliation commissions that nations around the world would launch more than one hundred years later.

The new commander of the district of Colorado, Thomas Moonlight, ordered a military investigation of Sand Creek to be headed by Samuel Tappan "to ascertain . . . who are the aggressors, whether the campaign was conducted by Colonel Chivington according to the recognized rules of civilized warfare," and "whether the Indians were under the protection of the government." Chivington sought to challenge the authority of the commission, but it began its hearings on February 15, 1865, in Denver. It called Soule as its first witness. He testified for six days. Cramer followed, testifying for five days. On March 20, Tappan moved his inquiry to Fort Lyon, where he took testimony from Wynkoop, for another five days.

When called on to testify, Chivington claimed that he had seen no mutilations, no dead children, and only two dead women. He claimed instead that his soldiers found settler scalps in the camp, proof that these Indians were truly hostile to settlers. He also claimed that the holes that Indians had dug desperately into the banks of Sand Creek for protection during the massacre were fortified positions they had prepared in advance from which to fight the soldiers. He, in short, insisted that this was a battle, not a massacre.

Two other investigations ensued, one by the Army's judge advocate general, Joseph Holt, and one by Congress's Joint Committee on the Conduct of War. They carefully weighed testimony from Soule, Cramer, Chivington, Wynkoop, Anthony, and many others. These inquiries were an important step in creating a government-sponsored process—a kind of proto-Truth and Reconciliation Commission—for responding to mass atrocities against Indigenous people. But they differed significantly from our modern TRCs because they did not seek out testimony from the Cheyenne and Arapaho survivors who had suffered the abuse directly.

Nevertheless, all of the investigations condemned Chivington in the most conclusive terms. Holt called Sand Creek "a coldblooded slaughter" that would "cover its perpetrators with indelible infamy." The Joint Committee concluded that Chivington had "deliberately planned and executed a foul and dastardly massacre," not a justified battle against hostile combatants. The investigation showed that despite Chivington's denials, three-quarters of the victims were women and children. It condemned officers for failing to restrain the "savage cruelty of the men under their command." It noted that "men, women, and children were indiscriminately slaughtered. . . . A few who endeavored to hide themselves under the back of the creek were surrounded and shot down in cold blood. . . . From the sucking babe to the old warrior, all who were overtaken were deliberately murdered. Not content with killing women and children, who were incapable of offering any resistance, the soldiers indulged in acts of barbarity of the most revolting character; such, it is to be hoped, as never before disgraced the acts of men claiming to be civilized."

Another government body, the Indian Peace Commission, concluded in its report to the president in 1868 that Sand Creek "scarcely has its parallel in the records of Indian barbarity. Fleeing women, holding up their hands and praying for mercy, were shot down; infants were killed and scalped in derision; men were tortured and mutilated in a manner that would put to shame the savages of interior Africa." (Notice that even when they are condemning the actions of white settlers and soldiers, the government cannot resist denigrating another group experiencing colonization.)

Like modern-day TRCs, the investigations sought to understand what had motivated the massacre. The Joint Committee Report stated that Governor Evans's order, enabling settlers to take Indian property, appealed to the "cupidity" of settlers. It asserted that Chivington was hoping to gain political office as a result of the massacre and that he had attacked Sand Creek in order to avoid more dangerous conflicts. Army officials recommended that Chivington be ousted from his position and court-martialed.

The investigations also examined the long-term consequences of the atrocity. The Indian Peace Commission determined that if Sand Creek was meant to bring the Cheyennes and Arapahos to heel, it had failed miserably. It reported that "no one will be astonished that a war ensued, which cost the Government $30,000,000, and carried conflagration and death into the border settlements. During the Summer and Spring of 1865, no less than 8,000 troops were withdrawn from the effective forces engaged in the Rebellion to meet this Indian war."

It was the eyewitness testimony of Soule and Cramer—first in their letters to Wynkoop and then in the first investigation—that led to the scrutiny of Chivington's actions and his censure. Their courage meant that the U.S. government could not cover up this crime, as they had so many other massacres. And at first it looked as if Soule's and Cramer's decisions to speak out might bring some vindication to the Cheyennes and Arapahos.

The Sand Creek investigations, in fact, prefigured modern-day truth and reconciliation commissions because they also considered how to make some form of redress for the massacre. General John Sanborn held council on October 12, 1865, with the remnants of Arapaho and Cheyenne bands that had escaped from Sand Creek. He formally and officially repudiated the actions of American soldiers at Sand Creek. He told them, "We all feel disgraced and ashamed when we see our officers or soldiers oppressing the weak, or making war on those who are at peace with us."

Acknowledging that the government, through Chivington, had committed a great wrong, General Sanborn even offered reparations to the Cheyennes and Arapahos. First he offered restitution, the actual return of lost property. "We are willing, as representatives of the President," he said, "to restore all the property lost at Sand Creek or its value. . . . [The president] has sent out his commissioners to make reparation, as far as we can." Then he offered compensation for the harms the soldiers had committed. He told the group of Arapaho and Cheyenne survivors, "So heartily do we repudiate the actions of our soldiers that we are willing to give to the chiefs in their own right 320 acres of land each to hold as his own forever, and to each of the children and squaws who lost husbands or parents we are also willing to give 160 acres of land as their own to keep as long as they live." Here was an early form of settler redress for

gross human rights abuses against Indigenous peoples. It included several of the key ingredients of truth and reconciliation today: an acknowledgment of the harm, some restitution, and compensation.

But this was not a thorough truth and reconciliation process that
sought to examine and reform U.S. government policy more deeply; it
was extremely limited. Vindication and modest reparations did not lead
to meaningful change in the way the government dealt with the Cheyennes and Arapahos, or other tribes. Just four years later, at the so-called
Battle of Washita, the U.S. cavalry, under the command of George Armstrong Custer, led another surprise dawn attack on Black Kettle's peaceable camp, on November 27, 1868, and this time the venerable chief did
not survive. At least one hundred of his band members also died in this
massacre.

Soule's and Cramer's actions did not lead to personal glory either. Instead settler courage could exact a high price. Many settlers ostracized
and stigmatized Soule when he returned to Denver in January 1865 for
speaking out against Sand Creek and for his supposed betrayal of
Chivington. He also gained a lot of enemies in his new role as assistant
provost marshal. After the Cheyennes and Arapahos increased their attacks on settlers in retaliation for Sand Creek, the governor declared
martial law in Denver. As assistant provost marshal, Soule was tasked
with searching for and taking possession of any government-issued sub-
sistence items found in Denver businesses. Soule also had to monitor
curfew, deal with crimes or disturbances by soldiers, and investigate
items stolen at Sand Creek to be returned to the Army.

Still Soule tried to get on with his life. He married Hersa Coberly on
April 1. One evening, three weeks later, as the newlyweds were returning
from a social occasion, Soule was called to deal with two soldiers shoot-
ing their guns in downtown Denver. When he approached them,
Charles Squier, an enlistee in the Second Colorado Cavalry, shot him
in the face. Soule, who had not yet turned twenty-seven, did not survive.
Tappan's military commission was still meeting when Soule died, and
"in respect to the memory of the deceased" they adjourned their meeting early on the afternoon of April 24. Authorities caught Squier in New

Mexico and brought him to jail in Denver for killing Soule. But at least two men broke him out of jail; they were caught and arrested, but Squier was never brought to justice.

Although we have no conclusive evidence that Squier killed Soule because of his outspoken criticism of Chivington and the Sand Creek Massacre, many Coloradoans believed that to be the case at the time of his death. The military commission noted in their transcripts that Soule had been assassinated. There had already been two attempts on his life prior to Squier's attack. Soule had confided to a friend that "he fully expected to be killed because of his actions at Sand Creek and his subsequent testimony."

Joe Cramer also died an early death. Soon after he testified to Tappan's commission, he mustered out of the military in the spring of 1865 and moved to Kansas, where he married Hattie Phelps. Cramer applied for a position as an Indian agent but was denied. Instead he and his wife moved to Solomon, Kansas, where he worked as a clerk. Just three years into their marriage, his wife died. Joe remarried the following year, in 1869, and won election as county sheriff. But a back injury he had suffered in one of the military campaigns against Indians in 1864 left him bedridden. He died at age thirty-three.

Chivington, in the meantime, escaped justice and lived to a ripe old age. He resigned his commission in January 1865, and the Army was thus unable to court-martial him. He was never tried in a civilian court either. Nevertheless, Sand Creek had marked him. He never regained the respect and esteem he had once enjoyed as a Methodist minister and anti-slavery crusader. He never achieved the political power he longed for either.

He remained a divisive figure for the rest of his life. For many, he was an object of scorn, for others a hero. He sought to parlay his notoriety—and support from many Coloradoans—into a political career. He ran for Congress from Colorado in October 1865, his former troops parading through Denver on his behalf. But he withdrew his candidacy shortly before the election. He shuttled between Nebraska and Colorado in 1866–67, engaging in the freighting business to make a living.

In June 1867, he addressed the Nebraska legislature on "the Indian question." While his old friends at the *Rocky Mountain News* claimed that "his vigorous sentiments were endorsed ... unanimously," the *Omaha Daily Herald* found it scandalous that he had addressed the legislature. They described him as "the author of deeds that in another day of our history ... would have been called ... high crimes against every law of Christianity and human feeling." They denounced his speech "as a slander upon the Christian name and a hideous insult and disgrace to human nature."

Sand Creek seems to have stained Chivington's personal life as well. Shortly after the massacre he suffered much personal tragedy in the space of just a year. His son perished in a ferryboat accident. His granddaughter also drowned when she fell from a Missouri River steamboat. And just a few months later, his wife died from a long illness.

For the rest of his life Chivington engaged in erratic personal behaviors and petty crimes and was mired in scandals. At the age of forty-seven, he seduced and married his deceased son's widow, in part, it seems, to gain the assets of his son's estate. The couple lived for nine months in Omaha and then returned to Nebraska City, where an arsonist set their home on fire. Some suspected that Chivington himself lit the blaze to collect on an insurance policy. When this proved unsuccessful, the newlyweds moved to Washington, D.C., where he continued to press his son's claims as a means to make a living.

Scandal continued to dog Chivington—he was indicted for forgery and arrested for knocking a woman down on the street in Washington. Chivington abandoned his second wife/daughter-in-law in 1870, and she sought a divorce from him in 1871, citing non-support. In subsequent years when he filed claims for a pension and for compensation for Indian depredations, she testified against him.

In 1873, Chivington married another widow, Isabella Arnzen. Their first home in Ohio mysteriously burned, and they moved to another county where Chivington became a newspaper editor. Isabella had him arrested on charges that he had stolen from and beaten her. Even though Isabella appeared in court with a black eye and a bruised face, she dropped the charges against her husband and remained married to him until his death.

Chivington tried to run for the Ohio State Legislature but Sand Creek and his personal scandals came back to haunt him, and he withdrew from the race, but not before the *Clinton County Democrat* alleged that "under the cloak of religion he seeks to hide the deformity of his moral nature."

But Chivington still had his defenders. Colorado's Sand Creek deniers remained steadfast Chivington supporters. The Pioneers of Colorado invited him to speak in Denver in 1883. He and Isabella relocated there. And he was elected president of the state's veteran's association and asked to preach in several churches. He also found work first as an under-sheriff and then as a coroner. Soon Chivington ran afoul of the law again, however, first for perjury charges in his role as bailiff and then for stealing $800 from a corpse. While he got off on the first charge, he was forced to return most of the $800 to the dead man's estate.

Chivington spent much of the rest of his life in litigation, attempting to extract a military pension from the government and a depredation claim against the Oglala Sioux for $32,850 in damages in 1891, the year after another famous massacre at Wounded Knee. Neither claim was successful, and Chivington died soon after at the age of seventy-three in 1894.

But if Chivington's personal life suffered after Sand Creek, his iconic status remained. Trinity United Methodist Church in Denver held a grand funeral for him. It took an hour for all the onlookers to parade past his open coffin. And still today you may pass through the town of Chivington, Colorado, if you take the lonely drive east from Pueblo, Colorado, on Highway 96. You'll see some old barns and houses overgrown with weeds, their windows broken, their roofs collapsed. You will not encounter any towns in Colorado named for Silas Soule.

Governor Evans was forced to resign his position in 1865 as a result of the investigations into Sand Creek, but still today you may hike up Mount Evans in Colorado or visit Evanston, Illinois, where Northwestern University, which Evans helped to found, still operates (although it did form a Study Committee to determine the extent of Evans's culpability in and financial benefit from Sand Creek). You will not find a peak named for Joseph Cramer. Nor is there a Black Kettle Avenue or White Antelope Boulevard.

Was it all in vain, then, that Silas Soule and Joseph Cramer bore witness to and spoke out against Sand Creek? The two men sought to tell
the truth of what had happened at Sand Creek but there were other
settlers bent on covering up the atrocity. Thousands of Colorado settlers, then and now, have chosen to live in denial, to forget the state's
founding crimes. Still the battle over the memory of Sand Creek rages.

CHAPTER 3

Spirits

The sun is just rising over the snow-dusted plains at the Monument Hill Overlook on the Sand Creek Massacre National Historic Site in Chivington, Colorado, on Thanksgiving, Thursday, November 28, 2019. Members of the Northern Cheyenne Tribe of Montana, the Northern Arapaho Tribe of Wyoming, and the Cheyenne and Arapaho Tribes of Oklahoma—descendants of Sand Creek survivors—perform a ceremony to cleanse the area of the negative spirits that still haunt the land. At 10:00 a.m. teams of volunteers begin the annual Sand Creek Spiritual Healing Run of 173 miles to downtown Denver, retracing the route that Chivington and his troops took on their way back to the capitol to celebrate their "victory."

Most other Americans are preparing turkey, watching football, and sharing a feast while these runners are remembering their ancestors and all that they suffered. The runners have a lot of ground to cover in three days, so they run in relays, passing their memories like batons every several miles to a new refreshed group of volunteers. They carry eagle staffs and their tribal flags along the way.

Lee Lone Bear, a Northern Cheyenne descendant of massacre survivors, started the healing run in 1999 "to honor and remember their ancestors and to ask the spirits for healing for all peoples." Cheyenne and Arapaho Elder Bobbie White Thunder explains why they run: "We're remembering our past when we run, healing the land and the youth so they know where they come from. It's also about sacrifice, these young runners are feeling the same elements, and experiencing pain, like their relatives before." Dean Wallowing Bull, Northern Arapaho and Northern Cheyenne, explains that "as you're running, you're praying for all the people back home, and for all the ancestors that were murdered."

Wallowing Bull and other race participants see the Spiritual Healing Run as a powerful means to connect the generations and to teach history. The ancestors "sacrificed their lives so that we could be here alive today, living," Wallowing Bull explains. "That's what we want all these younger ones to know, that we wouldn't be here today if it wasn't for [our ancestors]."

These are powerful healing events for the participants. White Thunder says, "This run comes from the heart, for me I still get very emotional because we're running to heal—but back then our ancestors were running for survival." "You feel proud when you run," one teenage runner says. "They tried to kill us off, but we are still here."

Painful as it is to remember, the Cheyennes and Arapahos know that healing is only possible through facing and commemorating their past. They know that their ancestors who survived the massacre carried the history of Sand Creek in their bodies, like bullets that burrowed so deep they could never be dislodged. Their descendants, too, would inherit the memory of these sufferings. Not only through the oral traditions among the Cheyennes and Arapahos but also through what American Indians, Holocaust survivors, and many psychiatrists call "intergenerational trauma." When survivors of atrocities do not have a chance to heal, they may develop self-destructive coping behaviors and pass these along to their children and grandchildren. Some neuroscientists, too, have posited that trauma even creates epigenetic change that can be inherited by children.

In contrast to the Cheyennes and Arapahos, however, most of us settlers are willfully forgetting Sand Creek. After the massacre, many soldiers and settlers immediately sought to deny the truth of what happened there despite multiple investigations that determined that Colonel Chivington, Governor Evans, and other authorities had conducted a grievous wrong against the Cheyennes and Arapahos at Sand Creek.

Shaping the memory of Sand Creek was crucial to the cover-up of the heinous crime that occurred there. Some media dismissed the investigations and celebrated Chivington as a hero. The *Nebraska City News*, in Chivington's old haunts, objected to the investigations: "If our National Capitol was located a little nearer the scenes of our Indian depredations, and members of Congress more familiar with the outrages perpetrated on Western settlers, by these dirty, lousy, thieving vagabonds, they would present [Chivington] with a sword, as a testimonial of their high appreciation, instead of censuring him."

William Byers, editor of the *Rocky Mountain* News, maintained a relentless crusade to reframe the Sand Creek Massacre as a justified "battle" against savage Indians who had murdered innocent settlers. In 1880, more than a dozen years after the massacre, Byers was still asserting that Chivington's soldiers "covered themselves with glory."

Throughout the twentieth century, many settlers continued to insist that Sand Creek had been a battle, not a massacre. In 1950, the chambers of commerce in Eads and Lamar hoped to attract motorists on State Highway 96 to stop in their small towns. They erected a marble slab on a privately owned hilltop, overlooking Sand Creek, featuring a carving of a silhouette of a Plains Indian warrior over the words, "Sand Creek Battle Ground."

Professional historians with the Colorado Historical Society were not entirely comfortable with this characterization of the event. They erected an obelisk at the same time near the town of Chivington. It included a bronze plaque reading, "North eight miles, east one mile, is the site of the Sand Creek 'Battle' or 'Massacre' of November 29, 1864. Colorado volunteers under the command of John Chivington attacked a village of Cheyennes and Arapahos encamped on Sand Creek. Many Indians were killed; no prisoners were taken. The white losses were ten killed and thirty-eight wounded. One of the regrettable tragedies in the conquest of the West."

While the Historical Society did not entirely erase the memory of the event as a massacre, it signaled that what mattered was the settler loss of life—carefully enumerated—in contrast to the "many Indians" who were killed. It was a "regrettable tragedy," they stated, but one necessary to the conquest of the West.

Historian Ari Kelman has written a riveting book about the battle over how to memorialize Sand Creek. He says that in 1986, the Historical Society posted a new interpretive marker that dropped the vague language of the earlier marker and unequivocally labeled Sand Creek a massacre. This did not go over well with the owner of the private land upon which Sand Creek sat or with other local settlers.

It took many more years for the National Park Service to gain the site from the private landowner and then to agree on a historical interpretation of the site. Many Coloradoans continued to object strenuously to calling Sand Creek a massacre rather than a battle. Establishment of the site foundered, too, because there was widespread disagreement among all the stakeholders about where the actual site of the massacre was.

Senator Ben Nighthorse-Campbell, a Northern Cheyenne and Democrat-turned-Republican from Colorado, spent years shepherding a bill through Congress to establish the Sand Creek Massacre National Historic Site. Finally, in November 2000, just months before leaving office, President Bill Clinton signed the bill into law. It set aside more than 12,000 acres and included space for a cemetery and special access to descendants for ceremonies. The bill enshrined into law the conclusions of the investigations that had been conducted over a century earlier: Chivington and his troops had attacked a peaceful village; at least 150 Cheyenne and Arapaho people had died; the majority of those killed had been women, children, and the elderly; and the soldiers committed atrocities on the dead.

But still many Colorado settlers resisted this interpretation. Ruthanna Jacobs (who is no relation of mine), head of the Kiowa County Museum, insisted Chivington "was just doing his duty." His men "were frightened for their lives." It wasn't a massacre, she maintained. "That's just politically correct nonsense." At a meeting of a group called the Order of Indian Wars in Colorado Springs in 2003, some history buff settlers also defended Chivington. One man gave a paper titled, "I Stand by Sand Creek: A Defense of Colonel Chivington and the Third Colorado."

The battle over Sand Creek's meaning was still not resolved in the 2010s. Another front opened in 2014, on the 150th anniversary of the massacre, in Jefferson County, the fourth most populous county in the state; it covers the western half of Denver. County school administrators sought to make the Sand Creek Massacre a part of the high school curriculum, at least through the adoption of new Advanced Placement (AP) textbooks that included a section on the massacre. (The vast majority of non-AP students would still not learn of the massacre.)

The Jefferson County School Board, however, objected to including such a damning view of the state's founding in the curriculum. School board members proposed a new "board committee for curriculum review" whose mission would be to "promote citizenship, patriotism, essentials and benefits of the free enterprise system, respect for authority and respect for individual rights." Implicitly referring to Sand Creek, they stated that educational "materials should not encourage or condone civil disorder, social strife or disregard of the law [but] should present positive aspects of the United States and its heritage." One member proposed that the committee identify and prohibit materials that "may reasonably be deemed" to be "objectionable."

The Jefferson County School Board could not tolerate any historical material that blemished the image of Colorado and the United States, that taught the complicated truths of history rather than a simplistic jingoistic narrative. Thus, it seemed that Colorado schoolchildren would receive the same sanitized version of history that I did as a child.

Admittedly, though, things have changed a bit since I was in high school. Decades of historical research on such atrocities as Sand Creek have escaped the Ivory Tower, entered popular consciousness, and reached many more Americans. High school students today are more aware that there is more to the history of the American West. They don't want the state to rob them of the truth.

In 2014, hundreds of Jefferson County students from twelve different high schools staged a walkout to protest the school board's moves. Some teachers joined them. Student protesters carried signs that read "We have a right to know history" and "Teach us the truth." Others declared, "I have the right to learn" and "First you take away my history and then you take away my rights." They gathered forty thousand signatures on a petition to stop the school board from censoring their education. The walkout and protest gained national attention, and the school board backed down initially.

Ultimately, however, the Jefferson County students did not win this battle. The school board stuck to its guns. Today in Colorado, there is still no requirement that Colorado students learn about Sand Creek. The National Park Service is "working with educators and tribal representatives to develop a permanent curriculum-based education program for grades K through 12 and beyond." In 2020, Governor Jared Polis signed a law requiring Holocaust and genocide education in public schools, "including but not limited to the Armenian genocide." Will this lead to coverage of the genocidal Sand Creek Massacre in Colorado's classrooms, or will another generation of Colorado settler children grow up in ignorance of the founding crimes of their state?

The Cheyenne and Arapaho runners are undeterred. They will never forget, and their remembering might eventually bring other settlers along. During their 2019 Spiritual Healing Run, the runners stop at small towns on the way, relying on the hospitality of settlers, some of whom may be descended from soldiers who took part in the carnage. They spend the first night in Eads. The next night, the group stays in Limon, and on the following day, Saturday, they arrive in Denver. That evening they have a pow-wow at the Sheraton in downtown Denver.

Sunday morning, as they have each year for two decades, the Spirit runners hold a special ceremony at 7:00 a.m. at the Riverside cemetery in Denver to honor the two soldiers, Captain Silas Soule and Lieutenant Joseph Cramer, who refused to allow their men to participate in the killing and spoke out so forcefully against the massacre.

From the Riverside ceremony, the runners go to the corner of 15th and Arapahoe Avenue in Denver, the site where Soule was assassinated a few weeks after giving testimony against Colonel Chivington and other war criminals at Sand Creek. In 2019, the participants celebrated a new memorial plaque to commemorate Soule before running the last mile to the Colorado State Capitol Building.

There, state dignitaries, tribal elders, and descendants of both Sand Creek survivors and of Soule and Governor Evans all pay tribute to the survivors and remember the massacre. Leaders of the Methodist Church, for whom Chivington was a minister, have also started to take part in the commemorative event. In 2019 the Lieutenant Governor Diane Primavera spoke of the need to acknowledge "this dark chapter in our history, teach our communities about our past, and work to create a better future for all."

What would it mean for Colorado's settlers to finally acknowledge and be accountable for this founding crime? Conversely, what will happen if we fail to remember? Lewis Hyde, in his book *A Primer for Forgetting*, asks, "Does unexamined history reappear in some form of collective acting out, nightmare, flashback, and so on? If so, then forced forgetting doesn't resolve or transcend a violent past but obliges it to live on by displacement." He reminds us that "violence denied and repressed doesn't disappear; it repeats. If 'America' is a nation created by organized forgetting, then by this logic its foundational violence will always be with us."

Most of us settlers are unaware that we, too, carry the painful histories of Sand Creek and other atrocities within us and that we, too, are in need of healing. The hundreds of settler soldiers who volunteered to kill Indians and who did so with such brutality at Sand Creek would never be able to banish from their minds, hearts, and bodies the sight of ghastly carnage and mutilation, the smells of blood and rotting flesh, the sounds of women and children screaming and pleading for mercy. And they, too, passed on these memories to their descendants.

And what about those of us who simply moved to Colorado after the Cheyennes and Arapahos had been brutally removed from the Front Range? My own family relocated to the area just about a century after Sand Creek. We may not have blood on our hands, but this bloody history flows in us, nevertheless. We cannot truly thrive until we face up to this past.

In setting up the Spiritual Healing Run, Lee Lone Bear was aware that settlers needed healing from Sand Creek, too; he made it open to everyone and declared that its purpose was "healing for all people, regardless of ethnicity, race, or religion."

Will we accept Lone Bear's generous gift?

CHAPTER 4

Bellies

My family and I moved from southern New Mexico to Lincoln, Nebraska, in 2004, when my sons were in second and fifth grade. As we drove northward in our moving van, we stopped at the Goodwill in Santa Fe to purchase down coats and snow pants, items of clothing we had never needed the previous seven years. We arrived in Lincoln on January 1. It was an unseasonable sixty degrees that day, but the next day it snowed a good eight inches.

Our cross-country migration was a jolt, and not just because of the climate. It was a culture and history shock, too. We moved from the high desert around Las Cruces, just forty miles from the U.S.-Mexico border, an area still redolent of the nations who once claimed it—Spain, Mexico, Comanche, Apache—before it was conquered by the United States. New Mexico's vibrant multicultural history was visible, and celebrated. The city sported a Farm and Ranch Heritage Museum that focused on Anglo settlers, but its Indian, Spanish, and Mexican history was ever-present.

In Lincoln, Nebraska, there has long been an African American community, urban Indians, Mexican families, and refugees from Vietnam, Iraq, Bosnia, and many other places, but white settler culture was predominant. During our son Cody's first week at his new school (named after General Philip Sheridan, the man credited with declaring, "the only good Indian I ever saw was dead"), his fifth-grade teacher marked him down on one of his worksheets for coloring a cardinal brown, not red. My son, with his blond hair, blue eyes, and pale skin, looked like a

typical Nebraska settler kid, so the teacher assumed he would have settler knowledge. He could have nailed a roadrunner (beep beep) or a
quail but had never seen a cardinal, a bluebird, or a meadowlark. (My
husband the birdwatcher protested to the teacher that our son was simply coloring a *female* cardinal.)

Here in Lincoln, our children got an education in settlerhood that
had not been so prominent in southern New Mexico. In the classroom
and on field trips, at museums and on the local PBS station, they
learned of the noble, hardworking, self-sacrificing pioneers who home-
steaded on the plains of Nebraska and brought the state into being.
Willa Cather, who grew up in Red Cloud, Nebraska, and penned books
like *My Antonia* and *Oh Pioneers!*, is practically the patron (or matron)
saint of the state.

In fourth grade, all children in the Lincoln public schools went to
"heritage school," a one-room schoolhouse transplanted to the city's
Pioneers Park, where they were further schooled in this version of history. They could act out the part of homesteader children for the day.
The city's public schools website states, "Girls may wear a long skirt or
a dress, apron, and a sunbonnet or hat. Boys may wear bib overalls, jeans
and suspenders, flannel, plaid, or checked shirts, and hats of the
period."

The day my younger son Riley's fourth grade class went to heritage
school occupies a prominent place in our family's lore alongside his
brother's failure to properly color a cardinal. My husband, Tom, and I
were called into the principal's office the next day to discuss Riley's inap-
propriate behavior on the field trip. Concerned, Tom and I each can-
celed our appointments and other work responsibilities and traipsed
sheepishly into the principal's office.

We tried hard to avoid each other's gaze when the principal told us
of Riley's infraction. He had called one of his classmates, and most
beloved friends, who had dressed in bib overalls for the class outing a
"hillbilly." Our son's friend had cried. We felt bad, and Riley did, too.
But in our family, we fondly joke about all of our hillbilly ancestors.
The principal encouraged us to have a talk with Riley about his
insensitivity.

The school system seemed strangely insensitive to how strange heritage school must be for American Indian children, like those of my Rosebud Lakota friends Susana and Kevin, or refugee or immigrant children. The district has obviously received complaints over the years and made some modifications. Their website states that while the children will reenact a typical day in a one-room schoolhouse and "bring a lunch that is similar to what children might have eaten on the prairie in 1892," children can also expect to discuss Native American foods. Hmmm. Foods? What about Native American *people*?

The school district also invites "students whose family heritage reflects clothing different from what might have been worn on the plains by European settlers in the 1800s . . . to dress in a manner reflecting their heritage, if they choose." Riley didn't tell us about the opportunity to dress up, but if he had, what would we have had him wear? Maybe some lederhosen with a green leprechaun hat or a jaunty beret? What about my friend Chantal's son, Daniel, descended from Tutsi lineage of Rwanda and Burundi on one side and German stock on the other?

This may all seem so innocuous. Just let the kids have some fun, for goodness sake. But such activities subtly elevate certain histories and erase others. What does it mean to not see your history reflected around you? Or, worse, to have to dress up as the people who displaced your ancestors from their homelands or sought to exclude your grandparents from settling in the state? The telling of our histories is one way that we gain a sense of identity, of belonging, of entitlement. What does a Rosebud Lakota kid, a Mexican immigrant, a Tutsi exile think when he or she has to go to heritage school?

My settler children never learned about Nebraska's Indians, nor their food, past or present. I don't remember them ever coming home with a homework assignment or a worksheet about the Poncas, for example. Our state's social studies standards require students to have some general skills, such as the ability to "analyze past and current events throughout Nebraska history." The standards suggest "Ponca Trail of Tears" as an example of such an event that they could analyze, but there is no requirement of such content. Some teachers want to include this material, but they might not feel well-versed enough in it. Or they may be consumed with preparing students for one of the many standardized tests that students must now take so frequently.

The Poncas certainly didn't rate a special day and a field trip. And maybe we should be grateful for this. No Indian person I know would appreciate a bunch of settler kids dressing up as Indians and reenacting a typical day in the life of a Ponca in the nineteenth century.

You'd think as a historian of the American West that I would have fully absorbed the history of the Poncas within a few years of moving to Nebraska. But that wasn't the case. It wasn't until the summer of 2018—more than fourteen years after I moved to the state—that I finally started to grasp the gravity of the Poncas' exile from Nebraska.

That summer, I had teamed up with Kevin Abourezk, a long-time journalist in Lincoln and a member of the Rosebud Lakota nation, and Boots Kennedye, a Kiowa filmmaker, on a new project to showcase Indigenous and non-Indigenous people who have been working together to reckon with and reconcile from the fraught histories of our nation.

One morning in early August, Kevin and I met at Boots's big old house on the west side of Lincoln. While the morning was still cool, we loaded up Kevin's minivan with Boots's tripods and video camera. This was our second road trip together, and we were starting to get into a rhythm. As we drove out of town we made a pit stop at a local convenience store so Kevin and Boots could get coffee refills. I still had plenty of hot tea in my shiny travel mug.

Kevin and Boots were already good friends. In their forties, they both wear their long hair tied back in a ponytail. Boots speaks with the slight southern lilt of his Oklahoma upbringing. Kevin has a soothing and gentle voice. As we drove west on the interstate, they talked of the intense heat of the sweat lodges they attended together with another friend, Leo, and critiqued recent superhero movies they had seen on their regular movie nights. They bantered about their stints as guitarists in heavy-metal bands. With their easygoing patter, I felt welcomed and at ease, as if I had known them for a long time.

We were headed about two and a half hours northwest to the Tanderups' farm near Neligh, to interview Art and Helen as well as Larry

Wright Jr., chairman of the Ponca tribe of Nebraska. Kevin and I had each been to the farm before, but when we grew near, we couldn't figure out which old county dirt road to turn down. Finally, we found the right road and pulled up into the shade of the Tanderups' yard.

As we interviewed Larry and the Tanderups over the next few hours, I came to realize that the history of the Poncas had as much to do with settlers like me as it did with the Poncas. Too often we settlers compartmentalize; we tend to think our families' and communities' histories are separate from those of the Indigenous families and communities that already lived on this land. After all, we are taught a triumphant view of settler history and we rarely learn of Indigenous history. We have been raised to believe that settler and Indigenous histories run on parallel, not intersecting, tracks. One of our tasks as settlers is to learn how inextricably our histories are braided together.

As Larry put it, of his friendship and partnership with the Tanderups, the couple have come to understand "how our people were removed as others came in," just as the pipeline threatens the Tanderups' removal from the land today. "There is that deep connection [with the land] for them as well," Larry explains. "Neither one can minimize it, and to understand what that has done to our relatives, . . . that's the connection we share."

The Poncas endured their own version of what the Cheyennes and Arapahos had experienced in Colorado. After the U.S. government passed the Kansas-Nebraska Act of 1854 and formed a new territory, incoming settlers and other tribes exerted intense pressure on the Poncas. Settlers soon moved onto land near the Niobrara River that the Poncas had farmed for hundreds of years. The Brulé or Sicangu Oyate Lakotas also regularly raided the much smaller Ponca tribe and terrorized them when they sought to hunt bison. Ponca tribal members began to suffer from starvation as a result of displacement from their farms and the increasing danger of hunting bison.

The Poncas' 1858 treaty with the U.S. government was meant to alleviate these hardships. In return for the Poncas giving up claims to over two million acres, the government promised to protect the Poncas against Lakota raids. They agreed to build a mill and a school and provide an interpreter and teacher to the Poncas. They said they would issue a one-time payment of $20,000 to build homes, buy farming tools, and fence the land. And they pledged they would provide the Poncas with annuities for thirty years and regular rations to replace bison and other traditional sources of food.

Many settlers today believe that the rations and annuities that Indian tribes received were government handouts, welfare. In reality they were payment for Indigenous lands. And what measly compensation they were for lands that would become the basis for American economic prosperity.

The Poncas must have hoped that this treaty would finally secure their lands, provide protection, and give them the economic resources they needed to survive the onslaught of settler colonialism. But it didn't turn out that way. As was so common in the treaty-making process, the government took the best land and relocated the Poncas to substandard land. They moved the Poncas twelve miles up the river, exiling them from their fertile fields, their burial grounds, their places of ceremony. A special agent to the Poncas later declared that the new land was "totally unfit for occupation of the Indians, not having a sufficient timber or good soil to afford them a home to sustain themselves." In the meantime, the government gridded out the Poncas' original village for white settlement. Five settler families eagerly took up their land.

The new treaty failed the Poncas in other ways, too. Part of the problem was the snail's pace at which the government operated. All treaties required the ratification of the U.S. Senate, and the legislators did not ratify the Ponca treaty for a year. (In the case of some other treaties, the Senate never ratified them, leaving American Indians who had negotiated in good faith in the lurch. This happened to nineteen treaties that California Indians negotiated with American officials in the 1850s.) The government's negligence meant that the Poncas received no annuities for eighteen months. Although the Poncas were skilled farmers, they could not produce viable crops on their poor reservation land. This meant that the group suffered once again from starvation. Moreover, the Poncas could not make up for poor crops and lack of annuities through hunting because the government reneged on another promise: to protect the Poncas from Lakota raids. The Poncas repeatedly asked why the government had failed to protect them, but the government never gave them a satisfactory reply.

Despite their poor treatment by the U.S. government, the Poncas outwardly conformed to American pressures to assimilate. The Ponca leader who would become famous, Chief Standing Bear, and his family lived not in an earth lodge or tepee but in a furnished frame house. Standing Bear sowed and harvested his crops with a steel plow, a departure from customary farming that was carried out primarily by Ponca women with tools made from wood and bones. Standing Bear also regularly wore the clothing of American settlers rather than his customary garb. (There were limits to this conformity, however. Standing Bear adhered to Ponca marriage customs and kinship arrangements. He lived with his two wives in his frame house.)

Agents—the government employees assigned to manage Indian affairs—admired and lauded the Poncas for their loyalty to the U.S. government and for their willingness to adopt so-called civilized ways. When the Poncas pleaded with the government to fulfill its treaty obligations, agents backed them up. They advocated that the government should reward the Poncas for their "constant fidelity." One agent wrote to his superiors, "I cannot speak in too high terms of the uniform good conduct of this tribe. While many other Indians are fighting the government and murdering the frontier settlers, this tribe . . . [has] remained faithful to their treaty stipulations, and stood as a barrier between the hostile Indian and the white settler upon the frontier."

Finally, in 1865, the government responded to all the entreaties of the Poncas and their advocates by proposing a supplemental treaty. The government required that the Poncas relinquish 30,000 acres from the western edge of their reservation, but in return they set aside a new 96,000-acre reservation near the confluence of the Niobrara and Missouri rivers, the site of the Poncas' former village, burial grounds, and fields.

But of course there was a hitch. Five settler families had already settled on those lands. The government required the Poncas to pay

$5,000 in compensation to the settlers from their treaty annuities, even though the Poncas were suffering from malnutrition and struggling mightily to support themselves. In essence, Indian people had to pay reparations to white settlers, even though it had been the U.S. government, not the Poncas, that had erred.

The Poncas soon transplanted their village to their newly reacquired lands. Tribal members must have been elated to return to familiar and fertile ground. Their 1866 harvest yielded a good crop. But elation soon gave way to frustration. The Senate took two years to ratify the new treaty. Infestations of grasshoppers ruined the Poncas' crops in subsequent years. And the government was still failing to provide the Poncas with protection against Lakota raids, making it impossibly dangerous for the Poncas to carry out their bison hunts.

The Poncas were starving and destitute again, so they had to rely once more on government rations. But the new treaty had not yet been ratified, and government rations were delayed. Once rations arrived, they were inadequate and often unfit for human consumption. The Arapahos and Cheyennes (and almost every other tribe) had all endured this same treatment.

What's more, the government was paying for the Poncas' rations out of the tribe's education fund, money meant to fund a school in their community. And their annuities were much lower than those of other tribes, even tribes that were considered hostile to the United States.

Perhaps the greatest disgrace—what government officials would later downplay as a "blunder"—occurred in 1868, when General William Tecumseh Sherman negotiated a treaty for the U.S. government at Fort Laramie with the Lakotas. As part of the deal to establish the Great Sioux Reserve, Sherman gave the Lakotas, who had attacked the Ponca relentlessly, the 96,000 acres of the Ponca Reservation. As Larry Wright Jr. puts it, this mistake made the Poncas "trespassers on our own land." Sherman's treaty also promised the Lakotas modern rifles, which they would later use to attack the Poncas again. Was this merely bungling ineptitude on the part of the government? Or was it a sinister plan to exploit long-standing conflicts between Indian tribes so that they would carry out the government's aims?

The Poncas struggled on. By the 1870s, eight bands of the Poncas—about 700 people in total—lived in three villages at the easternmost edge of their reservation. Their hold on the reservation was uncertain, however, and they were still at the mercy of raids by the Lakotas, frequent flooding of the Missouri River on the northernmost edge of their reservation, grasshopper invasions, and drought. In 1871, Poncas planted their spring crops, but the Lakotas raided them and uprooted all of their corn.

In the past the Poncas had compensated for a poor growing year with bison hunts, but they had not hunted off their reservation since 1870; their agent would not allow it. The U.S. government had confined a once free and autonomous people to a tiny reservation. Government agents sought to control their every move. They had reduced the Poncas to dependence on the government. To prevent utter starvation the government provided meager rations and annuities (just $11.50 a year for each Ponca). At one point, according to writer Joe Starita, the Poncas only had two weeks' worth of boiled corn to live on.

The Poncas felt a constant ache, deep in their bellies. Given this situation, some military authorities questioned the government. An Army garrison commander wrote, "Why [the Poncas] should be selected to starve to death, while their hostile neighbors (the Sioux) are bountifully fed and clothed is more than either the Poncas or I can understand."

Given the ongoing intransigence of the U.S. government, the Poncas sought to resolve their problems by negotiating directly with neighboring tribes. In 1873, they worked out an agreement with their relatives, the Omahas, who were prepared to sell part of their reservation to the Poncas so they would have a secure piece of land. Nebraska senators objected, however, and the plan went nowhere. In 1876, the Poncas signed a treaty with their long-time enemies; the Lakotas agreed to stop their raids and to allow the Poncas to live on their original reservation.

But the U.S. government did not recognize these intertribal agreements; it had other plans. Its ultimate goal was not peace but control through removal and confinement. In 1873, government agents suggested that the Poncas be moved once again so that their reservation could be used as an agency to oversee the so-called "wild bands of the

Sioux." In 1875, a government agent met with the Poncas and claimed that he had attained their consent to move to Indian Territory. (Chief Standing Bear thought the agent had agreed to let the Poncas move to the Omaha Reservation.)

In 1876, Congress appropriated $25,000 to move the Poncas to Indian Territory, just seven weeks after General George Armstrong Custer's defeat at the Battle of Little Bighorn. Settlers and their government were in a punishing mood, even against a tribe that had never been at war with the United States.

The plan to remove the Poncas came as a shock to the tribe. Congress stipulated that the relocation required the Poncas' consent, but the government never consulted with the Poncas. Instead, the Poncas did not learn of their fate until Government Inspector E. C. Kemble arrived at the Ponca Agency in January 1877 and informed the tribe that they were to be removed. "He called us all to church, and we went," recalled the head chief White Eagle. Kemble told them that the president "has sent me to tell you that you must pack up and move to Indian Territory."

White Eagle and the other Ponca leaders vehemently objected. White Eagle told Kemble, "I thought that when the President desired to transact business with people he usually consulted with them first." Kemble insisted, "When the President says anything it must be done. Everything is settled."

White Eagle grew increasingly angry with Kemble. "I have never broken any of my treaties with the government. What does the President want to take my land away for? . . . My people have lived and died on this land as far back as we can remember. . . . We have always been peaceful. The land is our own. We do not want to part with it. I have broken no treaties, and the President has no right to take it from me." Kemble replied, "You can do nothing. What the President has said will be done." But White Eagle continued to insist that he and other Ponca leaders must consult first with the president.

In response to the Poncas' continued objections, according to White Eagle, Inspector Kemble produced a telegram from the president; he told the Poncas that the president "wants ten of your chiefs to go to Washington, but he wants me first to take you to the Indian Territory and see for yourselves, so that you may select a piece of land there, and then go on to Washington afterwards to talk it over." This resolved the impasse, for the time being; ten Ponca leaders accompanied Kemble to Indian Territory to assess a potential new reservation.

Upon seeing the proposed new lands, first on the territory of the Osage and then that of the Kaws, the Ponca leaders told Kemble they thought the land was too rocky and the Indian people already there were sick and destitute. The Poncas also met with their old neighbors the Pawnees, who had been relocated to Indian Territory a few years before. The Pawnees warned them against moving to the territory. They told them that their move had been difficult; people had grown sick and died, and the tribe had become more impoverished.

Standing Bear later recounted what had happened when he and the other nine leaders told Inspector Kemble that they did not want to move to the Indian Territory. Kemble and his men "grew very angry, and said if we did not agree to come they would go off and leave us there to starve. They would not take us back home. We said it would be better for ten of us to die than that the whole tribe, all the women and little children, should be brought there to die, and die we all would, right there, rather than do what they asked."

The Ponca leaders then informed Kemble that they wanted to travel to Washington to speak with the president, as he had promised, but the inspector refused. Barring that, the leaders asked for money to return home to their Niobrara homelands. Kemble again said no and abandoned eight of the ten chiefs in Indian Territory (the other two were ill and traveled back to Nebraska with Kemble).

The eight Ponca leaders had to make their way back to Nebraska on their own, mostly on foot, in the middle of winter. Temperatures often plunged well below zero at night and barely returned to freezing during the day. The venerable Ponca men trudged along the railroad tracks and through snowdrifts and over crusted patches of ice while a fierce north wind stung their faces.

The group had little food or money and several chiefs were ill. A few days after they set out, Chief White Eagle recounted, they encountered a white settler who spoke the Lakota language. They pooled some of their resources and paid him to take them to Wichita. There, according to Standing Bear, the Ponca men offered a ticket seller at the train depot, who also spoke some Lakota, a pair of moccasins in exchange for train tickets home. The friendly vendor offered to let the men travel for free, but when they returned to the station the next morning to catch the train, he told them they could not board after all. He had received a message from Inspector Kemble to deny them passage. So, the group kept walking. "We had no interpreter," Standing Bear later explained, "so we could not speak a word to any man.... White men were suspicious of us. They thought we were vagabond Indians, who will travel round to beg and won't work. Very few of them would give us anything."

The group finally made it to Otoe Agency in southern Nebraska after forty to fifty days. Kemble had already told the agent there that they were bad Indians and not to accept them, but, Standing Bear recounted, "when the Agent saw how nearly starved we were, and looked at our bleeding feet, for our moccasins wore out [during] the first ten days, he took pity on us, and first gave us something to eat, and then asked us what bad things we had been doing." The agent reported that the group left bloody footprints on the floor as they came into the agency building. They were too depleted to walk any further.

The Poncas gave gifts of small tomahawks and beaded blankets to the Otoes. In return, the Otoes gave them some ponies. After ten days of rest, the Ponca men set out again. Riding their new ponies, they met a party of Omahas on the Platte River four days later. A few days later they arrived at the Omaha Agency. From there they worked with their Omaha relatives to send a telegram to the president about their ordeal. Reverend William Hamilton, a white missionary to the Omahas, and John Springer (an Omaha man who spoke English) went with Standing Bear to Sioux City to send the telegram.

Their lengthy telegram (which cost $6.25 to send; over a hundred dollars today) asked the president whether he authorized Kemble to "leave us there to find our way back as best we could, if we did not agree to go down there? This he told us, and left us without a pass, interpreter, or money, because we could not select one of three places, telling us if we did not go there peaceably we would be driven by soldiers, at the point of the bayonet, from our present homes. We were so left, and have been thirty days getting back as far as the Omahas, hungry, tired, shoeless, footsore, and sad at heart." Springer and Standing Bear also went to see the editor of the *Sioux City Journal*—who printed their story.

When they finally made it home to their villages on the Niobrara, on April 2, 1877, they found that Inspector Kemble had already started to round up the Poncas for removal, to the lands of the Quapaws in Indian Territory. In early March, having arrived in the Ponca homelands well before the Ponca chiefs, Kemble had begun his pressure campaign on the Poncas. He employed interpreters to harass the villagers, "Hurry and pack up. Be quick. Get ready and move." When the Poncas resisted, Kemble's instructions became increasingly harsh and intimidating. He sent an interpreter around the villages to threaten, "You must go, for the people will shoot you if you do not." The Ponca leaders were incensed. They told their tribal members to refuse to move.

Kemble called another council to insist that the Poncas must go. Many Ponca leaders vehemently opposed their removal. Chief White Eagle declared, "We would rather die here on our land than be forced to go. Kill us all here on our land now, so that in the future when men shall ask, 'Why have these died?' it shall be answered, 'They died rather than be forced to leave their land. They died to maintain their rights.'" The Ponca leader White Swan confronted Kemble, too. He said Kemble had been to the Ponca homeland before, as a missionary. "You professed to be a great Christian. . . . You preached to us and told us about God." Kemble had convinced White Swan to become baptized as a Christian. "You said that you wanted to save my soul from hell when I should die, but now I find that you wish to send my soul to hell while I am yet living."

The Poncas' forceful statements had no effect on the government inspector. Kemble called for sixty members of the cavalry to enforce removal. Immediately upon their arrival, the soldiers rode through the three Ponca settlements and insisted that the villagers pack for their forced removal. They threatened to kill the Poncas if they did not comply.

One village broke under the pressure. On the morning of April 16, its 170 members began the arduous crossing of the Niobrara River. Old people struggled to wade across the shoulder-deep water, the newly thawed waters chilling them, the swift current causing them to stumble. Soldiers pushed the wagons piled high with their only possessions through the water. They were the first contingent to walk the Poncas' Trail of Tears.

Poncas in the other two villages remained resistant. Standing Bear counseled his followers to stay in their homes, lock their doors, and refuse to leave. Standing Buffalo would later testify that Kemble retaliated by cutting off their rations for two months. He said, Kemble "tried to starve us into it." Soon the Poncas ran out of their stores of sweet corn. Standing Buffalo recounted, "We were starving, and so we had to sell some of our ponies to get provisions."

The government's actions devastated the Poncas. John Springer, who was staying in nearby Niobrara, told a Senate Sub-Committee later, "After [Kemble] had told them that they must go, the Indians were crying the whole night." Standing Buffalo testified, "We told [Kemble] that the land was very dear to us, because our fathers were buried there, and our fathers had left the land to us." Standing Bear confronted Kemble and told him, "This is my land. The Great Father [the U.S. government] did not give it to me. My people were here and owned this land before there was any Great Father. We sold him some land, but we never sold this. This is mine. God gave it to me." Standing Bear's brother, Big Snake, who was head of the Poncas' military society, told the inspector, "I want you to get off from this reservation. Drop your swords on the land here, and go across the river." Kemble was furious; he had Standing Bear and Big Snake arrested and imprisoned.

Many local settlers were appalled by the government's actions. Two local newspapers—the *Sioux City Journal* and the *Niobrara Pioneer*—registered their opposition to Ponca removal. The *Niobrara Pioneer* published a front-page editorial: "Swindled Poncas—An Act Too Base to Be Recognized by Honest People in a Free Land Like Ours." The Knox County commissioners passed a resolution against the removal.

One influential settler missionary, Alfred Riggs, who lived on the nearby Santee Sioux Reservation, wrote to the secretary of the interior: "The Poncas have a clear right to the land on which they now are; the right of original possession, guaranteed by two treaties with the United States." They are "wholly opposed to moving to Indian Territory." Riggs concluded, "We are therefore convinced that great wrong will be done these Indians and more disgrace accrue to our country by such ruthless disregard of our obligations."

With this intense opposition from settlers, the government questioned Kemble's actions. He returned to Washington, D.C., to convince the newly appointed secretary of the interior, Carl Schurz, of the necessity for Ponca removal. Ponca chiefs asked the local lawyer and newspaperman Solomon Draper to represent their case; they offered him thirty-two horses to travel to Washington to counter Kemble, and he agreed.

Kemble and Draper met separately with Schurz in April 1877. Some observers expected Schurz to be sympathetic to the Poncas, because he had been a strong opponent of slavery. But these observers were sorely disappointed. We've seen in the case of John Chivington that abolitionism did not always lead to standing up for Indian rights. Schurz decided after two days of rumination that he would base his decision on government reports—almost all written by Kemble—that claimed the Poncas had agreed to go and that some had already left.

General Sherman then ordered two companies from Fort Sully to the Ponca Agency to carry out the removal of the rest of the tribe. The government also sent Indian Agent E. A. Howard to help move the Poncas. Kemble finally released Standing Bear and Big Snake from jail. They found their people living in fear and dread of further government action.

Agent Howard arrived in early May. He set up headquarters on the south side of the Niobrara River. He summoned the Ponca chiefs across the river to a council on May 8 where he expressed sympathy to them. He said he knew that they had been treated unjustly but there was nothing he could do. But "when we came back from the council," Standing Bear would later testify, "we found the women and children surrounded by a guard of soldiers." Government duplicity seemed to be endless and shameless.

While Ponca leaders were away, soldiers had terrorized the Ponca villagers. They had gone to each home, broken down the locked doors, removed all the household items, and piled them in wagons. The soldiers had confiscated all of their farm equipment and locked it in a warehouse. When they finished, the military men pointed their bayonets at the defenseless Ponca people. Standing Bear remembered, "We told them that we would rather die than leave our lands; but we could not help ourselves."

The Poncas had done nearly everything the U.S. government had asked of them. They had abandoned their earth lodges for wooden homes. They had shed their loose buckskin garb and corseted and buttoned themselves up into American fashions. Ponca women had retreated from cultivating their fields and gardens, and Ponca men had taken up the plow. They had befriended and earned the admiration of the white settlers who had invaded their homelands. And yet, they had no power to stop this arbitrary removal.

The Poncas had played by the rules. They had been "good" Indians. But the rules kept changing. The government shifted maneuvers to dispossess Indian people of their land, under the guise of legality. The forced removal of the Poncas, as with so many other tribes, is so profoundly undemocratic. Like America's other founding crime of slavery, dispossession ran counter to all the ideals that the founding fathers had espoused and enshrined in the Constitution. It contradicts America's rhetoric on protecting property rights and individual liberties.

Standing Bear later catalogued all the property he lost, all the things he had to leave behind: "one house (I built it with my own hands . . .). It was twenty feet by forty, with two rooms; four cows, three steers, eight horses, four hogs (two very large ones), five wagon-loads of corn with the side boards on (about 130 bushels), one hundred sacks of wheat, . . . twenty-one chickens, two turkeys, and one prairie breaking plow, two stirring plows, two corn plows, a good stable and cattle sheds, three axes, two hatchets, one saw, three lamps, four chairs, one table, two new bedsteads, . . . [etc.] These things were mine. I had worked for them all. By [government] order I brought them all, except . . . such things I could not move, to the Agency, and they put them in a big house and locked them up. I have never seen any of them since."

Confiscation of their property was just the first step in the government's plan. On the morning of May 16, 1877, the Trail of Tears for the remaining Poncas began. Agent Howard and the soldiers made the Ponca people cross the overflowing Niobrara River. The current was so swift, and the wagons with the Poncas' few remaining possessions became trapped on the sandy bottom. Ponca men had to take all their goods out of their wagons and carry them across the rushing river on their backs. And many Poncas could not cross the river on their own. Helen Hunt Jackson, a sympathetic white settler, later wrote, "Let us dwell for a moment on this picture. [Hundreds of] helpless, heartbroken people beginning their sad journey by having to ford this icy stream with quicksands at the bottom. The infirm, the sick, the old, the infants, all carried 'by packing them on the shoulders of the men!' What a scene!"

The misery was just beginning. Once the Poncas crossed the river, they had to camp for two nights to wait out heavy storms before embarking on the rest of their journey. Torrential rains, thunderstorms, and tornadoes would torment the group during their entire six-hundred-mile journey. Hardly a day passed that they were not deluged. On many occasions, they had to stop and repair roads and bridges themselves to be able to continue their long march southward. On most days, the Poncas walked ten to twenty-five miles.

It didn't have to be this way. This was the 1870s. Steamships plied up and down the Missouri River, and railroad lines crisscrossed the Midwest. The majority of the exiles could have easily traveled on modern transportation. Later, a Senate investigation would point this out: "Was not the discomfort as well as the expenses greater than would have been to have gone by river and rail?" Kemble conceded that it would have been cheaper, but he declared that the "Indians themselves preferred" to go by land so that they could take "everything they had." Given that soldiers warehoused so many of the Poncas' possessions, Kemble's assertion seems disingenuous at best.

A smaller contingent of Poncas could have transported their livestock and wagonloads of goods. And the government could have freighted many of the possessions they left behind: their farming equipment, household goods, and other supplies for establishing a new home in a foreign land. But it was clear that the government wanted to inflict as much agony as possible on the exiles. They had carried out similar forced marches against so many other Native people.

Agent Howard kept a journal of the Ponca Trail of Tears. "On the morning of [May] 19th I broke camp and commenced the march from the Niobrara to the Indian Territory. Roads very bad. Marched twelve miles." Howard's entry for May 20 read, "Remained in camp. Rained heavily all day. Indian child died; about eighteen months old." The next day Howard made them trudge thirteen miles to Creighton, where they buried the child. The Ponca exiles could not stay and carry out a proper memorial for the child, however; the following day their captors marched them twenty-five miles, where they camped near Neligh—not far from the land that would become Art and Helen Tanderup's farm.

While they waited out another storm, White Buffalo Girl, just eighteen months old, died of pneumonia. The girl's father, Black Elk, implored settlers of Neligh, through an interpreter: "I want the whites to respect the grave of my child just as they do the graves of their own dead. The Indians do not like to leave the graves of their ancestors, but we had to move and hope it will be for the best. I leave the grave in your care. I may never see it again. Care for it for me."

The next victim was Standing Bear's adult daughter, Prairie Flower. She died of tuberculosis on June 15, after a march of fourteen miles, near the small town of Milford, Nebraska, on the Big Blue River. That evening a tornado hit the bereaved group, who were camped only in flimsy canvas tents. During the storm, a boiling kettle of water blew over onto Standing Bear's infant granddaughter. She, too, died that evening.

What did settlers who witnessed the 530 bedraggled and rain-sodden Poncas trudging through the settlers' newly acquired fields, accompanied by dozens of soldiers, make of this scene? Some undoubtedly supported the removal; others may have been horrified by it. Many may have regretted it but thought it necessary or inevitable. New European immigrants to the area, some of whom had fled persecution and hardship themselves, might have felt a sense of relief; this time, it wasn't them. Literary scholar and writer Beth Piatote noted to me that these public displays of government power must also have been meant to discipline new Americans during this time of rapid expansion, to show them what was possible if they, too, did not conform to American norms.

Some local townspeople responded in sympathy to the Poncas' tragedies. The white townswomen of Milford helped to prepare and decorate the body of Prairie Flower "for burial in a style becoming the highest civilization," according to one white woman. The people of Neligh, Nebraska, took the words of the grieving father Black Elk to heart. They have maintained White Buffalo Girl's grave at the Laurel Hill Cemetery north of Neligh for more than 140 years. If you visit, you will nearly always find fresh flowers there.

The Poncas' ordeal lasted 55 days and spanned 600 miles. They finally arrived at the Quapaw Reservation in Indian Territory on July 9. They were welcomed by yet another storm. Their new "home" offered little shelter. In perhaps one of its most callous moves, Congress had authorized funding for the Poncas' removal but not for their settlement in Indian Territory.

Agent Howard was disgusted when he saw that no provision had been made for the Poncas in their exile. He wrote to his superiors in Washington, D.C.: "It is a matter of astonishment to me . . . that the Government should have ordered the removal of the Ponca Indians from [Nebraska] to the Indian Territory without first having made some provision for their settlement and comfort." Howard believed that the government should have built a comfortable house for each family. Instead the Poncas had been "placed on an uncultivated reservation to live in their tents as best they may."

The Poncas had traded their villages, with their framed homes and cultivated fields, for a refugee camp. For more than a year, the exiles lived in canvas tents on the lands of the Quapaws, who had not been consulted with or compensated for the settlement of the Poncas on their land.

One Ponca leader, Chief White Eagle, dictated a letter to the people of the United States detailing all of the tribe's losses: "We left in our own land two hundred and thirty-six houses which we had built with our own hands. We cut the logs, hauled them, and built them ourselves. We have now, in place of them, six little shanties, built for us by the government." White Eagle continued, "We have now no stove, chairs, or bedsteads. We have nothing but our tents, . . . the tribe owned two reapers, eight mowers, a flour and saw mill. They are gone from us also."

Immediately, the Poncas faced hunger and starvation. They arrived too late to plant crops; and even if they had gotten there earlier, they lacked all the tools, equipment, and supplies needed to grow food. The land, too, consisted of a mix of stony ground and marshy swamp; it would be difficult to grow crops even in ideal circumstances. Inexplicably, the government did not provide food to the starving refugees. Standing Bear recounted, "When we got there the Agent issued no rations for a long time. For months we had to beg of the other tribes. We were all half-starved." The Poncas had always tried to grow or hunt their own food; it was yet another indignity for them to be reduced to dependency.

The Poncas also confronted disease, most alarmingly, malaria. Its victims alternated between high fevers and shaking chills. Nausea and vomiting wracked their bellies, their eyes sunk into their skulls, and their skin turned sallow. Agent Howard had warned the commissioner of Indian affairs that "a great mortality will surely follow among the people when they shall . . . become poisoned with the malaria of the climate." Standing Bear later testified, "We said we could go back, that we did not like it there. Then we were informed that we were prisoners. . . . Sickness commenced, several died. All my people were heart-broken. I was like a child. I could not help even myself, much less help them." Standing Bear again conveyed his feelings of powerlessness to lead and to help his tribal members.

Standing Bear's own family was as affected as all others in the tribe. Not only had he lost a daughter and granddaughter on the long trek to Indian Territory, but another daughter died while they camped on the Quapaw Reservation and his wife's mother and grandmother also succumbed. From the state of their new habitation, it's inescapable that the government wanted to utterly subjugate the tribe, even though the Poncas were so-called "good" Indians who cooperated with the United States.

This may seem like a familiar story. Cheyenne leader Black Kettle and Arapaho leaders Little Raven and Left Hand were "good" Indians, too. They had sought peace with the government. Colonel Chivington had massacred them at Sand Creek. And now the Poncas, who had never taken up arms against their colonizers, were forcibly marched six hundred miles from their homeland and left to starve and die in an inhospitable environment. It didn't seem to matter what Indian people did. The government was intent on taking their land, and it would do so whether Indians waged war against them or remained at peace.

But the Poncas did not give up. Standing Bear and nine other Ponca leaders, accompanied by Agent Howard, met with President Rutherford Hayes in November 1877 to plead to go back to their homelands in Nebraska. Hayes refused their request, but he did permit the Poncas to search for and choose new land in Indian Territory. A Ponca delegation located a more desirable spot in the spring of 1878, at the confluence of the Salt Fork River and Arkansas River, on the Cherokee Reservation to the west of the Quapaw Reservation. Establishing a new settlement at the point where two rivers met, just as in their prior villages, must have provided some comfort.

Still, old patterns prevailed in their new home. Once again, the government did not consult with or compensate the Cherokees for setting aside some of their land for the Poncas. Once again, the Poncas had to relocate overland, 185 miles, this time in midsummer in daily heat of 95–100 degrees. Once again, the Poncas arrived too late to plant crops, and many of their animals died. As Standing Bear described it, "After we reached the new land, all my horses died. The water was very bad. All our cattle died; not one was left." Once again, they had no homes; they still lived as refugees in tents.

And once again, malaria stalked them. This time, it may have been worse. Standing Bear later said, "There were dead in every family. Those who could walk around were sick. Not one in the whole tribe felt well.

I lost all my children but one little girl. A few more weeks and she would have died too. I was in an awful place, and I was a prisoner there. . . . I had been taken by force from my own country to a strange land, and was a captive." By the end of 1878, one-quarter of the tribe, or 158 people, had died. The mortality rate the Poncas faced in Indian Territory was greater than that of Union soldiers during the Civil War.

What did it mean to lose almost one-quarter of one's community in just eighteen months? In May 1879, Omaha leader Joseph La Flesche and his daughter Susette set out for Indian Territory to investigate the condition of the Poncas. They traveled by railway to Wichita and then by stage over four days to the Ponca reservation. A trip that had taken the Poncas several months took the La Flesches less than a week. As the La Flesches approached the reservation, on either side of the road ahead, Susette would later recount, "as far as the eye could see, were small mounds, each marked by a rough upright stone. Graves! But—all these—and the Poncas had lived in this new area only since July! When Standing Bear had spoken of all the deaths, they had been only a number. Now suddenly they became persons—men, women, and children whose names and faces [I] had known." How can we remember, like Susette, that these many numbers dead were not faceless ciphers but beloved kin?

For Standing Bear nothing was abstract about the situation of the Poncas. His only son, Bear Shield, was just sixteen years old when he died. Standing Bear told a journalist later, "As he was dying [he] looked up to me and said, 'I would like you to take my bones back and bury them there where I was born.' I promised him I would. I could not refuse the dying request of my boy."

After his son died, Standing Bear had had enough. He would later say, "I could see nothing ahead, but death for the whole tribe." So, on the night of January 2, 1879, Standing Bear "slipped away" with almost thirty other followers to return to Nebraska. Standing Bear's wife dressed Bear Shield in his best clothing and placed him in a coffin in one of the covered wagons the group took with them. Joe Starita notes that the temperature was 19 below zero with a steady north wind when they left their camp. On January 6, as they walked northward, the wind blew up to seventy miles an hour, dropping the wind chill to 41 degrees below zero.

The fugitives had saved a small quantity of rations. Standing Bear had ten dollars, as did another Ponca man, Buffalo Chip. So the group of thirty subsisted on less than a dollar a day for about three weeks; then they were without food or money for the rest of the trip. They had to beg for food from settlers for seven more weeks. Standing Bear would sum up the trip this way: "Some of the children were orphans. We were three months on the road. We were weak and sick and starved."

Omaha Indian leaders had been following the travails of their Ponca neighbors and kin since their removal. They had made clear that they would harbor and help the refugees if they returned to Nebraska. Standing Bear's group reached a camp just west of the Omaha Reservation on March 4, 1879. Their Omaha relatives proposed to give them some land on their reservation and incorporate them into the tribe. Close to home again and among kin, the Poncas gladly took up the Omahas' offer and planted crops in their camp.

But the U.S. government would not allow Standing Bear to get away with such disobedience. Troops under the command of General George Crook apprehended Standing Bear and his followers, as they were planting their crops, and insisted that they return to Indian Territory. Standing Bear remembered that "half of us were sick. We would rather have died than have been carried back [to Indian Territory]."

The government imprisoned the Poncas at Fort Omaha, confiscated all their belongings, cut off their annuities, and prepared to march them back to Indian Territory. The prisoners were despondent. Standing Bear recalled, "When we started back the scene among the women and children was heart-rending. They and their friends among the Omahas cried bitterly. It would break one's heart to look at them. Many were still sick, and all felt that we were going back to certain death. My efforts to save their lives had failed."

The Poncas appealed to the powers that be for some mercy. In 1879, as Crook was preparing to march Standing Bear's group back to Indian Territory, the Poncas' leaders requested a meeting with the general to make their case to him. Buffalo Chip (Ta-zha-but) spoke eloquently to him:

I sometimes think that the white people forget that we are human, that we love our wives and children, that we require food and clothing, that we must take care of our sick, our women and children, prepare not only for the winters as they come, but for old age when we can no longer do as when we are young. But one Father made us all. We have hands and feet, heads and hearts all alike. We also are men. Look at me. Am I not a man?

If we go back to Indian Territory, Buffalo Chip declared, "there will be not one left to tell the tale. It would be better for the government, better for us, to stand us out there in a line, bring the soldiers and tell them to shoot us all. Then our miseries would be ended, and the government would have no more trouble. It would be better that way."

Would it be different this time? Would Buffalo Chip and Standing Bear's appeals to morality and decency and justice have any effect on General Crook, the government he represented, or the settlers who had taken over the lands the Poncas had once called home?

On the day in August 2018 when Kevin and Boots and I traveled to the Tanderups' farm, Larry Wright Jr., chairman of the Ponca Tribe of Nebraska, told us how important it is to "remember our past, remember [where] we came from, the sacrifices [our ancestors] made." He says, "I owe that to my people, and to my children, and grandchildren." He concludes, "Everything that we do here affects all [of us]. . . . You know, we have in our language, . . . that we're [all] related."

This bedrock principle of Indigenous societies—we are all related—is a realization that many settlers resist. We erect boundaries between ourselves and Native people, thinking that their "plight," as we so often characterize it, has little to do with us. What would it mean if we settlers recognized, indeed, that we *are* all related? The Poncas' history of forced removal is also the story of Nebraska's settlement and founding. Ponca and settler histories are intimately intertwined. For me to dwell as a settler in Nebraska—and more than that, for me to fully live as a human being—I need to know this history, to feel it in my bones, to wear it.

CHAPTER 5

Tongues

The founding crimes of our nation—committed against the Poncas, the Arapahos, the Cheyennes, and all American Indian nations—would remain almost entirely hidden if it were not for the determination of many Indigenous people to preserve their histories and make these abuses known. Even if most settlers have actively forgotten this history and sought to silence counternarratives, Indian people have held on to their knowledge within their communities. They have kept their histories alive. They have passed on their stories to their children so their pasts would not be forgotten, so that healing could occur and justice could be sought.

Gathering testimony from Native survivors of settler abuses and bearing witness to their experiences is a crucial step in truth and reconciliation. When hundreds or thousands of Indigenous people testify to their common experiences, they build a new collective chronicle of our nation's ongoing history. But this is a lot to ask. It can be grueling, and sometimes hurtful, for many Indian people to recount the horrific abuses they or their ancestors suffered. It may re-traumatize survivors, especially if they cannot count on an acknowledgment of their pain or concrete actions of redress. Ideally our nation would create a safe, ritualized space for Indigenous people to tell their truths, where settlers would respectfully listen and learn the harsh and bitter truth. The United States has never designed such a place for confronting our past.

Yet many Indigenous people have taken every opportunity to tell their own histories, convey the truths of their experience, and challenge our winning-the-West narratives. It has often been difficult, however, to gain access to the venues—the courts, the news media, the popular magazines, the publishers of books, the film and television industry, the classrooms—where they could testify to the crimes committed against them and reach a non-Indigenous audience.

Even when Native Americans did obtain a platform, it was still a challenge to have their voices heard and understood. Settlers had written extensively about Indians and had created a lore about them. Their narratives were full of stock Indians—some bloodthirsty savages, some romantic figures—but all soon to be exited off the stage so the real settler drama could begin. When Indigenous people narrated their own lives and articulated their own grievances and their own solutions, translation and settler mediation could distort what they said. It is still difficult for Indigenous people to counter the weight and the staying power of settler colonial lore and plight narratives, to tell their myriad stories, unfiltered.

There was one unique moment in the nineteenth century when Indigenous people were able to finally reach a wide settler audience. In 1879 Chief Standing Bear of the Poncas found settler allies who helped him take his case to court in Nebraska and then go on a national speaking tour with a young Omaha woman, Susette La Flesche, who acted as his interpreter and then became a full-fledged speaker in her own right. Chief Standing Bear was, by all accounts, a gifted speaker who could transfix audiences with his vivid imagery and powerful metaphors. As with our modern truth and reconciliation efforts, telling the Poncas' truths was the first step in gaining acknowledgment for the harm the United States had done and for achieving some repair for the injustices they had suffered.

This was an improbable accomplishment. Standing Bear had tried on many occasions to gain an audience with the president and high-ranking officials in the government to make his case against Ponca removal, but he was often undermined by Indian agents and inspectors. He also didn't have the same public channels as settlers for making his voice heard. American Indians were barred from suing the federal government, so he couldn't go to court to make his case there. Settlers

controlled the press, too: newspapers, magazines, the publishing industry. Only a rare few American Indians—such as William Apess of the
Pequot nation, who published his autobiography in 1829—had managed to shape and circulate their own narratives. Public lectures became
a last resort. In the nineteenth century, abolitionists and women's rights
supporters regularly scheduled lecture tours. African American activists
such as Sojourner Truth and Frederick Douglass had become popular
orators. Before Standing Bear, however, few American Indians had
gained the stage to air their grievances.

There were other formidable barriers to spreading the truth of the
Poncas' story. In the 1870s Standing Bear represented just seven hundred souls in a country of over fifty million people. He did not speak
English. And the country was preoccupied; it was still confronting the
legacy of the Civil War and only recently had retreated from the promise
of greater equality for African Americans through Reconstruction. The
nation was convulsed by strikes and labor unrest. The defeat of Custer
at the Battle of Little Bighorn in 1876—the nation's centennial year—
and ongoing conflicts with Plains Indian nations fueled fear and hostility among settlers toward American Indians.

To gain a platform where he could make known the abuses the Poncas had suffered, Standing Bear needed settler allies. He found one such
ally, unexpectedly, in General George Crook, Commander of the Platte,
at Fort Omaha in 1879.

General Crook was a career military man who began his career in
California in the genocidal 1850s before becoming colonel of the
36th Ohio Infantry during the Civil War. Promoted to general in 1862,
Crook became famous for his role in the so-called Indian Wars, a settler
term for the subjugation of Indigenous peoples. He led several massacres in northeastern California, including the 1857 Pit River killings of
at least 89 Achumawi people and an uncounted number of Paiutes,
Modocs, and Achumawis during the three-day Battle of the Infernal
Caverns, as settlers call it, in 1867. He did not seem like a man who would
be sympathetic to the Poncas' experience.

But by the time that Standing Bear encountered him, Crook seems
to have become disgruntled about the U.S. government's handling of

Indian affairs. Even though he was a hardened military commander who had not hesitated to unleash brutal violence against Indians he deemed hostile, in this instance he seemed to believe that the government was treating the Poncas unfairly. He knew that the Poncas could not attain justice without having their story heard beyond the confines of his headquarters at Fort Omaha. So even before he met with Standing Bear, according to Joe Starita, Crook tipped off a journalist at the *Omaha Herald* about the Poncas' struggle. He supposedly even suggested a legal strategy to the journalist that might help the Poncas gain their day in court.

Thomas Tibbles was the thirty-nine-year-old journalist and assistant editor at the *Herald* whom Crook contacted. He became another important ally to Standing Bear and the Poncas. In his colorful autobiography, Tibbles chronicled his difficult childhood and early commitment to racial justice. He wrote that he had been indentured as a bound apprentice at age ten after his father died. He ran away from his employer when he was eleven years old. At age sixteen, he joined an emigrant wagon train to Kansas following the passage of the 1854 Kansas-Nebraska Act. He served in James Henry Lane's anti-slavery militia in 1856. Perhaps he even crossed paths with Silas Soule or John Chivington. Tibbles then claims to have lived for three seasons with a "mixed lot [of Indians] belonging to the tribes along the Missouri River," including some Omahas.

At age seventeen, in 1857, he "emerged from the wilderness." He gained a college education, became a journalist, and married an English woman named Amelia Owen. He served as a scout during the Civil War and covered the war as a journalist. After the war he became an itinerant minister, similar to Chivington, with the Episcopal Church in northern Missouri and then in Republican City in south-central Nebraska. He became well known for raising money for victims of the famine of 1874, caused by storms of grasshoppers that destroyed nearly all of the settlers' crops. He soon left his religious work and resumed a career as a journalist. He gained numerous positions at the *Omaha Herald* in the late 1870s and eventually became assistant editor and principal editorial writer for the newspaper.

Acting on General Crook's tip, Tibbles interviewed Standing Bear and other Ponca leaders in the spring of 1879. He became outraged by the Ponca saga of removal, attempted return, arrest, and detention. He used his position at the *Omaha Herald* to plead the Poncas' case. On April 1, he published his first article on the Poncas, titled "Criminal Cruelty, The History of the Ponca Prisoners Now at the Barracks" and an editorial, "The Last Indian Outrage." Tibbles followed this up by writing articles on the Poncas every day for two months.

Tibbles became passionate about the Ponca cause. He compared his zeal to that of what he had once felt for enslaved African Americans. He reflected on himself (in the third person): "he had made some hard campaigns for the liberty of black men with pistol and sabre, but this campaign for the liberty of the Indian, in which the pen was the only weapon, required just as much physical endurance."

Tibbles was clearly deeply sympathetic to the Poncas, and his advocacy was undeniably helpful to them. His journalistic campaign mobilized the white Christian community in Omaha to form the Ponca Relief Committee. He influenced nearby newspapers to support the return of the Poncas to Nebraska. Tibbles also transformed the Poncas' local story into national news.

But Tibbles also portrayed the Poncas in a way that denied them their own voice and silenced their tongues. In one editorial, for example, he wrote, "The wrongs of Government upon these Ponca Indians are lawless wrongs. They are monstrous wrongs. They cry to Heaven for redress from the lips of millions of good men and women all over our land, and a growing public opinion demands justice for a helpless and defenceless people." It was true that Standing Bear and the other Poncas often expressed a sense of powerlessness in the face of American might. And yet, Standing Bear was a tireless advocate for his people. He was not helpless, if only he could amplify his voice and find settlers willing to listen. In our own time, settlers who want to support Indigenous people may fall prey to the same tendencies as Tibbles. They may, too, portray Indians as defenseless victims who need settlers to speak on their behalf.

Tibbles could have printed Standing Bear's statements directly, albeit through a translator. Instead he appointed himself the spokesperson for

Standing Bear and the Poncas, and he selected and curated the chief's translated words. The Ponca leader rarely got to express himself and his concerns in a less mediated way to the public through the *Omaha Herald*. It must have been frustrating for Standing Bear to lack direct access to the media, but he undoubtedly appreciated the journalist's advocacy.

Tibbles also enlisted two settler lawyers in Omaha, John Lee Webster and Andrew Jackson Poppleton, to help Standing Bear pursue his case in court. Webster and Poppleton developed a novel legal strategy. They requested that a local judge grant a writ of habeas corpus against General Crook and the U.S. government for illegally holding Standing Bear and seven other Ponca men without trial.

The attorneys wanted the U.S. government to prove it had a legal right to arrest and detain Standing Bear and twenty-five other Poncas at Fort Omaha and prevent them from returning to their homeland on the Niobrara. If local judge Elmer Dundy granted a writ of habeas corpus, the Ponca prisoners would be required to appear in court, the Poncas could argue their case, and Dundy would then determine if they had been jailed and unlawfully detained. Before this time, no writ of habeas corpus had been filed on behalf of an American Indian.

This was an ingenious move, because otherwise Indians could not challenge federal Indian policy in court. Indeed, the attorney for the U.S. government, Genio Lambertson, argued that the court should not grant Standing Bear a hearing for habeas corpus because Standing Bear was not a citizen or a person under the law. Therefore, Lambertson declared, Standing Bear could not bring a suit against the U.S. government. Lambertson had extrapolated from the 1857 Dred Scott decision that had found a Negro was not a person before the law and had no access to a federal court. Surely an Indian would not have greater rights than a Negro, he argued. Judge Dundy was unpersuaded by Lambertson. He allowed Standing Bear and the Poncas to stand trial in April 1879.

Webster and Poppleton became as ardent in their defense of the Poncas as Tibbles. But like Tibbles, they mostly spoke *for* Standing Bear. As with Tibbles's newspaper coverage, the trial mostly involved the lawyers, not Standing Bear himself, articulating the Poncas' case. Standing Bear could only answer, through his interpreter, the questions that his defense lawyers and the district attorney posed to him. He could not make his case as he wished.

At the end of the trial, however, after two long days of legal wrangling, Judge Dundy allowed Standing Bear to speak on his own behalf. With his dramatic flair and oratorical skills, Standing Bear stood, faced the judge, and made an eloquent plea for Ponca freedom. We don't have a verbatim copy of this speech, so we don't know exactly what Standing Bear said, or at least what his translator said. Even when an Indian did gain a platform from which to testify directly of his own experience and perspective, it was not always assured that his words would be recorded properly.

Tibbles provided multiple accounts of Standing Bear's speech, all differing slightly. He reported in the *Omaha Herald* the next day that Standing Bear said to the judge and the courtroom, "God made me and he put me on my land. But, I was ordered to stand up and leave my land. . . . I objected to going. . . . I came away to save my wife and children and friends. I never want to go back there again. I want to go back to my old reservation to live there and be buried in the land of my fathers."

A month later, Tibbles published a more extended version of Standing Bear's remarks in *Standing Bear and the Ponca Chiefs*, an edited volume of transcribed letters and other documents. Tibbles quoted Standing Bear as declaring,

> From the time I went down there [to Indian Territory] until I left, one hundred and fifty-eight of us died. I thought to myself, God wants me to live, and I think if I come back to my old reservation he will let me live. I got back as far as the Omahas, and they brought me down here [on trial]. . . . What have I done? . . . I don't know. It seems as though I haven't a place in the world, no place to go, and no home to go to.

Asked why he had returned to Nebraska, his translator told the court, "He says it was hard for him to stay there, and he thought perhaps if he could come up here he could save his wife and child, the only child he has living." Upon cross-examination, Standing Bear said, according to his translator,

> he wanted to go on his own land, that had always been his own land; that he never sold it, and that is where he wanted to go to; that his son when he died made him promise if ever he went back there that he would take his bones there and bury him, and that he has got his [son's] bones in a box, and that if ever he goes there he will bury his bones there; that there is where he wants to live the rest of his life, and that is where he wants to be buried.

Standing Bear and the Ponca Chiefs also summarized the hours-long concluding remarks of each of Standing Bear's attorneys, as well as the district attorney, and then paraphrased Standing Bear's speech: "He claimed that, although his skin was of a different hue, yet he was a man, and that God made him. He said he was not a savage, and related how he had saved the life of a soldier whom he had found on the plains, starved, and almost frozen to death." Almost twenty-five years later, Tibbles produced yet another version of Standing Bear's speech in his autobiography.

So even in the best-case scenario—in which an Indian actually gained a platform to speak—his or her words were still filtered through multiple layers of settler intervention. It has thus been vitally important to American Indians to create their own independent media outlets, such as *Indian Country Today* and *Indianz.com*, to express their concerns and perspectives directly. The Indigenous Media Freedom Alliance, which journalist Jodi Rave Spotted Bear (Mandan, Hidatsa, and Minneconjou Lakota) started in 2016, is working "to advance American Indian rights to be seen and heard through independent media, language, [and] culture and to create an environment where citizens can control their destiny by making informed decisions." Vision Maker Media, which was established nearly fifty years ago, funds Native American filmmakers in a mission to create a world "changed and healed by understanding Native stories and the public conversations they generate." We could say that these organizations are seeking media sovereignty, the right to represent themselves.

We may not know exactly what Standing Bear said at his trial, but we do know that his remarks had an electrifying effect on the people who had crowded into the courtroom. Many sources report that in spite of efforts to maintain order in the court, Standing Bear's testimony elicited sustained applause. In his memoirs Tibbles said that Standing Bear's speech left Judge Dundy and General Crook in tears. Standing Bear, even through his interpreter, was able to tell his story in his own inimitable style.

Ten days later, the judge ruled in Standing Bear's favor, freeing him and his followers from their fifty-four-day detention in the custody of the U.S. Army at Fort Omaha. Dundy opened his ruling by stating, "During the fifteen years in which I have been engaged in administering the laws of my country, I have never been called upon to hear or decide a case that appealed so strongly to my sympathy as the one now under consideration." Dundy ruled that an Indian is a person within the meaning of the law and has a right to sue in federal court, that Crook had illegally detained the Poncas, and that the military had no legal authority to remove Standing Bear and his followers back to Indian Territory. He ruled that Indians have the same rights to life, liberty, and the pursuit of happiness as whites and that the Poncas must be discharged from custody.

Many settler Americans did not want to grant Indians such rights. As Joe Starita reports, the *Rocky Mountain News*, whose editor, William Byers, had supported the Sand Creek Massacre, called the decision dangerous. Its editorial complained that if the government could not control the movements of Indians, "the Indians will become a body of tramps moving without restraint wherever they please."

Dundy's ruling was a major victory for Standing Bear and the Poncas, and a legal turning point for other Indians, but it came with a cost and a catch. The *cost*? The judge had ruled that Indians were persons under the law, but only if they renounced their Indian status. Dundy explained that the case "present[ed] the question as to whether or not an Indian can withdraw from his tribe, sever his tribal relation therewith, and terminate his allegiance thereto, for the purpose of making an independent living and adopting our own civilization." He said that "if Indian tribes are to be regarded and treated as separate but dependent nations, there can be no serious difficulty about the question. If they are not to be regarded and treated as separate, dependent nations, then no allegiance is owing from an individual Indian to his tribe, and he could, therefore, withdraw therefrom at any time." Dundy concluded, "I think the individual Indian possesses the clear and God-given right to withdraw from his tribe and forever live away from it, as though it had no further existence." Thus, Dundy's ruling was based on the notion that Indian tribes were not sovereign nations. And it was premised on the settler colonial aspiration of eliminating Indian tribes.

In essence, Dundy's decision created a false choice. Either you could be a member of an Indian nation or you could enjoy the rights of an American citizen. The rights inherent in the Constitution and the Bill of Rights could apply to Standing Bear, and other Indians, but only if they ceased to be Indians, only if they shed their Indian identities and allegiances.

The *catch* was that Standing Bear and his group, now defined as non-Indians, could not legally inhabit reservation land. On May 19, upon their release, the Ponca captives were overjoyed, and they headed immediately back to their Niobrara homelands. Tibbles rushed after them. He realized that legally their old land still belonged to the Lakotas and they could be arrested as trespassers if they set foot on it. Tibbles reached the Poncas just in time before they could be apprehended, again.

So a new dilemma faced Standing Bear and his followers. Where would they live? The Omaha Indian leader Joseph La Flesche offered some land for Standing Bear and his band, but this presented the same problem. The government could arrest any non-Indian who ventured onto reservation land without government permission. So, Standing Bear was still unable to return to his homeland or to abide with tribal relatives to grow his crops, perform his ceremonies, and bury his son properly. Instead he and his small group set up a camp on private land near Decatur, Nebraska. By now, in the late spring, it was too late—again—to plant crops and they had to rely on the continued donations of the Omaha Ponca Relief Committee.

Standing Bear's settler advocates searched for a means to get the Poncas' land back and to help the venerable chief resettle on his homelands. His lawyers found that several islands in the Niobrara River had been excluded from Lakota ownership, so Standing Bear moved over the summer of 1879 to a "willow thicket on one of the larger islands, land owned by a private citizen in a nearby village," according to Starita.

Larry Wright Jr. put it this way: Standing Bear and his followers "had to go onto an island in the middle of the Niobrara that nobody claimed. And they had to sneak back into our homeland that didn't belong to us anymore." In short, they "made us trespassers in our own land."

At least the Ponca chief was finally able to bury his son on a bluff above the old village, but living on an island in the Niobrara River was not a sustainable solution. And what should be done about the Poncas who were still exiled in Indian Territory? And what would become of the Omahas, who feared government reprisal for helping runaway Poncas?

Settler allies in the city of Omaha's Ponca Relief Committee strategized after the trial about how to help the Poncas regain their land and to enable the Poncas in Indian Territory to return to their homelands. They decided to go national, to mobilize networks of influential settler reformers in the East. In the summer of 1879, they decided that Tibbles should travel to Boston to raise support for the Poncas among his old abolitionist friends. He resigned from the *Herald* and headed east. His meetings with influential eastern settlers generated some interest but not the groundswell of support that Ponca supporters had hoped.

The Ponca Relief Committee then determined that audiences in the East would be more moved by hearing from Standing Bear directly. His own eloquent orations would be more likely to mobilize non-Indians to support the Ponca cause than would those of a settler advocate like Tibbles. So the committee proposed that Standing Bear go on a lecture tour in the fall, with Tibbles. But the Ponca chief would need an interpreter. The committee suggested a young western-educated Omaha woman who had translated a letter for twelve Ponca leaders and attended one of their meetings: Susette La Flesche. (The Omaha and Ponca languages are related.)

Susette had been the only woman present at a meeting of the Ponca Relief Committee in a small hotel, just prior to Standing Bear's trial. At the meeting, members of the committee asked Willie Hamilton, the settler missionary's son on the Omaha Reservation, to tell what he knew of the Ponca case. He suggested that Susette speak instead. According to her biographer, Dorothy Clarke Wilson, "Susette shrank back terrified. She felt impaled on a barrage of probing eyes. When she tried to speak, her voice was little more than a whisper. But the glances, the nods, were encouraging. . . . She was soon leaning forward and talking eagerly, telling the story as she knew it."

Susette came from a prominent Omaha Indian family with many relatives among the Poncas. Her father, Joseph La Flesche—of mixed Ponca and French parentage—had grown up among the Omahas and been chosen by an older chief to be his successor. In 1854, when the Omahas moved to their reservation on the Missouri River, Joseph established a settlement of frame houses near the new Presbyterian mission and school that some other Omahas called the Make Believe White Men's Village. (Other Omahas established two other villages of more traditional earth lodges located to the west and south of La Flesche's settlement.)

Joseph promoted farming on new individually owned tracts of land and set up a police force to keep order. In 1866, he converted to Christianity and sent his children to the mission school. He ensured that all his children were well educated in American schools. His daughter Susan eventually became a medical doctor and his son, Francis, pursued a career as an ethnographer. Historian Susana Geliga (Lakota) asserts the La Flesche family were carefully observing the changing society around them and making preemptive and strategic choices to cope with the onslaught of settler colonialism, many years prior to the U.S. government imposing an assimilation program on Indians.

Susette may have been shy about public speaking, but she was a woman of many tongues; she could translate in an engaging manner. She also knew much about the Ponca cause and could speak eloquently about it herself. The Ponca Relief Committee soon called upon Susette to speak again on behalf of the Poncas at the Episcopal Church in

Omaha. This time she was not so reluctant. She had allegedly grown depressed after Standing Bear's trial. According to Wilson, she "felt incredibly helpless and remote, stranded in a backwash, while strangers were fighting for her people." She was still very nervous about public speaking, but she readily accepted this invitation to make the Ponca cause known to settlers.

Tibbles was not supportive; he thought inviting Susette to speak at the Episcopal Church was a bad idea. She was too timid, he believed, and her presentation might offend the conservatives who opposed women speaking in churches. Perhaps he realized that Susette, who was fluent in Ponca, Omaha, and English, might replace him as Standing Bear's spokesperson.

Susette spoke at the church, despite Tibbles's objections. Susette was "visibly trembling" before her address, but then expressed herself forcefully and movingly when she took the lectern: "Why should I be asked to speak? I am but an Indian girl, brought up among the Indians. I love my people. I have been educated, and most of them have not. I have told them that they must learn the arts of white people and adopt their customs, but how can they, when the government sends soldiers to drive them about over the face of the earth?" Susette boldly exposed the painful contradictions between government policies and practices. Even when the Poncas had followed its edicts, the government had capriciously and violently removed them.

The Ponca Relief Committee remembered Susette's eloquence and powerful statement when they were discussing an interpreter for Standing Bear's tour. They invited her, now twenty-five years old, to go east with Tibbles and Standing Bear, as both the chief's interpreter and a speaker in her own right. Tibbles, perhaps threatened, opposed the idea, as did Susette's father, Joseph. He worried about the propriety of allowing his daughter to tour with two unrelated men. Susette was also reluctant to travel so far from her home.

But the Poncas had asked Susette and her father for help. The La Flesches had visited their Ponca relatives in Indian Territory, and they had hosted Ponca families in their home on the Omaha Reservation. Susette later testified that "they said they could not talk English but that

I could talk English, and they asked me to use all my power to tell the white people of the United States the condition in which they were." Moreover, when legislators introduced a bill in Congress to remove the Omaha Indians to Indian Territory, Susette and her father thought it urgent that she join the tour. Joseph suggested that his son, Francis (or Frank), could chaperone his older sister.

And so, in the fall of 1879, the Ponca chief, the two Omaha Indian siblings, and the journalist Tibbles embarked on a months-long trip to provide a firsthand account of the Poncas' travails to settler audiences. The group made their first public appearance on October 19 at Chicago's Second Presbyterian Church and then headed directly to Boston.

Standing Bear and Susette may have thought that they would now finally have the opportunity to present their case on their own terms, without the intervention of settler translators, journalists, and attorneys. But it became apparent almost immediately that Standing Bear, Susette, and Frank would not be entirely free to present themselves, their grievances, and their solutions to their problems as they wished. To be effective, the tour group had to carefully calibrate not only what they said but also how they represented themselves and appeared in public.

They quickly learned to use to their advantage the romantic notions that some settlers had about Indians. Outside of their family, Susette and Frank had gone by their English names from their births, but eastern audiences preferred their Anglicized Indian names. They became Bright Eyes and Woodworker for the duration of the tour.

Standing Bear, Susette, and Frank came to know, too, that they were exotic figures to many easterners. On one memorable evening, Henry Houghton (cofounder of Houghton Mifflin publishing) and his family hosted Tibbles and the three American Indian speakers. Guests included some of the leading literary lights and social influencers of the era: John Greenleaf Whittier, James Russell Lowell, Oliver Wendell Holmes Sr., Henry Wadsworth Longfellow, Ralph Waldo Emerson, William Dean Howells, Samuel Clemens (aka Mark Twain), Harriet Beecher Stowe, Helen Hunt Jackson, Edward Everett Hale, Wendell

Phillips, the Bronson Alcott family (including the budding author Louisa May), the Boston mayor, and the Massachusetts governor.

When Susette walked in the door of the Houghtons' elegant home for dinner, Henry Wadsworth Longfellow declared that "this is Minnehaha," the beautiful Indian maiden in his famous epic poem, *The Song of Hiawatha*, a romantic depiction of American Indian life. Longfellow escorted Susette to a quiet corner, where the two conversed at length. Later he would share a stage with Susette and present her with an autograph album with a stanza from his famous poem.

For most easterners, by the late nineteenth century, virtually their only frame of reference for understanding an Indian woman was through the character of Minnehaha. Wherever she went, settlers insisted on referring to Susette as Minnehaha and the Beautiful Indian Maiden. Susette was dismayed; according to Wilson, Susette was "never quite able to establish her identity apart from that of 'Indian Maiden.'"

The three Indians also had to moderate their dress to fit the expectations of eastern audiences. At home in his Niobrara lands, Standing Bear had worn American-style dress, although he kept his hair long. As he traveled by train and attended receptions and dinners, he continued to wear a suit. But when he spoke publicly, he changed into his traditional garb: "a magnificent full costume of an Indian chief," according to Tibbles. "He had a red blanket, trimmed with broad blue stripes, a wide beaded belt around his waist, and wore a necklace of bear's claws."

The Boston *Advertiser* reported that Standing Bear wore his "civilized costume" until just before his speech, when he changed into "chief's official dress. His dignified figure showed to the best advantage in the picturesque costume, which was really handsome with its full draperies and strong colors—red, green, and goldwork predominating." Tibbles explained that wearing of chief's robes was like a military officer wearing his uniform on special occasions.

Standing Bear grew tired of conforming to Americans' ideas of an authentic Indian. After more than a month of this routine, Standing Bear wanted to have his hair cut and stop wearing his regalia. Tibbles forcefully opposed the change, ostensibly because it would distract

attention from the content of the Ponca leader's presentation. But perhaps Tibbles also believed Standing Bear's traditional dress was more
effective in moving audiences.

What Frank and Susette should wear was also a matter of discussion
and calculation. In this case, however, Tibbles did not want them to
appear in Omaha clothing. It might be preferable for the older chief to
wear his traditional garb, but the younger generation should don
American dress, as a sign of what settlers saw as the proper progress of
the "race." As western-educated Indians, Frank and Susette had long
worn American-style attire. So, they continued to do so. Frank had his
hair cut in the style of Americans as well. Some newspapers mentioned Frank's appearance—"a handsome young man of commanding
height and determined expression"—but did not dwell on it.

Reporters nearly always mentioned how Susette looked and how she
was dressed, as well as her public manner. (Some things never seem to
change.) Papers reported that Bright Eyes, as they always called her, was
"a handsome young woman of twenty-three" and "wore a mantilla coat
and black velvet bonnet neatly trimmed with beads." The Boston newspaper the *Woman's Journal* described her as "lovely and winning, refined
of great intelligence, and with singularly sweet, graceful, and simple
manners." Observers seemed to marvel at Susette's poise, at how this
"beautiful Indian maiden" conformed to late nineteenth-century gender
expectations at the same time as she shattered settler stereotypes of
American Indian women as "squaw drudges."

So, even before they spoke a word, Standing Bear, Susette, and Frank
realized they were communicating important messages to their audiences through their hairstyles, dress, and comportment. Knowing that
many settlers considered Indians as less than human, they maintained
a dignified and respectable presence. They conveyed that we Indians can
be just like you and therefore we are just as deserving of the same rights
as other Americans. This might have helped the Poncas' immediate
cause, but it also lent support to the growing settler reform movement
for the assimilation of American Indians, which insisted that Indians
become just like settlers if they hoped to enjoy rights and freedom. It
reinforced the message of Judge Dundy that Indians could gain equal

treatment under the law in America, but only if they abandoned their Indian heritages and nations.

The tour proved to be a great success in reaching a vast audience. The group spoke frequently to large crowds and influential movers and shakers during their four to five months in the East. They arrived in Boston by train at 6:00 a.m. on October 29 and stayed in the city for more than a month. They spoke almost every day to full houses in churches and meeting halls. They were feted by the most prominent Boston families. One of their most successful presentations occurred before almost five hundred businessmen at the Merchants' Exchange, in the middle of the workday. At their last public appearance in Boston, at Faneuil Hall on December 3, more than two thousand people had to be turned away. Susette was the first woman in its history to make a speech there.

The lecturers spent most of December in New York and then traveled to the seat of American power—Washington, D.C.—in the new year. Susette was invited to the White House to spend an informal evening with President and Mrs. Rutherford B. Hayes. In Washington, Standing Bear and Susette, along with several other Ponca leaders, testified to a Senate Committee.

During the new year, the group shuttled back and forth between Boston, Philadelphia, Wilmington, Baltimore, and Carlisle, Pennsylvania, the site of the first Indian boarding school, which had just opened the year before. The group also went to another boarding school—Hampton Institute in Virginia—which had admitted some American Indian children alongside African American students. Susette hoped Omaha children could go there, including members of her own family.

The busy schedule put a lot of strain on the speakers. The stress was compounded by personal events. When the group arrived in Boston on October 29, Tibbles and Standing Bear each received devastating news, via telegrams, that afternoon. Tibbles learned that his wife of eighteen years had died of peritonitis. Standing Bear was informed that his unarmed brother had been shot in the head by a soldier in Indian Territory for resisting arrest. The trio still had to speak that night and many days and nights after that.

Standing Bear and Susette made the most of their opportunities to speak. They used their platforms to testify to the wrongs the Poncas had experienced and to critique federal Indian policy. Susette, for example, told one audience,

> Your government has driven us hither and thither like cattle, and because poor human nature, unable to bear such treatment, retaliates in the only way open to it to free itself you call us savages and lay on us still more heavily that which we hate, the yoke of bondage. . . . Your government has no right to say to us, Go here, or Go there, and if we show any reluctance, to force us to do its will at the point of a bayonet. An Indian does not want to cultivate a piece of land, fence it in, build him a house, furnish and stock his farm, and just as he is ready to enjoy the fruits of it, to have it taken from him and be sent with his family to a southern clime to die. Do you wonder that the Indian feels outraged by such treatment and retaliates, although it will end in death to himself.

Susette also readily challenged misinformation. She used the occasion at the Merchants' Exchange to bust some of the prevalent stereotypes, prominent among them that Indians were receiving handouts from the government. After telling of how the Ponca tribe had been robbed of their property and annuities, she explained the nature of annuities: "It was money promised by the government for the land they had sold. I desire to say that all annuities paid to Indian tribes by the government are in payment for lands sold by them to the government, and are not charity."

Susette frequently responded to settler denials of massacres and representations of Indians as bloodthirsty savages. When a reporter claimed that U.S. soldiers only killed Indians in battle, Susette responded, "They kill men, women, and children, and you cannot deny it. It is true." When this reporter countered that Indians were more barbarous in war, Susette pointed out that white men taught Indians scalping—that it was first practiced in New England on the Penobscot Indians when the General Court of the Province of Massachusetts offered a bounty of forty pounds for every scalp of a male Indian and twenty pounds for that of a woman or child. She declared, "You never get but one side. We have no newspapers to tell our story. I tell you the soldiers do things with the prisoners and the dead as horrible as any Indian could think of. And you people are almost always the aggressors."

In addition to testifying to what they had endured and making appeals for funds and other assistance, Standing Bear and Susette often spoke of the importance of making their case on behalf of their people, rather than through the mediated voice of settler friends of the Indians. At the Merchants' Exchange in Boston, Susette declared, "For the last hundred years the Indians have had none to tell the story of their wrongs. If a white man did an injury to an Indian, the Indian had to suffer in silence, or, if exasperated to revenge, the act of revenge has been spread abroad through the newspapers of the land as a causeless act . . . just because the Indian delighted in being savage." She made it clear that Indians could speak for themselves. She told the history of the Poncas' struggle over the past two years, then stated, "This Ponca case is only a single specimen among hundreds of others. . . . We are thinking men and women. . . . We have a right to be heard in whatever concerns us."

Susette also fought against paternalism. At a February 2, 1880, meeting at the West Arch Street Presbyterian Church in Philadelphia, Susette admonished her audience, "Set aside the idea that the Indian is a child and must be taken care of, . . . give him a title to his lands, throw over him the protection of the law, . . . and the Indian will take care of himself. Then there will be no more wars in trying to settle the Indian problem, for there will be no problem to settle."

Their public speaking stirred eastern audiences in ways that Tibbles had not been able to achieve. Standing Bear's testimony, through the translation of Susette, mobilized many settlers to take up the cause of the Poncas and other Indians. As the Boston *Advertiser* put it, Standing Bear "spoke with great animation and earnest eloquence, using vigorous gestures," and they praised "the plain, simple interpretation of Miss Bright Eyes."

Public speaking was more challenging for Susette; as an Omaha woman, she had not been brought up to take on that role, although she had certainly heard many examples of outstanding oration. Susette felt more comfortable reading her speech than speaking off the cuff. But her words were affecting, too. The Boston *Advertiser* reported that "Miss Bright Eyes read her address from manuscript in a modest, natural manner, and with a sweet, girlish, and expressive voice which quite won the hearts of her listeners." The Boston *Woman's Journal* liked her style; they asserted Susette is "never bitter, never vindictive. She is calm, but full of animation and a very deep feeling." Lecturing eventually grew easier for Susette as she shared platforms with such luminaries as Longfellow, Holmes, and Phillips. "If I could speak before them, I could speak before anybody," she wrote. Tibbles claimed that Longfellow said to him, "I've been a student of the English language all my life, and I would give all I possess if I could speak it with the simplicity, fluency, and force used by that Indian girl."

It was taxing for Standing Bear and Susette to stand up before white audiences in Boston, Washington, D.C., New York, Philadelphia, and Baltimore and tell of the injustices the Poncas had suffered again and again, day after day, night after night from the fall of 1879 into the spring of 1880. On top of this, Tibbles and Susette became targets of "increasingly violent and vituperative attacks." After their exhausting tour the quartet returned to Nebraska in April 1880.

Standing Bear and Susette had overcome many of the obstacles to Native Americans speaking their truths to settler audiences. Hopefully their truth telling would be worth it. Hopefully all of the sacrifices they had made and the hard work they had done would be effective in gaining support from influential settler reformers who could help move the government to change its policies.

Indeed, their tour had profound consequences. Standing Bear and Susette found a settler audience that was eager to hear them. Many of these settlers had been active abolitionists who spoke out forcefully against slavery. They responded with concern and commitment to take action. But it would remain to be seen whether the Poncas would obtain justice as a result of speaking out and rousing settlers to take up their cause.

PART TWO

Promoting Reconciliation in Nineteenth-Century America

CHAPTER 6

Rousing the Conscience of a Nation

Today there are settlers who would excuse what the United States did to the Poncas in the 1870s by making the "man of his times" argument. It goes something like this: What happened to the Poncas, and to so many other tribes, was unfortunate, even tragic, but that's just how people (read: settlers) thought back then. They were not as enlightened as we are now, and they harbored prejudices against American Indians that were so strong that they could justify carrying out atrocities against them. We shouldn't judge these past actors by today's more "politically correct" moral standards, these settlers contend. Nobody back then would have batted an eye about the ill treatment of Indigenous peoples.

Notice first that this way of thinking does not consider the opinion of Indigenous peoples themselves, those like Chief Standing Bear and Susette La Flesche, who not only batted their eyes but vociferously opposed their dispossession and removal. It also rests on the assumption that it is merely politically correct to oppose violations of ancient and universal moral precepts like thou shalt not kill and do unto others.

But a powerful argument against the "man of his times" notion is that in those times, there *were* many settler men, and women, who did speak up for Indigenous rights. They became almost fanatical in their devotion to exposing the wrongs committed against Indian peoples. It is unlikely that you know their names because the cover-up of our founding crimes, through the creation of our settler lore, has been so complete that we are not even aware of the history of alliances between Indigenous people and settlers against such crimes. But in the nineteenth century, a large group of settler reformers spoke out forcefully against federal Indian policy. And they did so because of the activism of Standing Bear and Susette La Flesche.

Their lecture tour with Thomas Tibbles and Frank La Flesche over the winter of 1879–80 launched what we could regard as a truth and reconciliation initiative between settlers and Indigenous people in the United States. This may seem an odd phrase to use for a nineteenth-century movement. Truth and reconciliation, as an approach to making redress for historical wrongs, after all, did not enter our vocabulary until the late twentieth century.

Modern redress efforts have in common a desire on the part of those who have been wronged to tell their stories and give their testimony, to set the historical record straight, and to have others bear witness to the wrongs they have suffered. Truth and reconciliation processes have often involved lengthy investigations and reports and recommendations for redress. All of these elements were present in the late 1870s and early 1880s when Standing Bear and Susette spoke of the Poncas' grievances.

This was not the first such effort in American history. Many settlers had joined with members of the Cherokee nation in the early nineteenth century to oppose their removal to Indian Territory. And over the course of the twentieth century, there would be many more instances when Indigenous people told of the injustices they had experienced, settlers listened, and then they partnered to grapple with ways to make amends for such past abuses.

But the late nineteenth century was undeniably one of the most critical moments in American history for truth and reconciliation, not just for the injustices that the Poncas and other Native American groups had experienced but also, of course, for African Americans who had only recently gained their freedom from slavery. It was a moment in which the wounds of slavery were still fresh and a time when redress could have been speedily provided. The nation took halting steps toward such redress during the era known as Reconstruction, from 1863 to 1877. But ultimately, as David Blight charts in his heartbreaking book *Race and Reunion*, the nation prioritized a different kind of reconciliation—that between the former slave owners of the Confederacy and the Union. The nation missed an opportunity to reckon with and make amends to African Americans for slavery.

The potential for truth and reconciliation between settlers and Native Americans was also ripe in the late nineteenth century. The government was dispossessing and removing tribe after tribe in the West, and military forces and settler militias were still carrying out genocidal violence against Indian tribes. Rather than waiting decades or more than a century to make amends, the nation could have come to terms with its crimes against Native Americans in their immediate aftermath. It was a moment for *restitution*, which redress experts define as the restoration of victims to their original state before they had been subject to gross violations of their human rights.

At first this nascent truth and reconciliation movement *did* prioritize restitution; its members adhered closely to the expressed concerns of the Ponca leaders and the Omaha woman: helping the Poncas return to their homeland. Many settler reformers realized that other Indian tribes were suffering, too, and they sought to enforce treaties and help Indians retain or regain their land. A few settler activists became zealous in their support for restitution. But it was not to be. Until 1890 settlers continued to unleash deadly violence upon Indians and forcibly remove them from their homelands. And American Indians continued to lose land until well into the twentieth century.

This reconciliation movement was short-lived and ultimately failed, so it may be tempting to consign it to a footnote in American history. But we still have much to learn from it. It teaches us that the United States has a long history of reconciliation movements and a lineage of both Indigenous people and settlers who sought to overcome division and resolve conflict. It also shows us the contested nature of reconciliation, how it came to hold different meanings to Indigenous people and settlers over time. We learn, too, that reconciliation is a fragile and elusive process that can easily go awry. Rather than bringing justice to Indigenous peoples it can lead to further suffering and harm. We see that government officials can easily co-opt and pervert reconciliation for their own purposes. As we struggle to create meaningful truth and reconciliation processes in our own time, these lessons from the past are important to bear in mind.

Standing Bear and Susette's tour had created an opportunity for settlers to engage in truth and reconciliation with Indigenous peoples. Settlers could learn firsthand from Indian people who had suffered from and witnessed great injustice, they could become allies, and then they could work together with Indian people to challenge the federal policies that had wrought such injustice upon the Poncas. Indian people could voice their aspirations and ask for redress, and their settler allies could support their goals. For a brief time, this is what happened.

Standing Bear often expressed a powerful appreciation for and a desire to practice reconciliation with the allies who had helped him win his trial. After his release, he told Tibbles:

> When I was brought here a prisoner, my heart was broken. I was in despair. I had no friend in all the big world. Then you came. I told you the story of my wrongs. From that time until now you have not ceased to work for me. . . . I know if it had not been for what you have done for me I would now be a prisoner in Indian Territory, and many of these who are with me here would have been in their graves. . . . I owe all this to you. I can never pay you for it. It may be that some time you may have trouble. You might lose your house. If you ever want a home come to me or my tribe. You shall never want as long as we have anything. . . . While there is one Ponca alive you will never be without a friend. . . . You are my brother.

Tibbles was given to exaggeration and bragging, so it's not clear that Standing Bear actually said this, but we can infer from the chief's *actions* that he did feel gratitude for Tibbles and other allies. Standing Bear gave beaded buckskin leggings to Tibbles, a tomahawk to his attorney Webster, and a war bonnet to his other lawyer, Poppleton.

Another Ponca leader, White Eagle, had also articulated his appreciation of settler alliances. He had written a letter addressed to the American people that he gave to Susette and Joseph La Flesche when they visited him in Indian Territory in the spring of 1879, shortly after

Standing Bear's trial. "We thought that all the white men hated us," he wrote, "but now we have seen you take pity on Standing Bear when you hear his story. It may be that you knew nothing of our wrongs, and therefore, did not help us. I thank you in the name of our people for what you have done for us through your kindness to Standing Bear."

Susette also expressed gratitude for some white settlers who had become sympathetic to Indian people. She told one assembled crowd in Boston that the Omahas, the Poncas, and other Indians had suffered so much that they had almost given up hope. "I felt as though if there were a God he must have created us for the sole purpose of torturing us," she declared. Susette had attended a boarding school for girls—the Elizabeth Institute—in New Jersey for a few years with the support of many white women reformers. She told the audience that it was the memory of the white Christian women she had met while at Elizabeth Institute that sustained her through the trials of the Poncas. She struck a positive note: "I come to you with gladness in my heart and to try and thank you, for here, after a hundred years of oppression, my people have for the first time found public sympathy, and as soon as the truth of their story was known help was given them." These American Indian activists actively cultivated settler alliances.

Standing Bear and Susette's presentations particularly influenced white women. Standing Bear recognized this when he stated one night from the podium at the Boston Music Hall to a standing-room-only crowd, "For years the army did what it liked with us, and we had war and bloodshed. Then the Indians were turned over to the politicians, and they appointed our agents and rulers. That was a hundred times worse, and we had continual war. Then your great General who never talked [Grant] turned us over to the churches and divided us up among them. We still had war and bloodshed. . . . and we have had war and bloodshed ever since. Now I ask you to turn us over once more. Turn us over to the ladies, and they will not murder us or drive us from our lands." Many white women responded avidly to Standing Bear's request.

One night in Boston in November 1879, a settler woman named Helen Hunt Jackson listened with rapt attention to Standing Bear's,

Tibbles's, and Susette's riveting speeches. She went to the tour group's hotel early the next morning and asked for an interview with Tibbles. She simply wanted him to check an article she had written for accuracy. But she also inadvertently met Susette that morning. A bit starstruck, Jackson allegedly said to her, "My dear, you have given me a new purpose in life. You and I will work miracles together. You will see." Many settler historians assert that Helen and Susette became close friends.

Very few people know of Helen Hunt Jackson today, but at the time she was a well-known and beloved author. By the time she heard Standing Bear and Susette speak, she had written a dozen books. Ralph Waldo Emerson had dubbed her the "greatest American woman poet." Helen had married the banker and railroad baron William Sharpless Jackson in 1875, and the couple resided in Colorado Springs, near where I grew up. We often took visitors to the Helen Hunt Falls tourist attraction in Cheyenne Canyon Park. But as a child, I had no idea who this woman was. Her story did not fit into the western lore that passed for history during my childhood.

Up until the moment when she heard Standing Bear and Susette, Jackson had little interest in America's Indigenous people. Like many settlers, she had been both fascinated and repelled by Indians. She had referred to them in some of her writings as "loathsome," "abject," and "hideous." She had criticized Longfellow for "using the silly legends of the savage aborigines" in *Hiawatha*.

It was pure chance that Jackson attended one of Standing Bear and Susette's lectures. She had traveled from her home in Colorado Springs to the East Coast to attend the seventieth birthday party of the poet-physician Oliver Wendell Holmes Sr. in 1879. Her visit coincided with the Ponca tour. Her editor at the Boston *Advertiser*, for whom she had written literary reviews, encouraged her to attend one of the many presentations by the Ponca chief and his Omaha interpreter. She listened intently to the abuses they recounted. She seems to have shed, virtually overnight, her earlier prejudices against Indians.

Jackson was so moved that she began to do extensive research into government documents about Indian policy and violations of Indian treaties and to write numerous lengthy letters to the editors of some of the leading newspapers on the East Coast. And from that day when she met Susette, according to Dorothy Wilson, Jackson became "an almost constant companion of the Ponca party. She accompanied them on most of their speaking tours around New England." The California writer Joaquin Miller said Jackson had persuaded abolitionist Wendell Phillips to take up the cause of Indians as he had done for enslaved African Americans.

Jackson turned all of her writing skill and energy toward the cause of American Indians for the rest of her life, just six more years. According to historian Valerie Sherer Mathes, she took a "one-woman crusading journalistic approach" toward rectifying the injustices Indigenous people suffered. Thomas Tibbles in his memoir declared that Jackson threw "every ounce of her own strong influence into the scale in dealing with members of Congress, senators, editors, and writers." This required sacrifices on Jackson's part: she spent months away from her husband; traveled back and forth across the continent by train; and lived out of hotel rooms to research and write her books.

Jackson may have sacrificed, too, her literary career and reputation, and subjected herself to criticism, insult, and rejection. From some of her letters we can gather that some people, even her own husband, accused Jackson of sentimentality toward Indians. Many dismissed her as what we might call a bleeding-heart liberal today, a woman who lacked the pragmatism and toughness needed to deal with the so-called Indian problem.

Jackson fought back against such gendered constraints. She wrote to her husband to assure him, "I am not writing—& shall not write *one word* as a sentimentalist." She determined to present "verbatim reports, officially authenticated, . . . before the American people:—& are all which are needed, to rouse public sentiment. The ignorance of everybody on the subject is simply astonishing—my own included—till six weeks ago, & even now I am only beginning." Jackson did not let such belittling criticism deter her.

She used her extensive connections to advance the Ponca cause. She enlisted her friends in New York City to hold weekly receptions for the touring group. These were attended by the literati, including Ralph

Waldo Emerson, Edgar Allan Poe, Margaret Fuller, Horace Greeley, and many other leading authors.

Jackson focused her efforts on what Standing Bear, Susette, and other Ponca leaders said they needed and wanted. Over and over, the Indian speakers stated that keeping their land was their foremost priority. Over and over, they said that this was the way to bring justice to Indian people. In his letter to the American people in 1879, the Ponca leader White Eagle pleaded, "I ask of you to go still further in your kindness and help us to regain our land and our rights. I now ask the President . . . through this message, which I sent to all the white people of this land, to rectify his mistake [Ponca removal]. When a man desires to do what is right, he does not say to himself, 'It does not matter,' when he commits a wrong."

Upon his release from Crook's custody, after his trial, Standing Bear similarly articulated that it was the return of their land along the Niobrara River that the Poncas wanted. When he thanked Poppleton for representing him as his attorney, Standing Bear said, "I want to get my land back. That is what I long for all the time. I wish to live there and be buried with my fathers." Standing Bear also declared, "I thank God I am a free man once more, and I shall never forget those who have helped me. I would like to find some government land and take a homestead like the white people do. I am getting old but I can commence anew. The government has taken all my property, held me a prisoner a long time and now when it is too late to plant they say to me 'go.' But they do not give me back my land, my plows, or any property they have taken away." Tibbles printed Standing Bear's powerful words in the *Omaha Herald*.

Jackson followed the lead of the Indian activists. She wrote unceasing letters to advocate for restitution for the Poncas. In an editorial she titled "Justice," Jackson wrote to the *New York Tribune* in November 1879: "Standing Bear . . . seeks a response, and asks pecuniary aid to enable him to appeal to the courts to restore to his people the lands unconditionally ceded to them by the United States, from which they have been so unjustly and barbarously expelled." Jackson used language that is remarkably similar to that used by restorative justice advocates and theorists in our own era: she spoke of *restoring* land to the Poncas and noted that this constituted "justice" for the Poncas.

To Jackson, providing restitution to the Poncas was not only fair and just, it was also essential to the progress of the American nation. To the *Hartford Courant*, she wrote in November 1879, the Indians "are right & we are wrong—and the one chance the [Indian] race has for freedom and right—and our one chance for decency as a nation in our treatment of them, is just now, in this movement toward the courts, by the Poncas." For many modern-day advocates of truth and reconciliation, redress is as important for bolstering the legitimacy of the settler nation-state and the promotion of national unity as it is for righting historical wrongs. Jackson's observation that this was America's "one chance for decency as a nation" speaks to how she foreshadowed this future feature of truth and reconciliation efforts.

Jackson also became a student of other injustices against Indians. She wrote a series of letters to the *New York Tribune* over the winter of 1879–80 about the 1864 Sand Creek Massacre as well as the current situation in Colorado, where she lived: the withholding of rations from one thousand Utes at White River and the attempt to expel all four thousand Ute Indians from Colorado based on what is known as the Meeker Incident.

The Treaty of 1868 had already drastically reduced the Colorado Utes' land base (from 56 to 18 million acres) and confined them to a reservation. Then miners discovered minerals on Ute lands, and the government negotiated a new treaty with the Utes in 1873 that confiscated almost 3.5 million more acres from the tribe. Still Colorado settlers waged a relentless campaign to remove the Utes from the state entirely. They found their excuse to do so in 1879, when a small party of White River Utes killed their agent, Nathan Meeker, and ten other agency employees after Meeker had used heavy-handed methods to compel the Utes to abandon their traditional ways.

In retaliation, Secretary of Interior Carl Schurz had withheld rations for all of the White River Utes. And they were starving. Jackson sided with the Utes. "How many of the American people know anything about the true situation and experience of the White River Utes?" she asked readers in a letter to the editor of the *New York Tribune* in December 1879. She explained why a few of the Utes had revolted against Meeker: "the annual supplies for these Utes for the fiscal year ending 1877 lay in a store-house at Rawlings, Wyoming, one whole year" while the tribe was starving. Ute chiefs went to get their supplies but had been denied them. Moreover, the Utes, as guaranteed by treaty, were supposed to be paid $25,000 a year in annuities. The U.S. government had not paid them for three years; they were now owed $100,000 in payment with interest. Senator Teller from Colorado had sought to get the commissioner of Indian affairs to pay and had "warned . . . repeatedly that a Ute war would surely break out before long if this money was not paid."

A few weeks later, Jackson railed against an attempt by Colorado legislators in Congress to remove the Utes altogether from the state. She quoted from James Burns Belford, a representative of Colorado, who spoke in favor of a bill removing Utes from the state. As Belford spoke, he turned to representatives of Iowa, Illinois, Michigan, and other western states (who opposed his bill) and said that "'every one of those States had been stolen from the Indians, and it ill befitted those Representatives to preach morality and plead for the observance of treaties with the Indians.'"

Jackson asked her readers, "Did the Representative from Colorado realize . . . the hideousness of his logic? . . . Because we have broken more than 400 treaties, is it, therefore, no shame to break another?" Jackson answered emphatically to her rhetorical question: "Nay, it is all the greater shame. Treacheries repeated pile up infamy by a hideous geometrical ratio. The poison of baseness, of treacherousness, of cruelty is in a nation's character as in a man's like certain poisons in the body, cumulative. Unsuspected and unobserved, the slow process of dying goes on, till the one fatal moment, after which it is too late for any cure, and death is inevitable." Jackson had turned her poetic skills toward impassioned advocacy for the Utes. She also continued to advocate for the maintenance of the Ute land base at the same time as she insisted that America's emergence and legitimacy as a modern nation depended on creating fair relations with its Indigenous people.

Throughout January and February 1880, Jackson kept up the drumbeat about the 4,000 "well-nigh helpless" Utes in Colorado. She asked in a letter to the *Tribune*, "Shall we apply the same rule of judgment to the white men of Colorado that the Government is now applying to the Utes? There are 130,000 inhabitants of Colorado; hundreds of them had a hand in [the Sand Creek] massacre, and thousands in cool blood applauded it when it was done." She compared these hundreds of soldiers and thousands of their supporters to the dozen Utes who participated in the murder of Meeker and objected that the secretary of the interior had stopped rations to 4,000 Utes. Rations "are not, and never were, a charity, but are the Utes' rightful dues, on account of lands by them sold, dues which the Government promised to pay 'annually forever,'" she forcefully asserted.

Jackson also tried to get settlers to question why they should enjoy benefits and privileges while Indian people were suffering from starvation: "Shall we [white settlers] sit still, warm and well fed, in our homes, while five hundred women and little children are being slowly starved in the bleak, barren wildernesses of Colorado?" Jackson had a real flare for the dramatic. "Colonel J. M. Chivington's method was less inhuman by far," she wrote. "To be shot dead is a mercy, and a grace for which we would all sue, if to be starved to death were our only other alternative."

Jackson also refused to let past injustices be forgotten. She wrote an editorial for the *Tribune* in February 1880 that further compared the treatment of the Utes to the tragedy of the Cheyennes and Arapahos at Sand Creek. William Byers, founder and former editor of the *Rocky Mountain News*, rebutted her. He declared that in the present conflict, "Colorado soldiers have again covered themselves with glory." Byers claimed, too, that his state had been denied a fair hearing regarding Sand Creek, but Jackson marshaled 220 pages of official testimony based on 73 days of hearings in the state in 1865 to challenge him.

She reserved special animus for Carl Schurz, secretary of the interior, for his handling of the Poncas and his withholding of rations from the White Mountain Utes but also for his overall handling of federal Indian policy. She wrote to him in January 1880 and declared that for a hundred years Indians have been "victims of fraud and oppression on the part of the Government." She asserted that Indians must be given the legal right to protect themselves and vehemently critiqued his position.

Jackson eventually compiled all of her research and writings into a book, *A Century of Dishonor*, which scathingly critiqued American Indian policy. It included chapters on the Delawares, Cheyennes, Nez Perce, Sioux, Poncas, Winnebagos, and Cherokees, as well as detailed accounts of several massacres. Jackson completed the book in 1881, in record time, just a little over a year after first hearing Standing Bear, Susette, and Tibbles in Boston.

Here, Jackson returned to the theme that failure to do right by Indians constituted a moral stain on the American nation. Jackson contended that "the history of the U.S. Government's repeated violations of faith with the Indians . . . convicts us, as a nation, . . . of having outraged the principles of justice, which are the basis of international law." "It has been—to our shame," she asserted, "at the demand of part of the people that all these wrongs have been committed, these treaties broken, these robberies done, by the Government." In short, she condemned "a century's unhindered and profitable robbery." She used her book to "appeal to the heart and conscience of the American people" to demand that Congress reverse course toward American Indians. "There is such a thing as the conscience of a nation—as a nation's sense of justice. Can it not be roused to speak now?" By now, Jackson had become further convinced that in regard to its Indigenous peoples, the American nation needed a thoroughgoing process of what we would call truth and reconciliation today.

Many white middle- and upper-class Americans were moved by Standing Bear and Bright Eyes' speeches regarding the Poncas' struggles. But what would drive a settler to devote virtually every minute of her or his life to advocating for them? Helen Hunt Jackson pondered why this issue had taken such a hold on her. She wrote to Thomas Wentworth Higginson, an ardent white abolitionist who had helped form an all–African American Civil War unit, in January 1880:

I have done now, I believe, the last of the things I had said I never would do: I have become what I have said a thousand times was the most odious thing in life,—a "woman with a hobby." But I cannot help it. I think I feel as you must have felt in the old abolition days. I cannot think of anything else from night to morning and from morning to night. . . . I believe the time is drawing near for a great change in our policy toward the Indian.

Jackson trivialized her own advocacy as a "hobby," as well as that of thousands of white women who had similarly been engaged in condemning other forms of injustice in the nineteenth century. In reality she had become a full-time activist.

She recognized that not everyone looked with admiration on her newfound "hobby." She told Bishop Henry Whipple, an influential Episcopal Church leader and Indian advocate, that her sister-in-law was one of her dearest friends, but "she is not especially in sympathy with my work on this Indian Question, much as she loves me. She regards me as a variety of fanatic—only one degree less objectionable than the old Abolitionist."

It is no coincidence that Jackson kept drawing parallels between her "work on this Indian Question" with abolitionism. Many of the white settler Americans who became concerned with Indian injustices after the Civil War had also been anti-slavery advocates. But not all had as much sympathy for Indians as they had for blacks, as we have seen with Colonel Chivington.

Jackson often made comparisons between American Indian abuses and slavery against African Americans. In her January 1880 letter to Schurz, she asked him if he was "satisfied to have 250,000 human beings, with valuable possessions (however uncivilized), held as absolute slaves, with no rights, and at the mercy of a government like ours?"

Sometimes she engaged in a timeworn practice of comparing oppressions: she wrote to Higginson, "In some respects, it seems to me, [the Indian] is really worse off than the slaves; they did have in the majority of cases good houses, and they were not much more arbitrarily controlled than the Indian is by the agent on a reservation." To another friend she wrote, "The thing I can't understand is that all you who so loved the Negro, & worked for him, should not have been ever since, just as hard at work for the Indian, who is on the whole much more cruelly oppressed, with the name of a certain sort of freedom, but prisoner in fact—left to starve, and forced into poisonous climates to die— he is far worse off than the average slave ever was—and is a higher nobler creature." Jackson engaged in ranking the suffering of Native Americans versus that of African Americans, a practice that minimized the crime of slavery. And like other settler advocates of cultural evolution, she ranked Indians higher on the supposed scale of civilization than Africans. She may have been unusual in her outspoken defense of Indians and her opposition to slavery, but she was nevertheless beholden to the racial ideologies of her time.

Jackson continued to implore her relatives and friends who had been abolitionists to now demand justice for Indians. She even wrote to her husband, "By virtue of your organization, you ought to be as strong for *justice* to the Indians, as you were for *justice* to the Negro." Jackson recognized that some settlers—indeed, her own husband—had been swayed by anti-Indian propaganda. "Don't let the wicked & selfish atmosphere of the present Colorado talk about the Utes, warp your native instinct for justice," she counseled her husband. Jackson's family members, who had once outspokenly opposed slavery, may not have championed restitution for Indians because it meant questioning their own status as settlers and their own right to occupy and possess land that had only recently been in the hands of American Indians.

Jackson was undeterred by lack of agreement from her closest family members. She continued to seek to stop the ongoing land thefts and removals as they were happening before her very eyes. Her efforts resemble those of modern-day restorative justice advocates who respond with haste in the aftermath of atrocities. Jackson concluded *Century of Dishonor* with a strong and passionate contention. In regard to Indians, "cheating, robbing, breaking promises—these three are clearly things which must cease to be done. One more thing, also, and that is the refusal of the protection of the law to the Indian's rights of property, 'of life, liberty, and the pursuit of happiness.'" Until the U.S. government stopped these crimes and injustices, Indians would not be able to take their place in American life, she asserted. Thus, without first protecting

Indian land and treaty rights, she did not support Christian missioniza-
tion or assimilation projects.

Jackson continued to educate herself about ongoing efforts to dispossess Indians of their lands and made many forceful statements against
such policies. In a letter to the editor of the *New York Herald* in mid-
December 1880, she noted that the Office of Indian Affairs had drawn up
a bill providing for the removal of Indians in the states of Oregon, Colorado, Iowa, Kansas, Nebraska, Wisconsin, and Minnesota, as well as the
territories of Washington and Dakota. These removals would eliminate
25 reservations and 11 agencies and would "'restore . . . to the public domain 17,642,455 acres of land.'" She objected strenuously because these
lands rightfully belonged to the Indians through treaty, "but they are to
be compelled to sell them and move away." What's more, she declared,
Indians will have to use some of the profit they gain from sale to pay for
the cost of their own "involuntary, coerced" removal. Jackson was a master of using bureaucrats' own words to make her case. In this instance,
she quoted the commissioner of Indian affairs, who had written in his
1880 report, "'Every means that human ingenuity can devise, legal or illegal, have been resorted to for the purpose of obtaining possession of
Indians lands.'" She wryly noted, "It would seem so."

These statements might lead us to believe that Jackson was proposing
the outright return of land in North America to Indian nations and full
sovereignty for Indian peoples. But Jackson never went that far; she was
still a supporter of settler colonialism. She believed that Europeans had
sovereignty over North America by right of discovery. She believed in
the supposedly superior right of so-called civilized nations to have ultimate sovereignty; to question this is "feeble sentimentalism," she declared. Her point, however, was that all the European powers recognized
Indians' right of occupancy, "a right alienable in but two ways, either by
purchase or by conquest," and that Americans still needed to recognize
the lesser right of Indian occupation. Jackson was not ready to abandon
settler colonialism, but she did believe that the U.S. government needed
to live up to its treaty obligations. There was thus an inherent tension in
Jackson's support for redress, a tension that has continued to bedevil
truth and reconciliation efforts in settler colonial nations.

Despite its contradictions, Jackson's stance conformed to the stated wishes of Indian advocates like Standing Bear and Susette La Flesche. Many other settler reformers initially supported this position. Tibbles published *The Ponca Chiefs: An Indian's Attempt to Appeal from the Tomahawk to the Courts*, under the pseudonym Zylyff, with an introduction by Inshtatheamba (Susette's Omaha name) and a dedication by Wendell Phillips in Boston in 1880. It included an announcement on the back of the book that defined its mission as "devoted to securing, through the regular processes of the courts, the recovery of the lands taken by force from the Ponca Indians, and to settling the question, by a decision of the highest legal tribunal of the country, whether the life and property of an Indian can be protected by law."

Settler women in Philadelphia similarly followed the lead of what Standing Bear, White Eagle, and Susette had articulated as their greatest grievances and their greatest need: maintenance of their land base and adherence to treaty provisions. They had started the Central Indian Committee of the Women's Home Mission Circle of the First Baptist Church of Philadelphia in 1877. The Ponca tour emboldened them to become independent of the church. By 1881, they had renamed themselves the Indian Treaty-Keeping and Protective Association. The women sent petitions to Congress and the president to demand the United States live up to its treaty obligations, including the preservation of the Indians' land base. They gathered 13,000 signatures for the first petition and 50,000 for the second.

After hearing presentations from Standing Bear and Susette, businessmen in Massachusetts similarly proposed restitution for the Poncas. They asked the governor to appoint a five-member committee to look into Indian issues. This group, known as the Boston Indian Committee, initiated the first serious investigation into Indian claims. The Boston Indian Committee report, published in 1880, concluded that "the Poncas were unlawfully removed" and that "it is the bound duty of the Government to restore these Poncas to their homes without delay, and to make the most ample restitution possible."

In early 1880, Massachusetts senator Henry Laurens Dawes formed a Senate Select Committee to investigate the Poncas' case, and he introduced a bill to confirm the Ponca Treaty of 1865 and provide $50,000 for returning all the Poncas to their old reservation and restoring their homes. In February 1880, Standing Bear, Susette, and many other Ponca chiefs testified before the Senate Select Committee.

On the last day of May 1880, the Senate Select Committee released a 534-page report. It, too, concluded that the treatment of the Poncas "was without justification, and was a great wrong to this peaceable tribe of Indians and demands at the hands of the United States speedy and full redress." Even President Rutherford B. Hayes wrote in his diary in 1880, "A great and grievous wrong has been done to the Poncas." With this crucial support, in the immediate aftermath of Standing Bear and Susette's tour of 1879–80, it looked as if justice for the Poncas was on the horizon, that the tribe might be returned to their land and the land returned to the tribe. This was a moment in history when restitution—a bedrock principle of our modern-day notions of restorative justice—was still possible, before settlers had taken over all the land from which Indians had been so recently dispossessed.

But soon this movement of settlers morphed into something quite different. Reformers turned their energies to another solution to the "Indian problem," one based more on their own analysis of the problem and less on the stated interests of Indian people. And while they cloaked this new solution in the language of reconciliation, it closely aligned with the goals of the settler nation-state: further dispossession. This momentary commitment to reconciliation as restitution, living up to treaty promises and respecting Indian land rights, would fade from view among most settlers for many decades to come. Indigenous people, however, would retain this vision. They would use their treaties as a basis for challenging land loss up to our present time, even when settlers lost their way.

CHAPTER 7

Friends of the Indian

From 1883, members of the nascent settler movement for Indigenous rights gathered every summer in Lake Mohonk, New York, to discuss and coordinate their work. They called themselves the Friends of the Indian. Like Helen Hunt Jackson, many of the settlers in this movement had been deeply influenced by the speaking tour of Chief Standing Bear and Susette La Flesche. They had come to believe that the U.S. government had deeply wronged Indian people and that some form of redress and reconciliation was in order to make up for the many abuses that Indian people had suffered.

Within a few years, however, they had abandoned the most direct forms of restitution: return of lost land and treaty protections. Instead, they developed a near consensus about what would truly bring reconciliation between settlers and Indian people, what Cathleen Cahill refers to as "compensatory social programs": the allotment of Indian lands to individuals as private property and boarding school education for Indian children. Cahill notes that the Lake Mohonk reformers maintained "a sense of national obligation for wrongs committed against" Indians but now channeled their efforts toward "compensatory social programs intended to prepare . . . Indians for full citizenship" rather than upholding treaty rights. She also notes that Friends of the Indian adopted much of the same language and reform agenda they used in regard to newly freed African American slaves.

Now most Friends of the Indian redefined reconciliation, with little to no input from Indigenous peoples, in ways that supported settler

colonialism and white supremacy. They purported to be deeply dedicated to justice for American Indians, but, ironically, the measures they
ultimately proposed did not advance the cause of American Indians. Far
from it. What so many Friends of the Indian purported to be a form of
redress and a means of reconciliation resulted in further hardship,
deeper grievances, and legacies that are still haunting Indian people
today. How did this movement go so wrong?

Admittedly this movement was up against some powerful countervail-
ing tendencies. Restitution was at odds with the foremost goals of the
settler state: full acquisition of and control of all the lands and resources
on the continent. Government officials thus thwarted efforts at restitution at nearly every turn. Dawes's 1880 Senate bill to return the Poncas
to their land in Nebraska encountered fierce opposition and never made
it out of committee, and debate raged about what to do with the Poncas
who were still in Indian Territory. The commissioner of Indian affairs,
E. A. Hayt, and Secretary of the Interior Carl Schurz claimed that the
exiled Poncas were happy and well cared for in Indian Territory and
wished to remain. They asserted that Standing Bear did not represent
the Poncas who had remained in Indian Territory. Hayt vehemently
opposed the Poncas' return to Nebraska. He declared in April 1879 that
he had visited the tribe in Indian Territory in October 1878 "and found
their condition very much improved. . . . Every effort was made, and
large sums of money were expended to provide for their comfort." These
claims were patently false.

Hayt and Schurz were unmoved by the questions of fairness or justice to the Poncas that the Boston Indian Committee, the Senate Select
Committee, Standing Bear, Susette La Flesche, Tibbles, and Jackson
had raised. They were more concerned with not only transferring Indian
lands into settler hands but also maintaining control and authority over
Indian peoples. Hayt contended,

> If the reservation system is to be maintained, discontented and rest-
> less or mischievous Indians cannot be permitted to leave their reser-
> vation at will and go where they please. . . . the most necessary

discipline of the reservations would soon be entirely broken up, all authority over the Indians would cease, and in a short time the Western country would swarm with roving and lawless bands of Indians, spreading a spirit of uneasiness and restlessness even among those Indians who are now at work and doing well. . . . The task of transforming the nomadic habits of Indians into habits of permanent settlement and steady and self-supporting work, is a very difficult one at best, requiring the introduction and maintenance of certain rules of discipline which cannot be enforced . . . without sometimes producing individual hardships.

Thus, Hayt argued, the Poncas could simply not be allowed to return to their homelands; it would broadcast the wrong signal to Indians: that they could disobey government orders.

Settler allies initially fought back against the government's position and maintained their support for returning all of the Poncas to their homeland. The Ponca Relief Committee sought to keep up the momentum they had gained from the speaking tour of 1879–80. They sent Tibbles and Susette on another eastern speaking tour in the autumn of 1880. Standing Bear did not join them this time, but the "Boston committee insisted that [Susette's] presence was essential for the future success of the campaign." She and Tibbles again toured the whole eastern seaboard with another grueling schedule of lectures, receptions, and other social gatherings. (The tour did, however, lead to romance and eventual marriage for the pair.)

Tibbles and Susette vociferously contested the government's assertions that the Poncas were now happy to stay in Indian Territory. Susette testified in December 1880 before a Special Committee of the Senate to determine what should be done about Poncas: "They want to go back to [Nebraska]. . . . Not one of them is satisfied to live anywhere else. But, since the unprovoked murder of Big Snake [Standing Bear's brother], they are afraid they will be killed unless they acquiesce in the wishes of the Interior Department." She also pointed out that lands promised to the Poncas were the property of the Cherokees, "and are not for the United States government to bestow."

Susette also accused the government of intimidating the Poncas in Indian Territory and barring them from meeting with their advocates. She testified that government officials prevented her from visiting with her uncle in his Washington, D.C., hotel and that officials were pressuring him to testify that he wished to remain in Indian Territory. Although the missionary Reverend James Owen Dorsey confirmed Susette's testimony, the government called Susette a "phenomenal liar." The government subjected Susette and Tibbles to ongoing harassment, and their second eastern tour was perhaps even more exhausting than the first.

To address the impasse regarding the fate of the Poncas, President Hayes appointed a commission made up of General George Crook and General Nelson Miles, Walter Allen (a member of the Boston committee), and William Stickney (a member of the Board of Indian Commissioners). In January 1881, they interviewed Poncas from both Indian Territory and Standing Bear's band, who were still living on the island in the Niobrara River. The commission reasserted that the Poncas had been removed without cause. But they did not recommend that the Poncas who had relocated to Indian Territory be given restitution and be allowed to return to their homelands.

Instead, they favored a different kind of redress. Rather than restoring the lands that the Poncas had lost, they advocated giving some form of *compensation* for them. In this case, they advised an allotment of 160 acres to every member of the tribe, in either Nebraska or Indian Territory; cash compensation for their property losses; and congressional appropriations for homes and schools for the Nebraska Poncas. Their recommendations were included in a bill that Congress passed on March 31, 1881.

Allotment as a form of *compensation*, rather than *restitution*, was quickly gaining ground among Friends of the Indian as the preferred solution to what they called "the Indian problem." This involved the distribution of communally held Indian land in 40- to 160-acre plots to individual Indians.

Even in early 1880, as the Senate was conducting an investigation into the Poncas' removal, lawmakers were thinking about pushing this new policy. The chairman of the investigation, Senator Dawes, broached this

with a group of Ponca testifiers: "Some white people think that it would
be better for the Indians if they were required to select a certain quantity
of land for each family, for which patents should be given them the same
as are given to white people, . . . and then to have the rest of their lands
sold and the money applied to improve their farms, or invested for their
benefit; and in the future have them live under the same laws and have
the same privileges as the whites." Although Dawes would go on to become the foremost lawmaker who supported allotment, at this point in
his career, he still sought out the Poncas' feedback on the proposal. He
asked the Ponca leaders, "What is your opinion of such a plan?"

The response of the Poncas is telling. White Eagle and Standing Buffalo held a long consultation with their interpreters, Susette and Frank
La Flesche. The Ponca chiefs expressed skepticism at allotment. Susette
summed up their conversation: "They do not know whether it would
do to select the lands; they want to save their lands, what is left over after
they have chosen homes for themselves, for their children. . . . they do
not think it would be right to sell the land, so that when their children
grow up they will not have anything. They look upon the land as belonging to their children as well as to themselves, and they do not think it
would do to have white people come in and live between them." In
short, the Poncas wanted restitution: restoration of their communally
held land to manage as they saw fit, in perpetuity for generations to
come. Compensation for their losses, especially in the form of allotments, would not satisfy them.

But the senators continued to press the issue. And the Indian leaders
continued to confer among themselves. Finally, Susette summarized
their views: "They are between two horns of a dilemma. The one is the
present evil [the reservation system]; the other the evils that they know
not of that might result from the new plan." Indeed, the allotment system turned out to be another set of evils, not a measure of redress.

Yet Friends of the Indian were coming to believe that allotment was
a viable substitute for restitution. Their evolving reform agenda can
be seen by the third petition that the Indian Treaty-Keeping and Protective Association sent to Congress in February 1881. Now the white
women reformers asked not only for treaty fidelity but also for allotted

Indian land; U.S. citizenship; universal education for Indian children; and social welfare for Indian women. Far from providing Indians with a viable and fair compensation for their communal landholdings, however, allotment only led to further dispossession and deeper impoverishment.

One white settler woman became particularly influential in shifting the priorities of the settler reform movement toward allotment: Alice Cunningham Fletcher. Her support for and involvement in implementing allotment, and other assimilation policies, did tremendous damage to Indian nations. Yet she was a renegade in her time, at least when it came to being a white settler woman. She never married and instead pursued a career. She was involved in women's social reform throughout her life: she had participated in Sorosis in New York, one of the earliest women's clubs in the United States, and then helped to form the Association for the Advancement of Women (AAW) in New York in 1873. In 1878, because of her dire financial circumstances, Fletcher refashioned herself as a public lecturer, speaking to women's groups on topics related to American history.

As part of her public speaking, Fletcher developed a series called "Lectures on Ancient America," which led her to seek out training in the emerging field of anthropology. She corresponded with and later gained informal tutoring from Frederic Putnam, the director of Harvard's Peabody Museum of American Archaeology and Ethnology. As a woman, she could not pursue formal study. It was also unheard of for a single woman in the late nineteenth century to carry out anthropological research.

But Fletcher had finally found her chance to pursue this unprecedented endeavor when she attended a lecture by Standing Bear, Susette, and Tibbles in 1879. She approached Tibbles and Susette after the lecture and asked if they would assist her in learning more about Indians on the Great Plains if she came to visit them in Nebraska. She also struck up a friendship with Susette's brother, Frank La Flesche. The two shared an interest in the traditional culture of the Omahas. Probably the La Flesche siblings and Tibbles thought it unlikely that Fletcher, just over forty years old, would ever make the trip to the Great Plains. They probably forgot the seemingly eccentric woman who had approached them in Boston.

In 1880–81, when La Flesche and Tibbles returned to Boston for their second lecture tour, Fletcher came to see them again. She said she was still interested in going to live and study among Indians and asked if they would help her. I imagine that they smiled obligingly and nodded politely and thought little of it. They were probably surprised when Fletcher turned up in Nebraska later in 1881. Tibbles was skeptical that the now forty-three-year-old woman could travel in rough conditions, but he and Susette took Fletcher on an extended camping trip to the Omaha Reservation and to visit other Plains Indian tribes, as Fletcher wished.

Fletcher had used her connections with influential people to make careful preparations for the trip. When she first arrived in Omaha, Nebraska, in September 1881, she had letters of introduction from the secretary of war and the secretary of the interior to General Crook, still Commander of the Platte. Crook took an interest in her work and paid for her to travel by carriage with Susette and Tibbles eighty miles north to the Omaha Reservation, a trip that took two days. There the La Flesche family, led by the patriarch Joseph La Flesche, welcomed Fletcher.

Fletcher described approaching the La Flesche family compound from atop a hill. She wrote, "Down in the midst of trees, ploughed fields, and haystacks, nestled an unpainted house with a porch in front; the blue smoke curling from the chimney suggested supper time. A restful home-like look pervaded the picture. A tall woman [Susette's mother, Mary Gale La Flesche] stepped out of the house with a red shawl hanging over her shoulders." The carriage continued a few hundred yards further and came upon "another frame house, newly built . . . in the midst of a grove of tall oak trees." Susette's sister Rosalie stood at the door with a baby in her arms.

In her account of the extended trip, Fletcher never mentioned by name any members of the La Flesche family or Tibbles, although she did describe her interactions with them. "I had come at the invitation of the elder sister [Susette], my companion, whom I had known in the

East, where she had nobly pled for the rights of her Indian relations who had been driven from their homes to the Indian Territory. Fletcher referred to Susette throughout her chronicle as "my companion" and described her as "vivacious and brilliant."

She stayed with Rosalie and her settler husband, Ed Farley, while on the Omaha Reservation. The couple strung a hammock for her among the trees, and Fletcher enjoyed reclining in it while talking to her "sister-hostess" as she "rocked her baby or sewed on its little garments. We talked much of people and things during those hours." Fletcher marveled that Rosalie had learned such good English at the mission school. "Her low, gentle voice, pure English, saying such wise words [about human nature], made her like one of my own race," Fletcher remarked. She characterized the entire La Flesche family as a "singularly gifted family."

Over the rest of September and all of October, Fletcher, Tibbles, and Susette traveled several hundred miles between the Omaha Reservation, the nearby Winnebago Reservation, the Santee Sioux mission, and the Rosebud Sioux agency. Other Indians, such as an Omaha man named Wajapa, occasionally joined them.

On October 1, 1881, Fletcher ventured out to Standing Bear's island in the Niobrara River. "After the greetings the little Ponca tribe conducted their visitors to the village, fording the two swift channels with considerable excitement." She went to Standing Bear's tent "where all the afternoon the Poncas and their guests discussed tribal affairs and the future welfare of the people."

The cold, rainy weather as well as the worn camping equipment and old wagons may have led to tensions among the group. Wajapa had given Fletcher the name Sweep of an Eagle's Wing. Tibbles converted this name, derisively, to Highflyer. He seemed to dislike Fletcher; in his memoirs he returned her favor and never identified her by name but only as "the Highflyer." By the end of October, the relationships among the group had frayed as badly as the party's tents. Tibbles refused to let Susette serve as Fletcher's translator.

Perhaps Tibbles regarded Fletcher as a rival in his Indian reform work. She had the potential to displace him from his perch as foremost expert about and spokesperson for the Indians. He may have also dismissed her as a never-married woman. Many abolitionists and Indian rights supporters were also fierce women's rights activists, but Tibbles did not seem to be one of them.

Even though they seemed to intensely dislike one another, Fletcher and Tibbles eventually were in almost complete agreement when it came to their views about the need to reform Indian policy. Fletcher seemed to realize how much the Omahas revered their land. She noted that of the tribes living in Nebraska when white settlers came, the Omahas were the only Indians "remaining on their ancient homelands." In a rare moment of personal reflection, she wrote, "Their attachment to the locality is remarkable and made me feel, while among them, that I was but an emigrant on this continent; no part of the country had in the 250 years of my ancestral hold on it built itself into my thought and life as was this region interwoven with the customs, ceremonials, and myths of these Indians."

Fletcher seemed simultaneously to admire and to denigrate the Omaha's approach to land. "They possessed the land in their thought, in their love," she wrote. "They had companioned it, but they had not conquered and utilized it, mastered it, after the manner of the white race. The Indian lives on and passes over the land but leaves no felled forests, leveled hills, or dammed-up streams to mark his presence or ownership. His mounded graves seem to form a part of the landscape; his villages melt away, and only a sunken circle or an enhanced verdure marks the site of his ancient dwellings." While many an environmentalist today would extol the Omahas' light footprint on the land, Fletcher saw it to some extent as a waste of good land.

Fletcher was a kettle of contradictions in other ways. She was intensely interested in the Omahas' culture as well as that of other Indian tribes, but she also thought Indians must convert to Christianity, become educated in western ways, and shed their old religions and customs. Fletcher contended that "the Indian" (note the singular) "must acquire English and suffer his mother tongue to die; a hard sacrifice to make, but if he would survive, it must be made. . . . the winds, the water, the trees, and the animals must become his servants, not his

companions as in the olden time. . . . the present and the next generation must suffer much; there is no escape; they stand in the gap and are
called to combat their own inherent disabilities and a race prejudice that
will not and cannot abate until the equalizing seal of citizenship is
placed upon the Indian." For Fletcher, it was not possible that Indians
could keep their communal lands or maintain their long-standing lifeways. She did not favor restitution. Still, she felt regret about the use of
violence against tribes to acquire their lands, and she sought some form
of reconciliation.

Allotment offered a way out of these contradictions. And Fletcher
claimed that it was Indians who asked for it. In fact, she asserted it was
her time with the Omahas that led her to support the new scheme. She
claimed that one Omaha man, in reference to a house he had built and
land he had plowed on the reservation, said to her, "There is one thing
I am always thinking of—a title to my land. I may never know the good
it will bring, but my children will know, and for them I think and desire
this thing." Certainly the Omahas, like all Indians, wanted to retain their
land. Whether they thought in terms of individual "titles," a western
legal concept, is another matter.

In 1882, after having spent just a brief period of time with the Omaha
Indians, Fletcher advocated to Congress that their land be allotted in severalty (a legal term meaning "in separate"). Fletcher claimed that this
Omaha man was one among many she had talked to who had become
worried about the tenure of their lands, due to the removal of the Poncas.
She explained in a presentation to the American Society for the Advancement of Science that after the treaty of 1868, U.S. agents had issued certificates of allotment to a number of Omaha men. As the Ponca controversy
heated up, some of these men took their certificates of allotment to a
lawyer for examination. The lawyer concluded that the certificates granted
only occupancy rights, not legal title. Fletcher explained that "the Indians
felt themselves helpless in the grasp of a power to which they could neither reach nor appeal." She claimed that they wanted their land to be par-
celed out to individual Indians and to be given legal title to it.

The La Flesche family and some other Omahas supposedly approved
of the idea, according to Fletcher. They may have hoped that it would

secure their land claims and they would never be removed, as their Ponca relatives had been. Fletcher succeeded in 1882 in getting Congress to pass a bill that granted Omaha Indians patents to their lands in severalty. The following year, in 1883, the secretary of the interior appointed Fletcher as a special agent to carry out the land allotment program among the Omahas. Fletcher notes that "an educated Omaha accompanied me as my clerk" and that he had a "corps of assistants" who lent her "cordial and generous aid." This educated Omaha man was none other than Frank La Flesche, who also served as her interpreter. A government surveyor and a matron—a position established by the Office of Indian Affairs to help teach domestic arts (that is, *western* domestic arts) to Indian women—also assisted Fletcher in her work.

Fletcher's technique was to set up a campsite in the area that she intended to allot. She says that Omaha women made a tent for her, and as soon as it was completed and she had secured all her camp supplies, she went with her entourage to the western portion of the Omaha Reservation. She pitched her tent on a hill overlooking a creek. "The Indians gathered about me," she claimed. "The surveyor's tent was set up and before many days the white people over the line were filled with curiosity as to what the sudden encampment could mean." Settlers were intensely interested in Fletcher's work because the Omaha Reservation land to the west of the railroad was to be appraised and opened for settlement after Indians had made their selections.

The Omahas were successful farmers, and they were mainly living on the bluffs overlooking the Missouri River on the eastern side of their reservation, "where the land was unequal in value for farming," Fletcher acknowledged. But Fletcher told them they should select land far to the west in the Logan Valley near the new town of Bancroft, because it was close to railroad and therefore to markets. She claimed their other land was "too much isolated from the white settlers for any rapid progress in new ideas."

Was Fletcher just as duplicitous as other stealers of Indian land? Was she purposely steering the Omahas away from their most fertile lands so that eventually settlers could claim this land? Most reformers thought it was a good thing for Indians to be isolated from white settlers, because so often the settlers introduced alcohol and other vices to Indian reservations. So was Fletcher just making excuses for another land grab? It is difficult to know if settler reformers like Fletcher were simply overconfident, that they truly believed that they knew what was best for Indians, or if they were cynically manipulating Indians. It may be a combination of both of these factors, based on deeply embedded assumptions that settlers were superior to Indians and more deserving of the most fertile land.

The work of allotment proved to be exhausting. Fletcher rode for miles in her wagon in all directions from her tent to get selections settled. She crossed and recrossed Logan Creek. She notes, "I often had to be carried down by an Indian and placed in the boat to be poled over." (So the work of allotment was exhausting for Omaha people, too!) She realized it was impractical to float the wagon across each trip, so she arranged to have one wagon on each side of the creek.

Once she had allotted land in the Logan Valley, she moved on. "When the good land within a radius of six miles or more from my tent was taken, we moved to another locality," she explained. Fletcher's first set of allotments had gone fairly smoothly; it had primarily attracted Omaha supporters who hoped the new land scheme would help them secure their land. But she complained of her next set of allotments that "the region where my tent now stood was in the thick of the heathen and non-progressive element. The people were opposed to schools, to every sort of advancement, and were of the class most apt to be seen about an agency. They hated my work." These Omaha people feared—rightly, it turns out—that the new land scheme would be more evil than their current situation.

Fletcher soldiered on. Each morning the matron set up four crotched poles and tied a red blanket over them to create an awning. Fletcher erected her camp table and chairs under the awning and spread out the plats of land for Omaha allottees to "examine locations before going out to look at selections of land." She complained again that "men who gathered about me at this place were a motley crew and rather troublesome to deal with." She claimed that her work was eased when an Omaha man sang a song given to him forty years earlier that foretold the coming of white settlers and bid "his people make ready for the change and possess their land that they might not perish." He allegedly sang that the people should go to the white woman. As she carried out allotments, Fletcher also imposed other unrequested changes on the Omahas. She gave English names to all the allottees and even imperiously "declared that the last child born and allotted must be called Benjamin."

Just as she was nearly done with surveying all the allotments and assigning new names to each Omaha allottee, Fletcher became extremely ill. "Suddenly I found myself unable to rise and fire such as I had never known raging through my veins," she recalled. She later wrote that "non-progressive Indians" believed that "one of their magicians . . . had put a worm" in Fletcher and that she "would not be able to go on with" her work. One Omaha doctor offered to remove the worm, but she declined.

Her Omaha hosts took Fletcher to the mission for a month to be tended, then to the agent's house, where she lay on a mattress in his parlor. Fletcher writes that she was "ministered by a faithful woman" but does not mention that this woman was another La Flesche sister, Susan, who would go on to become the first Native American physician. Fletcher tried to do the second stage of allotment paperwork from her sickbed.

Finally, after months of recuperating, Fletcher was able to get back to her work. In June 1884, over the course of three days, she issued allotments of almost 76,000 acres to 1,179 members of the tribe: 564 men and 615 women. Under the terms of the bill, she sold 50,000 acres of Omaha Reservation and held 55,450 acres more for children born during the next twenty-five years—the period of trust during which the allotted land could not be sold.

But thousands of acres of the Omaha Reservation were still unaccounted for after Fletcher completed her work. Congress had not included a provision in the allotment bill regarding the surplus land. Local white settlers were squatting on it. Friends of the Indian divided over what to do with the land. Fletcher recommended a cooperative grazing space for both Indians at no fee and for settlers to lease. Tibbles opposed Fletcher's plan and the preservation of any communal land; he also opposed the maintenance of self-government among the Omahas. Tibbles's hard-line position alienated him (and Susette) from the rest of the La Flesche family and Fletcher.

The long-simmering tension between Tibbles and Fletcher erupted into open conflict in the mid-1880s. Tibbles complained to the Office of Indian Affairs and the Indian Rights Association that Fletcher was profiting from a cattle-ranching venture on surplus Omaha land. One scholar has found evidence that she did have a stake in a cattle enterprise owned by Ed Farley, the settler husband of Rosalie La Flesche. The Indian Rights Association investigated Fletcher, but she successfully defended herself.

By 1887, Fletcher had abandoned the idea that Indians should be able to attain any communal land. Later bills for the allotment of other Indian reservations would stipulate that all surplus lands would be returned to the so-called public domain, to be sold by the U.S. government. Fletcher explained the benefit of this, in 1884, from the point of view of many Friends of the Indian: The Indians "should be given their lands in severalty, the title thereto being properly secured for a term of years, and the remainder of the reservation should then be thrown open to white settlement. The Indians would thus be brought into daily contact with everyday, civilized living with its various activities, its opportunities for advancement, and its educated public opinion which recognizes the value of labor." Fletcher again spoke of the desirability of opening up remaining reservation lands to white settlers as a means of helping Indians assimilate into mainstream society and teaching them a work ethic.

Such comments by Fletcher and other Friends of the Indian were deeply ethnocentric and insulting. Indians had long grown corn, squash, and beans on this land. They had long roamed over the vast Great Plains to locate and hunt buffalo. They had turned buffalo hides into warm robes and snug homes. Fletcher, like many Friends of the Indian, believed that it was only American-style labor, performed in the service of an industrialized capitalist economy, that counted.

In 1887, Fletcher helped to convince Senator Dawes to amend his proposed allotment act to prevent the patenting of any Indian land to tribes as a whole. The resultant General Allotment Act, also known simply as the Dawes Act, granted male heads of family 160 acres, single Indians (including women) 80 acres, and children under the age of eighteen 40 acres. It stipulated that the land be held in trust for twenty-five years.

Eight years earlier, Dawes had been a foremost member of the Boston Indian Committee and the senator from Massachusetts who had initiated hearings into the Poncas' case. He had championed *restitution* for the wrongs that the Poncas had suffered: the return of their land to the tribe as a whole. Now Dawes, too, had gotten on the allotment train. In fact, he was now conducting the locomotive. Fletcher, Dawes, and almost every other settler reformer asserted that allotment was just what was needed to solve the so-called Indian problem.

In lieu of restitution, Friends of the Indian now promoted compensation for Indian land loss through allotment. They justified their new position in many ways, first by claiming that it was what Indian people wanted and then by asserting that it would promote justice for Indians. Fletcher and others claimed, "For the benefit of all concerned, the Indian should be given his just and individual rights to the land, to the law and to education. He is asking it and, as far as his power of discernment goes, using it." Dawes proclaimed in 1883, "To those who would do something in compensation for the wrongs that have been heaped upon [the Indian] in the past by the greed and avarice and inhumanity of so-called civilization, [allotment] opens a way for co-operation; . . . it opens the grandest field and promises the richest reward. . . . soon I trust we will wipe out the disgrace of our past treatment, and lift him up into citizenship and manhood, and co-operation with us to the glory of the country." Friends of the Indian presented allotment as a win-win situation for Indigenous people and settlers alike. It would bring justice to long-suffering Indians but not stand in the way of white settlement.

Friends of the Indian made other justifications that had more to do with pragmatism. They claimed that it was impractical for Indian people to live communally in their separate nations. Fletcher stated, for example, "It is hugging a delusion to suppose that any distinct Indian nation or nations can exist within the limits of the United States."

These supposed settler allies drew a stark choice for Indians—Fletcher put it this way: "the Indian must die or become absorbed in the body of citizens." Indians were not dying out, she remarked, so in order to be absorbed into American society, Fletcher and other Friends of the Indian reasoned, they needed to become "civilized" and assimilated. Owning and holding vast tracts of land, communally, was holding Indians back, Fletcher claimed. Large reservations are "harmful in their influence; the stretches of uncultivated land often block the path of enterprise. . . . it would be for the advantage of civilization to break the reservation up and make possible the conditions under which the Indians can become self-supporting," she asserted.

Some Friends of the Indian put it more bluntly. Colonel Richard Henry Pratt, for example, who had overseen a group of Indian prisoners of war in the 1870s, wrote, "I would blow the reservations to pieces. I would not give Indians an acre of land. When he strikes bottom, he will get up." This hardly sounds like the language of reconciliation. Indeed, the initial commitment to bringing justice to American Indians was reverting to a paternalistic and punitive lexicon.

Friends of the Indian were sure that allotment would fix all the problems that had beset Indian people. They made rosy predictions. Fletcher, for example, quoted the commissioner of Indian affairs, "in no case where allotments have been made and the title secured with proper restrictions have any other than the best results followed." Certain of the rightness of her actions, Fletcher continued her work to administer allotment after the Dawes Act passed. She won contracts from the commissioner of Indian affairs to conduct land allotments among the Nez Perce in Idaho and the Winnebago in Nebraska.

Fletcher's work to carry out government policy opened other doors for her; her time among the Omahas launched her ethnographic career. Fletcher notes that after her long season of illness, some members of the tribe "opened to me the meaning" of sacred pipes. They gave a pair of pipes, or calumets, jointly to her and Francis. Then, she writes, "I was permitted to learn the songs." Several leading men agreed to perform portions of the ceremony connected with the sacred pipes.

It is not clear whether there was an element of force involved in the transfer of the pipes from the Omahas to Fletcher. And it seems the

Omahas were as ambivalent about parting with these two calumets as they were about allotment. Fletcher writes that several Omaha men said at the ceremony that "their hearts were sorrowful because the pipes were taken up informally [taken away from tribe]." But she says they "had consented [to give them up] for a good reason and in no spirit of disrespect."

Fletcher brought the pipes to her home in the East, where she displayed them for all her houseguests to see. "Never before, so far as I can learn, have these sacred pipes been suffered to leave the Indians," she wrote proudly. She seemed unperturbed when Indians who visited her home "have looked at them as they hang in my eastern home and have said: 'We have heard that the Omahas had given you these pipes and our hearts are sad to see our sacred articles in the hands of strangers.'" She dismissed their concerns and retorted that the pipes were "still on their mission of peace and fellowship."

To some extent, Fletcher's ethnographic career helped her resolve other contradictions in her attitude toward Indians. She was working on behalf of the government to assimilate Indians through imposing a private property regime. She was advocating that Indians must give up their languages, their religions, their ceremonies, and their cultures. But she would help them preserve at least the *memory* of these old ways through her ethnographic work.

Through Fletcher's work as much as that of Senator Dawes, allotment became the preferred solution to the so-called Indian problem among white settler reformers. Many Friends of the Indian asserted that in supporting allotment, they were merely responding to the wishes of Indian people. They cast themselves as benevolent reformers who were making amends for past settler abuses of Indigenous people. As Amelia Stone Quinton, one of the founders of the Women's National Indian Association, put it, "Among the many noble endeavors of today, what is nobler than redemptive work among these native Americans, to whom we are under so great and so lasting obligation?"

At times these settler reformers noted opposition to the idea among some Indians, but they quickly dismissed it. Fletcher not only mentioned the "heathen and non-progressive" Omahas who opposed her in her journal. She also wrote derisively, "Chiefs oppose [allotment] because land in severalty breaks up completely their tribal power and substitutes civilization and law."

But there were many Indians who opposed the policy. Daniel Ross, editor of the *Cherokee Advocate,* feared that the Women's National Indian Association and its assimilation program in 1882 would "smother [Indians] to death in the exuberance of its misdirected friendship." He charged that in the white women's "zeal to be 'up and doing' there is some danger, indeed great danger of our friends doing some of us harm instead of good. . . . It is a mistaken idea to suppose that United States citizenship and the holding of land in severalty is the only panacea for all the ills to which we [Indians] are exposed."

There were also a few white settlers who took a dim view of allotment, among them Helen Hunt Jackson, before her untimely death. In a *New York Times* editorial in 1880 she stated that it was regrettable that Secretary of the Interior Schurz did not explain "how the giving to an Indian of 160 acres of land can clothe him with civil rights which he does not now possess." Thomas Bland, who published a pro-Indian rights newspaper, the *Council Fire,* and founded the National Indian Defense Association, a rival organization to the Women's National Indian Association and the Indian Rights Association, declared that his group's purpose was "protecting and assisting the Indians of the United States in acquiring the benefits of civilization, and in securing their territorial and proprietary rights." Rather than proclaiming that they were Friends of the Indian, they called themselves, according to historian C. Joseph Genetin-Pilawa, "friends of a sound and humane Indian policy."

Bland campaigned mightily against the Dawes Act. He labeled it "the embodiment of despotism and injustice," and said that "Dawes and his backers . . . exert their utmost abilities in efforts to clothe [the Dawes Act] in a garb of fictitious virtue." But Bland's voice, and that of many Indians, was drowned out by the Friends of the Indian. Herbert Welsh of the Indian Rights Association opposed Bland, in print, in the *Boston Herald,* regarding allotment. Welsh accused Bland of "want[ing] to keep 'the Indian as he is, his tribal relations untouched, his reservations intact; and [of] opposing the sale of his unused lands, upon no matter how equitable conditions, for white settlement.'" Bland, like Helen Hunt Jackson, was no radical who utterly opposed settler colonialism. But his stance in support of Indian land rights was quickly becoming marginalized among settler allies who had once promoted restitution.

Tibbles, Fletcher, and Dawes often referred to statements by Standing Bear and Susette La Flesche as evidence of Indian support for allotment. Tibbles claimed that Standing Bear, at their first meeting, told him, "All the Indians know the game is gone. They want land of their own, they want schools, they want to learn to work. . . . We want to be under the same law as the white man. We want to be free." Tibbles asserted that Standing Bear also said, "I represent in the Ponca tribe the foremost of those who want to support themselves, to send their children to school, to build houses, to get property and all kinds of stock around us, and to be independent." Tibbles took these comments to mean that Standing Bear supported allotment. But much was lost in translation.

In its 1881 bill to resolve the Ponca crisis, Congress had mandated the allotment of Ponca lands, north and south. But perhaps fearing a repeat of the debacle of 1877, now the government required the consent of three-quarters of all adult males. It took ten years to achieve this result, and the government began allotment of northern Poncas lands in 1889.

Friends of the Indian were deeply mistaken that Standing Bear had called for such a breaking up of reservation lands. He resisted allotment almost as fiercely as he had fought removal. In fact, he even left his Niobrara homeland and rejoined the southern Poncas in the late 1880s to avoid allotment. This time he did not succeed in challenging the juggernaut of U.S. government power. He returned to Niobrara to take up an allotment when he learned that he would become utterly landless if he refused. Standing Bear reluctantly accepted a family allotment of nearly three hundred acres on the Niobrara River near the agency; he lived there until his death in 1908.

These allotments may sound generous. Maybe they appear as appropriate *compensation* for the Poncas' sufferings and land loss. But after allotment, the government extinguished the northern Poncas' title to the remainder of their 96,000-acre reservation allotment. It sold most of the so-called surplus land to settlers or speculators in 1892 and 1893, leaving the allotted Poncas with just 30,000 acres total. And after the twenty-five-year trust period ended, Ponca allotments quickly passed into settler control. By 1939, the northern Poncas retained only 1,028 acres. Here, indeed, was the evil come to fruition that other Ponca chiefs had once feared. Many northern Ponca families scattered, mainly to other parts of Nebraska and to South Dakota.

In the 1960s, the government moved to eliminate the northern Ponca tribe altogether and confiscate its remaining lands through a policy known as termination. In 1966, the United States disenrolled 442 northern Ponca tribal members and dispossessed the tribe of its remaining 834 acres. (After lengthy legal battles, the tribe regained state recognition in 1987 and federal status in 1990.)

The Poncas were not alone in losing so much of their land. Overall, allotment led to further stealing of Indian land; the U.S. government took 90 million acres of supposedly "surplus" Indian land, or two-thirds of what Indian people still retained at the end of the reservation period. They then sold it to homesteaders, railroad magnates, and other speculators. As for the individual allotments, most—as in the case of the Poncas—also passed out of the hands of Indian ownership into settler possession.

What has remained within Indian hands has become so "fractionated" that it is virtually unusable for Indian people. Congress made no provision for what should happen to allotted land when the original allottee died. Instead Indian estates fell under the jurisdiction of state probate codes. What this has meant is that the allotted land remains physically undivided even though the land's title has been divided over many generations among increasing numbers of heirs. This has diminished the possibility for individual landowners to make use of the land. Usually Indian owners lease it to non-Indians or corporations.

The renowned anthropologist Margaret Mead conducted field research on the Omaha Reservation in 1930 and noted that allotment schemes had made "no attempt . . . to deal with the problems of inheritance. . . . The original allotments have been divided and subdivided in a fashion utterly incompatible with western farming. . . . The land, given to their grandfathers as a perpetual economic basis for their existence, is irretrievably lost and nothing remains in its place."

Land loss on this scale had dire consequences for both tribes and individual Indians. It undermined the long-standing spiritual connections that Indian people had to their lands. Without an extensive communal land base, it was also difficult for Indian nations to maintain their collective political and cultural sovereignty and cohesion. It was likewise almost impossible to develop cooperative economic ventures that would have benefited the tribe as a whole. And when individual Indians lost their holdings, many became unable to make a living on their reservation land. Allotment turned many Indians into landless laborers who eked out a living at the margins of the settler economy. Allotment did not foster independence and prosperity, as Friends of the Indian had touted; it furthered dependence and deepened poverty. The policy ultimately worked to the benefit of settlers, who acquired more land and resources and grew wealthy from the land that Indians lost and the cheap labor they provided.

Even Alice Fletcher soon realized that allotment and the assimilation policy of which it was a part had backfired. She broke ties with the Lake Mohonk Friends of the Indian in 1892, moving away from assimilation policy and concentrating more on the study and preservation of Indian cultures, in concert with Frank La Flesche. When she returned to the Omaha Reservation in 1899, she bore witness to the great damage that allotment had done. Yet she could never admit that she had supported—and been a primary administrator of—a deeply flawed policy, an "evil," as the Ponca leaders had predicted. She only commented, "No people can be helped if they are absolutely uprooted."

Were settler advocates of allotment trying to deceive Indian people, yet again? Some undoubtedly were. Allotment had wide support, far beyond the ranks of the Friends of the Indian, because it would open up so much more land to settlers. But some of the elite eastern reformers who had so avidly followed the Ponca case were probably sincere in their belief that allotment would help Indian people.

We could thus blame the failure of allotment entirely on the way in which the government and many white settlers perverted an idealistic program that was meant to benefit Indians into a boondoggle that merely enriched settlers. Other reconciliation efforts in our own time, too, have gone awry when settler colonial governments have co-opted them in this manner.

But allotment also failed in part because its architects had strayed far from the origins of the first truth and reconciliation movement. What began as an effort to respond to the grievances of Indians with meaningful restitution quickly became an effort by Friends of the Indian to give Indians only meager compensation for their lands and to reshape their behavior to conform to American norms.

Reformers lost touch with what it was that Indians wanted. They invited only a few Indians—those they deemed properly assimilated—to address the Lake Mohonk annual conference. They came to believe that they knew best what Indians needed and what would bring reconciliation between settlers and Indigenous people. You could say that they stopped listening to Indian people.

But it was more complicated than this. Settler allies thought the Poncas' problems derived entirely from a misguided government policy. They did not see that they were part of a much larger settler colonial phenomenon. They did not recognize the connection between their settlement and the displacement of American Indians.

Friends of the Indian moved to promoting a kind of reconciliation that required no sacrifice on their part. They would not have to give up their property or forgo new opportunities because Indians retained their land. They could continue to enjoy the benefits of settler colonialism while feeling that they were doing something of worth for Indian people. Such a limited and distorted view of reconciliation did not die out in the nineteenth century; it has frequently reemerged and persisted up to our own time.

Standing Bear and Susette had opened some settler eyes and unstopped some settler ears, but soon most settlers stopped listening, put words into Indian mouths, and only heard what they wanted to hear. Most Friends of the Indian no longer upheld land rights and treaty protections but now favored *saving* and reforming Indians. This was even more apparent in the other main initiative that settler advocates proposed: Indian boarding schools.

CHAPTER 8

Indian Boarding Schools

In 2016, a few of us at the University of Nebraska decided that we wanted to develop a new digital project to make accessible the historical records of the Genoa Indian Boarding School. The U.S. government had operated the school from 1884 to 1934 on land that had once belonged to the Pawnee nation, just about one hundred miles northwest of our campus in Lincoln.

Some settlers in the small town of Genoa, Nebraska, had already been preserving the school's history for decades. In 1990 they had established the Genoa U.S. Indian School Foundation and created an interpretive center in the school's old Manual Training Center.

Nancy Carlson later told me why she and other volunteers did this. She had been working at the local history museum. Indian people kept coming to Genoa, dropping by the museum, and asking about the school. Some were former students, others were descendants of those who had attended. They often expressed a desire to visit the school and reconnect with others who had attended the school. Nancy, her husband, Jerry, and a cadre of other historically minded settlers in town decided to create a space where Indian people could return to and remember Genoa.

Forty tribal nation flags hang from the rafters on the first floor of the Genoa museum and interpretive center, testament to all the Indian nations from which the students came. A diorama of the school occupies one corner of the first floor. It gives you a sense of the scale of the institution: thirty buildings sprawled over 640 acres. Local volunteers, all settlers, had created the diorama, along with all the other display cases full of student memorabilia around the museum. The second floor includes a re-creation of a classroom on one end and the industrial arts workshop, for boys, on the other.

Every summer since 1990, the Genoa Indian School Foundation has hosted a reunion for former students and their families. Visiting the school can be an overwhelming and bittersweet experience for Indian people. Many of those who attended the school shared their memories of warm friendships and typical teen pranks. Some praised the school for teaching them discipline and imparting a strong work ethic. But Genoa alumni also recounted deep loneliness as they labored under a strict military-style regime. They spoke of the anguish of losing their languages and familial connections.

Genoa was but one of more than 150 federal Indian boarding schools that operated from the late nineteenth century well into the twentieth. Many churches ran their own boarding schools, too. By 1900 nearly 21,000 Indian children, or about 78 percent of all Indian children who attended school, had been removed from their families to attend a boarding school. Memoirs by and oral histories of attendees reveal that boarding schools gave some Indian children new opportunities but also subjected many to abuse and exploitation. It pained many attendees, too, that the schools robbed them of their cultures and separated them from their families and tribal communities.

Paradoxically, Genoa and the other Indian boarding schools grew partly out of Standing Bear and Susette's lecture tour of the East in 1879–80. Friends of the Indian believed a system of education could serve as a form of redress for the abuses American Indian people had suffered in the past. But like allotment, the boarding schools became yet another government-sponsored cruelty inflicted on Indian people.

That is mainly because government officials, backed by settler reformers, required that children be removed from their families and communities, often for years at a time, to attend school. Most Americans were appalled at the Trump administration's cruel policy of separating children from their families at the U.S.-Mexico border. Yet the U.S. government carried out such a policy for at least fifty years in the

United States against American Indian families. And ironically, it had been Friends of the Indian, who professed to care so much for Indigenous people's rights, that helped design, promote, and carry out this policy that caused more damage to and hardship for American Indians. As they had with allotment, Friends of the Indian portrayed the boarding schools as a new and benevolent policy that could make amends for past abuses and serve as a viable substitute for restitution. Indeed, one man, referring to Helen Hunt Jackson's influential book, characterized the Friends of the Indian assimilation campaign in this way: "A century of dishonor is being succeeded by a century of justice and generosity."

When Standing Bear and Bright Eyes went on tour from the fall of 1879 to the spring of 1880 they made a stop at the recently opened Carlisle Indian Industrial School, the famous prototype for Genoa and the other Indian boarding schools. "Last week we were at Carlisle Barracks," Susette testified to Congress in 1880. "There are a lot of Indian children going to school there; among them were three Ponca boys that left the Indian Territory in October last—Captain Pratt has them in chase—and Standing Bear and my brother Frank spent all night with them."

Carlisle was the brainchild of Captain Richard Henry Pratt, a veteran of the Indian Wars, who later rose to the rank of general. Pratt had taken part in the 1868 Washita massacre that killed Black Kettle and other Cheyenne and Arapaho survivors of Sand Creek. He had then been involved in the Red River War against the Comanches, Kiowas, southern Cheyennes, and Arapahos in 1874 and 1875. The government put Pratt in charge of seventy-one Indian prisoners of war from the Red River campaign. He oversaw them at Fort Marion in St. Augustine, Florida.

Pratt claimed to have conducted a successful experiment on the prisoners; he said that he had rehabilitated them through "civilizing" them. By this he meant cutting their hair, outfitting them in military uniforms, instructing them in English, and converting them to Christianity. Pratt became famous for his quip that it was necessary to "kill the Indian to save the man." He arranged for seventeen of the young men to attend the Hampton Institute, a school in Virginia that General Samuel Armstrong had established for newly freed African American slaves.

Pratt became enthusiastic that he could solve the so-called Indian problem by extending his experiment to all American Indian children, if only they could be removed from what he considered the bad influence of their families and the backward environments of their tribal communities. "We have been told there are 35,000 or 40,000 [Indian] children to look after," he stated. "If we place these children in our American lines, we shall break up all the Indian there is in them in a very short time. We must get them into America and keep them in."

To scale up the scheme he had conducted with prisoners of war, he convinced the U.S. government to convert the Army barracks in Carlisle, once used as an arsenal for the Continental Army during the Revolutionary War, to an institution for American Indian children. The government brought at least 8,000 children to the school between 1879 and the school's closing, nearly forty years later.

The opening of Carlisle coincided with Standing Bear and Susette's tour. Pratt became a darling of the Friends of the Indian movement. Many settlers who heard and were moved by the Ponca chief and his Omaha translator also followed and admired Pratt's new initiative and put pressure on the federal government to establish more such boarding schools across the nation. Over the next twenty-some years, the government opened twenty-five off-reservation schools and dozens of on-reservation boarding schools. Many churches continued to run their own boarding schools on reservations, too. Given the size of reservations, even on-reservation and mission boarding schools often unduly separated children from their families.

Many "Friends of the Indian" saw the extension of boarding school education to Indian children as both a departure from the violence of past policies and a means for making some sort of redress for past injustices. The famous author of *Uncle Tom's Cabin*, Harriet Beecher Stowe, for example, who visited the Indian POWs at Fort Marion, asserted, "We have tried fighting and killing the Indians, and gained little by it. Might not the money now constantly spent on armies, forts and frontiers be better invested in educating young men [and women] who shall return and teach their people to live like civilized beings?"

White women reformers, in particular, became strong advocates for the schools. Many of them found new careers through implementing the government's new assimilation program. Alice Fletcher, for example, was as involved with the schools as she had been with allotment. Just a year after her first trip to Nebraska, in 1882, Fletcher earned fifty dollars a month by becoming a primary "recruiter" for Carlisle. Pratt ordered her to remove sixty-five Lakota children from the Rosebud and Pine Ridge reservations, as well as from Sitting Bull's Hunkpapa band. Fletcher also agreed to bring some Omaha Indian children to Samuel Armstrong's Hampton Institute.

Friends of the Indian often engaged in ventriloquism to justify the boarding school regimen, just as they did with allotment. Tibbles claimed, for example, that Standing Bear said to General Crook: "The Indian has no book. He cannot read. Here is where I am weak and you are strong. I never see a book or paper of any kind, but I think it is a good thing. It lets you know all that is going on in the world. I want my children to learn to read." Tibbles also asserted that Standing Bear said, "If the Indians are given lands and courts, with the same law as the white man, a few plows to start with, and a school teacher for the children, they need not be turned over to the soldiers, the civil authorities, or anybody else. That will be the end of our troubles. Ten years from now there will be no difference from the whites except in the color of their skin."

This quote sounds suspiciously like many of Pratt's own declarations. For example, in one speech to the Board of Indian Commissioners in 1889, Pratt declared, "I say that if we take a dozen young Indians and place one in each American family, taking those so young they have not learned to talk, and train them up as children of those families, I defy you to find any Indian in them when they are grown. . . . Color amounts to nothing. The fact that they are born Indians does not amount to anything." By this time, Pratt had implemented his outing program that placed Carlisle schoolchildren in local settler households for a portion of each day and for entire summers.

Standing Bear and other Indian leaders may have asked for schools and schoolteachers, and they may have seen some value in western education for their younger generations, but it is almost certain that they did not ask for *boarding* schools. Many Indian leaders requested *day* schools within their communities, often as a part of treaty negotiations, but nearly all came to oppose the removal of tribal children to boarding schools. Not only did they want to maintain their close-knit families and communities, but they also learned that the institutions imperiled their children. Tuberculosis and other diseases frequently swept through the schools and took thousands of children's lives. Thus many Indigenous communities and families fiercely resisted sending their children hundreds or thousands of miles away to school, for years at a time.

Government authorities often used incredibly brutal methods to force Indian people to send children to boarding schools. Sometimes they brought in the military or a police force to compel obedience. Other times they withheld rations and annuities, guaranteed by treaty, and Indian people were faced with the horrific choice of starving or losing their children.

Pratt and other Friends of the Indian did not listen to Indian people when they expressed their opposition to the remote schools. They pressed on with their plans to "recruit" Indian children to fill the boarding schools. Indian resistance only became further proof to Friends of the Indian that Native people were backward and in need of boarding school education. These supposed settler allies seemed impervious to the irony that it was often necessary to enforce their "benevolent" new compensatory program by separating children from their families at the point of a gun or by withholding rations that were guaranteed by treaty.

When I speak about my research on Indian boarding schools to non-Indian audiences, an audience member invariably asks me whether I am being overly negative and harsh in my assessment of the schools. When most settlers think of boarding schools, they imagine prep schools for members of the elite. Wasn't it a sign of the government's good intentions and benevolence that they established boarding schools for Indian children?

The Indian boarding schools were not focused on cultivating an elite, however, but on severing the children's associations with their kin, their tribes, their heritage, their land. Friends of the Indian called it "assimilation." What an innocuous word to describe a systematic program to strip children of their cultures, languages, and family and tribal associations.

Many Indian families sent their children, reluctantly, to boarding school in moccasins and garments sewn and beaded with the greatest care to protect their children and keep them safe. They had carefully combed and braided their children's long, lustrous hair. Upon arrival, authorities often burned the children's clothes and cut their hair close to the scalp, a sign of mourning in many Indian cultures. Zitkála-Šá, a Yankton Dakota, vividly recounted her own boarding school initiation when she was eight years old. When she learned that school officials planned to cut her hair, she hid under a bed: "I remember being dragged out, though I resisted by kicking and scratching wildly. In spite of my- self, I was carried downstairs and tied fast in a chair." Then, Zitkála-Šá continues, "I cried aloud, shaking my head all the while until I felt the cold blades of the scissors against my neck, and heard them gnaw off one of my thick braids. Then I lost my spirit."

This was step one in "killing the Indian." Then authorities gave newly arrived children a harsh bath and fitted them tightly into uniforms: step two. "When I came there the first thing you [had to do] was be mea- sured for a uniform, an army uniform," remembers one former Genoa student. School officials them stripped them of their names, too, and assigned them ID numbers and new American names.

Boarding school administrators punished children harshly for speak- ing their native tongues and sought to replace what knowledge they had already learned from their elders with Christianity and rudimentary literacy. Sidney Byrd of the Flandreau Santee Sioux tribe had gone to Genoa in 1925 as a six-year-old child after being brought up by his grand- parents. He returned to his home nine years later in 1934 when the school closed. His grandparents were waiting for him with open arms when his train pulled up to the station. "I practically leaped from the train, tears of joy streaming down my cheeks, and I ran to my grand- mother, and she embraced me," he described in the documentary *In the White Man's Image*. She greeted him in his Dakota language, tears streaming down her cheeks as well. Byrd said, "I suddenly discovered that the people that I loved and longed to be with, I could no longer communicate with them. My own language had been beaten out of me.... and I wept bitterly."

Following Pratt's model, all the schools required strict obedience to a military-style regimen. Byrd remembered, "We were controlled by whistles and bugles. A bugle sounded when we were to get out of bed. We got into formation, and we marched to our meals. At the dining room, a triangle was used. And when the first triangle sounded we sat down on stools. The second triangle indicated there was to be complete silence and we were to bow our heads and say our prayers. And at the third triangle we began to eat." No wonder that many former students compared the schools to prisons.

Children attended classes for only half of the day. They spent the remainder of the day learning vocational skills: domestic arts for girls and manual trades for boys. Once trained, children spent half their days laboring either for the school or for local families. Elizabeth Springer, an Omaha student, sewed uniforms for the Genoa school. Local families were required to pay the students wages, but the school garnished most of the students' earnings, putting them in trust accounts. Most students never recovered this money.

Many attendees reported hunger and ill health as well as emotional, physical, and sexual abuse. Frank La Flesche, Alice Fletcher's long-time colleague and friend, wrote about his experience at the mission boarding school on the Omaha Reservation in his memoir, *The Middle Five*. He witnessed and experienced firsthand many incidents of incredible brutality on the part of his settler schoolmaster. In one instance, his teacher, whom he referred to as "Gray-beard," took his friend Joe's hand and beat it furiously with a board. "Gray-beard dealt blow after blow on the visibly swelling hand. The man seemed to lose all self-control, gritting his teeth and breathing heavily, while the child writhed with pain, turned blue, and lost his breath." Frank soothed his friend: "I took him by the hand and tried to comfort him, and cared for his bruises." This incident stuck with Frank: "The vengeful way in which he [Gray-beard] fell upon that innocent boy created in my heart a hatred that was hard to conquer." Such brutal discipline often undermined the "civilization" efforts of institutions. As Frank remarked, "I tried to reconcile the act of Gray-beard with the teachings of the Missionaries, but I could not do so from any point of view."

Frank knew, too, how deadly the schools could be. He looked on helplessly while one of his friends, Brush, started to cough up blood and went into a steep decline at the mission school. Francis snuck in to the infirmary to see him in the middle of the night. "I knelt by the bedside, and Brush put his arm around my neck. We were silent for a while, finally he whispered in the Omaha tongue: 'I'm glad you came; I've been wanting to talk to you. They tell me I am better; but I know I am dying.'" Brush was one of thousands of children who died at the schools, far from home, sometimes to be buried on school grounds, sometimes in unmarked graves.

Indeed, one main difference between an Indian boarding school and other schools for children was the presence of a cemetery, as Bob Sam, a Tlingit man from Sitka, Alaska, put it at the National Native American Boarding School Healing Coalition's first conference in Carlisle in 2018. It was the frequency of death for children at the schools, as well as their burial so far from their homes, that set these schools apart from other institutions of education.

Frank La Flesche and Alice Fletcher became anthropological colleagues and close friends. Together they published an ethnography of the Omahas and a study of Omaha music. They rented houses next door to one another in Washington, D.C., in the 1880s, and they worked and socialized together almost every day. In 1891, Fletcher formally adopted Frank, who was seventeen years her junior. That same year Fletcher bought a home in Washington, D.C.; Frank lived there with her for the next sixteen years. In 1906, Francis married a Chippewa (now more commonly known as Ojibwe or Anishinaabe) woman in their parlor. Frank and his wife split up within a year, and he continued to live with Fletcher until her death in 1923. She left him most of her estate.

Yet despite her friendship with Frank, and the clear ambivalence he felt about boarding schools, Fletcher remained a steadfast proponent of the Indian boarding school system until at least the 1890s. She also exerted a great deal of influence within the government for support of the schools. Fletcher's biographer, Joan Mark, asserts, "The dramatic increase in federal appropriations for American Indian education in five years—from \$475,000 in 1880 to \$992,000 in 1885—was due in good measure to Alice Fletcher's efforts." As they had hired her to carry out allotment among the Omahas, Nez Perces, and Winnebagos, the government also employed Fletcher to conduct a comprehensive survey of Indian education. In 1888, she published a 693-page report for the U.S. Bureau of Education and the Department of the Interior titled *Indian Education and Civilization*. Commissioner of Indian affairs Thomas Jefferson Morgan, one of the most hard-line proponents of boarding school education, quoted Fletcher frequently in his annual reports during his tenure from 1889 to 1893.

Agents for the Genoa Indian School went into Ponca communities on the Niobrara and took children from their families to attend the school. They also removed children from the Omaha, Winnebago, and Santee Sioux reservations in Nebraska and from the many Sioux tribes in the Dakotas. Some students came from even further away. The Genoa Foundation has found records of students from the Penobscot nation in Maine and the Blackfeet in Montana. All told the government institutionalized at least 4,000 children at Genoa over the school's fifty-year history.

To get our digital project going, we formed a Community Advisors Council made up of Ponca, Winnebago, Omaha, Santee Sioux, and Pawnee representatives. We had one of our meetings at what remains of the Genoa Indian School in September 2018. Nancy Carlson led the group on a tour of the building before we began our business for the day. Larry Wright Jr., chairman of the Ponca Tribe of Nebraska, opened and closed our meeting with a prayer. He set a somber, respectful tone as we sat in a large circle near the diorama of the school on the first floor and discussed Genoa's history and how best to carry out our digital project. Two attendees from the Omaha Tribe of Nebraska—Orville Cayou and Clifford Wolf—shared their family stories of Genoa and how powerful and unsettling it can be to visit the Genoa school museum, to imagine their ancestors and all that they endured.

Later Kevin Abourezk and I visited Genoa to interview Nancy Carlson for our Reconciliation Rising podcast. It, too, was haunting for

Kevin to enter the school and to find several of his ancestors listed in the roster of students. He later told us, "I'm a father of five myself and I've thought many times what it'd be like if somebody came and knocked on my door . . . [and] just took [my children] without . . . asking whether I cared or what my opinion on the matter was. And then just left with my children. . . . It's just unimaginable this experience, and none of us I don't think can ever really understand what that was like."

Ironically, even though settler reformers proclaimed themselves to be deeply dedicated to justice for and reconciliation with American Indians, the assimilation measures they proposed—allotment and boarding schools—did not advance the cause of American Indians. Through allotment, Indian people lost ninety million more acres of land. The boarding schools created generations of traumatized children and undermined the strength and vitality of Indian families and communities. What Friends of the Indian portrayed as a form of redress and a means of reconciliation resulted in further hardship, deeper grievances, and legacies that are still plaguing Indian people today.

What went so terribly wrong? How was it that a group of settlers who had borne witness to Standing Bear and Susette's grievances, who had formed long-running advocacy associations, who had studied the "Indian problem," and issued multiple reports, had strayed so far from the original vision of reconciliation? Standing Bear and Susette had been clear about their priorities: restitution of their land and the government's adherence to its treaty promises. They wanted Indian people to be able to determine their own destiny, and they called on settlers and their government to respect the sovereignty and cultural integrity of Indian people.

Initially white settlers listened to and responded to these grievances by promoting legislation to return the Poncas to their homelands and to compensate them for their losses. But this first moment of truth and reconciliation proved fleeting. The white settler groups continued to work on behalf of Indians, but they drastically changed their focus and strayed far from addressing the original grievances of Indian people.

The white women who had formed the Indian Treaty-Keeping and Protective Association and submitted three petitions to Congress decided to change their name to the Women's National Indian Association (WNIA). Debate ensued within the organization about whether they should continue their efforts to lobby the government to live up to its treaty obligations or to go in a different direction—toward new assimilation and missionary activities within Indian communities.

Many WNIA members wanted to remain true to the organization's original mission and to the stated desires of Standing Bear and Susette. They insisted, "We should use all our Association's resources in urging the Government to give to the Indian truth and justice *practically*, before offering him a religion whose fruits, as he thinks, are robbery and cruelty towards himself."

Other WNIA members wanted the newly formed "gentlemen's association," the Indian Rights Association, to take up civil and political reforms, "thus leaving our own society free to devote . . . a portion of our work to uplifting Indian homes; to aiding the vastly needed work within Indian hearts, minds and souls." This vision prevailed, and the WNIA shifted its efforts from restitution of Indian lands toward reforming Indian people. The WNIA grew exponentially; it set up branches around the Northeast, in the Midwest and Great Lakes region, and on the Great Plains. In 1884 they established their first mission at the Ponca Agency in Nebraska for Poncas, Otoes, and Pawnees. Five years later they had established seventeen missions among fifteen tribes. Senator Henry Dawes (architect of the 1887 Allotment Act) reportedly declared that the "new Indian policy [of assimilation] . . . was born of and nursed by the women of this association [the WNIA]." The settler men's Indian Rights Association also supported an aggressive assimilation campaign for Indian people.

By and large settler advocates now campaigned *not* to make the government fulfill its treaty obligations to Indian people so that they could retain their land but to reform individual Indian behavior. They claimed that assimilation would enable Indians to become American citizens and to enjoy equality with other Americans. They shifted from identifying the problem, as Indian people saw it, as intransigence on the part of the government and loss of land and sovereignty to believing the problem to be Indian people themselves.

Even in promoting equality and citizenship, they demonized Indian people. They made Indian people responsible for becoming worthy of citizenship and equality through assimilation. They did not recognize Indian people's inherent human rights; nor did they identify white supremacist ideologies as the basis for Indian people's lack of equality and citizenship. It was now all on Indian people to prove that they deserved a place in the new nation. Friends of the Indian strayed far from Standing Bear and Susette's agenda, and they betrayed the fledgling truth and reconciliation process that the Ponca chief and his Omaha interpreter had helped launch.

Moreover, Friends of the Indian did not heed Susette's plea to "set aside the idea that the Indian is a child and must be taken care of." Instead settler advocates for Indians increasingly believed themselves to be experts about what was best for Indian people. They became indifferent to the expressed concerns of Indian people, often aping the racial ideologies and upholding rather than questioning the racial hierarchies of their day. Tibbles clearly had been deeply sympathetic to the Poncas, but he, too, increasingly took on a paternalistic attitude. "Like all uneducated people," he wrote, "[the Indians] frequently do not know what their own best interests are."

Ultimately, settler advocates did not treat Indian peoples as true partners but as objects of pity and charity, as dependent children who could not determine their own needs or make their own decisions. Alice Fletcher characterized the Omaha Indians she met as "children as faced toward us, [who] know nothing of the power of law and organization." Many Friends of the Indian cast themselves as the all-knowing parents who must guide the childlike Indians.

This family metaphor thinly concealed an underlying belief in white settler supremacy. In her speech "Our Duty toward Dependent Races," Fletcher contended,

In this march of progress thru the centuries the victory has been with the race that was able to develop those mental forces by which man is lifted above his natural life, which enabled him to discern the value of work.

> Looking back over the ages, there is little doubt that to the white race belong the great achievements of human progress. The religions of the world have sprung from this branch of the human family, the higher arts and sciences are its children, and it is also true that this race has held possession of the best portions of the Earth's surface.

Fletcher and other settler reformers not only insisted that white settlers were superior to Indian peoples but also ultimately justified white settler possession of land as the result of this supposed superiority.

With their embrace of white supremacy, Fletcher and many other settler reformers could talk themselves out of supporting Indigenous rights to land and sovereignty. If Indian people were lower on the scale of human evolution and were not properly using their land, and if the "white race" led the march of human progress, wasn't it only right that white settlers would eventually take over Indian land?

Yet, white settlers who espoused these views were also sympathetic to what they considered to be the Indian plight, or at least they felt guilty about the misery and degradation that dispossession and conquest had caused. As Fletcher put it, they had a "*duty* toward dependent races," a white man's and woman's burden. A genuine, if short-lived, movement for reconciliation, based on attaining restitution for Indigenous peoples through alliance and partnership, had morphed into a duty and a burden to uplift a "dependent race" by a superior white race.

Maintaining a focus on restitution and treaty adherence would have required a thoroughgoing internal evaluation of the very legitimacy of the American nation, a critique of its founding and ongoing crimes, a reckoning that few Friends of the Indian were ready for in the nineteenth century. Such a reconciliation movement would have required that settlers, not Indigenous people, change. It would have required them to question and abandon their view of Indians as childlike and dependent, that Christianity was the only true religion, that an industrial economy was inevitable, that private property was the only viable land tenure system. It would have required them to accommodate groups of people living within the United States with alternative land tenure systems, different religions, and their own autonomous governments. Most

of all, it would have required settlers to abandon the quest for the possession of all the land on the continent and the need to remove Indians
from this land, by hook or by crook, by gun or by law, or by assimilation.
It would have necessitated, too, a recognition and renunciation of white
supremacy. This was a long and rocky road. Only a few settlers, like Helen
Hunt Jackson, took tentative steps down this path. Most other settlers
took a long detour.

Many other settler colonial regimes have also removed Indigenous
children en masse to boarding schools or other institutions. Canada had
its own version of Indian boarding schools. Beginning in 1879, the same
year that Pratt opened Carlisle, the Canadian government partnered
with the Anglican, Catholic, Presbyterian, and United churches to develop a network of residential schools for Indigenous children. About
130 schools institutionalized close to 150,000 children over the course
of one hundred years. As in the United States, authorities deemed it
vital to their assimilation efforts that Indigenous children should be
separated, often forcibly, from their families. Officials claimed the
schools were necessary to save the children from their impoverished
communities and to prepare them for life in modern Canada. Many of
the schools closed in the 1960s and 1970s, but the last (the Gordon
School in Saskatchewan) did not close until 1996.

Just as in the U.S. boarding schools, everyday life for the students was
unduly harsh. School administrators often referred to children by the
numbers they had issued each of them. (Officials took some children as
young as five years old, and many forgot their given names.) They often
separated siblings and disallowed them from seeing one another. They
forbid the speaking of native languages. The schools did not develop a
curriculum, let alone any standards, until the 1930s. The children, as the
Canadian Truth and Reconciliation commissioner Murray Sinclair put
it, "received very little in the way of marketable skills while losing their
traditional knowledge." From the outset, too, the residential schools
never enjoyed sufficient funding. Many schools turned their pupils into
laborers who ran the institutions' own farming and dairy operations to
make up for insufficient funds. The schools quickly became overcrowded

vectors for deadly diseases, primarily tuberculosis. Children complained of being hungry all the time. If parents tried to withhold their children from school, they faced harsh punishment.

Australia followed suit. At the turn of the twentieth century, each Australian state (except Tasmania, which claimed it had no surviving Aboriginal people) enacted legislation that enabled an Aborigines Protection Board or a Protector of Aborigines to take guardianship over Indigenous children and place them within institutions. These Homes and Missions trained girls for domestic labor and boys for unskilled agricultural work. Authorities intended that Aboriginal children would make a permanent break with their families and communities. They justified these policies, which they labeled "protection," as a means of assimilating Aboriginal people into mainstream Australian society and ending their dependence on state support.

"Protection"—there's an evocative word. It makes me think of the loving arms of my mother, caring for me as a child when I had been hurt or frightened. For Aboriginal people in Australia, protection meant forcibly removing children from their families and "breeding out the color." Several Chief Protectors of Aborigines—A. O. Neville (portrayed by Kenneth Branagh in the film *Rabbit Proof Fence*) in Western Australia and Cecil Cook in the Northern Territory—supported the removal of so-called half-caste girls (of both British and Aboriginal descent) from their families just before puberty, training and placing them as domestics in white households and making them vulnerable to sexual exploitation and impregnation by white men. In so doing, Neville and Cook and a host of other officials believed that they could breed Aboriginal people out of existence. Protection, indeed.

Sadly, the practice of forcibly removing children has not ended. Now China is using boarding schools against its minority Uighur population. In Xinjiang, China, government authorities have separated almost half a million Uighur children from their mothers and fathers, who have been sent to detention camps. China aims to weaken the Uighurs' Muslim faith, assimilate the children, make them learn to speak Chinese instead of their own language, and instill loyalty to China and the Communist Party. Now, as we look at China's heavy-handedness toward its

Uighur population, we can see past settler policies of removing Indigenous children to boarding schools for what they truly were: efforts to control, discipline, punish, and ultimately eliminate Indigenous peoples.

It's hard to imagine that Friends of the Indian ever touted boarding schools as a measure of redress or as a gesture of reconciliation. In the irony of ironies, one hundred years later, at the turn of the twenty-first century, reckoning with the history of these institutions became the basis for a new global movement for truth and reconciliation.

PART THREE

Searching for Truth and Reconciliation in the Twenty-First Century

CHAPTER 9

America's Stolen Generations

It was still chilly on the morning of June 1, 2015, in Ottawa as I walked briskly from my Airbnb to the Delta Ottawa hotel for the first day of the Final Ceremony of the Canadian Truth and Reconciliation Commission (TRC). This event was the culmination of the commission's work over the previous six years to gain a fuller understanding of why Canada had set up the Indian residential school system and what it had wrought among Indigenous families and communities. I found one of the last available seats in the ballroom. Thousands of people, most of them Indigenous, sat expectantly as three Indigenous drummers surrounded and pounded a large floor drum to accompany the Grand Entry of the three commissioners, a group of decorated Indigenous veterans, government dignitaries, and honorary witnesses.

Justice Murray Sinclair, one of the three commissioners, stood before the lectern. Of Ojibwe heritage, he had been born and raised on the former St. Peter's Indian Reserve in the Selkirk area north of Winnipeg and became the first Indigenous judge in the province of Manitoba. He is an imposing presence who delivers his speeches in a calm bass voice and commands awed silence from his audience. He asked all the survivors in the audience to stand. I happened to be seated next to three elderly men and women who solemnly rose from their seats along with many hundreds more. I felt moved just to be near them. Sinclair honored the courage of the survivors, acknowledging that "sometimes it has been the first time that you have told your stories." The crowd stomped their feet in unison and thundered their applause.

Some critics thought the TRC's process of publicly gathering thousands of Indian residential school survivors' testimonies was an exploitative spectacle that put Indigenous pain on display. Undoubtedly, for some participants telling their stories was traumatic, especially if they did not gain therapeutic support after giving their testimony. But for others who testified the process was cathartic.

That afternoon I took the elevator up to a small penthouse room to attend a Sharing Circle for residential school survivors. Those who had decided to speak sat in a small circle in the middle of the room. Concentric circles of other former students and witnesses surrounded them. Two representatives from the TRC's Survivor Committee ran the meeting. One survivor spoke of the sexual abuse she had experienced at the hands of a priest. After sharing their stories, several survivors said it felt liberating to finally tell their truths. Some survivors said they forgave those who had abused them. Monitors wearing yellow vests wandered among the audience with tissues and glasses of water for people who were crying.

Through highlighting survivors' testimonies, the TRC has revealed deeply disturbing truths. Sinclair notes that *all* of the thousands of survivors who testified before the commission either experienced or witnessed brutal corporal punishment, often for trivial matters, even for speaking their native language. One woman described having to lick the floor. One survivor saw another child forced to eat his own vomit. Survivor testimonies are corroborated by a spate of past reports made by school employees who had been shocked by the cruel treatment of the pupils. Over the course of a century, the Department of Indian Affairs failed to respond to these allegations and instead hid such revelations from the public. Overall, the testimonies made it nearly impossible to deny the abuses of the Indian residential school system and their long-term ill effects.

The TRC's designers sought to achieve a tricky balancing act. They wanted to center and dignify Indigenous testimony, but they also knew it was essential for settlers to participate in the process. They initiated a program of "honorary witnesses," about eighty prominent Canadians, mostly settlers, who could bear witness to and advocate for the TRC and the residential school survivors.

The TRC had innovated other means to get non-Indigenous people on board, too. In Ottawa that morning, as they had at other national events, the TRC sponsored an "Actions of Reconciliation" session. Commissioners invited individuals and groups to put items symbolizing their commitment to reconciliation into the Bentwood Box that Coast Salish artist Luke Marston had been commissioned to carve. The large wooden chest has been a fixture at all the national events. Marston depicted his grandmother's residential school experience on Kuper Island on the front of the box. He had learned that a nun had thrown her down a set of stairs. She never received treatment for the broken fingers that resulted. His carving of her face boldly confronts the audience in earthy shades of brown, red, white, and black. Her eyes are closed but tears stream down her cheeks. She is raising her crippled hands beside her head as if under arrest.

Many of those who participated at the reconciliation session were representatives of churches that had been integrally involved in running the schools. Terence Prendergast, the Catholic Archbishop of Ottawa, expressed shame for the role of the Catholic Church and asked for forgiveness. He concluded, "I believe we have matured from paternalism toward Indigenous peoples to partnership." Some survivors undoubtedly snickered or rolled their eyes. But the Indigenous man sitting next to me wept uncontrollably. Representatives from two major Jewish organizations read a statement of solidarity with survivors. Bernie Farber, son of a Holocaust survivor, stated that "common histories of persecution, assimilation, and discrimination bind our two communities together."

On that first day of the final ceremony, Justice Sinclair emphasized how important it was that settlers acknowledged their role in the damaging policy and practice of the residential schools. He reminded the non-Indigenous people in the ballroom as well as the hundreds of thousands listening from home that the findings of the TRC were "not an Aboriginal problem, but a Canadian problem." He said, "We ask you to learn, to share, and to reflect on this tragic part of Canadian history. But more than that, we ask you to act." At other events, Sinclair had advised non-Indigenous people, "You must watch, you must listen, and you must respect."

The next day the commissioners released their findings and recom-mendations. I got to the hotel almost an hour before the scheduled ses-sion, but the ballroom was already full. I followed a crowd up to an overflow room on the third floor to watch the proceedings on TV. The session alternated between video clips and presentations by each com-missioner. More stomping and wild applause followed the introduction of each commissioner. Sinclair, in a light gray suit with a bolo tie gar-nished with an Indian-themed pin, seemed visibly moved. "I can see that you people are easy to please," he quipped to much laughter. He then turned to the grave matter at hand, declaring that Canada "sought to erase from the face of the earth the history and culture" of its Indig-enous peoples. "What took place in residential schools amounts to nothing less than cultural genocide," he stated unequivocally.

Chief Wilton Littlechild, another commissioner, dressed in his sig-nature cowboy hat and boots, shared some of his personal story. He had been brought at the age of six from the home of his Cree grandparents on the Ermineskin Reserve in Alberta to a boarding school. He spent the next fourteen years at Indian residential schools. "We were abused for using our own languages and practicing our spirituality," he told us. Memories of his grandparents' teachings and participation in sports helped Littlechild endure the cruelty, and he became an avid athlete, a lawyer, and an ardent advocate for the rights of Indigenous peoples as both a member of Parliament and a delegate to the United Nations. He emphasized the need for survivors to overcome their experiences through reclaiming their Indigenous languages and cultural practices.

I watched the broadcast with a few dozen other people, some of us Indigenous and some of us settlers, in that small windowless room. Tears brimmed in our eyes and sometimes spilled down our cheeks. Our hands shook as we reached out to clasp those of our neighbors. Volunteers roamed the crowd with bundles of burning sage to enable us to "smudge" or purify ourselves by gathering smoke in our hands and drawing it over our bodies. The volunteers also collected used tissues to later burn in a sacred fire. The magnitude of the cruelty of the Canadian government and churches' practice of Indigenous child removal weighed all of us down with a deep sadness. As an American, I felt another layer of grief. Even in the "yes we can" years of the Obama administration, I had a pervasive sense that a TRC that reckoned with our own history of Indigenous child removal was unlikely to ever happen in the United States.

For all the sorrow, there was another collective emotion that pervaded the room. We were not only witnessing something momentous, a nation remembering and taking responsibility for its past abuses. A potent kinship among strangers also welled up in the room. It called on us to honor and to care for one another. In a world of cynicism, calculation, manipulation, disillusion, and disappointment, it was surprising to experience this moment of deep connection, to feel what our lives could be if we could cherish and polish these moments like tiny beads and string them into a long necklace. The Canadian TRC's Final Ceremony in 2015 made me want to explore truth and reconciliation, no matter how fledgling, in the United States.

Carlisle, Pennsylvania, is a place of grief and mourning for most Native American people. In 2018, on the one hundredth anniversary of the boarding school's closing, the National Native American Boarding School Healing Coalition (NABS) held its first conference in the small town. A group of boarding school survivors, mental health practitioners, legal experts, activists, and scholars—nearly all of them Indigenous—responded to the call to gather and remember what happened in this place.

Since the site of the Carlisle school is hallowed ground to Indian people, it would have been fitting if NABS could have held its first conference on the site of the actual school. But the federal government repurposed Carlisle after it closed in 1918. Today the U.S. Army operates its War College there and access is restricted. We conference attendees were only allowed to take short tours of the grounds, after gaining security clearance. Traces of the school are interspersed throughout the sprawling campus, most of them legible only to those long schooled in the institution's history. The school's cemetery, however, occupies a prominent place on the campus, visible to all who enter the college. It is the part of Carlisle that causes the deepest distress to Indian people.

For most of the conference, we attendees are in a windowless basement of the Comfort Suites in Carlisle. Hundreds of people are attending the conference, with concurrent breakout sessions. We've scheduled
some sessions upstairs in two wings of the restaurant, known as the
Whiskey Rebellion, harking back to George Washington's presidential
administration. The rooms upstairs prove to be inadequate for conference presentations, and organizers quickly come up with a makeshift
solution to divide the big conference venue in the basement into three
or four smaller rooms.

It's hard to miss the symbolism that we are talking about the need for
healing from the Indian boarding schools in a cramped hotel basement
rather than a spacious ballroom as in Ottawa for the Canadian TRC's
final ceremonies, or in the halls of government, or actually on the historic site of Carlisle. The truths about Indian boarding schools still lie
hidden out of sight in the basement of our national house. The vast
majority of Americans, at least settler Americans, are unaware of the
harms that the boarding schools caused.

Christine Diindiisi McCleave, executive director of NABS and a
member of the Turtle Mountain Band of Chippewa Indians, opens the
conference by telling us about her grandfather, who was recruited to
play football on Carlisle's famous winning team in the final years of the
school. He, along with the other athletes, lived in a separate dormitory
from other Carlisle students. As an athlete, he may have had some positive experiences at the school and not only been subjected to the indignities and abuses endured by other Indian children.

Sandy White Hawk, a Sicangu Lakota and member of the coalition's
board, emceed most of the conference. She has a way of simultaneously
acknowledging the pain of boarding school survivors and their descendants while bringing healing laughter to the day. Through her humor, she
also has a way of both welcoming settlers like me and giving us a twinge
of discomfort. What are we doing here? How will we show up as allies?

Over the course of the two-day NABS conference, many boarding
school survivors shared their stories of pain and abuse. Their descendants told of how it continued to reverberate down through the generations. Maria Yellow Horse Brave Heart (Hunkpapa and Oglala Lakota)

has dedicated her career in psychiatry and behavioral sciences to identifying, understanding, and confronting this intergenerational historical trauma. She spoke about how, early in her career, she met Holocaust survivors and their family members. She immediately recognized that their experiences resonated with many American Indian people who had attended the boarding schools and passed trauma down through the generations.

Brave Heart identifies several features of "historical trauma response." They include hypervigilance, always being on alert and never able to truly rest; psychic numbing, an attempt to shut down the pain that also deadens other feelings; and a sense that any vitality in one's own life is a betrayal of the ancestors who suffered. These features have much in common with the post-traumatic stress disorder that many combat veterans and genocide survivors experience.

Brave Heart emphasizes the importance of helping Indian people move from the status of victim to survivor, and then beyond. She works to help people not just survive but thrive, by "returning to the sacred path." This conference is a collective effort to return to the sacred path through a complex process of telling truths, healing ceremonies and rituals, and raising the long-term possibility of reconciliation.

It took more than a century of agitation by Indigenous people to reach this point. The first couple generations of boarding school students started an organization, the Society of American Indians, to advocate for their rights. Some of them became ardent critics of the schools and the government's assimilation program.

Zitkála-Šá or Gertrude Simmons, a Yankton Dakota, was just eight years old when Quaker missionaries from White's Manual Labor Institute in Wabash, Indiana, showed up on her reservation to recruit children for their school. Rather than consulting with Indian parents, the missionaries went right to the children, hoping to lure them to school with carrots—or actually, apples—rather than force them with sticks.

They told Zitkála-Šá and her friend Judéwin "of the great tree where grew red, red apples" in Indiana, "and how we could reach out our hands and pick all the red apples we could eat." Zitkála-Šá later wrote, "I had never seen apple trees. I had never tasted more than a dozen red apples in my life; and when I heard of the orchards of the East, I was eager to roam among them." Zitkála-Šá begged her mother to let her go to White's Institute, and her mother eventually relented, with great reluctance.

Zitkála-Šá returned to Yankton three years later, but she felt out of place and decided to return to White's Institute at age fifteen to pursue further education in music—violin and piano. After graduation in 1895, she studied at both Earlham College in Richmond, Indiana, and the Boston Conservatory of Music. In 1899, Carlisle Indian School hired her as its music teacher. Carlisle's founder, Richard Henry Pratt, also employed her to recruit students from her reservation. For a time, Zitkála-Šá conformed with Pratt's directives.

But gradually she grew deeply critical of the boarding school enterprise. The shocking impoverishment of her reservation as well as the coercive assimilation program at the boarding schools led Zitkála-Šá to pen a series of critical articles in some of the most popular magazines of the day: the *Atlantic Monthly* and *Harper's Monthly*. She would later gather these in a collection called *American Indian Stories*.

In an essay she wrote in the *Atlantic Monthly* in 1900, Zitkála-Šá wrote movingly of her own sense of loss:

> For the white man's papers, I had given up my faith in the Great Spirit. For these same papers I had forgotten the healing in trees and brooks. On account of my mother's simple view of life, and my lack of any, I gave her up, also. . . . Like a slender tree, I had been uprooted from my mother, nature, and God. I was shorn of my branches, which had waved in sympathy and love for home and friends. The natural coat of bark which had protected my oversensitive nature was scraped off to the very quick.
>
> Now a cold bare pole I seemed to be, planted in a strange earth.

In 1902, Zitkála-Šá completely renounced her boarding school upbringing and its Christian orientation when she published "Why I Am a Pagan" in the *Atlantic Monthly*. Pratt fired Zitkála-Šá from her job at Carlisle.

Employment was limited for Indians, even ones who had excelled in their boarding school education. Zitkála-Šá, like many others, found work with the Office of Indian Affairs, first on the Standing Rock Reservation and then with her husband, Raymond Bonnin, at the Uintah-Ouray Reservation in Utah. She did not give up her music, however. She collaborated with a professor at Brigham Young University on *The Sun Dance Opera*, which re-created the sacred Lakota ceremony that the government had banned.

Zitkála-Šá also kept her critical perspective on Indian policy. She joined the Society of American Indians and became increasingly critical of the government's administration of Indian policy. When the Office of Indian Affairs fired Raymond Bonnin, the couple moved to Washington, D.C., where they became full-time activists. She edited the society's journal, *American Indian Magazine*, and frequently lectured across the country. She opposed assimilation and the separation of children from their families but also championed Indian citizenship. (The United States did not consider Indians citizens until Congress passed the 1924 Indian Citizenship Act.)

In the mid-1920s, Zitkála-Šá met a new generation of settler reformers through the General Federation of Women's Clubs. She helped to raise their concern with federal Indian policy. In 1926 she and Raymond also started their own advocacy organization: the National Council of American Indians. This was another ripe moment for truth and reconciliation in the United States, a time when Indigenous people gained a platform to express their grievances and promote their solutions, and when some concerned and impassioned settlers allied with them. Together they put pressure on the government to investigate all aspects of Indian policy.

As a result of these activists' efforts, the government commissioned a team of ten experts to survey conditions on reservations and in boarding schools. All of the experts were settlers except for Henry Roe Cloud of the Winnebago tribe of Nebraska, who had attended boarding school and gained his bachelor's and master's degrees at Yale University. The Rockefeller Foundation funded the independent inquiry and Lewis Meriam of the Brookings Institution led it. *The Problem of Indian*

Administration, or the Meriam Report, published in 1928, was scathing in its critique of all aspects of federal Indian policy. In regard to the boarding schools, the report deemed provisions for the care of children in them as "grossly inadequate," condemned school officials' use of cruel discipline and harsh punishment, and castigated the school system for destroying Indian family life.

The inquiry and its report helped lead to a new administration in Indian affairs in the 1930s, under President Franklin Roosevelt. John Collier, a settler who had taken part in the 1920s movement, became the new commissioner of Indian affairs. He helped revive the short-lived *restitution* movement that Standing Bear and Susette La Flesche's tour had launched. Collier ended the allotment program and returned land to some tribes during his Indian New Deal. He also promoted limited self-government among Indian tribes. Under Collier's administration, many of the boarding schools closed. His administration promoted both public school education for Indians and on-reservation day schools that taught Native languages, cultures, and histories.

But the boarding school era was not over for good. A number of schools remained open, particularly for the Navajos and Alaska Natives, well into the late twentieth century. These schools came under scrutiny again during the late 1960s and 1970s, another truth and reconciliation moment in American history. Attorney General Robert Kennedy led a Special Subcommittee on Indian Education, authorized in 1967, to investigate all aspects of Indian education. Its final report concluded that "our national policies for educating American Indians are a failure of major proportions."

The harshest aspects of the boarding school system ended, finally, in the 1970s, a century after the government had first set up the schools. In 1975, through the Indian Self-Determination and Education Assistance Act, the government contracted with many tribes to run their own schools. The vast majority of American Indian children—over 90 percent—now attend public schools. But still the Bureau of Indian Education (BIE), established in 2006 as an arm of the Department of the Interior, oversees education for about 40,000 Indian students in 183 schools on 64 reservations in 23 states. The BIE, often on a contractual basis with tribes, operates dozens of reservation day schools, 21 on-reservation boarding schools, and four off-reservation schools (Riverside in Oklahoma, Sherman in California, Chemawa in Oregon, and Flandreau in South Dakota).

The schools no longer focus on assimilation, but critics complain that they still have a "colonial mindset" and include very little Indian-centered curriculum. Moreover, many of the substandard conditions that plagued the earlier Indian schools are still present. In 2009 the government tagged 65 BIE school buildings as dilapidated, hazardous, and unsafe, with the presence of exposed asbestos and lead as well as water leaks near electrical outlets. And students attending the schools often have the lowest achievement outcomes of any children in their states.

The worst of the coercive assimilation program and abuses of the Indian boarding schools may now be over, but they have left bitter legacies for Indigenous people. Few settler Americans today are aware of how the schools separated Indian families and undermined Indian cultures and nations. There has been no sustained national reckoning with the United States' own history of child removal, as there was in Canada.

Many Indigenous people would like to change this. Survivors of the assimilationist era of boarding schools want justice for the indignities and abuses they suffered in the schools. Some former students tried to follow the route that their Canadian peers did; they sought to sue the federal government or the churches that ran the schools they had attended. But these court cases have gotten nowhere, partly because of the ubiquity of statute of limitations laws.

Frustration with the lack of legal recourse is what led a small group of boarding school survivors, legal scholars, activists, and service providers to come together for a Boarding School Healing Symposium over three days in May 2011 in Boulder, Colorado, home of the Native American Rights Fund, an advocacy group similar to the NAACP. Symposium attendees decided to form the National Native American Boarding School Healing Coalition (NABS) in 2012 to push for a national truth and reconciliation process that would ultimately "get the U.S. Government and churches to acknowledge their responsibility for the abuse and human rights violations that occurred in the boarding schools," director Christine Diindiisi McCleave told me. So it was that in the absence of a national truth and reconciliation process, NABS has initiated its own efforts at truth telling, healing, and redress.

Its first conference in Carlisle was a key event. Survivors and descendants are particularly concerned with the children who never returned from the schools. The school buried more than two hundred children from fifty different tribes in the Carlisle cemetery. The Army moved the children's graves from their original resting places to the present burial ground in the 1920s. Bob Sam, a Tlingit elder from Sitka, Alaska, has dedicated his life to the repatriation and re-interment of Indian remains, including members of his own family. He came in 2018 to Carlisle to help facilitate the return of fourteen Native Alaska children buried in the Carlisle cemetery.

The Northern Arapaho people, many of their members descended from Sand Creek survivors, were determined to bring home three boys— Little Chief, Horse, and Little Plume—who died shortly after arriving at Carlisle in 1881 and were buried at the school. Yufna Soldierwolf, a historic preservation officer with the Northern Arapaho tribe, led a long campaign to get the Army to return the children to their people on the Wind River Reservation. Finally, in 2017 the Army relented and allowed the tribe to bring home the three boys. Crawford White Sr., a Northern Arapaho elder, explained, "It's something that had to be done for our tribe, and the healing begins."

Unfortunately, when the children's graves were disinterred, Northern Arapaho tribal members discovered that the grave of Little Plume contained two other sets of remains, neither of which matched his description. McCleave commented, "It's extremely sad and disappointing for the family who's already grieving a loss that never should have taken place." She noted, "It's showing that there's more that needs to be looked into about the boarding schools, the treatment and care and responsibility that they had to our children, in life and in death."

Equally disturbing are the children who went to Carlisle, never to return home, but are *not* buried in Carlisle's cemetery. Louellyn White (Mohawk), a descendant of Carlisle students and professor of First

Peoples Studies at Concordia University in Montreal, discovered eleven children who were "outed"—placed with local families to work—and never returned to the school or their home communities. They just disappeared. After many years of research, White found them buried in local cemeteries near their outing placements in Pennsylvania and New Jersey. All but one was afforded a grave marker, and some were buried in pauper's grave sites. The government had been entrusted with the care of Indian children, and it had behaved with callous negligence and irresponsibility.

Government removal of Indigenous children persisted into the post–World War II era as well, even after the government shuttered most of the boarding schools. In the 1950s, as the government renewed its drive to assimilate Native Americans, the Bureau of Indian Affairs created the Indian Adoption Project to promote the adoption of Native children by non-Native families. Child welfare agencies in nearly every state also commonly removed Indian children to foster care or for adoptive placement in settler families. By the late 1960s, an estimated 25 to 35 percent of all Indian children were living apart from their families of origins.

Authorities insisted that they were separating Indigenous children from their families as a benevolent, caring act of rescue. In fact, as with the Friends of the Indian of the nineteenth century, they often used the language of reconciliation. One white settler who submitted a statement to the Senate committee investigating widespread Indian child removal wrote, "We *cannot* point with pride to the results of government policies during the past 150 years; in fact we should be ashamed of the way Indians have been treated. It seems to me that this present-day trend towards person-to-person assistance should be encouraged, not frustrated." Another settler who had adopted an Indian child told a researcher, "We have always been very moved by the story of the plight of the Indian and we gave up the idea of adopting a child from abroad on the basis of 'Let's solve our own problem first.' We feel that the American Indian owns the country by right and he has been pushed around and never given a break. In accepting the child, we feel we have done a little bit for the American Indian." Settler supporters of the fostering and adoption of

Indian children with non-Indian families characterized Indian communities as a "dead end" and the removal of children for placement in non-Indian families as a "chance" for a better life.

Despite its rhetoric of rescue, the government had more sinister, and financial, motives for placing thousands of Indian children for adoption in settler families. For government bureaucrats it presented the ultimate solution to the Indian problem. Indian children would grow up in middle-class homes where they would have no contact with their families, tribal communities, or peers (as they had in the boarding schools). Through adoption, authorities thought, Indian children would become truly assimilated into mainstream American culture. Over time, Indian peoples would cease to be distinct entities. And neither the federal government nor the states would have to contribute to the cost of raising the children.

Beginning in the 1960s, Indian leaders fought back against the removal of their children. They charged that welfare workers often used ethnocentric and middle-class criteria—like lack of indoor plumbing or caregiving by grandparents—as a basis for removing children from their homes without evidence of true neglect or abuse. Tribal officials conceded that there were occasions when parents could not properly care for their children, but they insisted that they could find Indigenous caretakers for these children within their own communities.

Indian nations and advocacy organizations organized to reverse the long-standing government policy and practice of Indigenous child removal. Congress held three sets of hearings on this egregious abuse, and in 1978, it passed the Indian Child Welfare Act (ICWA). The law enabled tribes to reclaim the care of their own children and to protect Indian families from unwarranted child removal. ICWA now enjoys widespread acclaim by dozens of child welfare organizations, who consider it the "gold standard" of care for dependent children.

Yet most Americans are completely unaware of the history of Indigenous child removal that led to ICWA's passage. And, despite ICWA, Indian families and communities still struggle against authorities who remove their children without cause. As the COVID-19 pandemic swept around the globe in 2020, for example, New Mexico authorities saw fit to single out Native American women for COVID-19 testing, separating them from their newborns until test results were available.

Indigenous children in Canada and Australia have also experienced unprecedented rates of removal into the child welfare system. Canada calls this phenomenon the Sixties Scoop, although it started in the 1950s and continues to this day. Unlike the United States, these nations have publicly confronted these abuses.

Beginning in 1996, the Australian Human Rights Commission held a comprehensive inquiry into the "Stolen Generations," Australians' evocative name for the thousands of Indigenous children who had been separated from their families over the course of a century, whether to institutions or for placement within non-Indigenous families. The commission's 1997 report, known commonly as the *Bringing Them Home* report, estimated that up to one in three Aboriginal children had been removed from their families. It included horrifying testimony from Aboriginal survivors about the brutal methods by which authorities often removed them from their families and the dreadful conditions they endured within the institutions. The *Bringing Them Home* report charged past state authorities with genocide based on the UN Convention on Genocide's definition, which includes the transfer of children from one group of people to another with intent to destroy their culture.

Sir Ronald Wilson, a distinguished non-Indigenous lawyer who had served on Australia's High Court between 1979 and 1989, and Mick Dodson, an Indigenous attorney of Yawuru descent and the Aboriginal Social Justice Commissioner, co-chaired the inquiry. They held hearings in every state capital and at many regional centers. They gathered testimony from over one thousand Aboriginal individuals and organizations and collected evidence from government and church representatives and adoptive and foster parents.

Just as with the Canadian TRC, the inquiry enabled many members of the Stolen Generations to tell their stories, unmediated by the hollow assurances of government officials that child removal had been done with the best of intentions and for the good of Aboriginal children. Indigenous people who testified did not so much want to pin blame on a perpetrator as to have their stories heard and believed. Dodson noted, "I know of no Indigenous person who told their story to the inquiry who wanted non-Indigenous Australians to feel guilty—they just wanted people to know the truth. They wanted to tell the stories of their lives. To have the truth of their experiences acknowledged. Many people who gave evidence to the inquiry said that the telling was itself healing—knowing that at last they were being officially heard."

Of the inquiry, Dodson later told me, "It was probably the toughest thing I've ever done in my life. It's very taxing to sit there day in and day out and listen to these stories. The sadness is almost overbearing. You find yourself weeping along with everyone, especially in the private sessions. They were very painful, but people wanted to tell their stories. It was an official validation that what they had been saying for generations was true. They are now in the official record of the history of Australia." Indeed, the accrual of thousands of such testimonies made it increasingly impossible to deny these histories.

Indigenous testimonies and the final report's interpretation undermined several cherished national mythologies. In a popular version of Australian history, it was the settlers who were innocent victims of cruel British authorities who sent their poorest, most benighted people—charged with all manner of petty crimes—to a remote convict settlement in the antipodes. Against all odds (including the presence of Aboriginal people), these accounts assert, these spirited settlers—"battlers" in Australian parlance—built a vibrant new nation. Now Australia had to reckon with the uncomfortable truth that its national heroes had also been its founding tyrants.

Testimony from members of the Stolen Generations also belied a common benevolent narrative. Australian authorities and the settler media constantly justified their programs as efforts to rescue Indigenous children and give them a better life, but now adults who had suffered through these policies as children were revealing how traumatic these misguided programs were. This has been an important dimension of all truth and reconciliation efforts: the unearthing of long-buried and silenced narratives that do not conform to national "myths of unity and identity."

I arrived in Australia's capital in 1998 to do some research, just a few months after the *Bringing Them Home* report had been published. Everywhere I went in Australia, people were talking about the Stolen Generations. A taxi driver would tell me how shocked he was to learn that the government had separated so many Indigenous children from their families. A stranger on a bus would reveal that she had been removed from her family as a child. During my two weeks in Australia in 1998, I couldn't help but marvel at the extent of public discourse about the Stolen Generations.

Moreover, the Stolen Generations inquiry occurred during Australia's reconciliation decade, 1991–2000. Legislators had set aside an entire decade to work toward resolving the long-standing grievances of Indigenous peoples. Sadly, it seemed inconceivable that the United States would hold a truth and reconciliation process to confront its own Stolen Generations and designate a decade to work toward reconciliation between Indigenous people and settlers.

Truth and reconciliation efforts are occurring in the United States, however. They just aren't happening at the national level or in the high-profile manner that they did in Australia and Canada.

The state of Maine and the Wabanaki federation of four tribes (the Passamaquoddy, Penobscot, Micmac, and Maliseet) held a truth and reconciliation commission for twenty-seven months from 2013 to 2015. It had been a long time coming. In 1999 the federal government singled out the state of Maine for its noncompliance with ICWA. Wabanaki children were vastly over-represented in the state's foster care system.

An ad hoc group of Indigenous and non-Indigenous social workers sought to address the problem. To convey the true meaning of Indian child removal, they contacted Denise Altvater, a Passamaquoddy who worked with the American Friends Service Committee, about video-taping her own story. Altvater recounted that when she was seven, "state workers came onto the reservation. My five sisters and I were home. My mother was not home. They took all of our belongings and they put them in garbage bags. They herded us into station wagons and took us to a state foster home and left us there for four years. During those four years, our foster parents sexually assaulted us. They starved us. They did some horrific things to us."

For seven to eight years the ad hoc group, which called itself Wabanaki REACH (Reconciliation, Engagement, Advocacy, Change, and Healing), held workshops and conducted trainings with social workers and court officials. But they did not feel that they were making lasting change. Penthea Burns, a settler social worker in the group, explains that "we were trying to move forward without understanding what had truly happened" to the Wabanaki in Maine. Carol Wishcamper, another concerned settler, told me "something more drastic was needed to make more profound structural changes in the system—to change attitudes toward Indian peoples, examine white privilege, and challenge institutional racism."

REACH decided a thoroughgoing truth and reconciliation process was needed, and they convinced representatives of the four Wabanaki tribes and the governor of Maine to sign a declaration of intent in 2011 to establish a statewide TRC. The declaration noted that "we have come to realize that we must unearth the story of Wabanaki people's experiences in order to fully uphold the spirit, letter and intent of the ICWA in a way that is consistent and sustainable." The commission sought "to give Wabanaki people a place where their voices will be heard, a place where they can heal, where they can be believed." It also aimed "to make recommendations for structural changes that will improve the way Wabanaki children and families are treated in the future."

The Maine-Wabanaki TRC commissioners visited the Canadian TRC as a potential model. Yet their TRC differed from Canada's because it addressed an injustice that is *still* occurring. And it did not have the financial backing of its state government. Instead, it had to raise all its funds from foundations and private donors.

The TRC had a small paid staff, but all five commissioners served on a voluntary basis. Carol Wishcamper, who became one of its commissioners, told me, "We have basically used a teaspoon to do the job of a front-end loader." The small TRC faced two main challenges: building trust among the Wabanaki so that survivors of the state's foster care system would come forward to tell their stories and cultivating interest among Maine's non-Indigenous population. They needed truth tellers and witnesses.

Through the help of Wabanaki REACH, the TRC visited Native communities, rather than asking Indigenous people to attend their meetings. Even then, few Native people showed up at their events at first. According to Wishcamper, "It took time to build trust. When we began, we would simply meet with Native community members in a circle and then later return to gather testimony." The TRC ultimately interviewed 93 Wabanaki people and 66 non-Natives who have been involved in child welfare: judges, lawyers, social workers, and adoptive and foster parents. Like the Canadian TRC they have supplemented oral testimony with archival and legislative research.

I attended one of the TRC's closing events in Portland, Maine, in May 2015. More than two hundred people, most of them settlers, crowded into a room at the public library. All the seats were filled, so latecomers stood in a ring around the edge of the room. Enacting Indigenous values of hospitality and reciprocity, the event's organizers had provided a full spread of food for all attendees at the back of the room. There was an electric buzz in the air as five representatives from Wabanaki REACH and the TRC took their seats on the stage. Carol Wishcamper introduced them. It was noticeable that all but one of the representatives were women.

Charlotte Bacon, the TRC's settler executive director, presented the commission's draft findings and recommendations. A slender middle-aged white woman, Bacon has written five novels and had been a tenured English professor at the University of New Hampshire. She exuded gentle yet earnest determination. Bacon explained that "we could have made a simple tool kit and checklist but we couldn't do it. We committed to doing something bigger and saying something larger." These included labeling the state's child welfare practices as racist and genocidal. Sensing that invoking genocide might cause unease, she told us, "I invite you in this difficult moment just to hold it, just to sit with it."

The crowd was not fazed, however. Audience members seemed eager to listen to Wabanaki people's concerns and get involved. Many might have felt as Wishcamper did. "I myself am not Wabanaki. Nor am I a social worker," she told me. "I heard an interview with Denise Altvater and could not get it out of my head. When I heard that the TRC was forming and looking for commissioners, I asked a Native friend of mine if it would be appropriate for me to apply. She encouraged me to apply and I did." Wishcamper joined two other settlers—Matthew Dunlap and Gail Weebach, and two Indigenous representatives—gkisedtanamoogk, a Wampanoag educator, and Sandy White Hawk, who is also active in NABS.

It's no wonder that Sandy White Hawk is involved in both NABS and the Maine-Wabanaki TRC, and served as an Honorary Witness for the Canadian TRC. For her, truth, healing, and reconciliation around American Indian child removal is a calling. She founded the First Nations Orphan Association (now the First Nations Repatriation Institute) in 2000 to help Indigenous people who were removed to foster care or adopted out of their families and communities to "return home, reconnect, and reclaim their identity."

American Indians use the term "repatriation" to refer to the return of sacred objects and burial remains to their nations. But White Hawk applies the definition of repatriation (the act or process of restoring or returning someone or something to the country of origin, allegiance, or citizenship) directly to adoptees and formerly fostered individuals. "We are returning to our place of origin; we are restoring our citizenship by enrolling in our respective tribes," she explains. "Even if one was not born on reservation homelands, it is still our homeland because it is our origin, the origin of the people we come from."

White Hawk experienced separation from her family firsthand. Social welfare authorities took her from her Sicangu Lakota mother on the Rosebud Sioux Reservation in 1953 when she was just eighteen months old. They placed her for adoption in an evangelical white Christian family where she experienced abuse from her adoptive mother. She points out in the documentary *Blood Memory* that once an adoption is finalized, no one checks to make sure that the child is being taken care of properly, that the placement is truly in the best interest of the child.

White Hawk links truth and reconciliation to healing. In 2003, she recounts, while at the Crow Creek Reservation in Ft. Thompson, South Dakota, a Lakota elder instructed her, "Don't talk about truth and reconciliation without including healing. If you do not leave time for healing, there will be no reconciliation." Chris Lieth, a Dakota elder from the Prairie Island Reservation in Minnesota, saw that White Hawk was envisioning a need for a new healing model. In his wisdom, White Hawk told me, he knew that an honor song would open the door to the conversation needed to begin bringing relatives home. He asked his good friend, Jerry Dearly, an Oglala Lakota from the Pine Ridge Reservation, to make a song for adoptees. This song became the foundation for the work that White Hawk began in 2001.

For about two decades, White Hawk has organized Truth Healing Reconciliation Community Forums. Her forums function in many ways like the Stolen Generations inquiry or the Canadian TRC as a means for survivors of abusive government policies to testify to their experiences while onlookers bear witness. At each forum, she invites adult adoptees and formerly fostered individuals as well as members of their birth families to sit in a Talking Circle and share their experiences with social workers, mental health professionals, adoption workers, and community members. White Hawk opens the sharing by asking, "What is one thing you want a social worker to know about what happened in your experience with child welfare?"

White Hawk's work simultaneously provides solace to adoptees, Indigenous families, and communities and provokes awareness among settlers. White Hawk describes her forums as providing "a therapeutic and spiritual healing of the intergenerational disenfranchised grief and trauma" caused by the removal of Indigenous children to foster care and adoption. They also help educate child welfare authorities about past practices. After attending one of the forums, one social worker reported back to the forum participants, "This will forever change how I advocate for Native children." White Hawk is clearly not waiting for the federal government to engage in truth and reconciliation with American Indians. Instead she is leading a grassroots reconciliation effort on multiple fronts to both heal and educate. And she emphasizes that reconciliation is not a one-time event but an ongoing process.

Most presenters at the NABS Carlisle conference in 2018 focused on truth telling and healing for Native people, but the organizers convened one session on reconciliation. McCleave, the moderator, immediately expressed the deep skepticism of many Native people about the concept. "Was there ever a time when relationships between Natives and non-Natives were actually conciliatory?" she asked. NABS organizers are concerned, too, that a "rush to reconciliation" could cut short the effort needed to bring out the truths of Indigenous child removal and the need for individuals, families, and communities to heal from a century of such policies and practices.

I could see why NABS members might be cautious about reconciliation, both at the national level and with the handful of settler allies who had come to their conference. After all, organizations like the Women's National Indian Association and the Indian Rights Association had grappled at the turn of the twentieth century with the government's role in Indian dispossession and dependence. They had determined to take steps toward reconciliation. Their vision of reconciliation, however, came to rest on cultural extinction and a set of policies and practices revolving around Indian child removal that proved as damaging to Indian cultures as the policies they rejected. Their efforts to make amends for abuses against American Indians, in short, led to new harms that now required another round of historical reckoning and redress.

What is to prevent latter-day reconciliation efforts from foundering or, worse, creating new harms? One key difference between that era and our own is that Indigenous people, not settlers, are in the driver's seat. It is Indigenous people who discuss, debate, and articulate what reconciliation means, how it should be carried out, and at what pace. We settlers are not in charge and we don't set the terms.

Despite a healthy dose of caution, all the presenters on the NABS reconciliation panel were moving in the direction of reconciliation. Sarah Eagle Heart, Oglala Lakota, and CEO of Native Americans in Philanthropy, seems weary of the question of whether the United States will ever have a TRC like Canada. We have statutes of limitations and can't bring a lawsuit like they did in Canada, she tells us. It will have to be a different process here. Like White Hawk she believes that Native communities need healing before action. She has carried out research on "Indigenous life courses," identifying assets within Native communities that can serve as protective factors for Native youth, including kinship bonds and extended families. Her organization has created a virtual reality game to help Indigenous youth envision healthy communities.

Vicky Stott, a member of the Ho-Chunk nation of Wisconsin, also works in philanthropy for the Kellogg Foundation. She helped launch their Truth, Racial Healing, and Transformation initiative, TRHT for short, in 2015–16 in twelve cities. She tells us that she realized the deep-seated trauma that needed to be addressed in Native communities and has since extended the program to Alaska through the First Alaskans Institute. She is adamant that neither Kellogg, nor the government, nor churches, nor non-Indian organizations can be prescriptive about what healing and reconciliation mean. Indigenous communities must "drive and define what healing is." Angela Gonzalez of the First Alaskans Institute doesn't use the word "reconciliation" in her work. Gonzalez believes we have to "let people empty out" by telling their truths, "but then we have to fill them up again with healing." Gonzalez declares, "We need to transform the trauma so we don't give it to the next generation."

What is clear from all of their presentations is that the paramount concern in the process of truth and reconciliation must be Indigenous healing. Indigenous people are the experts, and they themselves must direct any truth and reconciliation. This makes utter sense to me in my head. I am fully on board with this. But old settler habits die hard.

A year later, at the second NABS conference in Tulalip, Washington, I attended a session on reconciliation. I was full of fervor from writing this book and interviewing many people about truth and reconciliation. We broke out into small groups to discuss how to further reconciliation within church congregations. I told myself to sit back and relax, to listen and absorb. But I'd been *studying* this for several years now, right? Surely that makes me a fount of wisdom. A little voice in my brain said to remain quiet, but my mouth opened and words came tumbling out. "This is what reconciliation should look like in churches," I pontificated. "They just need to do this, then do that," I continued to blab. I couldn't stop myself, even as the little voice in my brain was saying, "Margaret, what the hell are you doing? Please stop." Thankfully, an Alaska Native elder in the group interrupted me. She gently but firmly stated that it is Indigenous boarding school survivors who are the experts and that we need to take a step back and listen to them. Embarrassed but also grateful, I thanked her later for her intervention.

How should a settler come into alliance with Indigenous people in support of Indigenous aspirations and reconciliation? One non-Native person on the NABS Truth and Reconciliation panel in Carlisle offers a model. Paula Palmer is the director of Toward Right Relationship with Native Peoples, in Boulder, Colorado, a project of the Quaker Friends Meeting. Palmer makes the point that work on reconciliation among settlers must start from a different point than that within Native communities. The first effort with settlers is *not* to alleviate the pain and bring about healing but the opposite: to encourage non-Natives to feel the pain, abuse, and trauma that Indian people have suffered. Palmer finds that as they learn about Indigenous experiences, settlers go through phases of denial, rejection, anger, and fear, but sometimes move on to empathy, recognition, and commitment to alliance. After learning the truth, Palmer queries settler audiences, what does that truth obligate us to do?

When faced with a federal government and a settler population that have been largely indifferent to the abuses they suffered, Indigenous survivors of child removal and their descendants took matters into their own hands. They formed a vibrant social movement to start telling their truths, to help one another heal, and to promote reconciliation. They are not *waiting* for the U.S. government to hold a formal truth and reconciliation process.

At the same time, they are still *calling* for the nation to finally face up to its history of abuse against Indigenous families and communities. The election of two Native American women to Congress in 2018 might have finally set this process in motion. NABS met with Representative Deb

Haaland (D-NM), member of Laguna Pueblo and now President Biden's Secretary of the Interior, to advocate for a national truth and reconciliation process. In September 2020, Representative Haaland partnered with Senator Elizabeth Warren to introduce the Truth and Healing Commission on Indian Boarding School Policy in the United States Act, which would establish the first formal commission in U.S. history to investigate, document, and acknowledge past injustices of the federal government's cultural genocide and assimilation practices. This commission, if it comes to fruition, would be an important step toward truth and reconciliation between settlers and Indigenous people in the United States. There are other essential elements that the United States needs to take toward that dream, too.

CHAPTER 10

The Hardest Word

When my family and I returned to Australia for eight weeks in 2008, our friends were eager to tell us about the Day of the Apology. There's a reason I capitalized that. It was a momentous day for almost everyone in Australia. It is like the Day that Kennedy was Assassinated or 9/11 in the United States.

On February 13, 2008, as his first official act, the new Australian prime minister, Kevin Rudd, issued a formal apology to the Stolen Generations and their families. He began with an acknowledgment of the wrongs that the Australian government had committed, a recognition of the new historical truths that had been revealed. "For our nation, the course of action is clear: that is, to deal now with what has become one of the darkest chapters in Australia's history," he declared. "In doing so, we are doing more than contending with the facts, the evidence and the often rancorous public debate. In doing so, we are also wrestling with our own soul. This is not, as some would argue, a black-armband view of history; it is just the truth: the cold, confronting, uncomfortable truth—facing it, dealing with it, moving on from it."

Rudd continued with a sincere expression of regret made on behalf of the government. "We apologise for the laws and policies of successive parliaments and governments that have inflicted profound grief, suffering and loss on these our fellow Australians," he asserted. "We apologise especially for the removal of Aboriginal and Torres Strait Islander children from their families, their communities and their country. For the pain, suffering and hurt of these stolen generations, their descendants and for their families left behind, we say sorry. To the mothers and the fathers, the brothers and the sisters, for the breaking up of families and communities, we say sorry."

Rudd delivered his apology before Parliament. Thousands of Australians, Indigenous as well as non-Indigenous, traveled to the capital and lined up outside Parliament House to watch the event. The apology also was broadcast live around the nation, and most communities planned events to accompany it. Many Australians were hungry for this official recognition of the nation's painful past.

Australia is but one of several settler colonial nations that have issued apologies to Indigenous peoples. Canada delivered an official apology to former students of the Indian residential schools in 2008, just a few months after Australia's apology, and has since offered another apology to members of the Sixties Scoop generation. New Zealand has made multiple apologies to many groups of Maoris since the 1990s for the taking of land and other resources.

There have been hundreds of such political apologies around the world since World War II. There are so many, large and small, that the Institute for the Study of Human Rights at Columbia University has created a database to document them. From 1947 to the end of 2019, they have chronicled 726 such apologies.

Apologies are a key part of any restorative justice process, but they are but one component of a comprehensive effort to make amends for past historical abuses. When I interviewed Mick Dodson in 2014, he told me that in designing the Stolen Generations inquiry and drafting its final report, he and his co-chair, Ronald Wilson, "relied on the van Boven principles." I didn't want to appear ignorant, so I nodded my head knowingly. I later learned that the van Boven principles (now known as the van Boven/Bassiouni principles) were developed by the jurists Theo van Boven and Mahmoud Cherif Bassiouni, members of the UN Human Rights Commission, and adopted by the United Nations General Assembly in 2005 to guide the process of making redress for gross human rights abuses.

Van Boven and Bassiouni believed that for a redress process to be successful, it needed to include attention to five principles: satisfaction, restitution, compensation, rehabilitation, and guarantees of non-repetition. The two international law experts were seeking ways to rebuild fragile societies after the fall of oppressive dictatorships or in the aftermath of extreme civil violence and conflict. Think Bosnia or Rwanda. Their principles do not apply neatly to the long-standing and ongoing abuses that Indigenous people have suffered as minorities in affluent settler colonial nations. But they do provide some insight and guidance.

What would it mean for people who have been collectively wronged to gain *satisfaction*? Van Boven and Bassiouni asserted that they needed widespread public acknowledgment by a national government of the human rights abuses that they had suffered. This included truth seeking and truth telling, commemoration, and public apologies.

But, many critics wondered, weren't these efforts merely symbolic? What could the expressions of regret, the apologies, do to provide redress, especially for so many years of abuse? Don't we really need some concrete actions? To van Boven, Bassiouni, and Dodson, apologies and other forms of satisfaction were certainly not the be-all and end-all of redress, but they were not just empty gestures either. The millions of words that spilled forth from testimonies, that were printed in reports and in new historical narratives, that resounded from apologies and were etched in public memorials mattered. And they mattered to both those who had suffered abuse and those in whose name the abuse had occurred. Apologies were a key component of any effort to heal and reconcile.

The Apology took on an outsized value in Australia, where reconciliation had stalled miserably after the hopeful reconciliation decade of the 1990s. The Stolen Generations inquiry's final report, *Bringing Them Home*, released in 1997, had called upon the state governments and the Commonwealth to make a formal apology to the Stolen Generations. It also urged churches and other nongovernment agencies that played a role in child removal to make their own apologies. All the state governments, as well as most churches and many private organizations, said they were sorry within a year. Even some local governments and police forces apologized. But the national Commonwealth government, now led by the conservative prime minister John Howard, refused.

Howard vehemently opposed any kind of apology for past policies and practices. He asserted, in his opening ceremony speech at the Australian Reconciliation Convention of 1997, no less, "I have never been willing to embrace a formal national apology because I do not believe the current generation can accept responsibility for the deeds of earlier generations." (Aboriginal delegates turned their backs on him at the event.) He also argued that no apology was necessary because past policies were believed to be in the best interest of children and were sanctioned by the laws of the time. Technically, it wasn't illegal to remove children, and if it wasn't illegal, there was nothing to apologize for, in Howard's logic.

Other settler Australians, following Howard, declared that there was nothing to be ashamed of or to apologize for in Australia's past. These doubters balked at the new histories that emerged from the findings of the Stolen Generations inquiry. Keith Windschuttle, an independent scholar, claimed, "In reality the New South Wales government was not stealing children, but offering youths the opportunity to get on-the-job training." Echoing Windschuttle, other conservative columnists claimed that the Stolen Generations should properly be called "the rescued generations."

P. P. McGuinness, the editor of the conservative *Quadrant* magazine, claimed that *Bringing Them Home* witnesses "suffered from a form of 'collective hysteria' or from . . . 'false memory syndrome.'" McGuinness asserted that there was no documentation to prove that there was a policy of breeding out the color. (This is patently false, as several such documents are freely accessible in the archives.) Historian Geoffrey Blainey claimed that the Stolen Generations inquiry had been distorted by a "black armband view of history," which Rudd referred to in his apology.

The conservative attempt to repress or discredit the new Stolen Generations narrative did not succeed. Another settler historian, Henry Reynolds, who had been integrally involved in exposing the violence and injustice of British colonization of Australia, countered that Stolen Generations deniers were purveyors of a "white blindfold" version of history. The Stolen Generations inquiry—and its hundreds of testimonies—had made it virtually impossible to still claim that the crime had not occurred.

It was tougher to deal with Howard's contention that the current generation held no responsibility for past abuses. Many Australian settlers wrestled with the question of what citizens are obliged to do about injustices of the past that they had little to do with but were done in the name of their nation. Janna Thompson, a philosopher, wrote an entire book on the subject: *Taking Responsibility for the Past*. She concluded, "The fact that our predecessors or forebears were the ones who did the wrongs does not excuse us from a responsibility for the reparation."

Her approach is grounded in a belief that members of a nation acquire intergenerational responsibilities. The "wealth of nations has been built on past injustices," she writes. "Non-Indigenous Americans, Australians, New Zealanders, South Africans, and Canadians are now benefiting from injustices done to indigenous communities—from the consequences of broken treaties, from land that was seized and settled." Moreover, Thompson argues, "transgenerational commitments [such as treaties] create transgenerational obligations." She contends, "It is not necessary that you be a descendant of someone who made or violated an agreement." Responsibility for past injustice derives from citizenship, today or in the past. Many settler Australians have come to share Thompson's conception of intergenerational responsibility. They believe it is essential that settlers today should be accountable for the policies and actions of past settlers.

National reconciliation in Australia, including an apology from the prime minister for the Stolen Generations, may have been stymied during the Howard years. But the genie had been let out during the reconciliation decade. Indigenous agencies and organizations were not about to let it be stuffed back into its bottle. The *Bringing Them Home* report recommended the commemoration of the Stolen Generations through an annual National Sorry Day, which was inaugurated on May 26, 1998. The government-sponsored Council on Aboriginal Reconciliation (CAR) created tool kits to assist communities in planning local reconciliation activities.

Many settlers sincerely embraced the spirit of reconciliation, even if the government was recalcitrant. In this era before social media, Australians for Native Title (ANT), a grassroots group that formed in June 1997 and primarily supported Indigenous land rights, created Sorry Books that served as a means for settler Australians to state their own personal regret for past policies even if the federal government refused to make a formal apology to the Stolen Generations.

Each Sorry Book began with these words: "By signing my name in this book, I record my deep regret for the injustices suffered by Indigenous Australians as a result of European settlement and, in particular, I offer my personal apology for the hurt and harm caused by the forced removal of children from their families and for the effect of government policy on the human dignity and spirit of Indigenous Australians. I would also like to record my desire for Reconciliation and for a better future for all our peoples. I make a commitment to a united Australia which respects this land of ours, values Aboriginal and Torres Strait Islander heritage and provides justice and equity for all."

Some signers simply added their names to a list. Others added lengthy personal messages. Trish Cowcher wrote, "It is hard to believe that it has taken us so long to understand and own up to the harm done to Aboriginal people. I hope that our apology can begin the healing. Hearing the stories of the Stolen Generation churns me up and makes me feel sorry that this went on and ashamed it happened in my lifetime. I promise to work towards justice for Aboriginal people in the future." The acclaimed Australian feminist author Germaine Greer wrote, "Forgive me for my ignorance. Now that I know the truth, I promise I will not cease from saying it." The Sorry Books were a powerful way to involve settlers in truth and reconciliation.

Demand was intense for the Sorry Books around the country; volunteers distributed around 650 official books to local councils, libraries, museums, churches, bookshops, art galleries, and schools. Many community organizations and individuals created their own books. Eventually an estimated half a million settlers added their signatures to one of the thousand Sorry Books.

The reconciliation decade culminated with Corroborree 2000, when 54 members of the Stolen Generations, each holding a recommendation from the *Bringing Them Home* report, led a march over the Sydney Harbor Bridge. Over 250,000 other Australians walked with them while skywriters puffed "Sorry" overhead. The grassroots fervor for apologizing to the Stolen Generations remained high in the first decade of the new millennium. When we lived in Canberra in 2001 my husband and I pedaled every day on our way to work over one giant Sorry after another, chalked into the bike path.

ANT eventually became Australians for Native Title and Reconciliation (ANTaR). It also developed another grassroots project called Sea of Hands that similarly sought to enable settler Australians, primarily schoolchildren, to express their regret for abuses against Indigenous people and their support for reconciliation. ANTaR installed an exhibit outside Parliament House in Canberra in 1997 that featured 70,000 hands in the colors of Aboriginal and Torres Strait Islander flags. Non-Indigenous Australians had signed their names to the hands as a show of support. Since 1997, ANTaR has brought the Sea of Hands project to communities all over the nation, and nearly 400,000 Australians have signed their name on a hand and planted it in community installations around the country.

It may be tempting to see the Sorry Books and the Sea of Hands as trivial symbolic actions that have little impact on creating reconciliation or promoting healing and justice for Indigenous peoples in Australia. Nevertheless, it was one way that settler Australians could express their alignment with reconciliation, and it could be an entry point for more sustained acts of reconciliation. It also built momentum for an official apology.

In 2008, the Labor Party gained power and Kevin Rudd issued the Apology. It had taken the Australian government more than ten years to apologize to Indigenous people for the policy and practice of separating children from their families. The Apology—as a national occasion— proved to be a deeply moving event to many Australians, Indigenous and settler alike. It mattered that the Apology emanated not from hundreds of thousands of individual settlers but from the prime minister.

For most of our settler friends, the Apology was freighted with deep meaning. It meant accepting responsibility and being accountable for the deeds of earlier generations.

For Indigenous Australians, the apology was more complicated. Some who had been in the thick of Stolen Generations politics lauded Rudd's gesture. Mick Dodson wrote, "What the apology has done is provide a cathartic and positive psychological effect for the peoples who are the subject of the apology and, indeed, for the nation as a whole." He noted the emotional impact of Rudd's apology. "What is real and important to Aboriginal people is how we feel about ourselves. It is immensely important to us that we can feel that our history and our culture are respected by the rest of the country. This is central in our capacity to face our problems and those that are shared with the rest of the nation. . . . Our spiritual and psychological health is just as important as our physical health." For Dodson, there was power in Rudd's words.

But other Indigenous people were more skeptical. They worried that the Apology, and the project of reconciliation more generally, might be all spectacle and no substance, purely a symbolic gesture that would make no meaningful difference in the lives of Indigenous peoples. Some Indigenous leaders suspected government talk of reconciliation was just the latest manifestation of an assimilation policy and that it thwarted rather than supported their quest for justice. Aboriginal activist Kevin Gilbert asked, "What are we to reconcile ourselves to? To a holocaust, to massacre, the removal of us from our land, from the taking of our land?" Gilbert and many other Indigenous activists called for a "treaty" instead that spelled out their unique status within the nation, clearly defined land rights and sovereignty, and codified the nation's unique responsibilities toward them.

In 2001, "Treaty" filled the antipodean air alongside "Sorry." My husband, our young children, and I often danced around our living room to the pulsating didgeridoo beat of "Treaty Now" from the Aboriginal rock band Yothu Yindi. We were not aware that for some Indigenous people, Sorry and Treaty were competing goals.

There were other Indigenous leaders, however, who were wholehearted proponents of reconciliation because they believed it could lead to a treaty, that it could help Indigenous people finally attain some form of justice. (Problematic as treaties proved to be in North America and New Zealand, they also formed the basis for Indigenous sovereignty and land claims.) The chairman of the Aboriginal and Torres Strait Islander Commission, Geoff Clark, practically equated reconciliation with treaty making: "True reconciliation means recognising we possess distinct rights. . . . Our right to self-determination is a core principle. The reconciliation process must lead us into a new era of constitutional consent." For Clark and doubtless for many others, genuine reconciliation would be based on attaining such constitutional consent through a treaty.

In June 2008, just a few months after Rudd said he was sorry to the Stolen Generations, Canada's prime minister, Stephen Harper, apologized for that nation's Indian residential schools and Indigenous child removal. As in Australia, there was practically a national holiday so that Canadian citizens could view the Apology at one of thirty major events across the nation. Many survivors also held their own ceremonies to mark the historic day.

Harper spelled out the specific wrongs that the residential school system had inflicted on Indigenous peoples:

> The Government of Canada now recognizes that it was wrong to forcibly remove children from their homes and we apologize for having done this. We now recognize that it was wrong to separate children from rich and vibrant cultures and traditions, that it created a void in many lives and communities, and we apologize for having done this. We now recognize that, in separating children from their families, we undermined the ability of many to adequately parent their own children and sowed the seeds for generations to follow, and we apologize for having done this. We now recognize that, far too often, these institutions gave rise to abuse or neglect and were inadequately controlled, and we apologize for failing to protect you. Not only did you suffer these abuses as children, but as you became parents, you were powerless to protect your own children from suffering the same experience, and for this we are sorry.

Without such specificity about the wrongs committed, an apology can seem meaningless. So, Harper's precise cataloguing of the abuses suffered by Indigenous people was important.

There were other welcome components of Harper's apology. He honored the eighty thousand remaining former students by noting "it has taken extraordinary courage for the thousands of survivors that have come forward to speak publicly about the abuse they suffered. It is a testament to their resilience as individuals and to the strength of their cultures." He then said unequivocally, "The government recognizes that the absence of an apology has been an impediment to healing and reconciliation. Therefore, on behalf of the Government of Canada and all Canadians, I stand before you, in this Chamber so central to our life as a country, to apologize to Aboriginal peoples for Canada's role in the Indian Residential Schools system."

For many Indigenous people the Apology had been a long time coming and was very powerful. Five Indigenous leaders and six former students were present in the House of Commons as Harper made the apology. Some of them cried softly. The Canadian Parliament broke with precedent that day and allowed the Indigenous leaders to respond to Harper's statement. Among them was Phil Fontaine, the leader of the Assembly of First Nations, whose admission on live TV of the sexual abuse he had suffered in residential school had helped to launch the truth and reconciliation movement around Indian residential schools.

Fontaine's comments were rich with meaning. He declared, "Our peoples, our history and our present being are the essence of Canada." Indigenous people, Fontaine insisted, should not be seen as a benighted minority or as strangers in their own land but as the very heart of the nation. He continued, "The attempts to erase our identities hurt us deeply. But it also hurt all Canadians and impoverished the character of this nation." This was an essential point that Fontaine and other Indigenous leaders emphasized. The residential schools and their attempt to eliminate Indigeneity had also damaged settler Canadians, albeit in different ways.

Fontaine, too, highlighted the importance of words and ceremony and how they could lead to action. "We must not falter in our duty now," he declared. "Emboldened by this spectacle of history, it is possible to end our racial nightmare together. . . . What happened today signifies a new dawn in the relationship between us and the rest of Canada. We are and always have been an indispensable part of the Canadian identity."

The Day of the Apology in Canada proved as momentous as it was in Australia. But there were some key differences between the two apologies. Unlike Australia's apology, which came *after* their truth-seeking inquiry, *after* a vigorous public debate, *after* the reconciliation decade, and *after* ten years of public agitation for an apology, Canada's apology came *before* the Truth and Reconciliation Commission's six-year odyssey. The apology, while it seemed long overdue to Indigenous survivors of the residential schools, may have been premature for settlers. The nation had not yet uncovered the full extent and impact of the Indian residential school system and most settlers still had little idea of how damaging it had been and how it continued to affect Indigenous people. It was up to the Canadian Truth and Reconciliation Commission to do this work, *after* the apology.

Moreover, the Australian apology, though recommended by the *Bringing Them Home* report, had not been a legislative requirement. It had grown out of the pressure of both Indigenous and settler Australians who wanted the national government to take responsibility for an abusive and damaging century-long policy. The Canadian apology, by contrast, had been mandated by the Indian Residential Schools Settlement Agreement of 2007, which the government and churches had negotiated with the Assembly of First Nations to avert class action lawsuits. The agreement stipulated that the government would issue an apology; fund a health support program for residential school survivors; develop a commemoration program for memorial projects; create a Truth and Reconciliation Commission (TRC); and provide reparations to residential school survivors.

The Canadian apology was thus the equivalent of your parents making you apologize to your sister. A kind of "Sor-ry," each syllable drawn out for ironic emphasis. It did not come from agitation on the part of settlers or from a place of deep collective national introspection and sincerity. On the other hand, it had a kind of "fake-it-till-you-make it" quality. Harper's apology may not have been freely given, but some set-tler Canadians may have gradually embraced its content and made it real, in part from the work of the Canadian TRC.

The Apology, in both Australia and Canada, was a significant sym-bolic break with the past. No longer would each nation deny its past abuses of Indigenous peoples. Yet there were some troubling aspects of both the Canadian and Australian apologies. Harper framed each part of the apology with the words, "we now recognize that it was wrong." This subtly indicated that the actors of the past did not know better, that they were acting with good intentions and should not be faulted for their behavior. (This is simply untrue. Over the decades many govern-ment agents had reported abysmal conditions and abuses in the resi-dential schools, but the government had ignored and buried these reports.)

Moreover, many skeptics think settler governments used the apolo-gies to close off conversation on Indigenous grievances without making any real substantive redress. This is evident in some of the rhetorical moves that both Australian and Canadian speechwriters made. Rudd had called the Stolen Generations a "dark chapter" in Australia's history. Harper stated that the "treatment of children in Indian Residential Schools is a sad chapter in our history." He also peppered his speech frequently with such phrases as "It is for the nation to bring the first two centuries of our settled history to a close, as we begin a new chapter." Harper and Rudd were both signaling that each of their nations could literally close the book on this episode in history and write a new his-tory together. They were saying, too, that Indigenous child removal was just an episode in each nation's history, not an underlying and long-standing practice, tied to each nation's founding crime.

There were many settlers in each nation who, indeed, looked at the Apology as the end of the conversation. My settler colleague Denise Cuthbert, a professor of sociology at Royal Melbourne Institute of Technology who researches in this field, told me, "The exquisitely poi-gnant thing is that somehow the recognition of the Stolen Generations took the political wind out of the larger movement. People say, we gave them an apology, we are done with that, let's move on. It is an invitation to believe that we are square." There is thus much to be skeptical about in these apologies.

Yet from within the United States, these apologies seem momentous. They represent a public acknowledgment that governments were culpable in the unjust removal of Indigenous children. There have been a few occasions when the United States, or one of its agencies, issued an apology to Native Americans, but if you are a settler, you have probably never heard of them.

In 2000, the Bureau of Indian Affairs' assistant secretary, Kevin Gover, a member of the Pawnee nation, used a ceremony marking the agency's 175th anniversary to issue an earnest apology for past policies and practices. Gover hoped to demonstrate that the BIA, which now had a majority of Indian employees, had changed in its orientation toward Indian peoples.

Many Indian people resented that the president had not issued the apology. Indeed, Gover acknowledged, "I do not speak today for the United States. That is the province of the nation's elected leaders, and I would not presume to speak on their behalf. I am empowered, however, to speak on behalf of this agency, the Bureau of Indian Affairs, and I am quite certain that the words that follow reflect the hearts of its 10,000 employees." Hoopa leader Lyle Marshall called the apology "inadequate because it came from the wrong person." Moreover, this event gained little media coverage, outside of Indian country.

Under the Obama administration, the government issued a more official apology. In 2009 President Obama signed a Native American Apology Resolution into law, which the bill's sponsor, Senator Sam Brownback (R-KS), then added to the 2010 Defense Appropriations Act. You can be forgiven if you have not heard of this apology. The press was not invited when the president signed it. Senator Brownback read the apology in 2010 at an event at the Congressional Cemetery where only *five* tribal leaders were present. Hardly the national holiday that occasioned the issuing of the Apology in Australia or Canada. Thus, unlike both Rudd's and Harper's apologies, made by each leader before their nations' governing bodies and broadcast nationwide, this apology seemed to be a half-hearted under-the-radar gesture.

This apology was vague, too. It "apologized on behalf of the United States to all Native Peoples for the many instances of violence, maltreatment, and neglect of Native Peoples by citizens of the United States." It lacked the kind of specificity about the true harms and abuses that the United States inflicted on Indigenous peoples.

Indigenous people deserve better. A national apology made by the president before Congress with Indigenous leaders present and televised nationally would go a long way toward a healing and reconciliation process. Imagine all American schoolchildren viewing this apology and learning more about why it was necessary. Envision every workplace making time to hear the apology and devoting a day of service to Native American communities. Alas, this seems like a distant dream.

While the United States has not made a national apology, some public officials at state government levels have apologized and made their own bids for truth and reconciliation. In 2019, Governor Gavin Newsom apologized to California's Native peoples and set up a truth and healing council "to provide an avenue for California Native Americans to clarify the record—and provide their historical perspective—on the troubled relationship between tribes and the state."

In Colorado, at the conclusion of the Sand Creek Spiritual Healing Run in 2014, Governor John Hickenlooper addressed the crowd on the steps of the capitol. He declared, "This has been a day too long in coming. On behalf of the State of Colorado, I want to apologize." Hickenlooper, the first Colorado governor to apologize for Sand Creek, added, "We will not run from our history. I will make sure this history continues to be told." Maybe there is hope for change at the state level.

These more localized apologies may actually have greater meaning for Indigenous people than a national apology. New Zealand has never made a national apology to the Maori people. But the Crown, as the government still refers to itself, has issued dozens of apologies to *iwis*, the Maori equivalent of tribes, or *hapus*, sub-tribes. Under intense pressure from Maori activists, the government created the Treaty of Waitangi Tribunal in 1975. (Representatives of the British Crown had negotiated the Treaty of Waitangi with a group of Maori chiefs in 1840 but had almost immediately violated it by a series of land grabs.)

By 1985, Maori were able to use the tribunal to bring their land rights claims and other grievances to the Crown. And in 1994 the Crown established an Office of Treaty Settlements to address the recommendations made in tribunal reports and negotiate redress packages with Maori groups to settle their historical Treaty of Waitangi claims. Each negotiation results in an Act of Parliament that includes a Crown apology, including a detailed historical account acknowledging the wrong.

The rituals and venues the Crown and Maori groups have chosen for apologies are also of significance. Maori *iwis* hold traditional ceremonies on the occasion of Crown apologies, either on their *marae*, Maori ceremonial spaces, or in places of historical significance. The Crown, for example, delivered its apology to the Ngati Ranginui *iwi* at Te Ranga, where in 1864 colonial forces attacked and killed over 120 Maori. The Crown and Maori claimants signed the agreement on the 148th anniversary of the killing. After the Crown's representatives have acknowledged and apologized for the wrong, Maori leaders usually accept the apology or express forgiveness.

Thus far, these more localized apologies have proven significant and meaningful. The 2008 minister of Treaty of Waitangi Negotiations, Michael Cullen, in fact, argued that a national apology was not appropriate. "Through our process of reconciliation and redress," he explains, "we seek to acknowledge specific cases of injustice. We seek to develop a shared understanding of exactly where we failed, how our failures impact on iwi and hapu, and how best we can move forward together." Maori leader Grant Hawke agrees; he has stated that he "prefe[rs] the process of iwi and hapu negotiating the terms of an apology because it [has] led to 'more intimate' and 'quite substantial' apologies." The apology process that has developed in New Zealand, or Aotearoa, its Maori name, may serve as a model for the United States. Indigenous people and settlers may have more success in generating a more heartfelt and specific apology at the state or local level than on the national stage.

Those of us Americans who are disappointed that our state and national governments are not yet taking steps to apologize to Indigenous peoples could follow the example of the grassroots reconciliation movement in

Australia. They show us that there are still many things we settlers can do to express our regret for past policies, to demonstrate that we want to be accountable and to promote reconciliation.

There are some American settlers who have already done this, but you may not know about them. Shay Bilchik, the president of the Child Welfare League of America (CWLA) from 2000 to 2007, delivered a heartfelt apology in 2001 for the league's role in the Indian Adoption Project as part of his keynote speech to the National Indian Child Welfare Association (NICWA) conference. Bilchik told me that the "dogged" effort of Terry Cross, a Seneca man who founded and headed NICWA for many decades, led to Bilchik and the CWLA taking a stand. This is key. Settler efforts should always come from the initiation of Indigenous people and in partnership with them.

Bilchik placed his apology in the context of other truth and reconciliation processes worldwide. "The spirit in which I stand before you today, as a representative of CWLA and as an individual, is the spirit of truth and reconciliation," he declared. "When the truth had been told as fully as possible, those who had been offended could have at least the knowledge that denial was at an end, and that the world knew what they had suffered. The perpetrators shared that knowledge."

Like all good apologies, Bilchik's acknowledged the specific wrong. In his apology, Bilchik noted that "while adoption was not as wholesale as the infamous Indian schools, in terms of lost heritage, it was even more absolute." He acknowledged that "no matter how well intentioned and how squarely in the mainstream this was at the time, it was wrong; it was hurtful." He stated unequivocally, "I deeply regret the fact that the League's active participation gave credibility to such a hurtful, biased, and disgraceful course of action."

Bilchik also gave the apology freely without any expectation of a specific response. This is the spirit in which we settlers must approach our work. Bilchik told me in an interview that when he decided to make an in-person apology, "I didn't know if it would lead to anger or would allow us to move forward." As he delivered his speech, he "sensed from the podium the power of the moment, the raw emotion in the room, the number of people who were crying. It was about taking ownership and moving forward together, to build new partnerships." His gesture could not take the place of a comprehensive national truth and reconciliation process, but it "led to more dialogue and more connectedness."

Bilchik realized, too, that an apology without some form of action would be meaningless. After Bilchik's apology, the league committed to developing meaningful responses to the continued over-representation of Indian children within the child welfare system. "We formed work groups with tribes and tribal organization and alliances with NICWA. We held a conference up in Canada on reconciliation," Bilchik recalls. Bilchik's apology is a moving example of taking action where we can to make redress and promote reconciliation.

But it also points to the limits of a grassroots approach. Without a *national* apology and a *national* commitment to Indian child welfare, Bilchik and the CWLA, as well as their tribal partners, were stymied in what they could achieve. Bilchik notes that "this was all happening in the context of a major upheaval in child welfare funding. It was a horrible time economically; organizations were folding, state budgets were crashing." The CWLA apology could only repair so much of the damage between settlers and Indigenous people; a national apology and truth and reconciliation process were needed, too.

Apologies have been a key component of truth and reconciliation efforts worldwide. They, in fact, link truth with reconciliation. Once truths have come to the surface but before reconciliation can occur, there must be a genuine expression of regret by representatives of those who inflicted suffering to those who have been harmed. For an apology to be effective, it must involve words of sorrow that are mindful of the specific grievance, and it must be delivered publicly by the right person to the right audience at the right time.

While words alone are insufficient to bring reconciliation and make redress, they are nevertheless powerful and contribute to healing. As Janna Thompson explains, reparative justice "always requires an acknowledgement of injustice, some act that makes it possible for members of the wronged nation to believe that those who have done them wrong are confronting their history and will henceforth treat them with respect."

Apologies are crucial. They are also not enough.

CHAPTER 11

Where the Mouth Is

Apologies and other symbolic actions may be meaningless without some form of substantive redress. Van Boven and Bassiouni's principles include four other important interventions: restitution, rehabilitation, compensation, and guarantees of non-repetition. These principles all involve concrete actions, deeds, and material recompense rather than mere words.

Restitution refers to efforts to restore victims to their original state before they had been subject to gross violations of their human rights. This, for example, might mean that members of a persecuted group who had lost property in a conflict could regain their homes and lands. We have seen that Friends of the Indian in the nineteenth century originally favored such an approach; they sought to return land to the Poncas and other tribes.

Rehabilitation includes the provision of legal and social services as well as medical and psychological care to victims of abuse. *Compensation* entails payments to victims of human rights abuses for whom restitution is not possible. *Guarantees of non-repetition* require new policies and laws aimed to prevent future harms.

Van Boven and Bassiouni designed these principles primarily with certain short-term conflicts in mind: civil wars, short-term genocides, and abusive dictatorships. They were thinking of places like Cambodia and Argentina. They were not imagining chronic abuses that occurred and accrued over a century or more. They were not envisioning policies and practices that became utterly normalized in settler colonial states— such as the removal of Indigenous children—over many generations.

They did not develop their principles for abuses that occurred over a century ago. Restitution may be nearly impossible in these cases. In New Zealand, for example, the Treaty of Waitangi Tribunal will not return land to *iwis* on which settlers now dwell.

Yet the other remaining van Boven/Bassiouni principles—rehabilitation, compensation, and guarantees of non-repetition—were very relevant to Dodson and other Indigenous truth and reconciliation leaders. Of these, rehabilitation sparked little to no controversy or opposition. The Canadian and Australian governments were willing, at least for a limited number of years, to fund healing foundations to support Indigenous-run rehabilitative services.

Compensation was much more controversial and was a long time in coming. Indian residential school survivors brought litigation and class action lawsuits for years before the government negotiated the Indian Residential School Settlement Agreement, which required that Canada pay reparations to survivors. Similarly, it took decades for members of the Stolen Generations to gain compensation in Australia, and then it came only from some states, not the federal government.

These reparations have not necessarily brought reconciliation and healing to Indigenous peoples. In many cases they have come too late. Thousands upon thousands of those who suffered under child removal policies died while government officials negotiated over compensation details. Some recipients, too, have had to relive their trauma in order to gain compensation. It has also been unsettling to have one's pain and suffering quantified. Reparations alone, without all the other components of restorative justice, can feel hollow.

Indeed, while Canada and Australia apologized and made monetary recompense for child removal, they failed to uphold van Boven/Bassiouni's guarantees of non-repetition, or "Never Again," principle. Interestingly, the United States, through the Indian Child Welfare Act of 1978, has implicitly recognized the wrongs of Indigenous child removal and committed to "never again" engage in such practices, even as it has failed to deliver an apology or compensation.

Mick Dodson knew that an apology alone would be an empty gesture without some form of material redress for all that the Stolen

Generations had suffered. Thus, the *Bringing Them Home* report recommended that the Commonwealth (or federal) government establish a National Compensation Fund to administer minimum lump-sum payments to members of the Stolen Generations as well as additional compensation for proof of "particular harm."

If you thought the conservative government under Prime Minister John Howard was utterly recalcitrant in offering an apology to the Stolen Generations, imagine how it reacted when asked to compensate victims. Howard even more fervently rejected calls for any kind of monetary reparations to those Indigenous people who had been separated from their families. He claimed to be concerned with "practical reconciliation," which he defined as improving the material circumstances of Aboriginal peoples. Australians call this "closing the gap," an effort to bridge the vast differences in health, housing, education, employment, income, and life expectancy between settler and Indigenous Australians. As but one example of this chasm, for Indigenous Australians born between 2015 and 2017, life expectancy was estimated to be 8.6 years less than that of the non-Indigenous population for males and 7.8 years for females.

Critics of Howard claimed that in focusing on "closing the gap," he had completely reduced the meaning of reconciliation. The influential historian Henry Reynolds asserted that Howard "appears to see reconciliation as being about improving service delivery. It is a narrow, unimaginative and essentially assimilationist view." Moreover, Howard envisioned only a limited role for Indigenous leaders in designing and carrying out "practical reconciliation." His policy perpetuated paternalism toward Indigenous people.

Howard emphasized, too, the granting of formal equality to Aboriginal people. This may sound progressive, but it was actually a means to evade Indigenous grievances. Howard asserted that Indigenous people should be treated no differently than other Australians, that they should not have what he called "special rights." This meant that the government refused to recognize the unique position of Indigenous peoples as the original inhabitants of Australia and to be accountable for the distinctive crimes and abuses it had committed against them. Howard's policy was still premised on destroying the unique nature of Indigenous peoples and undermining their land claims and rights to self-determination.

Because of the government's utter refusal to consider compensation, many members of the Stolen Generations took their cases to court. This was a difficult road. Courts required that Stolen Generations members prove that their removal was unlawful or that government authorities were negligent. Since removal was allowed by law, it has been hard going for Aboriginal people to make any gains in the court system. So far only one plaintiff has been successful: Bruce Trevorrow, who brought a case against the South Australia government in 1998. In 2007, nearly fifty years after being taken from his family, Trevorrow was awarded A$525,000.

When the Labor government took over in 2008, and Prime Minister Rudd swiftly delivered an apology to the Stolen Generations, many believed that the government would finally make some sort of compensation to Indigenous victims of child removal. Rudd had, in fact, declared, "unless the great symbolism of reconciliation is accompanied by an even greater substance, it is little more than a clanging gong."

Australia seemed poised to take this next step of restorative justice: substantive compensation for members of the Stolen Generations. Dodson declared, "Whatever happens now in Australia, there is one thing we cannot say, and that is: Now that the nation has apologized, the mistakes of the past do not matter. They matter even more now, and as a nation, we have an obligation to address and to correct those mistakes." Dodson added, "While the apology is hugely symbolic for our country, it does and should not end there; we still have to tackle all the unfinished business if we are to obtain a true and lasting reconciliation."

But Australia did not deliver on compensation. Just five months after Rudd's apology, an Australian Senate committee rejected a bill to compensate Australia's Stolen Generations, instead recommending an Aboriginal Healing Foundation. Such a foundation is an important and valuable government intervention, but it falls under van Boven/ Bassiouni's principle of rehabilitation. Experts in restorative justice believed that apology and rehabilitation alone would not bring full redress.

It turns out that the Australian government, and many of the settlers it represents, was reluctant to put its money where its mouth was. One government official explained the government's position: "The Commonwealth . . . did not . . . accept the recommendations concerning individual monetary compensation and a national compensation tribunal: first monetary compensation to individuals is not seen as the most appropriate way of dealing with family separation; second, given the varied and largely undocumented circumstances of the individual historical events in question, it would be impossible to devise and apply any such scheme in a practical and equitable manner." The minister insinuated that Indigenous testimony did not constitute legitimate documentation—a tried-and-true way of denying Indigenous grievances. He implied, too, that there were not copious written records to back up Indigenous claims, when in reality, historians had been uncovering these crimes through archival sources for decades.

Most gallingly, after subsequent inquiries into abuses against children, Australia made compensation for British child migrants and then for children who suffered from sexual abuse in institutions. Why was it appropriate to provide individual monetary payments to settlers but not to Indigenous people?

Some Australian states have made restitution for child removal. There is a logic to this, as Aboriginal policy administration fell to states, not the federal government, except for the Northern Territory. In 2006, Tasmania established a fund of $5 million for victims. But by that time, a decade after the Stolen Generations inquiry, only 106 applicants qualified, and 45 were rejected. Each successful applicant received about A$47,000.

Another state, Western Australia, in 2007 combined its reparations to the Stolen Generations into its more general Redress Scheme, which offered compensation for the "Forgotten Australians," children who were brought up in institutions or out-of-home care. To qualify for compensation, a claimant had to have suffered "very severe abuse and/or neglect with ongoing symptoms and disability." Removal alone was not sufficient grounds for making a claim. Over 10,000 people registered with Redress Western Australia; almost half of them were members of the Stolen Generations. However, many survivors refused to lodge a claim because they didn't want to relive the suffering and pain for what they considered to be menial returns, a maximum of A$45,000 per claim.

It wasn't until 2015 that South Australia announced an $11 million reparation fund (eight years after the Bruce Trevorrow decision). What had changed the state government's mind was a parliamentary committee report in 2013 that found a reparation fund would be cheaper for the government than fighting legal claims. An estimated 300 members of the Stolen Generations have been eligible for payments of up to A$50,000 under its program.

New South Wales followed in 2017 by agreeing to pay $75,000 to each survivor who came into the care of the New South Wales Aborigines Protection or Welfare Boards under the 1909 Aborigines Protection Act, which was in effect until 1969. An estimated 700–1,300 survivors were alive in NSW in 2017. Two states—Victoria and Queensland—and the Northern Territory have failed to provide any compensation to Stolen Generations survivors.

At the national level, Rudd and his Labor government were as opposed to reparations for individual members of the Stolen Generations as Howard had been. Rudd's "greater substance" called only for expanding services to help the Stolen Generations trace their families and "closing the gap" between Indigenous and non-Indigenous Australians.

To Mick Dodson and many other critics, Rudd's proposals merely echoed the Howard government's practical reconciliation program from the 1990s. "The Australian government has linked the apology to closing the gaps while dismissing the call to compensate the members of the Stolen Generations. The desire of government and just about every other Australian, including Indigenous Australians, to close the gaps is a given, but the grievance for compensation will not go away."

Ironically, while continuing to bemoan the ongoing settler-Indigenous disparities, Australian efforts to "close the gap" have failed miserably. In 2020, the 12th *Closing the Gap* report showed that the nation was on track to "meet just two of seven government targets to reduce the disparity in health, education and employment outcomes." The

Australian government has been talking about "closing the gap" since at least the 1990s, but it has made little to no improvement. Prime Minister Scott Morrison vowed in 2020 to replace the government's top-down approach with a plan developed by Indigenous people themselves. Will the government finally listen to Indigenous people and take their advice about what they really need?

Canada's reparations to Indian residential school survivors have been more extensive than those for the Stolen Generations in Australia. The Indian Residential School Settlement Agreement mandated reparations to survivors through two separate processes: the Common Experience Payment (CEP) and the Independent Assessment Process (IAP). To apply for and receive a CEP, a survivor simply had to prove attendance at one of the officially recognized residential schools. The CEP recognized that removal itself constituted a human rights violation that deserved compensation. Of the 105,530 survivors who applied for a CEP, 79,309 were successful in obtaining compensation. The CEP paid claimants an average of $20,457 based on attendance of 4.5 years.

The government set up the IAP to enable survivors who had suffered from sexual and/or physical abuse in the schools to make additional claims. The government expected only about 10 percent of survivors would apply for this extra compensation. Instead 38,087 people, or more than a third of all survivors, filed a claim with the IAP. By March 2016 the IAP had settled 91 percent of these cases, paying an average of $97,538 to each survivor, plus 15 percent lawyers' fees.

Compared to Australia's compensation schemes, Canada's process seemed far more comprehensive. But even there, reparations were not necessarily the panacea that survivors had hoped for. Most Métis and many Inuit people did not qualify because of technicalities. Because the IAP was overwhelmed by the number of claimants, the average claim took twenty-one months to resolve. Many survivors complained that they found little support for filling out CEP or IAP applications.

The primary problem with Canadian reparations, however, was the way in which the process retraumatized survivors. The Whose Settlement conference in Regina in October 2019 allowed me to hear firsthand from not only survivors but also adjudicators from the Independent Assessment Process. The chief adjudicator, Dan Shapiro, a settler, spoke during a keynote panel. He explained that the process was meant to be claimant-centered and not to replicate the cross-examination of a courtroom. He told us that their goal was that every claimant was to be respected and leave feeling as if they had been heard.

But the process may have inadvertently wounded Indigenous residential school survivors all over again. Adjudicators for the Canadian government, many of them non-Indigenous, used a crude point system (which critics dubbed the "meat chart") to determine the payment to be made to survivors. The chart assigned points to various levels of abuse, with 45–60 points for "repeated, persistent incidents of anal or vaginal intercourse," 36–44 points for "one or more incidents of anal or vaginal intercourse" and/or "repeated, persistent incidents of oral intercourse," 26–35 points for "one or more incidents of oral intercourse." And on and on. Severe beatings: 11–25 points. Fondling or kissing: 5–10 points.

The Independent Assessment Process required claimants to dredge up painful memories and talk about the details of sexual abuse, how long it had lasted, and how often it happened. It was less harsh than cross-examination in a court of law, but survivors still had to disclose a lot of difficult information. And then adjudicators quantified and scored their suffering.

Caron George, an adjudicator with the Independent Assessment Process, another panelist, told us that after adjudicating these and other claims for twelve years, she had learned from the IAP that the specificity and detail they had required had led to retraumatizing survivors. It took twelve years to learn this? Not twelve minutes?

Ry Moran, the Métis director of Canada's National Centre for Truth and Reconciliation, also was on the panel. He said that sometimes healing occurred through this process, but often it was harmful. Organizers of the Whose Settlement conference hoped that Sixties Scoop survivors would not have to experience the same trauma in gaining compensation for their suffering. As Moran sees it, the TRC had shone a light on violence within Canadian society. The TRC's aim was to make peace. So, he says, we need to use peace to bring peace. There should not be any processes that involve violence, such as the IAP.

The new settlement process for survivors of the Sixties Scoop might have a chance at getting reparations right, but it falls short in other areas. It shows how reparations without other crucial aspects of redress can be hollow and unsatisfying. Dan Shapiro is concerned that the new settlement does not include a truth commission. Thus, survivors of the Sixties Scoop are not getting the kind of "satisfaction" that comes from telling their stories and having them heard. Instead at hearings on the new settlement, organizers have allowed each survivor just three minutes to speak. Another keynote speaker, Robert Doucette, executive director of Saskatoon Indian and Métis Friendship Centre and a Sixties Scoop survivor, told us he hosted a gathering to find out what survivors wanted. "They didn't feel respected," he said. "They felt like no one wanted to listen to them."

The settlement's compensation scheme has also been problematic because many of the Indigenous people who were most affected by the Sixties Scoop—the Métis—were not included in the settlement. (They were also barred from receiving compensation under the Indian Residential Schools Settlement Agreement.) The Métis are a unique group in Canadian society, descendants of European fur traders and Indigenous women, primarily around the Red River colony in present-day Manitoba. But even though the Canadian government recognizes the Métis as one of three Indigenous groups in the nation, and even though adoption programs like the Adopt Indian Métis program in Saskatchewan explicitly targeted Métis children, only so-called "status Indians" are eligible for Sixties Scoop compensation.

Many Sixties Scoop survivors who are eligible for payments thought that the proposed compensation was simply inadequate. An audience member spoke up at the conference, "There's part of me that feels that [the proposed compensation] is an absolute insult." Many survivors have asked, how can you put a price on suffering? How can you ever provide enough money to compensate someone who was taken from her family for many years and subjected to a harsh upbringing, and often physically and sexually abused? Many survivors have come to feel that the payments were actually just another means of silencing them. Now that you have been paid, we don't want to hear this story ever again.

Reparations have also generated public discussions in Canada, and Australia, that reinforce and perpetuate old, tired representations of Indigenous people. Many conservative critics complained that survivors wasted their compensation on drugs and alcohol. Even liberal settlers have implicitly conveyed the view that most Indigenous people are alcoholics and drug addicts; they sympathize with their "plight," but they warn that a sudden infusion of money can just worsen survivors' drug and alcohol abuse.

These discussions rely on timeworn stereotypes of Indigenous people as dysfunctional and unable to care for their own affairs. This paternalistic undercurrent often accompanies any discussion of reparations for Indigenous peoples. It echoes discussions from the turn of the twentieth century that characterized Indigenous people as perpetual children who needed "protection." Earlier policies insisted on putting Indigenous assets—including money earned while working as domestic servants and cattle herders—in trust funds. Many of these funds have disappeared mysteriously; protecting Indigenous people's money became just another means to plunder them. Curiously there have been no such discussions about the potential damage that reparations can do for other recipients, such as Japanese Americans or Japanese Canadians who suffered internment during World War II, or the families of victims of 9/11.

In the United States, we have frequent and contentious discussions of monetary reparations for past historical wrongs but nearly always in the context of making amends to African Americans for slavery, Jim Crow, lynching, and other abuses uniquely suffered by blacks. At the national level, talk of reparations comes up periodically, including during the Democratic primary debates in 2019 and 2020. But the issue then recedes again into the background.

Nevertheless, some institutions are considering reparations to slave descendants. Mélisande Short-Colomb did genealogical research into seven generations of her family, discovering that she was descended

from one of 272 slaves that the Jesuit priests who administered Georgetown College sold to keep the college afloat in 1838. She connected with
Richard Cellini, founder of the Georgetown Memory Project, who has,
so far, identified 8,425 descendants of the 272 slaves. Cellini started the
project after a story about the Georgetown slave auction ran in the student newspaper. Short-Colomb became a student at Georgetown University in her sixties, under a program that the university started to give
admissions preference to the 8,000 descendants of those slaves.

Short-Colomb has perhaps taught other students and university faculty and administrators as much as she has learned. She has led efforts
by students to get the university to make amends to the 8,000 descendants. In April 2019 students voted for the university to pay reparations
to them, which would add $27.20 to their tuition and student fees. Not
all students support the reparations; some think the university, not the
students, should pay it. Others, particularly international students, don't
think they should pay for what earlier generations of Americans did.

Georgetown responded to the students' non-binding referendum in
October 2019 that it would raise $400,000 a year to create programs—
such as schools and health clinics—to benefit the descendants. It "embraced the spirit of the student referendum," according to the university
president, but it did not agree to pay individual reparations, much to the
disappointment of many Georgetown students.

Georgetown is not alone in reckoning with its past and mulling over
reparations. Many other universities, including Harvard, Yale, Brown,
and Princeton, have admitted that they profited from the slave trade.
Only a few so far, with religious ties, have taken steps similar to those of
Georgetown. Princeton Theological Seminary and Virginia Theological
Seminary have established reparations funds—in the millions—to
atone for their ties to slavery. They are using these funds for scholarships
and funding new faculty positions related to the study of African Americans. Positive as these steps are, some critics have questioned whether
scholarships really qualify as reparations, since the funds will be paid
back into the institution in the form of tuition payments.

Some municipalities have also weighed reparations for abuses against
African Americans. In 1997, the Oklahoma state legislature established

a commission to investigate the 1921 Tulsa Race Massacre. It hired a team of distinguished historians, including John Hope Franklin, a descendant of one of the riot's survivors. Commissioners documented how white supremacist mobs, including police officers and city leaders, slaughtered an estimated three hundred African Americans and looted and burned down their properties and businesses. They noted that no one had even been brought to justice for the violence and that victims had never been compensated for their losses. The Tulsa Race Riot Commission recommended a broad plan for reconciliation, including reparations.

But city and state residents did not favor *any* individual compensation. A 2000 poll found that 57 percent opposed any form of reparations payments, even if it came from private sources. Only 12 percent of respondents said reparations should be paid with tax money. The state legislature agreed to make a strong condemnation of the massacre; to provide money for scholarships for descendants (but not to be paid for with tax money); and to allocate $750,000 to a riot memorial commission. Historian Alfred Brophy notes wryly that the legislature "seemed willing to take any action, so long as it did not spend money on survivors." The city of Tulsa and the state of Oklahoma's refusal to pay reparations has continued to frustrate descendants. In September 2020, a group of black Tulsans filed a lawsuit to gain reparations from the city.

Many other communities across the United States have similar histories of heinous violence against African Americans. The Equal Justice Initiative has documented more than 4,000 lynchings between 1877 and 1950. In 99 percent of cases, the white perpetrators escaped justice and were never prosecuted for their crimes. Moreover, the lynchings were public spectacles that attracted extensive support from whites and engendered widespread terror among blacks. Since 1900, Congress has considered anti-lynching bills that would define the atrocity as a federal hate crime. But when a bill finally passed in 2020, Senator Rand Paul of Kentucky stymied it.

Sherrilyn Ifill, the director of the NAACP Legal Defense Fund, has written about communities that are trying to come to grips with their gruesome histories of white supremacy and lynching of African

Americans. Ifill sees such local initiatives not as a next-best alternative to some form of national reconciliation but as the only means by which we can truly heal the wounds of the past. "Reconciliation cannot be achieved at the national level," she writes. "Historically, racism was felt, lived, and perpetrated locally. Reconciliation, therefore, must also be local." She adds, "No 'national conversation' can take the place of a locally based dialogue in which members of a discrete community come together to talk about how specific instances of racial violence affected their community."

Ifill takes an expansive view of reparations. She believes that it may be more productive to consider reparations beyond individual financial compensation. She advocates for the importance of memorializing lynching in public spaces, as Bryan Stevenson has done in Montgomery, Alabama, and through new school curricula. Ifill also takes the long view. "Reparations, like reconciliation, must be regarded as a process, not an event," she concludes.

The nationwide and global protests spurred by George Floyd's murder at the hands of police in Minneapolis in 2020 added to the momentum around the urgent need for redress for the centuries of abuses that African Americans have endured, at both the local and the national level. But there seems to be little consciousness in the United States that reparations may be due to Indigenous peoples, too.

There are few models in the United States for substantive redress for historical injustices. Perhaps the closest example would be the story of Japanese Americans who obtained reparations for their internment during World War II. The Japanese American Citizens League (JACL) convinced Congress to establish a commission to investigate the internment of 110,000 Japanese immigrants and their children during World War II. As with the Canadian TRC process, it was the threat of a massive class action lawsuit that seemed to finally get Congress to face up to its moral obligations. The JACL had a powerful advocate in Senator Daniel Inouye of Hawaii (who incidentally was also a strong ally to Indigenous peoples). The commission not only established the truth of what occurred—Japanese Americans were unfairly interned for no security reason—and enacted a bill that made a formal apology to Japanese Americans. It also recommended reparations. Congress passed a separate bill that allocated \$1.2 billion in the form of per capita payments of \$20,000 for each survivor. Historian Elazar Barkan calls this combination of monetary and moral redress "the sine qua non of restitution movements everywhere."

Would a similar process work to make compensation to the Stolen Generations of the United States? There are many barriers to achieving such reparations for Indian child removal in the United States. The investigation of Japanese American internment and the awarding of reparations to its victims concerned a one-time event that had a clear beginning and end over a period of just a few years. Indian child removal, on the other hand, has spanned at least a century, has had multigenerational effects, and is even now still going on.

Moreover, the government had exact numbers and copious records for each Japanese American internee. Records of boarding schools are often buried deep in government archives dispersed across the nation. The boarding schools were at their most coercive and abusive before World War II, so the children who suffered in those institutions have long since died, and governments have been reluctant to compensate descendants.

And what about those American Indians who were put into foster care and up for adoption—the equivalent of Canada's Sixties Scoop? Do they deserve an apology and reparations, too?

Many of you might be convinced that the American Indian children that the U.S. government or state governments removed from their families and communities deserve some form of recompense for the abuses they suffered. But many of you might just think it's impractical and too expensive to engage in truth and reconciliation for Indigenous child removal survivors and their descendants.

But think about what we did for the victims of 9/11. Just two weeks after the tragedy, Congress passed the Air Transportation Safety and System Stabilization Act, which included the September 11th Victim Compensation Fund. This fund provided generous tax-free compensation to families of those who died or were injured during 9/11. How generous? Kenneth Feinberg, the special master in charge of the fund, had wide discretion to compensate victims and their families.

Congress did not even impose any limit on the amount of money to be distributed. It gave Feinberg only three instructions: (1) that he should consider pain and suffering and emotional distress; (2) that he should factor in economic loss to his compensation packages; and (3) that he should deduct any collateral sources of income available to claimants (such as life insurance) from their awards. The second stipulation meant that those making the most money would receive the highest compensation. That means that a stockbroker could be awarded $30–40 million more than a janitor.

Ultimately, Feinberg determined that at a minimum every legitimate claimant would receive $250,000. He claims, too, to have sought to narrow the gap between the highest and lowest compensation packages, although he is not forthcoming about the ultimate awards that he made. All told, Feinberg distributed $7 billion in public money to 5,562 people. You can do the math. That's an average of $1.25 million per person. Many of those compensated were already high-earning millionaires who worked on Wall Street. I don't recall that there was any debate about these reparations at all. I didn't even know about them until I came across Feinberg's book while writing this one.

Surely if we can make that form of compensation to the victims of 9/11, we can also come up with reparations for Indigenous people who were wrongly separated from their families as children, either to attend a boarding school or to be fostered or adopted in a non-Indian family. Whatever we may be able to achieve along these lines in the United States, we must be mindful of the Canadian experience with reparations. Compensation must be part of a comprehensive package of reckoning that addresses more of the van Boven/Bassiouni principles. It must also be done in a way that does not re-create the violence and abuse, as Ry Moran pointed out.

Australia's and Canada's truth and reconciliation processes have built some goodwill between settlers and Indigenous people, but they have neglected—or actually violated—van Boven/Bassiouni's final principle:

guarantees of non-repetition, or more simply, "Never Again." Rudd's apology had brought great hope to Indigenous people that finally the Australian government was taking their grievances seriously. But it soon rang hollow. He had declared with great fervor that "the injustices of the past must never, never happen again." But he soon intensified a government intervention into Northern Territory Aboriginal communities to respond to reports of widespread domestic violence and child abuse. Authorities again resorted to sweeping up children into the child welfare system and terrorizing families. Indigenous leaders were outraged. They did not deny that there were problems in Aboriginal communities, but they insisted that settler state authorities should be working closely with Indigenous leaders to create preventive and rehabilitative measures. Instead they were once again demonizing Indigenous families and forcibly removing their children.

Moreover, even as Australia sputtered toward an apology and states made recompense for the Stolen Generations, there has been little progress in lowering the numbers of Indigenous children that state social service agencies have taken out of their homes and into state care. As of June 2018, state authorities in Australia were sweeping up Indigenous children into the child welfare system at a rate 10.2 times that of non-Indigenous children. All the while, government officials were spending 83 percent of their budget on child removal and thus only 17 percent on family support services that would enable children to stay within their families. Jacynta Krakouer, a Noongar woman who teaches social work at the Melbourne School of Health Sciences, wonders if this is a second stolen generations or merely the continuation of earlier policies. The policy and practice of Indigenous child removal has quietly continued with no sustained effort to address its root causes and reverse it.

Similarly, in Canada, the rates of Indigenous children in care are higher than they have ever been. In 2016, Indigenous children were 7.7 percent of all Canadian children but were 52.2 percent of all children in foster care. At the Whose Settlement conference, Robert Doucette declared, "Now we are moving into a millennium scoop." He noted how troubling it is that this is still occurring in the age of reconciliation.

Australia and Canada are failing to carry out the Never Again principles in other ways, too. Despite its obvious need and value, both the Canadian and Australian governments have cut funding for rehabilitation in recent years. Their attitudes seem to be that we've funded that long enough and we can't do it forever. But this is immensely short-sighted. Healing, especially from a century of intergenerational policies of family separation, is a long-term proposition. And it is key to ensuring that these abuses Never Again occur.

Indigenous activists in Canada have successfully challenged their government's failure to resolve the Indigenous child welfare crisis. Due to the unceasing efforts of Indigenous activist Cindy Blackstock, the Canadian Human Rights Tribunal determined in September 2019 that the "federal government was willfully and recklessly discriminating against First Nations children in ways that contributed to child deaths and a multitude of unnecessary family separations." The tribunal ordered Canada to pay $40,000 to each victim of its discrimination, dating back to 2006.

The Canadian government, while professing support for reconciliation, has fought against this new ruling. Prime Minister Trudeau filed a court case to deny this compensation to victims. Faced with the government's recalcitrance, in September 2020, the Assembly of First Nations launched a class action lawsuit against the federal government over funding for Indian child welfare services and health care for children living on Indian reserves. In December 2020, Murray Sinclair, one of the TRC's commissioners, declared, "There are still far too many things this government is doing to diminish the position and rights of Indigenous people."

So, despite a robust truth and reconciliation commission, an apology, and reparations, Canada has not fulfilled the Never Again principle. Indigenous activists led by Blackstock have thus proposed legislation (An Act Respecting First Nations, Inuit and Métis Children, Youth and Families) that would build safeguards into the child welfare system to reverse the over-representation of Indigenous children and help strengthen Indigenous families and communities, and thus obviate the conditions that lead to removal. This legislation is similar to the Indian Child Welfare Act, a law that was enacted in 1978 in the United States.

Ironically, the United States unintentionally adhered to the Never Again principle. We have had *no* national truth and reconciliation around Indigenous child removal, *no* apology, and *no* reparations, but due to a ten-year campaign from 1968 to 1978 by Indigenous leaders and their settler allies, we have the 1978 Indian Child Welfare Act, a key piece of legislation meant to reverse child removal.

ICWA has a strong Never Again quality. It was meant to stop the unwarranted removal of Indian children from their communities and to prevent it from happening again in the future. It provides strong legal protections to families, requires the highest level of proof of neglect or abuse to remove a child from his or her family, and prioritizes the placement of a removed Indian child with an Indian family.

The law was supposed to also have a rehabilitative component; it included a provision for sufficient funding to Indigenous communities to run their own social programs to strengthen Indigenous families and reverse a century of child removal. However, Congress never appropriated enough money to fund Indian programs.

The legislation added a crucial element—tribal sovereignty—to the equation. It gives tribes exclusive jurisdiction over children domiciled on reservations and concurrent jurisdiction with states for children living off-reservation. Thus, ICWA has primarily functioned as a means for tribes to keep Indian children within Indian communities, if not within their own families.

But ICWA has been almost constantly under threat since its passage. Some states, especially South Dakota, have sought to evade the law and conservative groups have also been challenging the law for decades with the ultimate goal of having it declared unconstitutional. They were overjoyed by the Supreme Court's 5–4 ruling in the 2013 *Adoptive Couple v. Baby Girl* (or Baby Veronica) case that allowed a child to be placed for adoption against the wishes of her Cherokee father with a white settler family. In 2018, a district court in Texas ruled ICWA unconstitutional in the *Brackeen* case. The case is likely to go to the U.S. Supreme Court, where plaintiffs believe they will find sympathetic justices who are willing to overturn ICWA.

Thus, efforts to address Indigenous child removal in the United States have occurred almost exclusively in the legislative and litigative world and have primarily addressed the Never Again van Boven principle. ICWA has helped tribes stem the hemorrhaging of children from their families and communities, but the underlying settler attitudes, practices, and policies that led to Indigenous child removal are still in play in the United States. Court cases can bring meaningful victories, but they are costly, in both financial and emotional ways. And it is doubtful that legal challenges alone can bring true healing to Indigenous families and a wholesale change in attitudes among non-Indigenous people. The ongoing threat to ICWA, too, suggests that a more comprehensive national truth and reconciliation process is necessary.

The deeper one digs into truth and reconciliation between Indigenous people and settlers, the more it becomes apparent that there is no simple formula for success. The van Boven/Bassiouni principles provide a useful guide, but thus far no settler government has enacted all of them in regard to the abuse of Indigenous child removal. Moreover, the principles can only take us so far, designed as they were for very different kinds of conflicts. We can see that without regard for the unique status of Indigenous peoples, reconciliation may be doomed to fail.

When it comes to reckoning with settler abuses of Indigenous peoples, we need a more expansive framework. In the 1990s, Mick Dodson and Ronald Wilson could call on the van Boven/Bassiouni principles as they confronted the abuses the Stolen Generations had suffered. By the time of the Canadian TRC, its three commissioners had a new tool at their disposal, the 2007 United Nations Declaration on the Rights of Indigenous Peoples (UNDRIP).

In his book *In the Light of Justice,* Pawnee legal scholar Walter Echo-Hawk asserts that UNDRIP "is aimed at restoring the human rights of Indigenous peoples that fell by the wayside during the colonization of their homelands. . . . It defines human rights and fundamental freedoms in the unique Indigenous context, and it prescribes the duties of the state necessary to fully realize these human rights." Tellingly, there were only four nations that voted against UNDRIP when it came before the United Nations General Assembly in 2007: Canada, Australia, New Zealand, and the United States. In 2010, however, all four nations reversed their position. The last to do so was the United States, under President Barack Obama.

UNDRIP declares that Indigenous peoples are "equal to all other peoples," "should be free from discrimination of any kind," and retain a right to be different. It asserts self-determination as a fundamental human right, the notion that "all peoples are entitled to be in control of their own destinies and live within governing bodies that are devised accordingly." Echo-Hawk explains that this does not include a right to secede; "rather indigenous self-determination runs parallel to state sovereignty and takes place within the body of the state." UNDRIP affirms that Indigenous people have the right to participate in government decisions that affect their lives. We saw how devastating it was to the Poncas in the 1870s to be denied this right.

Article 8 of UNDRIP prohibits forced assimilation and the destruction of Indigenous culture. Article 14 stipulates that education may not be used to assimilate children or undermine their cultures. Several articles address the need to halt and reverse land dispossession and affirm Indigenous peoples' broad rights to land, territories, and resources. UNDRIP also notes the urgent need to respect and promote Indigenous treaty rights.

The Canadian TRC commissioners used UNDRIP to Indigenize truth and reconciliation and the restorative justice movement. Their *Final Report*'s Calls to Action incorporate UNDRIP's framework and vision. In December 2020 Commissioner Sinclair reiterated his support for UNDRIP and pointed out its foundational importance to changing the basis for reconciliation: "we will never achieve reconciliation when one side to the dialogue sees it as an act of benevolence and one side sees it as a recognition of rights."

Mick Dodson had relied heavily on the van Boven/Bassiouni principles as a means to bring justice, healing, and redress to Australia's Indigenous people. Valuable as the principles were, the two jurists had designed them with very different kinds of historical conflicts in mind. They were never a perfect fit for redressing the crimes of settler colonial nations, and they can only take us so far. They do not address the paternalism at the heart of settler colonialism and the desire on the part of Indigenous people to reclaim their sovereignty and gain a greater voice in determining their own destinies. They do not address the founding crimes at the heart of our settler colonial nations: the stealing of land and the dispossession of Indigenous peoples. By integrating UNDRIP's vision and provisions into its *Final Report,* the Canadian TRC explicitly connected the abuses of the residential schools with a broad agenda for respecting Indigenous rights.

Van Boven/Bassiouni's principles, too, have focused entirely on redress at a national level. But in settler colonial nations where abuses have been long-standing and ongoing, Sherilynn Ifill's insights about the need for local reconciliation seem particularly apt. And it is at the local level where we settlers may develop the relationships with and support the aspirations of Indigenous people for truth and reconciliation. I learned this firsthand in the place where I have settled: Nebraska.

PART FOUR

A Groundswell for Reconciliation

CHAPTER 12

Skulls

In October 2018 I boarded a plane in Omaha that was bound for Dallas. As the other passengers and I settled into our seats, the pilot informed us that this was a special flight. We were bringing home a soldier—after seventy years—who had not been properly buried. Ten minutes before the plane landed, we learned more of his story. The service member, who had died in battle during World War II, had been improperly identified and buried in Nebraska. Somehow, after so many decades, DNA tests had revealed the misidentification, and the man was now to be returned to his home and his kin in Idaho. His great-nephew, a private first class in the Army, was accompanying the soldier home. An honor guard met the plane in Dallas.

For once I was glad that I was seated near the back of the plane and by the window. As the plane pulled up to the gate, I could watch the ten or so members of the military standing at full attention to properly honor the service member. The honor guard carried out a solemn ceremony as the man's casket, draped in a flag, rolled out of the cargo hold and down the plane's conveyor belt. The passengers were all reverent as we disembarked. No one jostled for position to rush off the plane. No one spoke. A few covertly snapped pictures of the moving ceremony. Everyone understood the gravity of properly interring this man at his family's burial plot in Idaho.

As I watched this dignified ceremony, I thought of what I had learned only recently about what had happened to the graves of Pawnee people in the state I now call home. Just a few months before my Dallas flight,

Rosebud Sioux journalist Kevin Abourezk, Kiowa filmmaker Boots Kennedye, and I had interviewed Roger Welsch, a settler who lives in Dannebrog, Nebraska, a town that bills itself as the "Danish Park on the Prairie."

It was a milder day than most in July. We left Lincoln when it was still cool and pulled up into Dannebrog about midmorning, where Welsch was waiting for us on Main Street, just off Roger Welsch Way. Yes, the town named a street for Welsch, a lifelong Nebraskan of German descent, a retired professor of folklore, a raconteur who served as a former commentator on *CBS Sunday Morning*, and the author of over sixty books with titles like *Love, Sex and Tractors*.

Welsch told us that in 1988 he had become a member of the board of the Nebraska State Historical Society. It was "the highest thing I ever aspired to," he said, in an uncharacteristically solemn manner. At his very first board meeting, "the Pawnee were the last item on the agenda." They had come to ask the Historical Society to request that the bones of their ancestors be repatriated to the tribe so that they could properly rebury them. "We finished all of our business," Welsch recalled, "and it's, oh yeah, well these guys are here to ask the ridiculous!"

The board did not seem to think it odd that the Historical Society had thousands of Pawnee ancestral remains within their storage vaults. Moreover, they immediately rebuffed the Pawnees' request. All the board members, none of whom were of Indigenous descent, considered any bones and artifacts found in Pawnee graves in Nebraska to be the property of the Historical Society. Welsch explained to us how he went along with the rest of the board: "As a scholar and Historical Society board member, I'm there to protect the property of the State Historical Society." He thought, at the time, the Pawnees' request for the remains was "insane." The board members believed "these are items for scientific research; you don't bury them; some of these things are beautiful items: cradle boards and so forth. You don't just bury them. We have . . . unique historical pieces that are incredibly valuable."

It was this interview with Welsch, just a few months before, that came to my mind as I watched the reverent ceremony for the improperly buried soldier's casket at the Dallas airport. Why was the attitude of the

Historical Society so dismissive of the Pawnees, who simply wanted to properly rebury their ancestors? Why, by contrast, was so much effort being made to return the remains of this soldier from Nebraska to Idaho so he could be reinterred?

The Historical Society is in an innocuous-looking building on the very campus where I have taught history since 2004. Here was the place I brought students to get their first taste of archival research and to see if they had the history bug. I had never considered that this space had only recently been a mausoleum for the remains of the Pawnees and other Indian tribes. How had this come to be?

The Pawnees had been neighbors of the Poncas in the region that became Nebraska. They were a confederacy of four Caddoan-speaking tribes: the Chaui, Kitkahahki, Pitahawirata, and Skidi. Their population had once been around 45,000, but by the early 1800s, due to European American–introduced diseases, they numbered only about 12,000.

Their territory spanned the Platte River watershed from where the North and South Platte rivers meet in western Nebraska to where the Platte empties into the Missouri in the east, and from the Niobrara River in the north to the Arkansas River in the south, in what are now the states of Kansas and Oklahoma. The Pawnees lived in earth lodge villages near the rivers. Pawnee women were skilled farmers who grew the Three Sisters crops in the riparian zones and along the river bottoms. Pawnee men hunted bison and traded far out on the Great Plains.

The Pawnees experienced settler incursions and government intrusion beginning in the 1830s. Government officials negotiated a deceptive treaty with them. The Pawnee leaders who signed the treaty thought they had agreed to cede only a small piece of peripheral land on the Kansas River. The government claimed that the Pawnees had signed a treaty that ceded all of their lands south of the Platte River, more than twenty million acres of their most valuable hunting territories and fertile lands.

Like so many other treaties, this one did not give the Pawnees fair compensation. For the twenty million acres they insisted they had gained, the United States paid the Pawnees just $55,200 in trade goods over a twelve-year period and required them to move north of the Platte River. With the treaty in dispute, some of the Pawnees continued to live in three villages and to hunt south of the Platte River. But when Congress passed the Kansas-Nebraska Act of 1854 settlers moved into the Pawnee homelands, and they agitated against the continued presence of the Pawnees.

In 1857, under pressure from encroaching settlers, the Pawnees negotiated a new treaty with the United States. The tribe now agreed to exchange title for their remaining lands north of the Platte River (13 million acres) for an annuity of $40,000 a year for five years; then $30,000 a year in perpetuity. The Pawnees were to confine themselves to a reservation but still maintained their hunting rights in their old territories. The Pawnees, now just numbering about 4,500, selected a reservation thirty miles long and fifteen miles wide (285,500 acres) along the Loup River in central Nebraska for their permanent home. (Roger Welsch's 60 acres near Dannebrog was within the borders of the Pawnees' reservation.)

The story of the Pawnees' treaties followed a familiar script: first, the United States often tricked Indian people into giving away land or deceived them about the true nature of the treaty; second, the United States usually failed to provide adequate compensation for the worth of the land; third, the United States routinely violated the treaty; fourth, the United States renegotiated a new treaty. Then the cycle started all over again.

Indeed, conflict between settlers and the Pawnees did not end with the treaty's ratification in 1858. Some Pawnees still resided in their villages south of the Platte River. According to the Pawnee historian James Riding In, they were waiting to move to the new reservation until the government fulfilled its treaty promise to protect their new reservation from Lakota raids.

Settlers were incensed that the Pawnees had not vacated the area. In June 1859, while most of the tribe was off on a summer buffalo hunt, a group of hostile settlers attacked the Pawnees' three villages. They set fire to the earth lodges and killed all the Pawnee people still in the camp—small children, the aged, and the infirm.

When they learned of the attack, some Pawnees were understandably outraged and took retributive actions: they raided settlements, killed livestock, destroyed property, and looted homes. But, Riding In points out, they were remarkably restrained. They did not kill any settlers.

Settlers were not so restrained. John Thayer, a recent migrant to Omaha who became head of the territorial militia, led two hundred settlers on a surprise attack of a Pawnee camp. As the soldiers advanced, Pawnee leaders walked out to meet them and made gestures of peace. It could have been another gruesome Sand Creek–style massacre, another attempt to terrorize American Indian communities and force them to move. But this time, cooler heads prevailed. The territorial governor, one of those taking part in the planned attack, ordered a halt to the assault.

Like the Poncas, the Pawnees did not take up arms against the U.S. government or kill settlers. Far from it. They sought to make peace with the incoming flood of settlers in the 1860s. Riding In describes how they adopted a policy of peaceful coexistence and empowered members of a society known as *raripakusus* (those "fighting for order") to prevent crimes against settlers. Pawnee leaders also sought peace by entering into military alliance with the United States between 1864 and 1876. Three to four hundred members of the Pawnee nation served as scouts for the U.S. Army between 1864 and 1877 against their long-time enemies: the Lakotas, Arapahos, Cheyennes, Comanches, and Kiowas.

Most likely, then, some of the ancestors that the Pawnees sought to regain from the Nebraska State Historical Society in 1988 were members of the U.S. military. In other circumstances, the U.S. government would have been honoring them with a color guard, not boxing up their disinterred bones in a storage vault.

Neither Nebraska nor the U.S. government repaid the Pawnees for their loyalty. This is an old story, too. We saw that it happened to the Poncas as well. And it was true for Black Kettle's band of the southern Cheyennes, too. Nebraska officials refused to bring charges against white men accused of killing Indians or stealing timber from the Pawnees' reservation. And in the 1870s, just a few years after Nebraska gained statehood, the federal government relocated the Pawnees, now numbering just 2,376 people, to Indian Territory, as they did with so many other tribes.

The government sought to make way for a flood of settlers, land speculators, and railroad companies. Ironically, a uniformed battalion of 800 Pawnee men helped facilitate settler colonialism when they served as guards for the Union Pacific Railroad against Lakota and Cheyenne raiders as workers laid track across Nebraska. The government did not repay them for their loyalty.

In this case, the Pawnees agreed to the move; they were not forced into exile, as the Poncas would be only a few years later. But it's not accurate to present the Pawnees' move as voluntary. It had grown harder and harder for them to subsist on ever-shrinking plots of land, especially during years of drought and grasshopper invasions. They had grown tired of continual raids from Lakota warriors, which had contributed to their population decline and often prevented them from successful bison hunts. As my colleague David Wishart puts it, "There was no security left in their lives, no confidence that the next year would not bring yet another crushing famine or another terrifying attack."

Moreover, the government and churches were putting intense pressure on the Pawnees to give up their means of livelihood and some of their most cherished traditions. President Ulysses Grant, as part of his so-called Peace Policy, had put Hicksite Quakers in charge of administering Pawnee affairs. The religious order with a peaceful reputation instituted an aggressive assimilation program. They pushed for a western Christian education, the adoption of individual frame houses instead of communal earth lodges, and the transformation of Pawnee men, instead of women, into farmers. The Quakers also sought to stop the Pawnees from hunting bison. The Pawnees had usually conducted two annual hunts. In the summer of 1873, the Quakers allowed only one hunt. And that hunt ended disastrously, with a raid in which Lakota enemies killed sixty to eighty Pawnees who were hunting in the Republican River Valley.

In his novel about his Pawnee ancestors, *Sea of Grass*, Walter Echo-Hawk described it this way: "Our sacred covenant with Father Buffalo was broken at last by the hand of man. . . . Our common home was no longer the greatest grassland on the face of the earth. It was a war-torn land, bathed in blood and broken buffalo bones."

Indeed, on top of Lakota raids and overzealous Quakers, the Pawnees faced intense hostility from encroaching settlers. By 1870 there were 125,000 settlers in Nebraska compared to just 2,500 Pawnees. Many settlers advocated for either the Pawnees' extermination or their removal. The July 3, 1873, *Omaha Republican* opined: "The white man and red man cannot live together in peace. They have nothing in common. Every tribe should be removed from Nebraska and placed on a reservation. It would be better for both races. The savage race must submit to the inevitable." This was a classic settler colonial move: to portray injustices against Indigenous people not as the result of settler violence and relentless efforts to dispossess Indigenous people but as some inevitable outcome between a clash of two races.

The Nebraska legislature, its governors, and its two U.S. senators expressed the same racial antipathy toward the Pawnees as the *Republican* newspaper. Every year from 1867 to 1875, state legislators introduced resolutions and memorials asking Congress to remove one or more tribes from the state. They claimed the presence of Indians was deterring prospective settlers from moving to Nebraska.

Many European American newcomers to the area regularly complained about the Pawnees. Settlers accused them of grazing their horses on settler land or stealing their timber. In reality, it was settlers who were stealing huge amounts of timber from the Pawnee Reservation. Armed settlers began stealing 60 to 100 loads of wood a day from the Pawnee Reservation beginning in the fall of 1873. Three-quarters of all Pawnee timber had been stolen by settlers by the fall of 1874. The Pawnees had no legal recourse against such depredations. The courts refused to prosecute settlers who committed crimes against the Pawnees. Conversely, Nebraska usually held *all* Pawnees responsible for a crime committed by just one Pawnee individual and meted out collective punishment accordingly.

Riding In details one example of the intense hostility that Pawnees faced from settlers: the Mulberry Creek Massacre of January 29, 1869. Soldiers attacked and slaughtered a party of fourteen Pawnee scouts who were traveling through Ellsworth County in Kansas, shortly after being discharged from the U.S. Army. Pawnee eyewitnesses said that soldiers opened fire on the Pawnees without provocation while the Army insisted that the victims had fired the first shots. Nine Pawnee men died from their wounds. Five survived and escaped, but three of them suffered frostbite and died from the effects of exposure.

Many Kansas newspapers wrote in support of the attack on the Pawnee scouts, as part of their call for the extermination of all American Indians. Several newspapers urged the Kansas governor and the commander of the state militia to carry out a massacre of the Pawnees, as Colonel Chivington had done at Sand Creek in Colorado in 1864. Riding In notes, "The [Kansas] Republican state convention issued a . . . proclamation in 1868: 'We demand in the name of our frontier settlers, that the uncivilized Indians be driven from the state, and the civilized tribes be speedily removed to the Indian country.'"

Nebraska settlers similarly campaigned for the removal of the Pawnees. They still coveted the four hundred square miles of fertile land on the Pawnee Reservation. They claimed the Pawnees were not using it properly. In 1871 Governor David Butler described the reservations that had been set aside for the Pawnees and other Nebraska Indians as "some of the choicest agricultural lands in the state." He declared that Indian title to the land should "be extinguished and the Indians removed . . . to Indian Territory or some other place." The next governor, Robert Furnas, who had once been an agent for the Omaha Indians, insisted that "the valuable land now held by these aborigines should be permitted to pass into the hands of intelligent, enterprising citizens, who would render them productive."

This was the harsh social climate in which the Pawnees lived in the late 1860s and early 1870s and which led them to agree to removal to Indian Territory. A Pawnee man named Ese-do-to-des, who left Nebraska in the fall of 1873, told the Fifth Annual General Council of Indian Territory (a gathering of Indian leaders in the territory) in 1874 about why he and some other Pawnees had moved away from their beloved homelands: "We can scarcely move without disturbing some white person. If a Pawnee lays his hand on a stick of timber or grass, the white man says, 'Hold, this is mine!' If a Pawnee horse gets beyond the limits of his narrow reserve, he need not hunt him. We [were] surrounded up there on all side[s] by the white man, I and my people will come here and surrender our part [of land] to him."

The Pawnees were desperate to be free of the pressures of settler invasion and Lakota raiding, to have land of their own where they could rebuild their earth lodges, grow their crops in peace, and continue to perform their ceremonies. Some bands of Pawnees moved to the Wichita Agency in Indian Territory in 1873; a year later most of the other bands followed. In the summer of 1875, the Pawnees moved to their newly allocated lands, 150 miles away from the Wichitas, their relatives along with the Arikaras. The last remaining Pawnees in Nebraska joined them that autumn. But, as with the Poncas who would follow a few years later, Congress had not appropriated any funds for their establishment in their new home. The Pawnees had no food supply; they had to subsist on emergency rations.

Dispossession of the Pawnees—and their increasing impoverishment—contrasted with the enrichment of settlers who took over their land in Nebraska. The federal government sold the Pawnees' reservation lands along the Loup River at auction in 160-acre plots, beginning in 1878. (Sixty acres of this land would eventually pass into the hands of Roger Welsch.) By 1883 settlers owned all of the Pawnees' former reservation lands. In this case, the restrictions that had governed homesteading did not apply. Bidders could buy as many tracts as they wished, they did not have to live on the land or erect a dwelling on it, and they could resell it. So the area largely went to speculators rather than individual yeoman-style farmers.

The sale grossed $750,000 for the Pawnees, but the government subtracted $300,000 from the proceeds for the cost of supporting the Pawnees in their new home. They also deducted about $177,000 from the total to pay the Muscogee (Creek) and Cherokee nations for the Pawnees' new lands in Indian Territory. So, the Pawnees netted just $280,000, or about a dollar an acre, for what remained of their precious Nebraska lands.

Removal, too, did not improve the Pawnees' fortunes. It proved, in fact, to be disastrous. Malaria and influenza plagued members of the transplanted nation as they tried to adjust to their exile. By 1877, 855 Pawnees (or 36% of the remaining tribal members) had died. Just about 1,500 Pawnee people remained, and their agent expected them to become extinct. When Kevin and Boots and I visited Pawnee, Oklahoma, in March 2020, Pawnee elder Herb Adson told us, "When we came [from] Nebraska, it was a . . . real time of depression for our folks here. And so we lost a lot of our ceremonies, a lot of our old folks."

The Pawnees defied these expectations and refused to be eliminated. They had brought with them their corn seeds, their knowledge of the stars, their songs and ceremonies, their skill at building homes from the soil. They made the best of this very bad situation. Adson told us that despite so much loss, "we gained a few more new ceremonies, which were really good for us." But it was devastating to become exiled from their homelands, the places where they had planted their earth lodges, sowed their crops, hunted bison, and prayed and performed their religious ceremonies in the Pawnee tongue along the rivers of what had become the state of Nebraska.

It was particularly heart-wrenching for the Pawnees to move so far from the graves of their relations. The Pawnees, like humans everywhere, took great care to bury and mourn their dead. Families would request the services of a holy man to prepare the recently deceased for burial. According to James Murie, a nineteenth-century anthropologist of Pawnee descent, the holy man "anoints the body with fat and red paint, places offerings of meat fat in his hands and mouth, and finally dresses the body in the regalia worn during life."

Pawnee women had historically been responsible for digging graves, transporting the departed to the grave, and burying the dead. Lieutenant John Dunbar (the namesake and possible prototype for the Kevin Costner character in *Dances with Wolves*) observed that "the women bore . . . [the corpse] to the grave. The relatives and friends followed, howling and weeping."

Deaths and burials were occasions of intense heartache and anguish. In 1834, a missionary recounted, "One cold morning as I was returning from my walk, I saw several women, bearing the lifeless remains of a little child, that had died the preceding night, to his burial. They carried it a short distance, then placed it on the ground, stopped and wept awhile, then took it up and went forward, all the while howling sadly. The father, a young man, followed at a little distance, apparently, in an agony of grief."

It was not uncommon for the Pawnees to bury their dead with their personal possessions. Anthropologists Murie and James Owen Dorsey wrote that some Pawnee "women were buried with the umbilical cords of their children, wrapped 'in a buckskin in a work-box.'" Roger Echo-Hawk, a prominent Pawnee attorney, noted that one "account of the burial of a young woman mentions the piling of 'buffalo robes and all her dresses' in the grave."

The Pawnees visited the graves of their ancestors frequently. They often left offerings or performed ceremonies there. Dunbar wrote that "women continued for years to resort to the grave of a brother, husband, or child, to mourn. Seated beside the grave they would give utterance to their feelings in plaintive wailings . . . or in a sort of monologue, *talking* to God they termed it. Sometimes they also placed food at the grave, or if a man, a bow, for the use of the dead."

Roger Echo-Hawk reports that until their exile to Indian Territory, the Pawnees in Nebraska "continued to visit tribal cemeteries long after abandoning nearby earth lodge towns. Stories related by the descendants of white settlers in southern Nebraska describe delegations of Pawnees traveling from their reservation north of the Platte River to visit the ruins of a Pawnee town on the Republican River . . . each spring and fall in order to perform certain ceremonial and religious rites at the 'sacred hill' where the Pawnee chiefs and important men were buried."

Even after their exile to Indian Territory the Pawnees sought to visit the graves of their ancestors in Nebraska. In 1898, for example, according to settler historian Orlan Svingen, "Harry Coons, a Pawnee visiting Nebraska from his home in Oklahoma, stopped at Wild Licorice Creek, a former Pawnee town [near present-day Genoa], to visit the graves of his two sisters." Now, however, the Pawnees often found that their ancestors' graves had been disturbed. Coons observed, "Where my sisters graves were is now cornfields[;] what few graves I did find were open and robbed of what little—if any[—]trinkets were found on the dead."

As homesteaders plowed up their newly appropriated Pawnee land to plant crops, they routinely found, and disturbed, the graves of Pawnee people. Svingen writes that "in his *Early History of Webster County*, Emanual Peters described how a neighbor built a dugout and in the process 'several skulls were thrown out.' The same neighbor later fenced in a hog lot. 'The hogs soon rooted out so many skulls,' Peters claimed, '[that they] would roll down and form a drift against the fence.'"

Landowners eventually found that it was foolish to simply let these skulls and skeletons bleach in the sun and rattle in the wind. Money could be made by hocking the remains to scientific institutions. Careers could be built by systematically digging up Pawnee cemeteries. Asa T. Hill, for example, was a car salesman in Nebraska who in his non-work hours pursued a hobby of finding and excavating Pawnee cemeteries. In 1925 he purchased 320 acres in Webster County, Nebraska, where he had "discovered" the remains of a Pawnee village. He allegedly bought the land to preserve the site and protect it from other looters.

Digging up Pawnee graves soon became a genteel Sunday leisure pastime. Hill himself told the *Omaha World Herald*, "I don't play golf. . . . My only recreation is this Indian investigation. I come out here Sundays and dig up Indians. . . . This hill is my golf course." Svingen writes that "some excavations took on a sporting event atmosphere." He notes that Hill placed notices in newspapers to invite people to "visit his farm and to 'join in the further hunt for finds.' On one occasion, one hundred people responded and spent the afternoon digging, with two graves located and opened that day. A note by Hill indicated that sightseers were common: 'We are having good luck finding skeletons. Have lots of visitors.'"

It was not only in Nebraska that private archaeological sites containing Indian remains became a big tourist draw. The Echo-Hawks feature a few of these enterprises in their book *Battlefields and Burial Grounds*. At the Dickson Mounds Museum in Illinois, for example, from 1927 to 1945 a local farmer charged admission to visitors on his land to gawk at Indian skeletons; then the state took over the tourist site's operation. When neighboring Indian tribes objected, local settler descendants complained that reburial of the exposed skeletons would harm tourism. A settler near Salina, Kansas, found a 700-year-old burial site of 146

Caddo Indians on his land in the 1930s. He sold the site to a local grocer who dug up and shellacked the bones, constructed a metal shed over the area, and charged tourists to view the burial site.

Back in Nebraska, Asa T. Hill eventually parlayed his gravedigging hobby into a new career; in 1933 he retired from the car dealership and moved from Hastings to Lincoln, where he was appointed by the Nebraska State Historical Society as director of the Museum and Field Archaeology. Throughout the Great Depression he conducted several excavation projects in Nebraska and Kansas, with the help of federal funds from the New Deal's Works Progress Administration. Hill and his crews removed at least sixty-five bodies from the property he owned along with thousands of grave goods. These were some of the ancestors that the Pawnees sought to bring home from the Historical Society in the late 1980s.

Clearly Nebraska's settlers, amateur pothunters, and professional archaeologists did not regard the Pawnees' relatives in the same way as they did their own. Settler burial grounds were sacred sites for paying one's respects to the dead; cemeteries for Indians were sites of curiosity, amusement, and profit. This was an attitude shared by most white settlers toward most American Indian people, for centuries. When the Stephen H. Long expedition, a government-sponsored exploration into the Rocky Mountains, passed through Nebraska in 1820, it obtained the skull of a Pawnee who had been killed in 1818. According to Edwin James, a botanist who chronicled the journey, "we thought it no sacrilege to compliment [the skull] with a place upon one of our pack-horses."

Such disrespect toward Pawnee burials betrayed a view that Indians were less than human. James Riding In told Kevin and me, "When you deem someone a savage, whether they're your friend or not, it's like issuing a death warrant against them. You can do anything to them because they're inferior and whites are superior."

Indeed, many settlers may have felt justified in such careless treatment of Pawnee burials due to the dominance of dehumanizing rhetoric regarding American Indians in the nineteenth century. Many nineteenth-century men of science were bent on creating racial theories of European superiority. In 1854, for example, Josiah C. Nott, a surgeon and early anthropologist, concluded that "certain savage types can neither be civilized or domesticated. The Barbarous races of America . . . although nearly as low in intellect as the Negro races, are essentially untameable. Not merely have all attempts to civilize them failed, but also every endeavor to enslave them. Our Indian tribes submit to extermination, rather than wear the yoke under which our Negro slaves fatten and multiply."

To add insult to injury, many so-called scientists also used the skulls they had looted from Indian graves to "prove" that Indians were intellectually inferior to whites. Dr. Samuel George Morton, who helped establish the discipline of American physical anthropology, examined and measured the Pawnee skull from the 1820 Long expedition, along with those of 143 other Native Americans and hundreds of African American skulls. He asserted in his 1839 book, *Crania Americana*, that Caucasians had the biggest brains, averaging 87 cubic inches, Indians were in the middle with an average of 82 cubic inches, and Negroes had the smallest brains with an average of 78 cubic inches. Morton believed that brain size correlated with intelligence, and as Stephen Jay Gould has written in *The Mismeasure of Man*, he hypothesized that "a ranking of races could be established objectively by physical characteristics of the brain, particularly by its size." (Gould and other critics have utterly debunked Morton's work. Gould went so far as to study Morton's calculations and concluded that he had engaged in "fudging and finagling" to support his preconceptions.)

Scientists like Morton and doctors who worked for the Army Medical Museum particularly coveted Indian skulls for their medical research. Wars and massacres against Indian people offered a prime means of procuring Indian crania. Doctors in Minnesota drew lots for the bodies of 38 Dakota men the government hanged in 1862 for their alleged role in the so-called Minnesota Massacre of 1862. William Mayo, the founder of the Mayo Clinic, perhaps the most famous medical facility in the United States, was delighted to procure the skull of Cut Nose, one of the Dakota 38.

Soldiers who took part in the 1864 Sand Creek Massacre beheaded a number of Cheyenne, as well as Arapaho corpses; military leaders deposited several of their skulls in the Army Medical Museum's collection.

Many of the body parts that Colorado volunteers cut off from other Sand Creek victims ended up in the Smithsonian.

By the late 1860s, Indian skull collecting was no longer just an incidental sideline of the federal government's wars against Indian peoples. It was now official policy. According to Riding In, "The surgeon general's office issued, in 1868, a memorandum ordering army field surgeons to collect Indian crania for scientific study. It noted that 'a craniological collection was commenced last year at the Army Medical Museum, and that it already has 143 specimens of skulls . . . to aid the progress of anthropological science by obtaining measurements of a large number of skulls of the aboriginal races of North America.' The memorandum particularly urged 'medical officers stationed in the Indian country or in the vicinity of ancient Indian mounds or cemeteries in the Mississippi Valley or the Atlantic region' to become involved in gathering human remains."

Riding In has detailed the troubling history of how six Pawnee crania came to be in the collection of the Army Medical Museum. Remember the Mulberry Creek Massacre, the attack on the fourteen Pawnee men who had dared to venture into Kansas in 1869? On January 30, 1869, one day after the massacre, the surgeon at Fort Harker, B. E. Fryer, sent a civilian guide from the fort to go get the victims' heads. Dr. Fryer wrote to Brevet Lieutenant Colonel George A. Otis, the curator at the Army Medical Museum, of what transpired, on February 12:

> I had already obtained for the [Army Medical] museum the skull of one of the Pawnees killed in the fight . . . , [and] would have had all had it not been that immediately after the engagement, the Indians lurked about their dead [and] watched them so closely that the guide I sent out was unable to secure but the one. Until within a day or two the snow has prevented a further attempt. Yesterday I sent a scout who knows the spot and [I] think I can get at least two more crania— that number being reported to me as left unburied by the Pawnees, and it may be that if the remaining five (eight not seven were killed) are buried or have been hid near where the fight took place—about twenty miles from here, I can, after a time, obtain all. I shall certainly use every effort.

Fryer used words like "obtaining" and "securing" the crania. Let's drop the euphemisms and call this what it was: Fryer's guide *decapitated* six of the Pawnee corpses. Then the severed heads had to be prepared for scientific study. This also entailed a dehumanizing process. Riding In quoted from one man who "described his method of treating the head of a recently slain Kiowa Indian: '[H]is scalp and the soft parts of the face and neck were carefully dissected up from the skull, atlas and axis, and these were subsequently boiled and cleaned for the Army Medical Museum. The skull was carefully cleaned and then steeped in solution of lime for 36 hours.'"

According to Riding In, on March 11, 1869, Fryer shipped to Washington the six Pawnee crania together with twenty other Native American skulls he had "obtained," including those of three Cheyennes, three Caddos, six Wichitas, and two Osage Indians. Riding In found that this was only the beginning of Fryer's collecting of Indian ancestral remains. He notes that "from 1868 to 1872, Fryer shipped Otis at least forty-two human remains belonging to the Cheyenne, Wichita, Caddo, Osage, and Kansa tribes, among others."

Such practices deeply offended the Pawnees and other Indians, and settlers knew it. Riding In found that Fryer contended that "a good deal of caution is required in obtaining anything from the graves of Indians, and it will have to be managed very carefully to prevent the Indians from finding out that the graves of their people have been disturbed—as this might be offered as an excuse (of course, a trifling one) for taking the 'War Path' again—which is always walked each year, however, as soon as the grass is high enough for the ponies." Fryer's comment reveals both how seriously American Indians took the raiding of their graves and how Fryer and other white settlers dismissed and trivialized Indian concerns.

Roger Echo-Hawk explains that there are "strong Pawnee proscriptions against grave-tampering" and that "the Pawnee regard the unsanctioned removal of grave offerings as a spiritually dangerous violation of the dead." Riding In concurs. "Equally critical to our perspective are cultural norms that stressed that those who tampered with the dead did so with profane, evil, or demented intentions," he writes. "From this vantage point, the study of stolen remains constitutes abominable acts of sacrilege, desecration, and depravity."

It wasn't just the Army that procured skulls for science. Physical anthropologists such as Morton and his disciples also became more directly involved in the procurement of skulls. Even Franz Boas, the renowned anthropologist who came to be known as a critic of the racism of physical anthropology and the founding father of a new kind of cultural anthropology, wrote in the 1880s, "it is most unpleasant work to steal bones from a grave, but. . . . someone has to do it." Historian Ann Fabian notes that "peddling skulls helped to finance his studies."

Any natural history museum worth its salt needed its own collection of American Indian remains. The Field Museum in Chicago, for example, sent out its assistant curator, anthropologist George Dorsey, to gather Indian remains and sacred burial objects in the late 1890s. Dorsey ventured to the northwest coast of Canada to collect Haida remains. After Dorsey and his Canadian accomplices had swept through the area, a local missionary wrote to an area newspaper to complain that he had found coffins and some discarded human remains scattered about where these men of science had raided Haida graves.

Museums knew that their practices were deeply troubling to American Indians, but they went ahead anyway. Roger and Walter Echo-Hawk detail the elaborate scheme that New York City's American Museum of Natural History developed to attain the remains of Qisuk, an Inuit man from Greenland, who had died in New York City. Qisuk had accompanied Arctic explorer Robert Peary to the city in 1897 but died there unexpectedly.

The museum saw this as a great opportunity to obtain an Eskimo specimen, in the chilling lingo of the time, for study and display. Qisuk's family was, of course, concerned that he should be properly buried. So, museum staff "staged a phony funeral to make Qisuk's son Minik believe that his father had been respectfully buried." Behind the scenes, however, doctors at the nearby medical college quickly dissected Qisuk and removed his brain for future study. They took his remains to a "bone house" where they were boiled to remove flesh from the bones. Qisuk's skeleton ended up in the museum's collection.

It was not just American Indian or African American crania that scientists sought. They were interested in proving that there were differences between and a hierarchy among "races." So they also sought the
skulls of European Americans, albeit very poor white ones. An uproar
developed over this practice, however. Roger and Walter Echo-Hawk
note that there were protests and riots when, in 1788, medical students
in New York dug up the graves of European Americans. Legislatures
drafted new laws to protect white burials.

By contrast, the federal government passed a law to formalize and
regulate the desecration of Indian graves that settlers had been carrying
out for some time. In 1906, President Theodore Roosevelt signed into
law the American Antiquities Act, ostensibly to conserve and preserve
archaeological sites on public lands and to prevent the looting and desecration of American Indian burial grounds and other sites. Critics
charge that the act had little effect on looting by private individuals—
only a handful of people were ever charged with violating the act. Certainly, it didn't deter settlers from digging up Pawnee graves in Nebraska. On the other hand, the act sanctioned the idea that Indian
remains were for public consumption and could be permanently removed from their sites and ensconced in museums.

By the 1950s, the Nebraska State Historical Society was warehousing
an estimated 500 to 1,000 Pawnee bodies and thousands of funerary
goods. After stealing Pawnee skeletons and burial remains, according to
Svingen, "archaeologists had separated the deceased Pawnee from their
burial possessions. The funerary goods became 'artifacts' that were identified and placed in an ethnographic collection, and [Historical Society]
personnel routinely incorporated selected grave goods into a variety of
museum exhibits over the years." Authorities with the Historical Society
put the skeletal remains of Pawnee bodies in small storage boxes, mea-
suring one foot by one foot by two feet.

But the desecration of Pawnee graves did not stop there. During road
construction south of Genoa, Nebraska, in the 1960s, crews found and
exposed five burials and removed three bodies. In September 1970, archaeologist Carl Hugh Jones learned from landowner Allen Atkins that
he and others had been "land leveling on the [Genoa site] and were

hitting burials." Jones and other archaeologists arrived at Genoa and found "six or eight pothunters gathered around a couple of burials trying to dig out the bones before the other guy could."

This time the Pawnees' cemetery became the site of a field trip for schoolchildren. "A rural school showed up and kept us company much of the morning," Jones noted. "Some of these kids," he continued, "collected bones from the area where they had been scraped and dumped." This isn't ancient history, far removed from our own time. Many of us settlers may have participated in such field trips ourselves.

The Pawnees were not alone in having their graves so disrespected. Nearly every tribe suffered from the same practice in which settler looters—some amateur, some professional—dug up their graves. And nearly all of the remains and burial goods that the raiders stole from the graves ended up in American or European museums.

Indian grave robbing is a long American tradition. Anthropologist and museum curator Chip Colwell (of settler descent) points out that the first probable grave looting in American history likely occurred in 1620 when Pilgrims "despoiled the grave of a man and a child out of curiosity" not far from Plymouth Rock. They took away, according to one of the Pilgrims, "sundry of the prettiest things." Even our founding fathers got in on the act. Thomas Jefferson dug up an Indian burial mound in Virginia in the late 1700s.

How disturbing it must feel to go to a museum and see your ancestors or their possessions on display. Riding In recalls a trip in 1970 to the National Museum of Natural History at the Smithsonian with a Navajo (or Diné) friend. "As soon as you walked through the door . . . [there were] glass cabinets, there were a collection of Indian crania [in them]. And they were identified by the Indian nation from which they came from," Riding In told Kevin and me. "It was an awful feeling to see that. While I was there, one of my Diné friends, from Crown Point, had come to DC and [that] was hell for him, and you know, even today, he has these strong feelings about the deceased. So, we were both upset about that. But we didn't say anything, you know, and I felt powerless to say anything in those years."

Even in death Indigenous people on this continent could not stay on their homeland or rest in peace. Settlers and their government were not content to appropriate 98 percent of the continental United States. They also removed the dead far from their homelands and institutionalized them. Settlers categorized and racialized Indigenous ancestors, too, just as they did with their living descendants.

No one knows exactly how many Indian graves have been dug up by settlers—for science, for profit, or for amusement. The museums offer modest estimates. The Smithsonian says that it had 14,000–18,000 Indian bodies. The National Museum of Natural History: 17,000. Colwell estimates that 1,500 museums hold 200,000 Native American skeletons and one million grave goods and sacred objects.

American Indian groups put the number much higher. American Indians Against Desecration estimates that 300,000–600,000 Indian bodies were, or still are, in university, museum, and lab collections across the United States. Two attorneys who have long studied the issue, Jack Trope and Walter Echo-Hawk, conclude that 100,000 to 2 million deceased Indigenous people have been "dug up from their graves for storage or display by government agencies, museums, universities, and tourist attractions."

Why did so many settlers think it was acceptable to dig up Indian graves? We could chalk it up to the common "man of the times" argument. You remember that: everyone (read: *settlers*) thought this way at the time. You can't judge settlers of the past by today's standards. But we know this wasn't true. Army field surgeons, anthropologists, and museum curators knew they were deeply offending American Indians. They went to great lengths to cover up their crimes of obtaining skeletons and burial goods, such as staging funerals of Indigenous people while covertly keeping their bodies for science.

Did settlers think it was acceptable because they believed that Indians were dying out, becoming extinct? Under this logic, their skeletons and burial goods were of no consequence to the few remaining Indians. And at the least, their remains could be preserved for posterity, for western science.

It was true that the Indian population was in decline at the turn of the twentieth century, but it rebounded after that. And Indian populations were in decline primarily because the U.S. government had failed to fulfill its treaty promises and had enacted policies—such as forced removal and confinement to reservations without adequate food supplies—that all but assured starvation, disease, and high rates of mortality among Indian populations. On top of that, the government and settlers often killed Indians with impunity. Population decline was not inevitable; settlers were largely responsible for it.

Other settlers believed, and still do today, that such desecration of graves was justified in the name of science. Sure, the practice was culturally insensitive, but scientists, if not amateur pothunters, had good intentions. They simply wanted to contribute to the store of knowledge about human history.

This argument just doesn't hold up, because such different standards have been used in regard to Indigenous versus settler bodies. We don't allow the digging up of non-Indigenous graves to be studied in this way, unless they are of extremely ancient peoples, such as Egyptian mummies, or pre-human hominids like Lucy.

The destruction of burial sites is actually a tactic of colonization everywhere, a common means of erasing the history of a people from the land. In 2019 intrepid journalists reported that the Chinese government has been destroying Uighur burial grounds in northwest China as part of its ongoing attempt to suppress the Muslim Uighur minority within its borders. Journalists found that the government has rounded up an estimated one million Uighur and other Muslim ethnic minorities in China and sent them to so-called reeducation camps, all in the name of opposing religious extremism. And since 2014 the Beijing administration has been smashing Uighur graves, scattering Uighur bones, and flattening at least forty-five Uighur cemeteries. Satellite imagery shows that the cemeteries have been overlaid with parks, parking lots, new cemeteries, and housing developments.

Uighur activists have protested. "This is all part of China's campaign to effectively eradicate any evidence of who we are, to effectively make us like the Han Chinese," said Salih Hudayar. The graveyard where his great-grandparents had been buried was demolished. "That's why they're destroying all of these historical sites, these cemeteries, to disconnect us from our history, from our fathers and our ancestors," Hudayar added.

"The destruction is not just about religious persecution," said Nurgul Sawut. She has five generations of family buried in Yengisar, in southwestern Xinjiang. "It is much deeper than that," she said. "If you destroy that cemetery . . . you're uprooting whoever's on that land, whoever's connected to that land," she explained. Hudayar and Sawut could be talking about the desecration of American Indian cemeteries as well.

American Indian grave desecration grew out of brutal Indian massacres. It morphed into a pseudoscientific enterprise and then a tourist bonanza. A huge number of settlers took part in this desecration of graves, as they appropriated the land of Native peoples, up to the late twentieth century. The effect has been to eliminate the physical evidence of Indigenous people from the land, to make it possible to narrate American history as if it begins with European settlement.

How we tell our history and remember our past is not so different from how we bury our dead. The past is a vast cemetery. Some of our pasts have been exalted with lavish headstones and memorialized with bronze statues, or even sandblasted into the side of a mountain. These pasts dominate our historical narratives, whether in the pages of a textbook, in the popular history books on the shelves of our bookstores and libraries, in our museum exhibits and films, or cast in bronze outside our courthouses and city halls. But many other of our ancestors languish in unmarked graves. Their tombs have been desecrated. Their pasts have been plowed up and displaced.

In 2018, on that flight to Dallas, there was proper respect for a man who had died and been buried improperly. Strangers made a great deal of effort to make sure that he came home to where he belonged. Strangers paused from their usual routines and obsessions to honor him. Even if they did not know him personally, they recognized him as a fellow human being. That is what the Pawnees were asking for in 1988 when they came to the Nebraska State Historical Society. Would strangers respond to them, too? Would there be some who listened to the Pawnees' history, who heard their grievances, and acknowledged their humanity?

CHAPTER 13

Bones

It was the first week of March 2020. News of the coronavirus was creeping around at the periphery of our lives, but most of us were still reeling from the Trump impeachment trials and wondering what would happen on Super Tuesday. Could Bernie maintain his lead? Would Joe build on his South Carolina blowout? Would some other Democrat suddenly surge to the front? Kevin, Boots, our sound engineer Joe, and I decided to meet in Pawnee, Oklahoma, that week to interview the Pawnees about how they were regaining a presence in Nebraska.

We had talked on the phone with a few Pawnee tribal members before our trip, but we just showed up unannounced at the Pawnee Museum that first day. First we met Matt Reed, the tribe's Historic Preservation Officer, and then he invited two coworkers to join us: Herb Adson and Adrian Spottedhorsechief, who serve in the Cultural Division for the tribe. We chatted for a while in the cool, dimly lit museum, larger-than-life portraits of several Pawnee tribal members in their resplendent regalia peering down on us. Then the three men took us on a tour of the six hundred or so acres that the tribe owns.

We lingered a little while at the old boarding school and the new dance grounds and then drove past a baseball field named for Mose Yellow-horse, a Pawnee man who played for the Pittsburgh Pirates in the 1920s, the first Indian to play for a professional baseball team. And then we continued up the hill to the tribe's cemetery. Matt, Herb, and Adrian brought us to a site of sixteen graves, fifteen of them marked with wooden crosses, the final grave marked with a small white marble pillar.

Matt gamely agreed to do an impromptu interview with us. As the wind blew across the hillside, the grass brown, the trees still leafless, he told us about the Pawnee scouts that had been buried here. These were the men James Riding In had written about, who had just been discharged from the U.S. Army and were on their way home to the Pawnee village near Genoa, Nebraska. At Mulberry Creek, soldiers massacred them, and soon after the Army surgeon at the fort nearby had their heads decapitated. It had taken the Pawnees decades to get these bodies of their relatives back from the Army Medical Museum. They stayed on this hilltop for a while, but ultimately the tribe decided to rebury them in their homelands in Nebraska.

During our time at Pawnee we learned more and more about how the Pawnees had grown increasingly upset about the fate of these and other ancestors. Pat Leading Fox, a prominent member of the Nasharo, or Chief's Council, told us that many Pawnee elders believed that the Pawnees were experiencing many problems and hardships "because our ancestors were in museums, they were crying out." The attorney Walter Echo-Hawk, who became the Pawnee nation president in 2020, explained that "we had no sooner left [Nebraska] than people started digging up our cemeteries . . . and carting the remains off to . . . universities and museums. So when that became known down here in Oklahoma, our people were naturally upset and experienced a lot of spirit sickness about that." So in 1988, a delegation of Pawnee Indians approached the Nebraska State Historical Society to request that the remains of their ancestors be repatriated to them for reburial.

Nebraska tribes had raised this issue many times before. The Nebraska Commission on Indian Affairs had called for legislation in 1971 to stop the desecration of Native American graves in the state, but the legislature had failed to respond. Native American Rights Fund attorney Robert Peregoy, a member of the Flathead tribe, notes that Nebraska tribes renewed their efforts in the 1980s. "Between 1981 and 1986," he writes, "the Omaha and Winnebago tribes worked to preserve, protect, and salvage unmarked burial sites in Nebraska from archaeological excavations, grave robbing, and construction projects." However, "their efforts met with little success."

The Nebraska tribes tried again in 1987 to get a bill (LB 612) passed through the state legislature that would protect their grave sites. The Nebraska State Historical Society (NSHS), according to Peregoy, "bitterly opposed the bill on the basis that it allegedly would 'cripple' forensic research and the 'science of archaeology' and would force the NSHS to lose 'more than 10,000 irreplaceable artifacts.'" The Historical Society sent a legislative alert to its 4,000 members that decried the bill's "absurd provisions." Director James Hanson sent an alarmist message to the society's membership saying that "if LB 612 becomes law, you could go to jail for a year and be fined up to $1,000 for giving an arrowhead, a piece of pottery, or a chip of flint to a child, a friend, or even a Nebraska museum!"

Momentum had been building for some time among Nebraska's Indian nations, then, for putting a stop to the looting of Indian graves and returning the ancestors to their people. It was the Pawnees' request in 1988 that amplified the concerns of Indigenous people and vaulted the issue into Nebraska's public consciousness. In March 1988, Chairman Lawrence Goodfox Jr. of the Pawnee Tribe of Oklahoma wrote to the Nebraska State Historical Society to explain why the Pawnee nation wanted the Historical Society to repatriate the remains and burial offerings of hundreds of Pawnee people it held in its storage vaults:

> the remains of our ancestors are in Nebraska. In our culture their grave sites are sacred to the Pawnee people. When our people die and go on to the spirit world, sacred rituals and ceremonies are performed. We believe that if the body is disturbed, the spirit becomes restless and cannot be at peace. . . . our ancestors have been in the Historical Society's possession for decades. The Historical Society has already gone on record in opposition to the reburial of our ancestors. This we do not understand. . . . Why do you impose your values on us when we do not impose our values on you? All we want is reburial of the remains of our ancestors and to let them finally rest in peace, and for all people in Nebraska to refrain from, forever, any excavation of any Native American graves or burial sites.

This is the request the Pawnees made at the first board meeting that Roger Welsch attended for the Nebraska State Historical Society. The board and the society's executive director, James Hanson, swiftly rejected the Pawnees' request. Hanson claimed that the Pawnees' request threatened science and the pursuit of knowledge. He asserted, "A bone is like a book . . . and I don't believe in burning books." He told a reporter that the Pawnee remains were crucial to "discovering how people lived" before settlers arrived in Nebraska.

When we interviewed Adrian Spottedhorsechief at the Pawnee nation, he had a ready response to this viewpoint. "If you want to know how the Pawnee people lived," he said, "just ask us." Pawnee people are stewards of their own histories and cultural traditions. They have passed down knowledge from generation to generation. Why not accept them as experts on their own lives? Even though living, breathing Pawnee people had come before the Nebraska State Historical Society Board—albeit in modern American business suits—Hanson was unmoved by such arguments.

Hanson also fought back against the Pawnees' request by asserting that the Historical Society owned the bones. According to Peregoy, the society claimed that it held title to a certain number of Pawnee dead bodies and burial offerings on the basis of a bill of sale from Asa T. Hill to the society from 1942. Peregoy and the Echo-Hawks countered that "under American common law, there is no property interest or ownership right to a dead body. . . . Once duly interred, a dead body is in the custody of the law and may be removed only pursuant to proper legal authority." Similarly, common law considers burial offerings to be owned by descendants, not landowners.

In their fight against the Pawnees' repatriation request, Hanson and a new group who called themselves Citizens to Save Nebraska's History questioned the Pawnees' religious beliefs. They opposed the return of the items included in Pawnee burials because, they said, these "are not religious objects like crucifixes, rosaries and bibles." This citizen's group seemed unable to imagine the legitimacy of a non-Christian religion.

Hanson went even further in deriding the Pawnees' religious beliefs and practices. He in fact publicly dared the Pawnees to "prove their religion is being affected by our possession of these things." He seemed to subscribe to the notion that the Pawnees no longer truly existed as a

distinct people with their own religion, language, cultures, and sovereign government.

I wish Hanson and members of Citizens to Save Nebraska's History could
have traveled to Pawnee, Oklahoma, with us in March 2020. It's true that
the Pawnees had lost over a third of their tribe after the U.S. government
removed them to Indian Territory. And proselytization and boarding
school education had sought to root out their religion, language, culture,
and identity. By 1900 they had just 650 tribal members. Yet the Pawnees
have persisted. They now number about 3,500 members.

One night we attended a Pawnee language class, taught by two lively
twenty-something Pawnee men who are obtaining PhDs in linguistics
and are actively reviving the language. The next day Matt Reed and Deb
Echo-Hawk, who runs the tribe's Seed Preservation Project and is Walter
and Roger's sister, brought Kevin, Boots, Joe, and me to the tribe's newly
refurbished round house. The building squats between the tribe's new
elder center and its towering hospital. From the outside, it looks rather
nondescript—it has few windows and looks like it could be a giant stucco
storage unit. But when you enter through one of the doors, you come
into a spacious arena. Sunlight streams through skylights and ricochets
off an intricate pattern of wooden braces holding up the ceiling. Benches
ring the central dance area. A huge mural encircles the walls. Portraits
of four epic Pawnee singers, one from each of the four bands, look out
on the dance floor. Matt and Deb allow us to interview them, the late
afternoon sun creating an aura around each of them.

Matt tells us about the big sandy dance floor. "We have a drum keeper
that takes care of this. And even when we're in here dancing, . . . you
give this floor, you pour some water on it. 'Cause . . . the dirt is our ancestors. So by watering them, you're giving them a little drink, especially
when we're doing something, that's basically a big, giant prayer, the
whole ceremony. So when this was built, . . . there's no telling how many
different trips have been made up to Nebraska to obtain our [soil], bring
it back here and put it on this floor. There's, you know, there's Oklahoma
dirt here too. It's not all from Nebraska, but you know, we kind of mix
it together."

Just down the hill from the round house, the Pawnees have recently finished a new outdoor dance ground, nestled in a grove of majestic oaks and elms. It sits fifty yards or so away from the old boarding school superintendent's house—now abandoned, the roof collapsed in, vines climbing the walls, saplings sprouting up out of the broken windows. It's hard to miss the symbolism: the crumbling monument to a failed policy next to a vibrant new dance arena where the Pawnees continue to carry out their ceremonies and practice their religion. Pawnee culture, language, and religion are alive and well.

In the late 1980s, as the Historical Society continued to respond with contempt and hostility, the Pawnees protested to the media and then took their case to the Nebraska state legislature. Chairman Goodfox told reporters that his people were devastated by the "indignant, insulting, and sacrilegious treatment" of their ancestors. Two other Nebraska tribes, the Omahas and Winnebagos, joined the Pawnees in their efforts. Reba White Shirt, director of the Nebraska Commission on Indian Affairs, asserted that Indigenous people "want the graves of our ancestors to be treated with the same dignity and respect as anyone else's grave."

The Pawnees who came to Nebraska to request the return of their ancestors from the Historical Society faced other indignities as well. Once a restaurant refused them service. Walter Echo-Hawk writes that "a group of about thirty tribal elders. . . . were refused service in one busy café after sitting there for about an hour. We finally got up to leave the diner without being served." Deb Echo-Hawk told Kevin and me that it "was kind of scary going to Nebraska" and that this incident had traumatized her son.

At first there were few non-Indigenous Nebraskans who were ready to listen and to really hear what the Pawnees had to say. Roger Welsch had initially been skeptical of the Pawnees' request. He told Kevin and me that when as a freshman at the University of Nebraska he took an introductory anthropology class, his professor "passed around a cigar box of Indian fingers and ears because they've been buried with copper on them and they've been preserved, and so we could make jokes about [them] . . . just before lunch . . . wow!!"

Gradually Welsch had a change of heart, though, and became one of the most ardent supporters of the Pawnees and their request for repatriation. What made Welsch change his mind? It started, ironically, as he listened first to the other members of the board. "[I'd] reached the pinnacle of my dreams of what I wanted to be—on the board of the State Historical Society," but "the worse [the controversy with the Pawnees] got the madder I got!" He explained, "What really set me off was how rude the bastards were on the [board]."

Welsch started to compare the Pawnees' quest for their remains with that of others. He wondered—aloud—why Americans treated the dead of white settler Americans differently than those of American Indians. He would ask the other board members, "Are we worried about remains in Korea and Vietnam? Are we digging [up] any pioneers? Are we digging up anybody in the Oregon Trail to see what they've died of? What kind of things were they buried with?" The other members of the board ridiculed Welsch's concerns, and gradually, Welsch said, "I realized the people on my side of the board . . . were not the kind of people I cared to be associated with. My mother said, 'You're judged by the company you're keeping.' I sure as hell [didn't want to be] judged by these people."

Welsch became deeply moved by the integrity and honor of the Pawnees and other Indians who requested the return of their ancestors. Welsch was probably unique among the board members in that he had already established ties with members of the Omaha Tribe earlier in his life, and he was already predisposed to listen to Indians. He invited "a couple of Omaha people down here, my relatives," for a meeting of the Historical Society Board and their Indian petitioners at the capitol building.

It was at this meeting that Welsch had his greatest moment of revelation. "We had a break. . . . in the [capitol] rotunda, there were some benches, and . . . my [Omaha] brother Buddy Gilpin [was] sitting there crying . . . and I sat down beside him, and I asked him why was he crying? Was he crying because the board had been so rude to him? . . . Or was it the disrespect for the dead? Why was he crying? And he said, he was crying because he felt bad about what was going on with the people in the [Historical Society]. He felt bad for what they were bringing down on themselves. And that just kicked me over the edge. And that was when I resigned—I wrote a long letter of resignation. They told me to go fuck myself pretty much essentially and then I was full tilt Pawnee, Winnebago, Omaha, and I was ready to fight anybody for it."

Questioning settler actions and becoming an ally to Indian people could be costly, as we have seen with Silas Soule, the soldier who witnessed the carnage of Sand Creek, blew the whistle on Colonel John Chivington, and then was assassinated. Welsch recounts, "I almost lost my job, the governor attacked me, the State Historical Society attacked me, the legislators attacked me. But I knew I was on the right side."

Gradually other Nebraskans came to agree with Welsch, including at least one state legislator: Senator Ernie Chambers, an African American representative from Omaha who had learned every arcane rule of the state legislature so as to thwart the efforts of his conservative peers and to further his progressive causes. Senator Chambers made it his mission in life to champion the underdog. (This is literally true; he regularly introduced bills to stop the poisoning of prairie dogs, a routine procedure among ranchers and farmers in rural Nebraska.) He led a decades-long fight against the state's death penalty and has always stood up for racial justice.

So Chambers gravitated to the Pawnees' cause and sought a legislative solution to the conflict. He introduced Legislative Bill 340 in January 1989 to the Nebraska state legislature to stop the practice of looting Pawnee and other Nebraska Indian graves and to create a process to return most ancestral remains and some burial goods to tribes.

Senator Chambers was not only a good listener with a particular radar for injustice. He was also an outstanding orator in the tradition of Ponca Chief Standing Bear. On the day that LB 340 came before the Nebraska state legislature, a group of fifty schoolchildren were in the balcony of the capitol. The president of the legislature invited Chambers to speak. His speech went to several single-spaced pages in the legislative record. Perhaps the most powerful part of his speech was this:

What we are talking about with this bill is nothing less than human dignity, and what we are asking for is common decency. The same concern accorded to those that we identify as Native Americans accorded routinely to every other group on this planet and certainly in this country. It should not be necessary for a group who were wronged in the first instance to be required to bring out their religion and have it pass muster before those who may have wronged them in the first instance. They should not be required to prove every tenet of their creed, or their doctrine, or their dogma as no other member of any religion is required to do before he or she is allowed to say that "I reverence and respect my dead and I want the same respect from you." We must be able to conceive of the idea that to Native American people there can be as much concern on their part of their ancestors who are departed as we have for ours.

Further, Chambers saw the bill as a means to make amends for the past: "We didn't need a bill like this to protect the ancestors of white people or any other group, and I think the very fact that we have to do it in this fashion is a shame upon all of us, but we can rectify a long-existing wrong as much as lies within our power."

Senator Dennis Baack was equally adamant that the bill represented an opportunity to rectify a historical wrong. "We're talking about doing something that is right and doing something for a people who have been put down all of their lives and throughout much of their history. We need to do this to try and correct some of the mistakes that we have made in the past. You can't totally correct those, I realize that. But we do have here a chance to correct some mistakes that have been made and to do absolutely the right thing."

LB 340 proved to be controversial, but Chambers and Baack were persistent, as were the Pawnees and their settler allies and advocates. Walter Echo-Hawk remembers, "That was very difficult, probably the biggest political battle in that session of the [legislature]. . . . It was the first state law in the country that actually repatriated dead Indians that were in the possession of state museums back to their tribes of origin for reburials. It was a very fraught campaign."

In May 1989, Nebraska's legislature passed LB 340, the Unmarked Human Burial Sites and Skeletal Remains Protection Act, the first state to pass a repatriation act. It had far-reaching consequences. As Echo-Hawk explains, "The [Nebraska state legislature] passed this landmark law. It became a precedent for other states and got into the national level. It became a precedent for the law that was passed in 1990, Native American Graves Protection and Repatriation Act (NAGPRA)." Echo-Hawk adds, "It all came from our heartland here, where peoples could see quite quickly the need for a respect to honor our own dead and our Indigenous Nebraskans. It rose from our heartland and established a nationwide legal standard, and now it's taken for granted as the order of things."

Despite this clear victory, the Historical Society, still under the direction of Hanson, refused to comply with the law. Just one month after the law went into effect, Hanson refused to let Pawnee researchers review burial records. The Pawnees requested access to the documents under Nebraska's open records law in January 1990. Hanson responded by filing a lawsuit against the Pawnee tribe; he claimed the Historical Society was a private agency that was not subject to state's open records law. (This of course was news to Nebraska's taxpayers, as the state budget provided the society with over $3 million each year.)

Hanson and the Historical Society lost every court case but still sought to thwart the Pawnees from regaining their ancestral remains. Hanson finally released an inventory of Pawnee remains in 1990, but it was incomplete. The tribe filed a grievance, but a mediator could not resolve their dispute. The state ombudsman ruled in the Pawnees' favor in 1991 and ordered the Historical Society to repatriate all Pawnee skeletal remains and burial offerings that it held. Finally defeated, Hanson resigned the following year.

The Historical Society and the University of Nebraska, with which it was closely connected, thereafter became responsive to and cooperative with Indian nations who sought the return of their ancestral remains. They also became remorseful and sought to make amends. Beginning in 1998, following revelations that some Indigenous remains in the university's anthropological teaching collection had been incinerated surreptitiously in the 1960s, the university convened major NAGPRA meetings of sixteen tribal nations on the Great Plains. The university chancellor apologized to the tribes, and in 2001, he established a memorial on

campus to honor "an unknown number of Native Americans whose remains had been taken from their graves for inclusion in the University of
Nebraska's archaeological collections" and "to remind future generations
of this cultural injustice." The memorial ends by stating, "May we learn
from this and treat all persons with honor and respect."

It took several more years for the Pawnees to conduct an inventory
of the Pawnee ancestors in the Historical Society's vaults, and then to
repatriate and to rebury them. It was thus a long ordeal for the Pawnees
to regain their beloved relatives. They had had to confront disrespect,
insensitivity, and outright hostility from influential settlers. They had
ultimately prevailed, but this battle could have left the Pawnees embit-
tered. It would have been understandable if they wanted nothing more
to do with Nebraska settlers. But the Pawnees did not bear a grudge,
and their long dispute with the Historical Society did not lead to further
enmity but in an unexpected direction.

CHAPTER 14

Hands

Kevin, Boots, Joe, and I pulled up to the nursing home, perched atop a tree-covered hill, in Pawnee, Oklahoma. The staff had reserved a small conference room for us right off the dining hall. When we arrived Boots and Joe immediately started scurrying about the small room to set up all their video and sound equipment. Soon a Pawnee elder, Francis Morris, came into the room, his daughter and nephew pushing his wheelchair. Mr. Morris smiled broadly and greeted us heartily. In his eighties, and suffering from multiple health problems, it is still clear that he was once an all-star athlete.

Playing football and basketball and running track as a child in Pawnee enabled Morris to get a college scholarship. Then he became a teacher and spent most of his adult life in California. When he retired, he came back to Pawnee, where he became involved in the Pawnees' efforts to properly rebury their relatives.

When the Pawnees finally won their battle against the Historical Society, teams of Pawnee leaders then had to engage in the emotionally and spiritually grueling task of identifying the remains of their ancestors. On many occasions Morris went up to Nebraska with two of his closest friends to help repatriate his Pawnee ancestors. He told us how Ronnie Good Eagle, a spiritual leader, would burn cedar and smudge Morris and other Pawnee men before they went to the Historical Society to visit their ancestors.

"And then we would go in into the rooms and look over the inventories" of their relatives, Morris told us. "And lots of times we would go to the storage facility and then we'd be able to go through and handle the [remains] if we wanted to, and we usually did." Often Pawnee caretakers would open a storage box to find only a small part of an individual. Morris lamented, "Some of those remains are just a few bones, not even, you never get a complete skeleton. Sometimes it's a cranium, sometimes just teeth." Morris gestured as if cupping the head of a baby and commented, "It makes you think when you have a little skull that big, you know, and you had to put him down, and they're usually just in little brown sacks or some kind of wrapping paper."

Pat Leading Fox, chief of the Skidi band, had a similar experience when he went to the Historical Society to retrieve the remains of Pawnee people. He told Kevin and me, "Here was stacks of boxes and boxes, . . . bones, skulls. So we were having to open them, make sure what was [recorded in the inventory] . . . was in there. Well, I grabbed this one box and I opened it and it was a baby skull. And that's when it hit me, . . . and I started crying. This baby, I could have been related to him."

It was disturbing for the Pawnees and their Nebraska Indian friends to see how the Historical Society had dehumanized their ancestors. Louis LaRose, of the Winnebago tribe of Nebraska, helped with the repatriation work. He told his Oglala Lakota friend Chuck Trimble, who later served as president of the Nebraska State Historical Society's Board from 1995 to 1997, "Those remains were from a museum and were in plastic bags numbered with codes that would tell a researcher the gender, age and other facts that could be discerned, as well as the geographic coordinates of the location where the bones were unearthed." Trimble recounts LaRose's "deep sorrow that those individuals had names, loving names that told of exploits, of lineage and of endearment; and those names were obliterated and replaced by cold numbers."

To the bitter end, some staff members of the Historical Society still refused to respect Indigenous concerns. As the Pawnees and their friends packed up their ancestors' remains, LaRose said to a salvage archaeologist for the state of Nebraska "that the return of the Pawnee remains in the wooden coffins was a reason for celebration. The archaeologist countered that 'those aren't coffins; they are storage boxes.'" The Pawnees persevered, despite such disrespect. At last they were able to discard the cold numbers and invoke the names of their beloved ancestors again.

But now the Pawnees faced a new challenge: where to rebury their relatives. They could bring them to Pawnee, Oklahoma, but then they would be far from their homelands. They could try to bury them in their homelands along the rivers of Nebraska, but they had no designated space.

Roger Welsch had by this time developed a strong alliance with the Pawnees. He realized that he could do something to support the Pawnees' repatriation. He offered them a hillside cemetery plot on the sixty acres on the Loup River that he owned in Dannebrog, Nebraska.

The day Pawnee leaders and dignitaries came to see Welsch's land stands out in his memory. Welsch had researched the local history and found that the first Danish settlers who had come to the area had interacted with Pawnee people on this very spot. This was land where the Pawnees had once built their earth lodges, where they had planted the Three Sisters and potatoes, too. They had not visited for more than 120 years.

The day that Kevin and Boots and I met with Welsch, after touring the hamlet of Dannebrog, he brought us to this land. The path from Welsch's old cabin to the river is now overgrown with mostly deciduous trees. But Welsch helped us imagine the day when the Pawnees returned: "The first time the [Pawnee] contingent came out here to survey a place for the reburials, I showed them all kinds of places down here." He pointed in the direction of the river. Welsch was stunned when "leading men in the tribe in suits, good clothes" simply waded into the river. "They cr[ied] and pull[ed] the water over their hair," Welsch recounted. They drank the water "because it was their River—the Loup River, the Loup Pawnee River, it's Plenty Potatoes River."

Welsch was deeply affected by the Pawnee leaders' profound and abiding connection to their homelands. He told us, "I got home that night, and [my wife] Linda and I both looked at each other, and said, 'You know they're not visiting us on our place, we're visiting them on their place.' And that sealed it." The couple decided, "We're going to leave [the land] to them in our will." The Welschs were not going to wait for the U.S. government to finally make amends for their violation of treaties, their violence, their appropriation of Indian lands. They were going to take matters into their own hands.

What moved Welsch from words to deeds (literally, deeds)? What would inspire other settlers to take similar action? This question has occupied many people who live in societies that are trying to transition from bitter enmity to social harmony, from stark inequality to egalitarianism. Pumla Gobodo-Madikizela, a black psychologist who served on the South African Truth and Reconciliation Commission, at one time believed that if white South Africans simply learned the factual evidence of what happened to black South Africans it would change their perspectives. They would want to support policy changes and transform their society.

Many of us have shared Pumla's faith in education. We have assumed that if settlers learn the truth of our painful histories, they will be moved to support reconciliation. But is this the case? Pumla came to feel that evidence and knowledge were not enough to get white South Africans to care and take responsibility. Now, she insists, what is needed is resolve and a willingness to engage. But what is it exactly that builds resolve and leads to a willingness to engage? How do we move from words to action, from hearing and accepting the truth to taking part in reconciliation?

The Pawnees did not immediately take Welsch up on his offer of a burial ground on his land along the Loup River. They decided on a different place near the town of Genoa for the first re-interment of their ancestors. But over time they acquired the remains of hundreds of their ancestors, and they approached the Welschs again.

But this time the couple did *not* want to leave the sixty acres to the Pawnees in their will. This time, they had an even better plan. Welsch explains, it "was Linda's idea, she said why don't we give it to them now and that way instead of missing all the fun 'cause we're dead, we can be here in it and celebrate with them all of these things." So, in 2007 the Welschs transferred the deed of their sixty acres to the Pawnees.

The return of this small acreage to the tribe has enabled a powerful reconnection between the Pawnees and their homelands. In October 2008, the Pawnees held a reburial of their ancestors' remains on the hill over the Loup River. As he sat in his wheelchair at the nursing home, Morris told us about that event. He describes how Welsch and one of his friends dug a huge grave, "about twice the size of this room. And we had a couple guys that were with us and we had all those remains and boxes, different size boxes. And, the University of Nebraska gave us . . . two dozen blankets, Pendletons." The Pawnees lowered the boxes into the grave and then placed a layer of Pendletons over them. Then, Morris explained, "we put . . . another layer of [boxes and] blankets until we put them all down there and were able to cover them all with Pendletons."

Attendees at the burial ached with sadness for the treatment of their ancestors, but the reburial brought some relief. A young Pawnee man, Warren Pratt, gave a prayer in Pawnee on the occasion. Chuck Trimble was in attendance. He later shared the translated words of the prayer:

> Old Ones, I want to speak to you. I am Pawnee. My grandparents were Pawnees. . . . I speak for the Pawnee people. We're glad that you are home. We are sorry that you have had to be gone so long. It hurt us to know that you were in museums. It hurt us to know that you were away from the Pawnees. We don't live here anymore. We live in Oklahoma. All our people are there. We are well. It is a good home. But this is Pawnee land. This is our home, too. Our people walked here a long time ago. We walk here again. We look and see our people. We listen and hear them speaking. This is our home. We want you to rest here. You won't be disturbed anymore. God has brought you here. Old Ones, you are home. It is good. We are happy.

Thus, the reburial was filled with a sense of tempered solace that the Pawnees could finally bring their ancestors home. Trimble shared that "at the graveside, several people spoke of their feelings of sorrow for those whose spirits were held captive by researchers and curious collectors, and joy at seeing and participating in a solemn ceremony to bring them home and free their spirits." This was a bittersweet moment of intimate reconciliation, the culmination of a long engagement that started in 1988.

A settler—Welsch—had listened to a group of Indigenous people—the Pawnees—when they told of the harms they had suffered. He had changed his mind. He had used his voice to advocate for change. Together with his wife he had joined in partnership with Indigenous people. But the Welschs had gone beyond words. They took a concrete action to rectify a past harm. The Pawnees had regained some of what they had lost through this gesture.

Cynics and critics among us could dismiss Welsch's gesture as the result of white savior syndrome or the product of liberal white guilt. But speaking with Welsch—ever witty, eternally self-effacing—it is clear that it was not guilt or paternalism guiding his actions. It was both a result of the friendships he had formed with Pawnee people and a sense of justice, accountability, and the desire to make things right, as much as was in his power.

But the real test of Welsch's gesture is not anything he may say about it. It is how the Pawnees see it. In the nursing home, Morris tells Kevin and me, his eyes tearing up, that he and Roger Welsch became *iraris* to one another. Francis explains that "*irari* is a Pawnee word that means if you had twenty good friends, good friends, then the one you would take to be your brother, is your *irari*. And it's that strong a word, and it's not to be tossed around. You could call your friends, whatever you want to . . . but your *irari* is different. And so, . . . Roger and I adopted each other that way."

Pat Leading Fox, a former cop, was direct with Kevin and me when we asked him about Welsch. "Roger? I love Roger. I love him. At first, when this all was getting started, I was like, what's his motive? . . . He's got to have a hidden agenda. Nobody does this. Nobody just gives their land like that without something in return, you know? And, as we sat and talked, he told us basically this was y'alls land. . . . I'm just here to take care of it." Pat and other Pawnee leaders "spent a couple of days up there [with Roger] and just talked," Pat tells us, "and then I knew he was sincere, I knew it."

Walter Echo-Hawk publicly extolled Roger Welsch's contribution at an event in Lincoln in 2018. "Thanks to Roger," he said, "the Pawnees are still here [in Nebraska] today. We may live in Oklahoma, but we are landowners in the State of Nebraska, you know, on Roger's Place. Despite all the big efforts to take our land, Roger . . . gave his land back to the Pawnee Nation."

Everyone we met in Pawnee, Oklahoma, conveyed similar sentiments about Welsch and how much they appreciated his return of the land. It's not often you find such consensus among a group of American Indian people, or anyone. The attitude of the Pawnees to the return of their land makes it clear that they saw Welsch's act as a genuine gesture of respect that had meaningful material consequences.

To express their gratitude, on a sunny Saturday in late April 2007 at the Pawnee nation headquarters in Oklahoma, one hundred tribal members gathered to receive the Welschs' gift and to induct them into their tribe. A tribal nation isn't usually open to new members, except through birth. Kevin and I asked if the Pawnees had adopted other non-Pawnees recently. Only Billy Graham, decades ago, they told us. The Pawnees began with a Pipe Ceremony, then a feast and an honor dance, concluding with a cedar ceremony to adopt Roger and Linda. Now that they had regained a presence in Nebraska the Pawnees even chose Welsch to represent them on the Nebraska Commission on Indian Affairs.

Chuck Trimble had also become close to Welsch and brought him into his Lakota family in 2005. He gave him the name Clown Medicine. Trimble explained that "in Lakota culture, as in many Native American societies, the clown is an important member of the clan or band. He brings happiness, and sometimes his humor brings ridicule on anyone who tries to seize power and bully the people. The *heyoka* is the Lakota clown, a holy man of sorts. Because Roger Welsch uses his humor to give joy and laughter, but also uses it as a weapon in defense of the Indian people and their tribes, and all oppressed people, I give him the name, Heyoka ta Pejuta, Clown Medicine."

The Welschs' actions inspired other Nebraska landowners. Two other settlers, one in Grand Island and one in Aurora, read about the return of the Welschs' land to the Pawnees and decided to repatriate their properties to the Pawnees as well.

And across the nation, other individuals and communities came up with the same idea and took similar action. Kevin and I have come across more and more individuals, groups, churches, municipalities, corporations, and other entities that have handed back land to Indian communities, from Kansas to California, from New York to Colorado. Interestingly in the United States it is at the grassroots that this type of reconciliation is proceeding apace. We may not have a formal truth and reconciliation process, but we have a nascent social movement.

What's more, it is a movement that is making what may be the most meaningful type of reconciliation possible: true restitution, the return of land. As Walter Echo-Hawk expressed to Kevin and me, "If a person is wanting to heal a historical injury or to bring about a reconciliation or a true atonement of a painful past, when it comes to our native people, it's all about the land. And there's nothing better that one can do than to return the land. And that would be the highest and best thing that a person of goodwill could do."

Not every settler is on board, of course. Whenever I give a talk, a member of the audience invariably says, "This talk of reconciliation is all very nice, but what can we really do? Give the land back?" And then he (or sometimes she) laughs nervously and looks around through the crowd to gain their affirmation.

"Well, yes, actually, you can!" I've taken to saying.

My flip answer doesn't sit well with many settlers, particularly rural residents who have grown deeply attached to the land that their family may have owned for several decades. Welsch, like many settlers, also loved his land. "It's a piece of ground I've had for forty-five years," he says of the sixty acres he returned to the Pawnees. "I love it with all my heart, on that beautiful river, the wildlife is spectacular." The Welschs wanted to live out their days there, but they didn't know what would happen to the land after their deaths. Their children were living far away in cities and had no intention of coming back to rural Nebraska.

Welsch did not want to sell the land, either, because he feared that a new landowner would undo all the work he had done to restore it to its pre-settler habitat. "More importantly to me, was that land, and I didn't want someone to come in there and destroy everything I've worked so hard all my life for planting trees, returning it to native grasses, to native plants, to making it a wildlife refuge." Welsch knew the Pawnees would take care of the land, as they had for centuries before he had owned and occupied it.

Undoubtedly, the thought of returning land to Indian people feels threatening to many settlers, as if they are losing something. But Welsch insists that returning the land has been more of a reward than a sacrifice. Handing back the land has "been the best thing I've ever done in my life," he tells us. "And I've come to the point where I really believe that's why I'm on this Earth. Everything I've done in my life has led to this place and this thing—returning the Pawnee nation to their homeland. And this is the first land they owned [in Nebraska] since 1873."

At a 2018 event in Lincoln with Walter Echo-Hawk, Welsch stood up and declared, "The rewards are immense. . . . I was asked when I decided to return our land and home to the Pawnee, 'What would [we] leave our children with?' I said, 'I would leave them with a better world,' and I believe that's exactly what we've done. . . . the kindness of the Pawnees has been immense, and my hope is that we can correct some of the errors that were committed on the frontier." New friendships, even better ways of being in the world, have developed as a result of Welsch's offering, and the gift the Pawnees gave to him in return. As Dawna Riding In Hare, a member of the Pawnee business council, puts it, "It's not just the land that we've received back. It's the relationships that we've developed in doing that with Roger."

The Pawnees have not just used the land for reburying their ancestors. They return frequently to their repatriated land and have re-Indigenized their old camping grounds. Welsch tells us that now the land "is holy, . . . it's been blessed many times, and we sat around this fire and had a lot of good talks; had singers in the backyard celebrating battles of hundreds of years ago; and hearing stories and hearing songs." During the solar eclipse of August 2017, a large group of Pawnees trekked up to the Loup River, erected sixteen tents, and camped on their land. "And we had ceremonies going on down at the river," Roger recounted, "and ceremonies here and up on the hill in different ways of celebrating the eclipse."

It is not unsettling but gratifying for Welsch to see the Pawnees back on their land. Many of the Pawnees "who come back here," Welsch explained to Kevin and me, "have said that they never came back to Nebraska [before] to visit because they heard so much from their grandparents about how wonderful a place it was that they had lost. They couldn't bear to come back and see it gone. And now they're coming back because now they can see what they have again, and it's a blessing."

That's what the Pawnees we met in March 2020 conveyed, too. Pat Leading Fox calls Nebraska his "motherland." When he learned of the return of Roger's land to the Pawnees, it moved him powerfully. "To think that, you know, my ancestors, . . . walked that place, [were] living there, camping, . . . it made it feel very special that that was going to be ours."

Electa Hare-RedCorn experiences a complicated mixture of feelings whenever she travels to Nebraska. She says, "It's really hard to explain other than it's just breathtaking and it's a sense of peace and it's a heavy, heavy sense of sadness." She elaborates: "Pawnee people . . . some of our values are service and reverence, and we've always been service-oriented. So all of the dedication that we had put into . . . serving and protecting our people, but also protecting the expansion of the railroad at the time, . . . we were doing that to protect our people, protect our villages and protect our families. So it's really disheartening and sad to see that through all the service and the reverence, we still lost what we would consider our Homeland."

Yet Electa regularly takes groups of Pawnees back to Nebraska. She told Kevin and me, "It's been really nice to have these trips back to the Homeland and to . . . see [how the Pawnee visitors'] breath gets taken away when we cross the river or get close to those rivers. And I felt that same feeling the first time I went in 2012."

It's not just adults. We visited a school in Pawnee, Oklahoma, and talked with middle schoolers in a Pawnee language class who had visited their repatriated land on the Loup River and other sites in

Nebraska. Tyrone is a bit of a class clown. We had already heard about him several times before we met him. On a class trip to Nebraska in the cold spring, he had fallen into the Platte River, twice. Of what the trip meant to him, he told us, "I was looking in the woods and I was like, is this where some of my ancestors used to live? Is this where they used to walk? It was pretty cool for me."

Welsch's return of the land has not only affected the Pawnees, giving them a small place to return to, but in the spirit of reconciliation it has also had an impact on the townspeople, nearly all white settlers, of Danne-brog. Welsch tells us, "I was worried for a long time about what the people in this little town are going to think when the Indians come back. You know there is guilt, there is uneasiness, there is all kinds of strange feelings going on." Welsch remembers that "one half [of] the people were saying: 'is there going to be a casino down there?' and the other half were saying: 'is there going to be a casino down there?!'" Many Dannebrog settlers had probably never met any Indians.

"We decided we better tell them what was going on," Welsch remembers. "So, we had a meeting over here in the town hall, and opened it up to questions." One person asked, "What's it going to be like when the Indians are in town?" Welsch knew what she was thinking. Having been fed a diet of stereotypical images all of her life, she wanted to know, "Are there going to be drunks laying out here, and the gutter with brown paper bags, and all of that?" Welsch replied, "Well, I'll tell you what. I think you'll see a lot of people with better education and better dressed than you usually see around town." Welsch believed that the Pawnees who returned to Dannebrog would overturn local settlers' preconceptions about Indians.

Indeed, Welsch's predictions have come true.

When the Pawnee are here and it's becoming more and more frequent—not just for special occasions like reburials or ceremonials or the eclipse—but just coming back because this has now become a second home. The Pawnee flag flies on Main Street. There's a new mural over here on the American Legion building, and while there is a picture of the Danes coming to America, there's also a picture of the Pawnee who were here before. And more and more the Pawnee have become an integral part of this community, which means that the community has accepted them. But, I think equally important, is that the Pawnees have accepted this town. . . . I knew we passed a huge threshold when the Danes had their annual Danish Festival, the first weekend in June, and the marshal of the parade was the Pawnee tribal council chairman.

The little town even boasts the Pawnee Arts Center, a place run mostly by settler volunteers where Pawnee artisans sell some of their wares and which sponsors a lecture series.

Welsch's act has had ripple effects, many of which he might never have imagined. The return of land to the Pawnees by Welsch and several other settlers has bolstered another major reconciliation effort: the growing of Pawnee corn varieties in Nebraska again after more than a century. Deb Echo-Hawk, Walter and Roger's sister, started the Pawnee Seed Preservation Project. She explained to Kevin and me, one winter day in Lincoln, how it came about:

Well, in the 1980s . . . my brother Walter Echo-Hawk had received some seeds from Diana Henry . . . that she had acquired out of a Kansas museum. And she said they were pretty well tucked away in a basement. And so, she felt like it was important to see if the Pawnees wanted them back. So, she had given some to my brother. At the time, we were living in Boulder, Colorado. And so, we started to grow out the seed. . . . My older brother grew it around Lyons, Colorado. My younger brother grew his in Longmont and I was in Boulder.

It's as if Deb is telling an ancient Pawnee story as she recounts what happened next. "My younger brother ate all his," she laughs. "And he said it was beautiful and wonderful. Raccoons and deer made use of some of my oldest brother's garden. And when I felt like it was ready, I called my oldest brother and said, 'Hey, let's go ahead, I could fix some up for us.' He said, 'No Deb, you better hang on to those seeds because this is our tribe's, and we don't know if they have any or not, so just hang on to them.' And that's what I did."

In 1997, Deb moved back to Pawnee, Oklahoma. She and her cousin Alice "went around to different elders and said, 'Hey, we're people of the corn; we're people of the buffalo, where's all the corn?' Because when you read any kind of story or books about the Pawnees that was all that they talked about. We got the help of the culture committee at the time to ask the same question, 'Do you have any of these seeds? [Do] the families?' And they did, they started turning them in to me."

Soon the traditional council of chiefs from the four Pawnee bands "got on board with the project," Deb explains, "and made me the keeper of the seeds. And we just started collecting them from families. And some had seeds in sacred bundles. We'd wait three years or so before they would open them, and there would only be a little handful of seeds there. So, we didn't start out with very much. We had elder Nora Pratt, a beautiful Pawnee woman. She was very elderly at that time that she remembered all of our corn and talked about it. We asked her to please bless these seeds. And so, we laid out a blanket on a lawn and she sat down and held the seeds in her hand and started praying. About an hour and a half later, she was finished praying. And it's really that prayer alone where she had talked about the seeds and hope that one day our people will eat it and enjoy the food of our ancestors again. That started the project."

While Deb was finding and preserving ancient seeds in Pawnee, a Nebraska settler, Rhonda, or Ronnie, O'Brien, was becoming interested in planting traditional Pawnee corn in Nebraska. Ronnie had grown up on a farm but then moved away and gained a business degree. In 2000, the little city of Kearney, Nebraska, opened an Archway that bridges Interstate 80 as both museum and tourist attraction, primarily to commemorate the pioneers who had traveled along the great Platte River Road that the interstate now covered. Ronnie, a history buff, was excited to get a managerial position there.

"So it wasn't very long after we opened that people would come and find me that worked for me and say somebody wants to talk to the manager," Ronnie tells Kevin and me as she sits cozily beside Deb, "and it would be someone who was Native and they would say, 'You're doing a great job of telling the history of all the trails and all the transportation routes, but you're missing about a thousand years.'" This happened many times.

Local teachers also approached Ronnie. "And then I had fourth-grade teachers saying to me, 'You have great programs here at the Archway, could you develop a Native American program because we're afraid to teach anything beyond what we read in the book, in our textbooks. We don't want to get anything wrong,' which I thought was honorable of them."

Ronnie shared a sensibility with Roger Welsch. She did not become defensive when Native people criticized the museum; nor did she ignore their requests. She listened, she heard, and she got curious. These ideas germinated within Ronnie, and she thought about what action she could take. "Then I finally decided three years after we were open that it was time to start a program. So, if I was going to start a program about Natives, I was going to have it be about the Pawnee because their territory was large, and we were right in the middle of it."

Ronnie had good instincts. She hadn't had many interactions with Native people in her life, but, she says, "I thought if I'm putting on a program about Pawnee history and this being their area, I want them to help tell their story. I don't want to read what some white man wrote in the late 1800s, early 1900s. I want the Pawnee, if they're willing to help me put together a program about their homeland, and them being in Nebraska."

Ronnie also sensed that she might do more to convey Pawnee history, culture, and survival with a hands-on project than with a traditional exhibit. "I knew they had a lot of different varieties of corn and it was sacred to them," she told us. "So I wanted to have the Pawnee help me start a program. And I wanted to have a garden as part of it because my mom was a big gardener and we all grew up gardening, all four of us still gardening. So . . . I contacted the Pawnee Nation; it took three attempts to find someone that they thought I could talk to."

That someone was the Pawnee keeper of the seeds, Deb Echo-Hawk. They spoke for an hour during that first call and Deb told her of how she had collected, preserved, and grown some ancient Pawnee seeds. Ronnie was amazed and heartened. "To me, the biggest miracle of all of this is that they kept [their corn] viable somehow, even though it wasn't home,"

Ronnie told us. "But they were to the point where they were afraid to do anything with it. And I said, well, maybe we can try it here in your homeland." Deb was intrigued, but it wasn't her decision to make. She would have to clear this with the tribe's Culture Committee.

Deb tells us that at first the committee was wary. "They were saying, 'Okay, well we don't have that many seeds. Why do you want to trust this chatty woman to grow up our seeds?' And I said, 'I don't know; you look at a package of seeds and on the back, it says it grows best in this region. And so, with our seeds, it needs to go back home. You know, because that's where our seeds were best grown. We talk about all the hundreds of acres we had, and so let's grow it back in the region that it belongs.'"

The Culture Committee eventually approved Deb and Ronnie's project and since then, for sixteen years, the Pawnee farmers, nearly all of them women, have been partnering with Nebraska settlers to grow Pawnee corn on its homeland. Deb laughs and says, "I love to remind Nebraskans that we were the first Cornhuskers," the name of the University of Nebraska's football team, which inspires such fierce devotion across the state.

Ronnie and Deb's mutual interest in growing Pawnee corn sprouted into a deep friendship and a reconciliation project. Ronnie says, "For the last sixteen years, we've talked almost daily. It's interesting that our friendship, if we hadn't done that, Deb says if we hadn't had these constant communications, we wouldn't be where we are today. I mean, it's amazing the things that have happened. It's layers and layers and layers deep now, this project and all of the things that's impacted and affected. We still talk every day and really the center of our conversations, our friendship, everything that we've developed around it, the center of all of that is Pawnee corn. Because believe it or not, every day we have things going on to talk about with the Pawnee corn."

A number of Pawnee women have joined Deb and Ronnie in what they call a rematriation movement. Deb has mentored Electa Hare-RedCorn, who told Kevin and me, "we held onto that corn from that walk all the way from Nebraska down to Oklahoma, a really difficult, challenging time where many of our people were lost, but some of us still held those seeds, then it's just a really beautiful thing to me that decades later, we found a way for those seeds to still germinate, even if they were down to like a handful of seeds. We know that each seed had been prayed over, had been thought over. And so that's part of the values I see in our Pawnee people. And it's an easy parallel to seed work, but it takes a little bit of thinking about it, thinking how we lost it, and then thinking how we've come to the point where we needed to preserve it, to perpetuate and move it forward."

Cynics and critics among us could dismiss the Welschs' gesture, or Deb and Ronnie's Pawnee Seed Preservation Project, as proverbial drops in the bucket. The Pawnees lost millions of acres of land. What good is the return of just sixty acres by a few settlers? Or why bother to grow a few fields of Pawnee corn on a few acres of their once vast territory? In the large scheme of things, these intimate and grassroots (literally, grassroots) acts of reconciliation between Nebraska settlers and the Pawnees may seem trivial.

Critics could say, too, that these are merely futile actions meant to compensate for lack of progress on the national level. Australian historian Peter Read, who was so involved in his nation's reckoning with its Stolen Generations, a term he coined, believes not. He once told me, "The incremental grassroots approach achieves more than the grand gesture." I'd like to believe that is true. But without policy reform and big structural changes, are these just feel-good efforts that make little difference in the lives of Indigenous people?

Such questions get to the very heart of how social change occurs. Often, I hear the criticism that Action X or Gesture Y is useless, because it doesn't address the systemic disparities that are embedded in the structure of American society. It is true that Welsch's hand-back of sixty acres does little to address the foundational crime committed against the Pawnees and the ongoing inequities that resulted from it. But it does do something. It acknowledges the abuse and makes one small step toward rectifying it. It is an act of transformative reconciliation, albeit a small one. This step is no small thing to the Pawnees.

And how exactly *do* we change the structures and systems that undergird our society? What role do individual and localized acts play in moving the big ship of state? Sometimes it seems that arguing that we need structural change, and that nothing less will do, can become an excuse to retreat into cynical inaction. It's also a classic settler colonial move: a belief that we need to come up with the all-encompassing solution that will finally resolve "the Indian problem" once and for all. The comprehensive solutions that past settlers came up with—war, removal, reservations, allotment, boarding schools, termination, relocation— were utter disasters. Designed by settlers at a far remove from Indigenous people, they delivered blow after blow to American Indians and failed to reckon with the root of the problem: dispossession.

There might be many of us settlers who want to do what Welsch did. We'd like to give back what was taken to Native Americans. But maybe we don't own land to return. What can we do? A group of Indigenous and non-Indigenous Australians in the state of Victoria came up with an ingenious way for settlers to still take accountability: the Pay the Rent campaign, a kind of grassroots reparations. Settlers commit to paying 1 percent of their income to a nonprofit Indigenous organization that then redistributes the money.

The organizers explain their motive. "Saying Sorry isn't enough. We live, work and play on land that was forcibly taken from Aboriginal people. There has been no Treaty with the First Nations of this place and the effects of colonisation continue to this day. We could wait for years for the government to sign a Treaty and commit to justice and restitution for Aboriginal people. But we don't want to just sit and wait. We want to act now in solidarity with Aboriginal people."

Some Americans have created something similar. Corinna Gould, a member of the Confederated Villages of Lisjan, a group of Ohlone people, created the Sogorea Te' Land Trust to regain some of their land in the East Bay of the San Francisco area. She invites settlers in the area to pay a Shuumi land tax. "Shuumi in our language means gift," Gould explains.

This is happening elsewhere, too. Northern California settlers in the Humboldt Bay region initiated an "honor tax" that individuals can pay to the Wiyot people. In Seattle, the Coalition of Anti-Racist Whites started the Real Rent Duwamish campaign. More than 6,800 settlers have signed up to pay the Duwamish Tribe rent. One of them explains, "I pay Real Rent to the Duwamish Tribe monthly because as a white settler on this land, it is my responsibility to acknowledge the land I live on belongs to the Tribe and they deserve to be compensated by all of us, regardless of what our government has determined."

Some communities are taking action on a collective scale. The Wiyot people had been asking for the return of some of their ancestral land—the Duluwat Island in Humboldt Bay—since the 1970s. Finally the city of Eureka returned the 280-acre island in October 2019 to its Indigenous owners. The Wiyot had considered this island the center of their universe. It had been in their possession until the night of February 26, 1860, when a group of white male settlers from Eureka massacred about 250 Wiyot people while they performed an annual ceremony that is designed to heal the world and restore balance.

Some churches, too, are returning property to Indian communities or organizations. The Rocky Mountain Synod of the Evangelical Lutheran Church in America transferred the deed of the Bethany Danish Lutheran Church, on a prime lot in downtown Denver, to an urban Indian group, the Four Winds American Indian Council. Sky Roosevelt-Morris, a Shawnee and White Mountain Apache member of the council, now calls it "decolonized land" and "a liberated zone."

This kind of small and local intimate reconciliation, based on the return of actual land, may not be just a second-best alternative to a grand and national reckoning. It might actually be the road to truth and reconciliation in the United States. It keeps control within the hands of Indigenous people but engages settlers. It leads to specific and meaningful actions rather than more vague and general apologies and promises. It is premised on an Indigenous ethos of relationality and reciprocity rather than on western conceptions of reconciliation that are often framed and guided by financial metaphors and considerations: tallying up offenses, calculating what is owed, and paying debts. Those of us who are settlers can do something, however small, here and now. We have to constantly remind ourselves that we must do it under the leadership and in partnership with Indigenous people. Together with others doing their own small part, our work starts to swell into something larger and more powerful.

CONCLUSION

Hearts

Too often discussions about the painful histories between settlers and Indigenous peoples devolve quickly into defensiveness and denial. The script goes something like this:

TRUTH TELLER: "The United States needs to face up to its history. As a nation we need to talk about the historical abuses Indigenous peoples suffered."

SETTLER DESCENDANT SKEPTIC: "What's the point? We can't go back to the way it was. The past is past."

TRUTH TELLER: "Indigenous people are still suffering from the legacies of those earlier abuses. Settlers need to take responsibility."

SETTLER DESCENDANT SKEPTIC: "The government may have dispossessed Indian people of their lands, but my ancestors had nothing to do with it. They were just poor farmers who needed the homestead they gained to survive."

TRUTH TELLER: "The government represented your ancestors. They were acting in their name."

SETTLER DESCENDANT SKEPTIC: "Ok, maybe my ancestors had some responsibility—in the nineteenth century. But I had nothing to do with it. Why should I feel guilty or shameful about that past?"

MORE RECENT IMMIGRANT: "Yeah, and my ancestors weren't even in this country when all those abuses happened. Why should I be held responsible for those actions?

TRUTH TELLER: "Because settlers—whether they are descendants of the pioneers or more recent immigrants—have benefited from the dispossession of Indian people. And we still do. Don't we settlers owe something to Indigenous people?"

SETTLER DESCENDANT SKEPTIC: "Well, maybe what happened wasn't right. But we can't just pay every Indigenous person reparations. And we can't give back the land. You can't expect settlers to give up what they have worked so hard for."

TRUTH TELLER: "We need to at least start the conversation about acknowledgment and accountability."

MORE RECENT IMMIGRANT: "You are just trying to make people feel guilty and ashamed. People don't want to be hit over the head with a club."

This script has been written and distributed widely. We settlers readily audition for and accept our roles in the epic saga. We mouth the platitudes we've heard over and over. Many of us settlers think that if we acknowledge this history, we will walk around in a state of perpetual shame, a big red T (for thief, trespasser) emblazoned on our chest. We fear that we will be forced to give up something—land, money, or at the least a view of ourselves as the heroes of history. Many of us prefer continued denial.

But not one settler I've interviewed who has taken part in reconciliation has ever mentioned shame or guilt. They commonly speak instead of gaining life-affirming friendships and a sense of interconnectedness with Indigenous people. For those settlers who have repatriated land to Indian nations, not one has represented themselves as giving up or losing their land. Each reconciler has, in fact, expressed that it is they, not the Indian people they have known, who has been given a gift.

Of all the conceptualizations of reconciliation that I have come across, it is that of Galarrwuy Yunupingu, the Yolngu land rights campaigner from Arnhem Land in northern Australia, that has most captivated me. He declared in 2016 to the settler inhabitants of his nation, "Let us be who we are—Aboriginal people in a modern world—and be proud of us. Acknowledge that we have survived the worst that the past has thrown at us, and we are here with our songs, our ceremonies, our land, our language, and our people—our full identity. What a gift this is that we can give you, if you choose to accept it in a meaningful way."

Galarrwuy Yunupingu wants settlers in Australia to acknowledge his pain and that of other Indigenous people, but he does not expect them to wallow in guilt or bathe in shame. Nor does he want settlers to see him and other Indigenous people as objects of pity and charity cases. Instead he wants them to be aware of and accept the great gifts that he and his Aboriginal sisters and brothers have to share. Few people I know—in the midst of long-standing abuse—could be so forgiving and so generous.

Yunupingu's conception of reconciliation is not just his individual view; it is rooted in values that are common to Indigenous societies around the world. We could sum up these values with three R words: relationship, respect, and reciprocity. How deeply humbling it is to learn as a settler that many Indigenous people conceive of reconciliation not in a transactional western sense as a way to settle old scores but as a life-affirming and ongoing process of building respectful relationships and sharing gifts through reciprocity.

When Kevin and Boots and I interviewed Electa Hare-RedCorn in Pawnee, Oklahoma, in March 2020, she similarly recommended using Pawnee concepts and values to guide truth and reconciliation efforts. When we asked her if she saw her Pawnee seed preservation work as reconciliation, she told us, "I feel like I lean toward the word reciprocity . . . because when you talk about . . . reconciliation, . . . sometimes that lifts the responsibility, like once it's reconciled, it's done. . . . So I like the word . . . rematriation. I like the idea of reciprocity and, building those relationships. But I think acknowledgment is part of that reconciliation. It's just those are probably all big English words and I want to help us find the Pawnee words that will help us frame that out."

Galarrwuy Yunupingu is but one of many Indigenous leaders in Australia who is promoting this type of reconciliation. After the nation's settler leaders failed to deliver on reconciliation, after many decades, a group of Indigenous leaders met in 2017 at the center of the nation, at Uluru, the giant red rock at the center of the continent (formerly known

as Ayers Rock). They drafted the Uluru Statement from the Heart, ostensibly to call for constitutional reforms: a voice in Parliament and a
commission to supervise a truth-telling and treaty-making process. But
their manifesto goes far beyond a mere call for policy change. It eschews
the bureaucratic language of most government statements. The one-
page declaration lays out in language as beautiful and generous as
Galarrwuy Yunupingu's a compelling vision for reconciliation.

The drafters assert that Aboriginal people have an "ancestral tie" to
the land. This is the basis for their "ancient sovereignty," which "has
never been ceded or extinguished, and co-exists with the sovereignty of
the Crown." They ask, "How could it be otherwise? That peoples possessed a land for sixty millennia and this sacred link disappears from
world history in merely the last two hundred years?" The statement's
writers speak of the "torment of our powerlessness" and the desire for
constitutional reforms "to empower our people and take a rightful place
in our own country." They conclude, "When we have power over our
destiny . . . [our] culture will be a gift to [our] country."

When settler media sources cover Indigenous issues at all, they rarely
represent Indigenous people through the capacious visions of Electa
Hare-RedCorn, Yunupingu, or the Uluru Statement from the Heart.
Instead they so often portray Indigenous peoples as mired in deficits.
Reporters recite the grim statistics that beset Indigenous communities:
lower life expectancy, higher incarceration, elevated suicide rates,
greater unemployment, worse poverty.

We settlers are missing so much when we only ever read or view such
limited representations. They encourage us to continue to see ourselves
as distant from Indigenous people, only connecting with them when we
bestow from our superior position our pity or our charity. They prevent
us from seeing the inextricable connections between settlers and Indigenous people. They wall us off in a shrunken box, with a few air holes
and tiny windows. We cannot even see the gifts that Indigenous people
bear; we certainly cannot accept them.

The drafters of the Uluru Statement assert their vision of what reconciliation should encompass. They use a Yolngu word to express their
desire for their version of a Truth and Reconciliation Commission: a

Makarrata commission. Makarrata means "the coming together after a struggle." The drafters asserted, "It captures our aspirations for a fair and truthful relationship with the people of Australia and a better future for our children based on justice and self-determination." They end by saying, "We seek to be heard. We leave base camp and start our trek across this vast country. We invite you to walk with us in a movement of the Australian people for a better future."

Indigenous people have suffered so much injustice at the hands of settlers. They have endured well more than one hundred winters of hardship and oppression. They could be bitter and angry, and some are, understandably. Given our histories, it would not be surprising if Indigenous people wanted nothing to do with settlers. Indeed, some have sought to disengage with settlers, as much as is possible in our modern society. So, it is all the more heartening to know that some Indigenous leaders have not given up all hope that we settlers will finally come to our senses. They have extended us an invitation to walk with them, and we would do well to accept it.

Indigenous conceptions of reconciliation are not punitive. They do not seek vengeance or retribution. They do not threaten the existence of settlers. Indigenous people want acknowledgment of their history, recognition of their sovereignty, support for their self-determination, and return of some of their land. This will enable them to flourish and to share their gifts. A group of Canadian scholars and activists have asserted that one of the most important gifts that Indigenous people have to share is not only a strong attachment to the land but deep knowledge of how to sustain the land. This, more than ever, is a gift that we all need.

Today in the United States, there are settlers and Indigenous people who are engaging in building Yunupingu's world. You may find them in unexpected places. My husband, Tom, and I went to the planting of Ponca corn on the Tanderups' farm in Neligh, Nebraska, in the spring of 2019. About fifty people, both American Indians and settlers, showed up. After sharing a potluck meal in the Tanderups' utility shed, we headed out to the Ponca cornfield. Many of us piled onto a flatbed trailer, which Art pulled with his tractor up to the field. We gathered in a circle near a row of cottonwood trees. A Ponca elder led a prayer. The circle of people then unfurled into a long line along the edge of a plowed field. A Ponca woman and her child came down the line with a bucket of scarlet corn kernels. Each of us took a handful, cradling them carefully in our palms. On the signal from Art Tanderup, each of us bent down, nestled three seeds into three holes in the loose earth, and then stood again. After everyone had planted their seeds, the line took one step forward and repeated the process until all the corn was planted. A group would gather again in a few months to harvest the sacred corn.

After more than one hundred winters, this corn is growing in its homeland again. And through planting the long-dormant seeds together, people Indigenous to this land as well as the settlers who displaced them are starting to build small relationships that may grow into thriving and nurturing friendships.

Other seeds were planted by the Tanderups' alliance with the Poncas. Reconciliation did not end with planting and harvesting Ponca corn. It was not a fixed end point but an ongoing practice. The Tanderups decided, like Roger Welsch before them and countless Americans around the nation, that they could do more. So, in 2018, they returned ten acres of land to the Poncas.

Art told us how that came to be:

Kind of the seed was planted there, too, back in that spirit camp in that tepee. Because Mekasi [Horinek] talked about [how] his grandfather was eight years old when he walked this land south. And he talked about how the land was theirs. . . . this farm is also part of that trail of tears. Someone is ashamed of the history that happened in the past and the things that were done that shouldn't have been done. I guess we came to the realization that this is just a small thing. It's not a very big thing. Just a small thing that maybe we can do to help the relationships. This was their land, . . . and now, they can have this land again. We can utilize it; they can utilize it; and we can work together on this project to have the land back, to have part of that sacred trail of tears back, and to work together in the future.

The Tanderups do not know Roger Welsch and are not familiar with his own return of land to the Pawnees. But the Tanderups have developed similar sentiments to Roger's about how returning the land is "the right thing to do."

Many people would consider the Tanderups' repatriation of land to the Poncas and Roger Welsch's return of land to the Pawnees as great sacrifices. As Welsch notes, "I absolutely love that piece of ground, and now we are giving it away and what some people consider to be the most stupid thing anybody could conceivably do." But, Welsch says, "it actually turned out to be the other way around." Their gestures set in motion a series of events that had led to a new kind of community, not one of thieves and trespassers but of kin and neighbors.

Let us return to that hot and windy June day in 2018 on the Tanderups' farm when the Tanderups and the Poncas held a ceremony to repatriate ten acres to the Ponca people. When Art signed the deed over to the Poncas, he said, "We hope again that we can grow more seed, that once again can be given to the people. . . . what we harvest this year [can be planted] in their land in Niobrara. . . . We're so thankful. We're honored and humbled to be a part of this and just to know some good things are going to happen."

A few months later, Art and Larry Wright Jr., chairman of the Ponca Tribe of Nebraska, reflected on that day. Art told Kevin and me, "To me, it was so powerful. Larry was here to represent the northern Ponca and Casey Camp[-Horinek] was there to represent the southern Ponca. It was like, here we were the four of us together. We were doing something almost magic; it was powerful. At one second, I had to hold back the tears, and the next second, but those tears were of joy. Here was something happening I thought it was almost unimaginable."

Larry agreed.

Yeah, same feelings, almost surreal! But when I was sitting there and I'm thinking about where we are today, we're coming up on the twenty-seventh anniversary of the tribe being restored, after being terminated in the 1960s. That's why I'm thinking of my relatives, my father, aunts, uncles that went through that loss of land. Again, our property was sold off and allocated. My relatives were being told you're no longer Ponca—Ponca tribe doesn't exist anymore. And then here we are. At that time, I'm sitting at this table and for the second year in a row, accepting a donation from somebody who is giving land back to the Ponca. We wouldn't have thought about that thirty years ago, twenty years ago. We had to scrap and fight for all of the resources that we've been able to get since the tribe has been restored. Here we are on that event, on land that our people roamed, called home, died for and were ultimately removed off. From that context, this is one more thing that helps restore a people and pride in being a Ponca; pride in who we are as Natives; and again, pride in working with somebody who is willing to help our people, and bringing us together.

Mekasi Horinek ended the ceremony on the Tanderups' farm by beating a small hand drum and singing a Ponca song: a gift. He told the people gathered there, "All my life I dreamed for my people to be able to come home. My entire life I've watched my people suffer in Oklahoma. I've watched as a refinery and other environmental stressors have taken the lives of my relatives," at a rate of one death a week, in a community of just eight hundred people. He tells us he has nine children and fifteen grandchildren. He just buried a granddaughter and his father is a cancer survivor. "Every family in my tribe has suffered from some type of illness that's been brought on by our environment, from our forced removal to Oklahoma—malaria, whooping cough, smallpox, to the cancer of today." He explains, "So throughout my lifetime I've dreamed of bringing my people home, of us having a place to be able to come home and breathe this clear air that I smell today. To have this wind blow in our faces and not stink the way it does at home, from the refinery. To be able to drink the water from the aquifer, because our aquifer's contaminated where I live. You're all blessed with what you have."

Then Mekasi spoke of what reconciliation meant to him. "In my lifetime I didn't know I would see a day like this come. . . . Art and I have had a lot of conversations throughout our travels together over the past five years. We got to spend time with each other and know each other's families, know each other's children and grandchildren. To know each other's heart. And I know that what he's doing is from his heart. From my heart I just want to say I love you my friend."

The ceremony on the Ponca homelands and Tanderups' farm shows us that Indigenous-led intimate reconciliation is not an occasion for settler guilt or humiliation but a practice that is life affirming, empowering, and enriching. It calls on us settlers to take risks and make ourselves vulnerable and accountable, but it also challenges us to live more fully, to truly connect, to thrive. Facing our history, together, is not an exercise in shaming. It is an act of respect, integrity, and interconnectedness. The Poncas and the Tanderups are showing us just how much we have to gain by confronting and learning from our history, not denying and evading it.

Reckoning with our painful histories also leads us in creative new directions. It can be so easy to retreat and to stay within the confines of our own communities, to only associate with those people we identify as like us. We cower from difference. At best we call for "tolerance." But reconciliation challenges us to do better and promises, too, a richer life. Writing in another context, African American feminist author Audre Lorde declared, "Difference must be not merely tolerated, but seen as a fund of necessary polarities between which our creativity can spark like a dialectic."

The alternative to practicing reconciliation is living in denial. When we live in a community of thieves, in a place built on lies, denial is our religion, our diet. Not only do we deny our history, but we also deny our interconnectedness to other humans, other creatures, and the natural world. In reality most of us are living in denial most of the time. We are disconnected from others, atomized, although we may have a false sense of connection because we have a thousand Facebook friends or five hundred followers on Twitter and Instagram.

Practicing reconciliation is not easy and it will not always make settlers feel good. Engaging in reconciliation will, at least at first, probably make us uncomfortable, vulnerable, and uncertain. How could it not?

It requires us to face the worst of ourselves and our history, to acknowledge that our advantages and privileges have been built on disadvantaging Indigenous people.

Practicing reconciliation as a settler also relies on a delicate balance. At the same time that we settlers must reach across boundaries and divides, we must also speak less and listen more. We will have to give up the notion that we know best and stop rushing to fix things. Our lack of control will feel disorienting. We can't expect that Indigenous people will immediately, if ever, forgive or trust us. We cannot seek their approval. We will make mistakes, and we will need to be humble and apologize.

But practicing reconciliation is also co-creating a new world, a world in which we extend ourselves out to those around us, not one in which we shrink in fear from one another. This is a world in which we seek out and learn from one another. In this world we don't just tolerate one another and our differences. We do not stagnate in isolation. We thrive in interconnectedness.

On the Tanderups' farm on that June day, Mekasi Horinek bears his gift: he sings his song "to honor this day, that we could all be together in unity, in strength and power, as one family and one people." Wearing jeans and a turquoise T-shirt made for the occasion, he beats out a steady drumbeat. His mother, Casey, ululates during certain parts of the song. He tells us afterward that the song says, "to the Creator, it's a beautiful path, or a beautiful road, that you've given this warrior to travel." He ends the ceremony by saying, "My children and grandchildren are here today. And they're going to remember this and they're going to carry this throughout our oral history, what took place here today. I hope this is just a beginning, a new beginning for our people to come together in unity."

As Art Tanderup says, in returning ten acres of land to the Poncas, "it's something that makes our hearts feel good."

ACKNOWLEDGMENTS

While working on this book, I have received many gifts and gotten to know many generous spirits.

For the gift of time to learn more about truth and reconciliation, at home and abroad, I thank the Carnegie Corporation of New York for an Andrew Carnegie Fellowship and the University of Nebraska at Lincoln.

For the gift of sharing ideas and passion for truth and reconciliation, I thank Sherry Smith for our long-ago conversation over dinner one autumn evening in Albuquerque.

For their gifts of hospitality, in all senses of the word, I am grateful for my far-flung friends who shared their worlds with me. In the UK, I thank Sarah Pearsall for her warm companionship and for her reading of my first musings on the subject of this book, along with Seth Archer. In Canada, much gratitude to Tricia Logan, Paulette Regan, Allyson Stevenson, Adele Perry, Jarvis Brownlie, and Andrew Woolford. In Australia, many thanks to Kat Ellinghaus, Lynette Russell, Ann McGrath, Denise Cuthbert, Kim Mahood, Mandy Martin, and Guy Fitzhardinge. In New Zealand, I am very grateful to Erica Newman, Barry Rigby, Dolores Janiewski, Paerau Warbrick, Lachy Paterson, Angela Wanhalla, Vincent O'Malley, and Joanna Kidman.

Back home in Nebraska, I have been blessed to get to know, learn from, and work with Will Thomas, Dawne Curry, Liz Lorang, Judi gaiashkibos, James Riding In, Boots Kennedye, Georgiana Ausan, and Christine Lesiak. In particular, I want to thank Kevin Abourezk, who cofounded Reconciliation Rising with me in 2018. It is a pleasure and honor to work with you, Kevin.

Thanks also to Priscilla Grew, who as I was preparing the final manuscript, taught me much more about NAGPRA and repatriation in Nebraska.

I especially want to recognize my PhD students and research assistants, Baligh Ben Taleb and Susana Geliga, who have also been my teachers.

Profound thanks to all the people who agreed to be interviewed for this book and for the Reconciliation Rising project.

For taking time away from their busy lives to read and comment on the first draft of this book, I thank my first readers and dear friends: Kelly Lytle Hernández, Ari Kelman, and Beth Piatote. I also thank my second readers, Chris Rogers, Priya Nelson, and Sherry Smith, for their support and astute insights. I appreciate, too, the team of committed and competent book producers at Princeton University Press and copyeditor Jenn Backer. To the Ponca/Lakota artist, Sarah Rowe, my deepest thanks.

For the gift of many decades of friendship and her help coming up with a title, I thank Isabel Velázquez.

For his loving care of our mother in the last year of her life, I thank my brother James and his wife, Amy. For their gifts of love and companionship, I thank Tom, Riley, Cody, Alicia, and Abigail.

NOTES

Introduction

PAGE NOS.

3   "A bunch of us would stay": Art Tanderup, Helen Tanderup, and Larry Wright Jr. interview with Kevin Abourezk and Margaret Jacobs, August 8, 2018, Neligh, Nebraska. Edited audio version at https://soundcloud.com/indianz/a-farm-family-and-a-gift-to -two-tribes.

5   "The soldiers got on their horses": U.S. Senate, *Removal of the Ponca Indians*, 46th Cong., 2nd sess. (Washington, DC: Government Printing Office, 1880), 500.

7   "not a nation, but a community of thieves": Xavier Herbert, "Australia Has the Black Pox," in *Xavier Herbert: Episodes from* Capricornia, Poor Fellow My Country, *and Other Fiction, Nonfiction, and Letters*, ed. Frances de Groen and Peter Pierce (St. Lucia, Queensland: University of Queensland Press, 1992), 228.

9   "we became strangers in our own land": Tanderups and Wright interview, August 8, 2018.

9   "Our bodies are the texts that carry the memories": Katie Cannon, quoted in Bessel van der Kolk, *The Body Keeps the Score: Brain, Mind, and Body in the Healing of Trauma* (New York: Penguin, 2014), 186. Neuroscientists such as van der Kolk have found a physiological basis for this theory in the emerging field of epigenetics.

10 "Other groups have difficulties": Vine Deloria Jr., *Custer Died for Your Sins: An Indian Manifesto* (New York: MacMillan, 1969), 1.

11 "Our people lost the sacred corn" and other quotes by Art Tanderup: Tanderups and Wright interview, August 8, 2018.

12 This day on the farm "has been many years in the making" and other quotes by Casey Camp-Horinek and Larry Wright Jr.: Land return ceremony, Tanderup family farm, June 10, 2018, Neligh, Nebraska, https://www.youtube.com/watch?v =3idIs5sufcE.

16 "All nations depend on forgetting": Michael Ignatieff, *The Warrior's Honour: Ethnic War and the Modern Conscience* (New York: Henry Holt, 1998), 166.

16 "some things ha[ve] to be forgotten": Roger Epp, *We Are All Treaty People: Prairie Essays* (Edmonton: University of Alberta Press, 2008), 134.

17 "This whole pipeline thing is something we wish didn't happen": Tanderups and Wright interview, August 8, 2018.

Chapter 1

PAGE NOS.

24 **"The prominent feature of this region" and a** (25) **"smothered passion for revenge agitates these Indians":** Quoted in Bureau of Indian Affairs, *Annual Report of the Commissioner of Indian Affairs* (Washington, DC: Government Printing Office, 1860), 138–39.

27 **"Those that perpetrate such unnatural, brutal butchery":** *Weekly Commonwealth,* Denver, June 15, 1864, available at https://www.pbs.org/weta/thewest/program /episodes/four/whois.htm.

27 **"The conflict is upon us":** Proclamation of Governor John Evans, August 11, 1864, United States Congress, Senate, *Reports of the Committees,* 39th Cong., 2nd sess. (Washington, DC: Government Printing Office, 1867), 47, available at https://www.kclonewolf .com/History/SandCreek/sc-documents/sc-evans-second-proclamation.html.

27 *all* **the tribes "on the plains":** Quoted in Tom Bensing, *Silas Soule: A Short, Eventful Life of Moral Courage* (Indianapolis: Dog Ear Publishing, 2012), 76.

28 **"What shall I do with the Third regiment":** Wynkoop's testimony in United States Congress, *Report of the Joint Special Committee to Inquire into the Conditions of Tribes* (Washington, DC: Government Printing Office, 1867), 77, https://quod.lib.umich.edu /m/moa/ABB3022.0001.001?rgn=main;view=fulltext.

29 **"carriages of many of the leading citizens tagged along the rear of the formation":** Bensing, *Silas Soule,* 88.

29 **"no war would be waged against them":** Major Scott Anthony, Report, November 16, 1864, in United States War Department, *The War of the Rebellion: A Compilation of the Official Records of the Union and Confederate Armies,* ser. 1, vol. 41, *Reports,* part 1 (Washington, DC: Government Printing Office, 1892), 914.

32 **"From down the creek a large body of troops was advancing at a rapid trot" and other eyewitness accounts by George Bent and Little Bear:** George E. Hyde, *A Life of George Bent Written from His Letters* (Norman: University of Oklahoma Press, 1968), 151–54, 157.

Chapter 2

PAGE NOS.

37 **"I've been trying to tell our story for my whole life" and other quotes:** Interview with Darren Parry by Margaret Jacobs, Friday, October 18, 2019, Las Vegas, Nevada.

40 **"The day you wrote" and other quotes:** Silas Soule to Sophia Soule, December 18, 1864, and January 8, 1865, available at http://www.kclonewolf.com/History/SandCreek /sc-documents/sc-soule-letters.html.

40 **"hundreds of women and children were coming toward us" and other quotes:** Silas Soule to Edward Wynkoop, December 14, 1864, available at http://www.kclonewolf .com/History/SandCreek/sc-documents/sc-soule-to-wynkoop-12-14-64.html.

41 **"Bucks [Indian men], women, and children were scalped" and other quotes:** Joseph
Cramer to Edward Wynkoop, December 19, 1864, available at http://www.kclonewolf
.com/History/SandCreek/sc-documents/sc-cramer-to-wynkoop-12-19-64.html.

45 **a "commanding presence"; "herculean frame"; "making rapid advancement as a
public speaker"; "regret . . . in the loss of so valuable and worthy a citizen"; "have
learned to respect and esteem him"; "I feel compelled to strike a blow in person";
and "crazy preacher who thinks he is Napoleon Bonaparte":** Lori Cox-Paul,
"Chivington," *Nebraska History* (winter 2007): 129–31.

46 **"they are stealing large numbers of stock":** George Stillwell, Acting Assistant
Adjutant-General, Colorado Territory, April 13, 1864, quoted in U.S. War Department,
*The War of the Rebellion: A Compilation of the Official Records of the Union and Confeder-
ate Armies* (Washington, DC: Government Printing Office, 1880–1901), 150.

46 **promising to "'kill and scalp all [Indians], little and big'":** Quoted in Bensing, *Silas
Soule*, 95.

47 **"thieving and marauding bands of savages" and advised "a few months of active
extermination against the red devils":** "Its Effect," *Rocky Mountain News*, December 31, 1864, and "To Fight Indians," *Rocky Mountain News*, August 10, 1864, available
at https://www.kclonewolf.com/History/SandCreek/sc-reports/rocky-editorials
.html and https://www.kclonewolf.com/History/SandCreek/sc-documents/rmn-to
-fight-indians.html.

47 **He "berated the assembled men" and "believed it to be right or honorable":**
Quoted in Bensing, *Silas Soule*, 97, 98.

48 **"to ascertain . . . who are the aggressors":** Report of the Secretary of War: Sand
Creek Massacre, S. Exec. Doc. No. 39–26 (1867), 3, available at https://play.google.com
/books/reader?id=MVFHAQAAIAAJ&printsec=frontcover&output=reader&hl
=en&pg=GBS.RA13-PA1.

49 **"a coldblooded slaughter" that would "cover its perpetrators with indelible
infamy":** Quoted in Ari Kelman, *A Misplaced Massacre: Struggling over the Memory of
Sand Creek* (Cambridge, MA: Harvard University Press, 2013), 194.

49 **Chivington had "deliberately planned and executed a foul and dastardly massacre"
and other quotes:** "Massacre of the Cheyenne Indians," in United States Congress, *Report of the Joint Committee on the Conduct of the War*, 38th Cong., 2nd sess., vol. 3 (Washington, DC: Government Printing Office, 1865), iii–v, available at https://babel.hathitrust
.org/cgi/pt?id=miun.aby3709.0003.001&view=1up&seq=5.

49 **Sand Creek "scarcely has its parallel in the records of Indian barbarity":** Quoted
in Helen Hunt Jackson, *A Century of Dishonor: A Sketch of the United States Government's Dealings with Some of the Indian Tribes* (New York: Indian Head Books, 1994),
357–58.

50 **"no one will be astonished that a war ensued":** Quoted in Valerie Sherer Mathes,
ed., *The Indian Reform Letters of Helen Hunt Jackson, 1879–1885* (Norman: University of
Oklahoma Press, 1998), 108.

50 **"We all feel disgraced and ashamed" and other quotes:** Quoted in Mathes, *Indian
Reform Letters*, 103.

52 **"he fully expected to be killed"**: Quoted in Bensing, *Silas Soule*, 112.

53 **"his vigorous sentiments were endorsed"; "the author of deeds that in another day of our history"; "as a slander upon the Christian name"; and** (54) **"under the cloak of religion"**: Quoted in Cox-Paul, "Chivington," 135, 143.

Chapter 3

PAGE NOS.

56 **"to honor and remember their ancestors and to ask the spirits for healing for all peoples"**: Sand Creek Massacre National Historic Site, National Park Service, https://www.nps.gov/sand/planyourvisit/annual-spiritual-healing-run-walk.htm.

56 **"We're remembering our past when we run"**; (57) **"as you're running, you're praying"; and other White Thunder and Wallowing Bull quotes**: McKayla Lee, "Spirits Run Deep at Healing Run," *Southern Ute Drum*, December 6, 2019, available at https://www.sudrum.com/top-stories/2019/12/06/spirits-run-deep-at-sand-creek/; Savanna Maher, "Healing Run Honors Victims of the Sand Creek Massacre," *Wyoming Public Media*, November 29, 2019, available at https://www.wyomingpublicmedia.org/post/healing-run-honors-victims-sand-creek-massacre#stream/0.

57 **"You feel proud when you run" and "They tried to kill us off, but we are still here"**: *We Are Still Here: Sand Creek Massacre Healing Run*, trailer, https://www.facebook.com/wohehivfilms/videos/trailerwe-are-still-here-sand-creek-massacre-spiritual-healing-run/235285137422930/.

57 **Some neuroscientists, too, have posited that trauma even creates epigenetic change that can be inherited by children**: The science of epigenetics is still in its infancy and has many skeptics. Still there are a growing number of scientific studies that show how the trauma experienced by one generation can alter the expression of a gene and be passed on to future generations. See van der Kolk, *Body Keeps the Score*.

58 **"If our National Capitol was located a little nearer the scenes of our Indian depredations" and "covered themselves with glory"**: Quoted in Cox-Paul, "Chivington," 133; quoted in Mathes, *Indian Reform Letters*, 14.

59 **Chivington "was just doing his duty" and "I Stand by Sand Creek"**: Quoted in Kelman, *Misplaced Massacre*, 191, 218–19.

60 **educational "materials should not encourage or condone civil disorder" and other Jefferson County quotes**: Nicky Woolf, "US 'Little Rebels' Protest against Changes to History Curriculum," *Guardian*, September 26, 2014, available at https://www.theguardian.com/world/2014/sep/26/-sp-colorado-ap-history-curriculum-protest-patriotism-schools-students; Lindsey Bever, "After Weeks of Student Protests, Colorado School Board Gives a Little on 'Positive' History Curriculum," *Washington Post*, October 3, 2014, available at https://www.washingtonpost.com/news/morning-mix/wp/2014/10/03/after-weeks-of-student-protest-colorado-school-board-gives-a-little-ground-on-positive-history-curriculum/?noredirect=on.

62 **"this dark chapter in our history"**: Lee, "Spirits Run Deep at Healing Run."

62 **"Does unexamined history reappear in some form" and "violence denied and repressed doesn't disappear":** Lewis Hyde, *A Primer for Forgetting: Getting Past the Past* (New York: Farrar, Straus and Giroux, 2019), 233–34.

62 **"healing for all people, regardless of ethnicity, race, or religion":** Sand Creek Massacre National Historic Site, National Park Service, https://www.nps.gov/sand/planyourvisit/annual-spiritual-healing-run-walk.htm.

Chapter 4

PAGE NOS.

67 **"how our people were removed as others came in":** Tanderups and Wright interview, August 8, 2018.

68 **"totally unfit for occupation of the Indians":** Quoted in David Wishart, *An Unspeakable Sadness: The Dispossession of the Nebraska Indians* (Lincoln: University of Nebraska Press, 1994), 137.

69 **"I cannot speak in too high terms":** Agent J. A. Potter quoted in U.S. Senate, *Removal of the Ponca Indians*, 13.

70 **"trespassers on our own land":** Tanderups and Wright interview, August 8, 2018.

71 **"Why [the Poncas] should be selected to starve to death":** Quoted in Joseph Starita, *"I Am a Man": Chief Standing Bear's Journey for Justice* (New York: St. Martin's, 2008), 35–36.

72 **"He called us all to church" and other White Eagle quotes:** U.S. Senate, *Removal of the Ponca Indians*, 458–59.

73 **Kemble and his men "grew very angry"; (74) "We had no interpreter"; and "when the Agent saw how nearly starved we were":** Transcription of Standing Bear's remarks to General Crook, Fort Omaha, April 13, 1879, quoted in Thomas Henry Tibbles, *Standing Bear and the Ponca Chiefs*, edited and with an introduction by Kay Graber (1880; Lincoln: University of Nebraska Press, 1972), 7–8.

74 **"leave us there to find our way back as best we could":** Telegram from White Eagle, Standing Buffalo, Standing Bear, Smoke Maker, Frank La Flesche [White Swan], Little Chief, Big Elk, and Gohega to the President of the United States, March 27, 1877, in U.S. Senate, *Removal of the Ponca Indians*, 432.

75 **"Hurry and pack up":** Quoted in U.S. Senate, *Removal of the Ponca Indians*, 8.

75 **"We would rather die here on our land than be forced to go" and "You professed to be a great Christian":** Quoted in U.S. Senate, *Removal of the Ponca Indians*, 461.

76 **"We were starving"; "After [Kemble] had told them that they must go"; and "We told [Kemble] that the land was very dear to us":** Quoted in U.S. Senate, *Removal of the Ponca Indians*, 461, xiii, 222.

76 **"This is my land":** Quoted in Tibbles, *Standing Bear*, 10.

76 **"I want you to get off from this reservation" and "Swindled Poncas":** Quoted in Starita, *"I Am a Man,"* 53, 58.

77 "The Poncas have a clear right to the land on which they now are": Quoted in U.S. Senate, *Removal of the Ponca Indians*, 428.

77 But "when we came back from the council" and (78) "We told them that we would rather die": Quoted in Jackson, *A Century of Dishonor*, 203.

78 "one house (I built it with my own hands . . .)": Quoted in Tibbles, *Standing Bear*, 13.

79 "Let us dwell for a moment on this picture": Jackson, *A Century of Dishonor*, 212.

79 "Was not the discomfort": Quoted in U.S. Senate, *Removal of the Ponca Indians*, 78.

80 "On the morning of [May] 19th I broke camp" and other Howard quotes: Howard to Commissioner of Indian Affairs, May 30, 1877, included in U.S. Senate, *Removal of the Ponca Indians*, 446–47.

80 "I want the whites to respect the grave of my child just as they do the graves of their own dead": Quoted in Starita, *"I Am a Man,"* 68.

81 "for burial in a style becoming the highest civilization" and "It is a matter of astonishment to me": *Annual Report of the Secretary of the Interior for 1877* (Washington, DC: Government Printing Office, 1877), 494, 496.

82 "We left in our own land two hundred and thirty-six houses": Quoted in Tibbles, *Standing Bear*, 119–20.

82 "When we got there the Agent issued no rations": Quoted in Starita, *"I Am a Man,"* 91.

82 "a great mortality will surely follow": *Annual Report of the Secretary of the Interior for 1877*, 496.

82 "We said we could go back": Quoted in Tibbles, *Standing Bear*, 14.

83 "After we reached the new land, all my horses died": Quoted in Jackson, *A Century of Dishonor*, 203.

83 "There were dead in every family": Quoted in Tibbles, *Standing Bear*, 15.

84 "as far as the eye could see, were small mounds": Dorothy Clarke Wilson, *Bright Eyes: The Story of Susette La Flesche, an Omaha Indian* (New York: McGraw-Hill, 1974), 202.

84 "As he was dying" and "I could see nothing ahead, but death for the whole tribe": Quoted in Tibbles, *Standing Bear*, 25, 15.

85 "Some of the children were orphans"; "half of us were sick"; and "When we started back": Quoted in Jackson, *A Century of Dishonor*, 203–4.

86 "I sometimes think that the white people forget that we are human": Quoted in Tibbles, *Standing Bear*, 20.

86 "remember our past, remember [where] we came from, the sacrifices [our ancestors] made": Tanderups and Wright interview, August 8, 2018.

Chapter 5

PAGE NOS.

90 "mixed lot [of Indians] belonging to the tribes" and "emerged from the wilderness": Thomas Tibbles, *Buckskin and Blanket Days: Memoirs of a Friend of the Indians* (1905; Lincoln: University of Nebraska Press, 1957), 74; Wilson, *Bright Eyes*, 168.

91   **"he had made some hard campaigns for the liberty of black men"**: Tibbles, *Standing Bear*, 32.

91   **"The wrongs of Government upon these Ponca Indians are lawless wrongs"**: Thomas Tibbles, "A Perturbance in the Indian Ring," *Omaha World Herald*, May 15, 1879.

93   **"God made me and he put me on my land"**: Quoted in Hugh J. Reilly, *The Frontier Newspapers and the Coverage of the Plains Indian Wars* (New York: Praeger, 2010), 105.

93   **"From the time I went down there [to Indian Territory] until I left" and other quotes**: Quoted in Tibbles, *Standing Bear*, 93, 94, 100.

94   **"to advance American Indian rights to be seen and heard through independent media" and "changed and healed by understanding Native stories and the public conversations they generate"**: websites of Indigenous Media Freedom Alliance and Vision Maker Media, https://www.imfa.us/ and https://visionmakermedia.org /about/.

95   **"During the fifteen years" and "present[ed] the question as to whether or not an Indian can withdraw"**: U.S. Circuit Court, District of Nebraska, *Standing Bear v. Crook*, May 12, 1879.

95   **"the Indians will become a body of tramps"**: Quoted in Starita, *"I Am a Man,"* 159.

97   **"willow thicket on one of the larger islands" and "had to go onto an island in the middle of the Niobrara"**: Quoted in Starita, *"I Am a Man,"* 176; land return ceremony, Tanderup family farm, June 10, 2018.

98   **"Susette shrank back terrified";** (99) **"felt incredibly helpless and remote"; and "Why should I be asked to speak?"**: Wilson, *Bright Eyes*, 189, 210–11.

99   **"they said they could not talk English"**: Quoted in U.S. Senate, *Removal of the Ponca Indians*, 31.

101   **"this is Minnehaha"**: Tibbles, *Buckskin and Blanket Days*, 218.

101   **"never quite able to establish her identity apart from that of 'Indian Maiden'"**: Wilson, *Bright Eyes*, 258.

101   **"a magnificent full costume of an Indian chief"**: Quoted in Tibbles, *Standing Bear*, 29.

101   wore his **"civilized costume";** (102) **"a handsome young man of commanding height and determined expression"; "a handsome young woman of twenty-three"; "wore a mantilla coat and black velvet bonnet neatly trimmed with beads"; "lovely and winning, refined of great intelligence, and with singularly sweet, graceful, and simple manners";** (104) **"Your government has driven us hither and thither like cattle"; "It was money promised by the government"; "They kill men, women, and children";** (105) **"You never get but one side"; "For the last hundred years the Indians have had none to tell the story of their wrongs"; "Set aside the idea that the Indian is a child and must be taken care of";** Standing Bear **"spoke with great animation";** (106) **"Miss Bright Eyes read her address";** Susette is **"never bitter, never vindictive"; "If I could speak before them"; "I've been a student of the English language all my life"; and "increasingly violent and vituperative attacks"**: Quoted in Wilson, *Bright Eyes*, 227, 224, 223, 217, 228, 240, 220, 221, 240, 250–51, 227, 217, 239, 236, 254.

Chapter 6

PAGE NOS.

111   *restitution,* **which redress experts define as the restoration of victims to their original state:** Theo Van Boven, "The United Nations Basic Principles and Guidelines on the Right to a Remedy and Reparation for Victims of Gross Violations of International Human Rights Law and Serious Violations of International Humanitarian Law," *United Nations Audiovisual Library of International Law* (New York: United Nations, 2005), https://legal.un.org/avl/ha/ga_60-147/ga_60-147.html. Incorporated into UN Resolution 60/147 of December 16, 2005, https://www.ohchr.org/EN /ProfessionalInterest/Pages/RemedyAndReparation.aspx.

112   **"When I was brought here a prisoner, my heart was broken"** and (113) **"We thought that all the white men hated us":** Quoted in Tibbles, *Standing Bear,* 112–13, 120.

113   **"I felt as though if there were a God he must have created us for the sole purpose of torturing us":** Quoted in in Starita, *"I Am a Man,"* 185.

113   **"For years the army did what it liked with us"** and (114) **"My dear, you have given me a new purpose in life":** Quoted in Wilson, *Bright Eyes,* 232, 233.

114   **"greatest American woman poet":** Quoted in Mathes, *Indian Reform Letters,* 5.

114   **"loathsome," "abject," and "hideous"; "using the silly legends";** (115) **and Jackson became "an almost constant companion":** Wilson, *Bright Eyes,* 234.

115   **"one-woman crusading journalistic approach":** Mathes, *Indian Reform Letters,* 6.

115   **"every ounce of her own strong influence"** and **"I am not writing—& shall not write *one word* as a sentimentalist":** Quoted in Mathes, *Indian Reform Letters,* 10, 65.

116   **"I ask of you to go still further in your kindness"** and **"I want to get my land back":** Quoted in Tibbles, *Standing Bear,* 120, 116.

116   **"Standing Bear . . . seeks a response"** and (117) **the Indians "are right & we are wrong":** Quoted in Mathes, *Indian Reform Letters,* 26, 22.

117   **"How many of the American people know anything";** (118) **"'every one of those States had been stolen from the Indians'";** and (119) **"Shall we apply the same rule of judgment to the white men":** Quoted in Mathes, *Indian Reform Letters,* 34, 51, 92.

119   **"Shall we [white settlers] sit still, warm and well fed, in our homes":** Jackson, *A Century of Dishonor,* 346.

119   **"Colorado soldiers have again covered themselves with glory"** and **Indians have been "victims of fraud and oppression":** Quoted in Mathes, *Indian Reform Letters,* 14, 78.

120   **"the history of the U.S. Government's repeated violations of faith"** and **"There is such a thing as the conscience of a nation":** Jackson, *A Century of Dishonor,* 29–30, 346.

120   **"I have done now, I believe, the last of the things I had said I never would do":** Quoted in Mathes, *Indian Reform Letters,* 84.

121   **"she is not especially in sympathy with my work"; "satisfied to have 250,000 human beings"; "In some respects, it seems to me, [the Indian] is really worse off than the slaves"; and "The thing I can't understand is that all you who so loved the Negro":** Quoted in Mathes, *Indian Reform Letters,* 136, 78, 84, 135.

122 **"By virtue of your organization, you ought to be as strong for *justice* to the Indians" and "cheating, robbing, breaking promises—these three are clearly things which must cease to be done":** Quoted in Mathes, *Indian Reform Letters*, 63; and Jackson, *A Century of Dishonor*, 342.

123 **"'restore . . . to the public domain 17,642,455 acres of land'" and "but they are to be compelled to sell them and move away":** Quoted in Mathes, *Indian Reform Letters*, 153, 154.

123 **to question this is "feeble sentimentalism":** Jackson, *A Century of Dishonor*, 10.

124 **"devoted to securing, through the regular processes of the courts":** Quoted in Tibbles, *Standing Bear*, 138.

124 **"the Poncas were unlawfully removed" and (125) the treatment of the Poncas "was without justification":** Quoted in *The Indian Question: Report of the Committee appointed by Hon. John D. Long, Governor of Massachusetts* (Boston: Frank Wood, 1880), 11–12; and U.S. Senate, *Removal of the Ponca Indians*, xviii.

125 **"A great and grievous wrong has been done to the Poncas":** Quoted in Mathes, *Indian Reform Letters*, 16.

Chapter 7

PAGE NOS.

126 **"a sense of national obligation for wrongs committed against":** Cathleen D. Cahill, *Federal Fathers and Mothers: A Social History of the United States Indian Service* (Chapel Hill: University of North Carolina Press, 2011), 26.

127 **"and found their condition very much improved" and "If the reservation system is to be maintained":** Quoted in Tibbles, *Standing Bear*, 47–48.

128 **"Boston committee insisted that [Susette's] presence was essential":** Wilson, *Bright Eyes*, 269.

128 **"They want to go back to [Nebraska]" and (129) "phenomenal liar":** Quoted in Wilson, *Bright Eyes*, 272, 274.

130 **"Some white people think that it would be better for the Indians"; "They do not know whether it would do to select the lands"; and "They are between two horns of a dilemma":** Quoted in U.S. Senate, *Removal of the Ponca Indians*, 277–79.

132 **"Down in the midst of trees, ploughed fields, and haystacks" and subsequent quotes:** Alice C. Fletcher, *Life among the Indians: First Fieldwork among the Sioux and Omahas*, ed. Joanna C. Scherer and Raymond J. DeMallie (Lincoln: University of Nebraska Press, 2013), 234, 235, 244, 94, 95.

134 **Omahas were the only Indians "remaining on their ancient homelands"; "Their attachment to the locality is remarkable"; and "They possessed the land in their thought":** Fletcher, *Life among the Indians*, 253.

134 **"must acquire English and suffer his mother tongue to die" and (135) "There is one thing I am always thinking of—a title to my land":** Fletcher, *Life among the Indians*, 329, 261.

135 **"the Indians felt themselves helpless in the grasp of a power":** Alice C. Fletcher, *Lands in Severalty to Indians: Illustrated by Experiences with the Omaha Tribe*, proceedings of the American Association for the Advancement of Science 33, September 1884 (Salem, MA: Salem Press, 1885), 8.

136 **Fletcher notes that "an educated Omaha accompanied me as my clerk" and that he had a "corps of assistants" who lent her "cordial and generous aid" and subsequent quotes:** Fletcher, *Life among the Indians*, 321–28.

139 **The Indians "should be given their lands in severalty"; (140) "For the benefit of all concerned, the Indian should be given his just and individual rights to the land"; "It is hugging a delusion"; "the Indian must die or become absorbed in the body of citizens"; and (141) Large reservations are "harmful in their influence":** Fletcher, *Lands in Severalty*, 11–13.

140 **"To those who would do something in compensation for the wrongs":** Quoted in 15th Annual Report of the Board of Indian Commissioners (1883) reprinted in Francis Paul Prucha, *Americanizing the American Indians: Writings of the Friends of the Indian, 1880–1900* (Lincoln: University of Nebraska Press, 1973), 30.

141 **"I would blow the reservations to pieces. I would not give Indians an acre of land. When he strikes bottom, he will get up":** Quoted in David Wallace Adams, *Education for Extinction: American Indians and the Boarding School Experience, 1875–1928* (Lawrence: University Press of Kansas, 1995), 53.

141 **"in no case where allotments have been made and the title secured with proper restrictions":** Fletcher, *Lands in Severalty*, 13.

141 **some members of the tribe "opened to me the meaning" of sacred pipes and other quotes:** Fletcher, *Life among the Indians*, 331–35.

142 **"Among the many noble endeavors of today":** Amelia S. Quinton, "The Women's National Indian Association," in *The Congress of Women: Held in the Woman's Building, World's Columbian Exposition, Chicago, U.S.A., 1893*, ed. Mary Kavanaugh Oldham Eagle (Chicago: Monarch Book Company, 1894), 71–73.

143 **"Chiefs oppose [allotment] because land in severalty breaks up completely their tribal power":** Fletcher, *Lands in Severalty*, 12.

143 **"smother [Indians] to death in the exuberance of its misdirected friendship":** Quoted in John Rhea, *A Field of Their Own: Women and American Indian History, 1830–1941* (Norman: University of Oklahoma Press, 2016), 95.

143 **Schurz did not explain "how the giving to an Indian of 160 acres of land can clothe him":** Quoted in Mathes, *Indian Reform Letters*, 11.

143 **"protecting and assisting the Indians of the United States in acquiring the benefits"; "friends of a sound and humane Indian policy"; "the embodiment of despotism and injustice"; and "want[ing] to keep 'the Indian as he is'":** Quoted in C. Joseph Genetin-Pilawa, *Crooked Paths to Allotment: The Fight over Federal Indian Policy after the Civil War* (Chapel Hill: University of North Carolina Press, 2012), 125, 144, 142.

144 **"All the Indians know the game is gone" and "I represent in the Ponca tribe the foremost of those who want to support themselves":** Quoted in Tibbles, *Standing Bear*, 26, 52.

145 **allotment schemes had made "no attempt . . . to deal with the problems of inheritance":** Quoted in Fletcher, *Life among the Indians*, 58–59.

146 **"No people can be helped if they are absolutely uprooted":** Quoted in Rhea, *A Field of Their Own*, 119.

Chapter 8

PAGE NOS.

150 **"A century of dishonor is being succeeded by a century of justice and generosity":** Warner van Norden statement at 16th Annual Meeting of the Friends of the Indian, 1898, reprinted in Prucha, *Americanizing the American Indians*, 86.

150 **"Last week we were at Carlisle Barracks":** Quoted in U.S. Senate, *Removal of the Ponca Indians*, 36.

151 **"We have been told there are 35,000 or 40,000 [Indian] children":** Quoted in David H. DeJong, *Promises of the Past: A History of Indian Education in the United States* (Golden, CO: Fulcrum Publishing, 1993), 110.

151 **"We have tried fighting and killing the Indians, and gained little by it":** Quoted in Richard Henry Pratt, *Battlefield and Classroom: Four Decades with the American Indian, 1867–1904* (New Haven: Yale University Press, 1964), 162.

152 **"The Indian has no book":** Quoted in Tibbles, *Standing Bear*, 29.

152 **"I say that if we take a dozen young Indians":** Quoted in DeJong, *Promises of the Past*, 110.

154 **"I remember being dragged out":** Zitkála-Šá, *American Indian Stories*, foreword by Dexter Fisher (Lincoln: University of Nebraska Press, 1921), 55–56. This story originally appeared in the *Atlantic Monthly* in 1900.

154 **"When I came there the first thing you [had to do] was be measured for a uniform":** Nebraska Educational Television, *White Man's Way: Genoa Indian School*, documentary (1986), available at http://netnebraska.org/interactive-multimedia /none/white-mans-way-genoa-indian-school.

154 **"I practically leaped from the train, tears of joy streaming down my cheeks"** and (155) **"We were controlled by whistles and bugles":** Christine Lesiak, dir., *American Experience: In the White Man's Image* (Boston: WGBH Boston Video, 1992).

155 **"Gray-beard dealt blow after blow"** and (156) **"I knelt by the bedside":** Francis La Flesche, *The Middle Five: Indian Schoolboys of the Omaha Tribe*, with a foreword by David A. Baerreis (Lincoln: University of Nebraska Press, 1978), 138, 150–51.

156 **"The dramatic increase in federal appropriations":** Joan Mark, *A Stranger in Her Native Land: Alice Fletcher and the American Indians* (Lincoln: University of Nebraska Press, 1988), 85.

158 **"I'm a father of five myself":** Interview with Nancy Carlson by Margaret Jacobs and Kevin Abourezk, Genoa, Nebraska, February 10, 2020.

159 **"We should use all our Association's resources"** and subsequent WNIA quotes: *Annual Meeting and Report of the Women's National Indian Association* (Philadelphia: Women's National Indian Association, 1883), 10, 11.

160 **"Like all uneducated people":** Tibbles, *Buckskin and Blanket Days*, 112.

160 **children as faced toward us" and "In this march of progress thru the centuries":** "Our Duty toward Dependent Races," draft of lecture, n.d., Box 11, Alice Cunningham Fletcher and Francis La Flesche Papers, National Anthropological Archives, Smithsonian Institution, Washington, DC.

162 **"received very little in the way of marketable skills":** Presentation by Murray Sinclair, Indigenous Enslavement and Incarceration in North American History Conference, November 15, 2013.

Chapter 9

173 **They told Zitkála-Šá and her friend Judéwin "of the great tree where grew red, red apples" and** (174) **"For the white man's papers, I had given up my faith in the Great Spirit":** Zitkála-Šá, *American Indian Stories*, 41–42, 97.

175 **Henry Roe Cloud of the Winnebago tribe of Nebraska:** Renya Ramirez, *Standing Up to Colonial Power: Henry Roe Cloud and Elizabeth Bender Cloud* (Lincoln: University of Nebraska Press, 2018).

176 **deemed provisions for the care of children in them as "grossly inadequate":** Lewis Meriam et al., *The Problem of Indian Administration* (Baltimore: Johns Hopkins University Press, 1928), 11.

176 **the late 1960s and 1970s, another truth and reconciliation moment in American history:** Sherry Smith, *Hippies, Indians, and the Fight for Red Power* (New York: Oxford University Press, 2012).

176 **"our national policies for educating American Indians are a failure of major proportions":** United States Senate, Senate Committee on Labor and Public Welfare Kennedy Special Subcommittee on Indian Education, *Indian Education: A National Tragedy*/A National Challenge Report, (Washington, DC: Government Printing Office, 1969), xi.

177 **critics complain that they still have a "colonial mindset":** Denise Juneau, "The Bureau of Indian Education Is Broken," *Education Week*, February 6, 2018, available at https://www.edweek.org/leadership/opinion-the-bureau-of-indian-education-is-broken/2018/02.

177 **"get the U.S. Government and churches to acknowledge their responsibility":** Telephone interview with Christine Diindiisi McCleave by Margaret Jacobs, January 29, 2016.

178 **"It's something that had to be done for our tribe" and "It's extremely sad and disappointing for the family":** Liz Navratil, "The Northern Arapaho Boys," *Pittsburgh Post-Gazette*, August 11, 2017, available at https://newsinteractive.post-gazette.com/northern-arapaho-boys/.

178 **Louellyn White (Mohawk) . . . discovered eleven children who were "'outed'":** Jeff Gammage, "A Search for Native Children Who Died on 'Outings' in PA,"

Philadelphia Inquirer, May 2, 2018, available at https://www.inquirer.com/philly/news/indian-school-carlisle-native-quaker-cemetery-outing-20180502.html?photo_10&mobi=true.

179 **"We *cannot* point with pride"**: Mrs. Winifred Kromholtz to Senator Warren Magnuson, *Indian Child Welfare Act of 1977*, Hearing before the United States Senate Select Committee on Indian Affairs, 95th Cong., 1st sess. on S. 1214, August 4, 1977 (Washington, DC: Government Printing Office, 1977), 493.

179 **"We have always been very moved by the story of the plight of the Indian"**: David Fanshel, *Far from the Reservation: The Transracial Adoption of American Indian Children* (Metuchen, NJ: Scarecrow Press, 1972), 92.

179 **Settler supporters . . . characterized Indian communities as a "dead end"**: Arnold Lyslo, "The Indian Adoption Project: An Appeal to Catholic Agencies to Participate," *Catholic Charities Review* 48, no. 5 (May 1964): 13. See also Margaret D. Jacobs, *A Generation Removed: The Fostering and Adoption of Indigenous Children in the Postwar World* (Lincoln: University of Nebraska Press, 2014).

180 **New Mexico authorities saw fit to single out Native American women for COVID-19 testing and separating them from their newborns until test results were available:** Bryant Furlow, "Federal Investigation Finds Hospital Violated Patients' Rights by Profiling, Separating Native Mothers and Newborns," *New Mexico in Depth*, available at http://nmindepth.com/2020/08/22/federal-investigation-finds-hospital-violated-patients-rights-by-profiling-separating-native-mothers-and-newborns.

182 **"I know of no Indigenous person who told their story to the inquiry"**: Mick Dodson, "Now for Real Action on Reconciliation," *Sydney Morning Herald*, February 7, 2009, available at https://www.smh.com.au/politics/federal/now-for-real-action-on-reconciliation-20090206-7zyw.html.

182 **"It was probably the toughest thing I've ever done in my life"**: Interview with Mick Dodson by Margaret Jacobs, July 21, 2014, Australian National University, Canberra.

183 **"state workers came onto the reservation. My five sisters and I were home"**: American Friends Service Committee, "Conversation with Denise Altvater on Truth and Reconciliation in Maine," n.d., ca. 2011, https://afsc.org/resource/conversation-denise-altvater-truth-and-reconciliation-maine.

184 **"we were trying to move forward" and "something more drastic was needed"**: Burns presentation for Maine-Wabanaki Truth and Reconciliation Commission, May 27, 2015, Portland, Maine; telephone interview with Carol Wishcamper by Margaret Jacobs, March 9, 2015.

184 **"we have come to realize that we must unearth the story of Wabanaki people's experiences"**: Maine-Wabanaki Declaration of Intent, available at https://static1.squarespace.com/static/5c2e615b4611a08076e730e4/t/5cdc6794e4966b24c8f312ba/1557948308240/Declaration+of+Intent+to+Create+a+ME%3AWabanaki+Truth+%26+Reconciliation+Process.pdf.

184 **"We have basically used a teaspoon to do the job of a front-end loader"; (185) "It took time to build trust"; and "I myself am not Wabanaki"**: Interview with Carol Wishcamper, March 9, 2015.

186 **"We are returning to our place of origin"; (187) "Don't talk about truth and reconciliation without including healing"; "What is one thing you want a social worker
to know"; "a therapeutic and spiritual healing of the intergenerational disenfranchised grief"; and "This will forever change how I advocate for Native children":**
Interview and correspondence with Sandy White Hawk by and with Margaret Jacobs,
February 2015 and February 2021. See also Sandra White Hawk, "Generation after
Generation, We Are Coming Home," in *Outsiders Within: Writing on Transracial Adoption*, ed. Jane Jeong Trenka, Julia Chinyere Oparah, and Sun Yung Shin (Boston: South
End Press, 2006), 291–301; and Drew Nicholas, dir., *Blood Memory: A Story of Removal
and Return* (Row House Cinema, 2019).

Chapter 10

PAGE NOS.

192 **"For our nation, the course of action is clear" and other Rudd quotes:** Transcript
and video of Rudd apology, available at https://www.sbs.com.au/news/transcript
-rudd-apologises-to-stolen-generation.

193 **van Boven principles (now known as the van Boven/Bassiouni principles):** Van
Boven, "The United Nations Basic Principles and Guidelines on the Right to a Remedy
and Reparation."

195 **"I have never been willing to embrace a formal national apology":** Howard quoted
in Justin Healey, ed., *Stolen Generations: The Way Forward*, vol. 289 in *Issues in Society*
(Thirroul, New South Wales: Spinney Press, 2009), 4.

195 **"In reality the New South Wales government was not stealing children" and "the
rescued generations":** Keith Windschuttle, "Don't Let the Facts Spoil the Day," in
Healey, *Stolen Generations*, 30. Windschuttle's essay ran in the *Weekend Australian* on
February 9–10, 2008, just before Rudd's apology.

195 **"suffered from a form of 'collective hysteria'"; "black armband view of history";
and "white blindfold" version of history:** McGuinness quoted in Damien Short,
Reconciliation and Colonial Power: Indigenous Rights in Australia (Hampshire, England:
Ashgate, 2008), 104. Blainey and Reynolds quotes explained in Patrick Brantlinger,
"'Black Armband' versus 'White Blindfold' History in Australia," *Victorian Studies* 46,
no. 4 (summer 2004): 655–74.

196 **"The fact that our predecessors or forebears were the ones who did the wrongs"
and "wealth of nations has been built on past injustices":** Janna Thompson, *Taking
Responsibility for the Past: Reparation and Historical Injustice* (Cambridge: Polity, 2002),
xviii.

199 **"What the apology has done is provide a cathartic and positive psychological effect":** Mick Dodson, "When the Prime Minister Said Sorry," in Gregory Younging,
Jonathan Dewar, and Mike DeGagné, *Response, Responsibility, and Renewal: Canada's
Truth and Reconciliation Journey* (Ottawa: Aboriginal Healing Foundation, 2009),
113–14.

199 **"What are we to reconcile ourselves to?"** and (200) **"True reconciliation means recognising we possess distinct rights"**: Quoted in Short, *Reconciliation and Colonial Power*, 132, 144.

200 **"The Government of Canada now recognizes that it was wrong"**: Stephen Harper, "Statement of Apology to Former Students of Indian Residential Schools," available at https://www.rcaanc-cirnac.gc.ca/eng/1100100015644/1571589171655. For video of apology and other statements, see https://www.c-span.org/video/?205172-1/apology -native-canadians.

201 **"Our peoples, our history and our present being are the essence of Canada"**: Quoted in "Aboriginal Leaders Look to Apology," *CBC News*, June 11, 2008, available at https://www.cbc.ca/news/canada/aboriginal-leaders-look-to-future-after-historic -apology-1.700098.

203 **"The exquisitely poignant thing is that somehow the recognition of the Stolen Generations"**: Interview with Denise Cuthbert by Margaret Jacobs, University of Nebraska, Lincoln, September 5, 2014.

204 **"I do not speak today for the United States"** and **"inadequate because it came from the wrong person"**: Gover apology available at https://vimeo.com/404428918; Marshall quoted in Melissa Nobles, *The Politics of Official Apologies* (Cambridge: Cambridge University Press, 2008), 86.

205 **"This has been a day too long in coming"**: Patricia Calhoun, "Sand Creek Massacre: Governor John Hickenlooper's Apology, Story behind It," *Westword*, December 9, 2014, available at https://www.westword.com/news/sand-creek-massacre-governor -john-hickenloopers-apology-story-behind-it-6052146.

206 **"Through our process of reconciliation and redress"** and **"prefe[rs] the process of iwi and hapu negotiating the terms of an apology"**: Quoted in Maureen Hickey, "Apologies in Settlements," in *Treaty of Waitangi Settlements*, ed. Nicola R. Wheen and Janine Hayward (Wellington, New Zealand: Bridget Williams Books, 2012), 83.

207 **"The spirit in which I stand before you today"** and other quotes by Bilchik: Shay Bilchik, "Working Together to Strengthen Supports for Indian Children and Families: A National Perspective," keynote speech for the NICWA conference, April 24, 2001, Anchorage, Alaska, http://www.cwla.org/execdir/edremarks010424.htm, now available at http://blog.americanindianadoptees.com/2010/03/apology-cwla-shay-bilchik .html; interview with Shay Bilchik by Margaret Jacobs, June 17, 2014.

208 **reparative justice "always requires an acknowledgement of injustice"**: Thompson, *Taking Responsibility for the Past*, 96.

Chapter 11

PAGE NOS.

211 **Howard "appears to see reconciliation as being about improving service delivery"**: Quoted in Andrew Gunstone, *Unfinished Business: The Australian Formal Reconciliation Process* (North Melbourne: Australian Scholarly Publishing, 2007), 143.

212 **"unless the great symbolism of reconciliation is accompanied by an even greater substance"**: Transcript and video of Rudd apology, available at https://www.sbs.com.au/news/transcript-rudd-apologises-to-stolen-generation.

212 **"Whatever happens now in Australia"**: Dodson, "When the Prime Minister Said Sorry," 114.

213 **"The Commonwealth . . . did not . . . accept the recommendations"**: Phillip Ruddock, "Reparations for Stolen Generations: The Government Responds," presentation at Moving Forward conference sponsored by the Australian Human Rights Commission, 2001, available at https://oldahrc.humanrights.gov.au/reparations-stolen-generations-government-responds-philip-ruddock.

214 **"The Australian government has linked the apology"**: Dodson, "When the Prime Minister Said Sorry," 113.

214 **the nation was on track to "meet just two of seven government targets to reduce the disparity in health, education and employment outcomes"**: Isabella Higgins, "Closing the Gap Report Shows Only Two Targets on Track as PM Pushes for Indigenous-Led Referendum," *ABC News*, February 12, 2020, available at https://www.abc.net.au/news/2020-02-12/closing-the-gap-report-2019-indigenous-outcomes-not-on-track/11949712?nw=0.

216 **the "meat chart"**: J. R. Miller, *Residential Schools and Reconciliation: Canada Confronts Its History* (Toronto: University of Toronto Press, 2017), 127.

220 **"seemed willing to take any action, so long as it did not spend money on survivors"**: Alfred Brophy, "The Tulsa Race Riot Commission, Apology, and Reparation: Understanding the Functions and Limitations of a Historical Truth Commission," in *Taking Wrongs Seriously: Apologies and Reconciliation*, ed. Elazar Barkan and Alexander Karn (Stanford: Stanford University Press, 2006), 245.

221 **"Reconciliation cannot be achieved at the national level" and other Ifill quotes:** Sherrilyn A. Ifill, *On the Courthouse Lawn: Confronting the Legacy of Lynching in the Twenty-First Century* (Boston: Beacon Press, 2007), 127, 131.

222 **"the sine qua non of restitution movements everywhere"**: Elazar Barkan, *The Guilt of Nations: Restitution and Negotiating Historical Injustices* (New York: Norton, 2000), 37.

225 **"federal government was willfully and recklessly discriminating against First Nations children"**: Cindy Blackstock, "Canada Must Stop Normalizing Inequality for Indigenous People," *Maclean's*, December 9, 2019, available at https://www.macleans.ca/opinion/canada-must-stop-normalizing-inequality-for-indigenous-people/.

225 **"There are still far too many things this government is doing"**: Quoted in Christian Paas-Lang, "Liberals Have Not Yet Lived up to Reconciliation Promises: Sinclair," *CBC News*, December 12, 2020, available at https://www.cbc.ca/news/politics/murray-sinclair-undrip-the-house-1.5839195.

227 **UNDRIP "is aimed at restoring the human rights of Indigenous peoples"**: Walter R. Echo-Hawk, *In the Light of Justice: The Rise of Human Rights in Native America and the UN Declaration on the Rights of Indigenous Peoples* (Golden, CO: Fulcrum, 2013), 11.

228 **"we will never achieve reconciliation"**: Paas-Lang, "Liberals Have Not Yet Lived up to Reconciliation Promises."

Chapter 12

PAGE NOS.

234   **It was "the highest thing I ever aspired to" and other Welsch quotes:** Interview with Roger Welsch by Margaret Jacobs and Kevin Abourezk, July 31, 2018, Dannebrog, Nebraska.

238   **"There was no security left in their lives":** Wishart, *An Unspeakable Sadness*, 175.

238   **"Our sacred covenant with Father Buffalo was broken":** Walter Echo-Hawk, *Sea of Grass: A Family Tale from the American Heartland* (Golden, CO: Fulcrum, 2018), 249.

239   **"The white man and red man cannot live together in peace":** Quoted in James Riding In, "Pawnee Removal: A Study of Pawnee-White Relations in Nebraska" (MA thesis, University of California, Los Angeles, 1985), 56.

240   **"The [Kansas] Republican state convention issued a . . . proclamation":** James Riding In, "Six Pawnee Crania: Historical and Contemporary Issues Associated with the Massacre and Decapitation of Pawnee Indians in 1869," *American Indian Culture and Research Journal* 16, no. 2 (1992): 103.

240   **"some of the choicest agricultural lands" and "the valuable land now held by these aborigines":** Quoted in Wishart, *An Unspeakable Sadness*, 188.

240   **"We can scarcely move without disturbing some white person":** Quoted in Riding In, "Pawnee Removal," 111.

242   **"When we came [from] Nebraska, it was a . . . real time of depression for our folks here" and "we gained a few more new ceremonies":** Interview with Herb Adson by Margaret Jacobs and Kevin Abourezk, March 4, 2020, Pawnee, Oklahoma.

242   **"anoints the body with fat and red paint"; "the women bore . . . [the corpse] to the grave"; "One cold morning as I was returning from my walk"; (243) some Pawnee "women were buried with the umbilical cords of their children"; one "account of the burial of a young woman"; "women continued for years to resort to the grave of a brother, husband, or child, to mourn"; and "continued to visit tribal cemeteries":** Roger C. Echo-Hawk, "Pawnee Mortuary Traditions," *American Indian Culture and Research Journal* 16, no. 2 (1992): 78, 79–80, 82, 88, 82, 90.

243   **"Harry Coons, a Pawnee visiting Nebraska from his home in Oklahoma" and (244) "in his *Early History of Webster County*, Emanual Peters described how a neighbor built a dugout":** Orlan J. Svingen, "The Pawnee of Nebraska: Twice Removed," *American Indian Culture and Research Journal* 16, no. 2 (1992): 125, 127–28.

244   **"I don't play golf" and (245) "we thought it no sacrilege to compliment [the skull] with a place upon one of our pack-horses":** Quoted in Svingen, "The Pawnee of Nebraska," 128, 124.

245   **"When you deem someone a savage, whether they're your friend or not, it's like issuing a death warrant against them":** Interview with James Riding In by Margaret Jacobs and Kevin Abourezk, April 11, 2019, Lincoln Indian Center, Lincoln, Nebraska.

246   **"certain savage types can neither be civilized or domesticated":** Quoted in Riding In, "Six Pawnee Crania," 104.

246   **"a ranking of races could be established objectively by physical characteristics of the brain":** Stephen Jay Gould, *The Mismeasure of Man* (New York: Norton, 1981), 51.

247 **"The surgeon general's office issued, in 1868, a memorandum"; "I had already obtained for the [Army Medical] museum the skull of one of the Pawnees"; (248) "described his method of treating the head of a recently slain Kiowa Indian"; "from 1868 to 1872, Fryer shipped Otis at least forty-two human remains"; and "a good deal of caution is required in obtaining anything from the graves of Indians":** Riding In, "Six Pawnee Crania," 104, 107, 108, 109.

248 **there are "strong Pawnee proscriptions against grave-tampering":** Roger C. Echo-Hawk, "Pawnee Mortuary Traditions," 85.

248 **"Equally critical to our perspective are cultural norms that stressed that those who tampered with the dead did so with profane, evil, or demented intentions":** James Riding In, "Repatriation: A Pawnee's Perspective," *American Indian Quarterly* 20, no. 2 (spring 1996): 240–41.

249 **"it is most unpleasant work to steal bones from a grave":** Quoted in Roger C. Echo-Hawk and Walter R. Echo-Hawk, *Battlefields and Burial Grounds: The Indian Struggle to Protect Ancestral Graves in the United States* (Minneapolis: Lerner Publications, 1994), 21. See also Ann Fabian, *The Skull Collectors: Race, Science, and America's Unburied Dead* (Chicago: University of Chicago Press, 2010), 189.

249 **museum staff "staged a phony funeral":** Roger Echo-Hawk and Walter Echo-Hawk, *Battlefields and Burial Grounds*, 26–27.

250 **archaeologists had separated the deceased Pawnee from their burial possessions"; "land leveling on the [Genoa site] and were hitting burials"; and Jones quotes:** Svingen, "The Pawnee of Nebraska," 129, 127.

251 **Pilgrims "despoiled the grave of a man and a child out of curiosity":** Chip Colwell, *Plundered Skulls and Stolen Spirits: Inside the Fight to Reclaim Native America's Culture* (Chicago: University of Chicago Press, 2017), 5.

251 **"As soon as you walked through the door . . . [there were] glass cabinets":** Interview with James Riding In, April 11, 2019.

252 **Indigenous people have been "dug up from their graves for storage or display":** Jack F. Trope and Walter R. Echo-Hawk, "The Native American Graves Protection and Repatriation Act: Background and Legislative History," in Devon A. Mihesuah, *Repatriation Reader: Who Owns American Indian Remains?* (Lincoln: University of Nebraska Press, 2000), 125.

253 **"This is all part of China's campaign to effectively eradicate any evidence of who we are" and (254) "The destruction is 'not just about religious persecution":** Nicola Smith, "China Destroys Dozens of Uighur Cemeteries in Drive to 'Eradicate' Cultural History of Muslims," *The Telegraph*, October 9, 2019, https://www.telegraph.co.uk/news/2019/10/09/china-destroys-dozens-uighur-cemeteries-drive-eradicate-cultural/.

Chapter 13

PAGE NOS.

256 **"because our ancestors were in museums, they were crying out":** Interview with Pat Leading Fox by Margaret Jacobs And Kevin Abourezk, March 5, 2020, Pawnee, Oklahoma.

256 **"we had no sooner left [Nebraska] than people started digging up our cemeteries"**: Interview with Walter Echo-Hawk by Margaret Jacobs and Kevin Abourezk, March 4, 2020, Pawnee, Oklahoma.

256 **"Between 1981 and 1986," he writes, "the Omaha and Winnebago tribes worked to preserve, protect, and salvage unmarked burial sites" and other quotes:** Robert M. Peregoy, "Nebraska's Landmark Repatriation Law: A Study of Cross-Cultural Conflict and Resolution," *American Indian Culture and Research Journal* 16, no. 2 (1992): 151.

257 **"if LB 612 becomes law, you could go to jail for a year and be fined up to $1,000 for giving an arrowhead"**: Legislative Alert from James A. Hanson to Historical Society members, February 2, 1988, S61, S1 File LB612, Box 294, Nebraska State Historical Society Papers, RG014, History Nebraska, Lincoln.

257 **"the remains of our ancestors are in Nebraska"**: Statement of chairman Lawrence Goodfox Jr. of the Pawnee Tribe of Oklahoma to the Board of Directors, Nebraska State Historical Society, March 25, 1988, LB 340 file, Box 36, Nebraska State Historical Society Papers, RG014, History Nebraska, Lincoln.

258 **"A bone is like a book . . . and I don't believe in burning books" and Pawnee remains were crucial to "discovering how people lived"**: Quoted in Peregoy, "Nebraska's Landmark Repatriation Law," 141.

258 **"If you want to know how the Pawnee people lived," he said, "just ask us"**: Interview with Adrian Spottedhorsechief by Margaret Jacobs and Kevin Abourezk, March 5, 2020, Pawnee, Oklahoma.

258 **"under American common law, there is no property interest or ownership right to a dead body"; these "are not religious objects like crucifixes, rosaries and bibles"; and "prove their religion is being affected by our possession of these things"**: Peregoy, "Nebraska's Landmark Repatriation Law," 143, 141.

259 **"We have a drum keeper that takes care of this"**: Interview with Matt Reed by Margaret Jacobs and Kevin Abourezk, March 3, 2020, Pawnee, Oklahoma.

260 **"indignant, insulting, and sacrilegious treatment" and Indigenous people "want the graves of our ancestors to be treated with the same dignity"**: Quoted in Svingen, "The Pawnee of Nebraska," 132.

260 **"a group of about thirty tribal elders" and it "was kind of scary going to Nebraska"**: Walter Echo-Hawk, *Sea of Grass*, 393; interview with Deb Echo-Hawk by Margaret Jacobs and Kevin Abourezk, March 3, 2020, Pawnee, Oklahoma.

260 **"passed around a cigar box of Indian fingers and ears" and other Welsch quotes:** Interview with Roger Welsch by Margaret Jacobs and Kevin Abourezk, August 26, 2018, Center for Great Plains Studies, Lincoln, Nebraska; interview with Roger Welsch, July 31, 2018.

262 **"What we are talking about with this bill is nothing less than human dignity" and** (263) **"We're talking about doing something that is right"**: Chambers and Baack quotes in Transcripts of Floor Debate, Nebraska State Legislature, 91st Legislature, First Session, 1700 and 1710, https://www.nebraskalegislature.gov/transcripts/view_page.php?page=1&leg=91.

263 **"That was very difficult, probably the biggest political battle in that session of the [legislature]" and other Echo-Hawk quotes:** Interview with Walter Echo-Hawk, March 4, 2020.

265 **to honor "an unknown number of Native Americans whose remains had been taken from their graves":** Communication with Priscilla Grew, long-time NAGPRA coordinator at the University of Nebraska, by Margaret Jacobs, February 2021.

Chapter 14

PAGE NOS.

266 **"And then we would go in into the rooms and look over the inventories":** Interview with Francis Morris by Margaret Jacobs and Kevin Abourezk, March 5, 2020, Pawnee, Oklahoma.

267 **"Here was stacks of boxes and boxes, . . . bones, skulls":** Interview with Pat Leading Fox, March 5, 2020.

267 **"Those remains were from a museum and were in plastic bags":** Quoted in Chuck Trimble, "Pawnee Nation Reburies Ancestors," *Indianz.com*, October 31, 2008, https://www.indianz.com/News/2008/011742.asp.

268 **"The first time the [Pawnee] contingent came out here to survey a place for the reburials" and subsequent Welsch quotes:** Interview with Roger Welsch, July 31, 2018.

269 **believed that if white South Africans simply learned the factual evidence:** Pumla Gobodo-Madikizela, *A Human Being Died That Night: A South African Woman Confronts the Legacy of Apartheid* (New York: Houghton Mifflin, 2004).

270 **dug a huge grave, "about twice the size of this room":** Interview with Francis Morris, March 5, 2020.

270 **"Old Ones, I want to speak to you" and "at the graveside, several people spoke of their feelings of sorrow":** Trimble, "Pawnee Nation Reburies Ancestors." Matt Reed, Tribal Historic Preservation Officer for the Pawnee Nation, explained to me that at the time of this reburial, the Pawnees did not have protocols and ceremonies for reburials. They have since developed them and would not allow them to be publicly shared with non-Indians.

271 **"*irari* is a Pawnee word that means if you had twenty good friends":** Interview with Francis Morris, March 5, 2020. Thanks to Matt Reed for giving me more background on *iraris* (pronounced ee-dah-dees).

271 **"Roger? I love Roger":** Interview with Pat Leading Fox, March 5, 2020.

272 **"Thanks to Roger," he said, "the Pawnees are still here [in Nebraska] today":** Walter Echo-Hawk presentation at the Center for Great Plains Studies, University of Nebraska, Lincoln, August 26, 2018.

272 **"in Lakota culture, as in many Native American societies, the clown is an important member of the clan or band":** Trimble, "Pawnee Nation Reburies Ancestors."

273 **"If a person is wanting to heal a historical injury":** Interview with Walter Echo-Hawk, March 4, 2020.

273 **"It's a piece of ground I've had for forty-five years" and other Welsch quotes:** Interview with Roger Welsch, July 31, 2018.

274 **"It's not just the land that we've received back":** Interview with Dawna Riding In Hare by Margaret Jacobs and Kevin Abourezk, March 5, 2020, Pawnee, Oklahoma.

275 **"To think that, you know, my ancestors, . . . walked that place":** Interview with Pat Leading Fox, March 5, 2020.

275 **"It's really hard to explain other than it's just breathtaking":** Interview with Electa Hare-RedCorn by Margaret Jacobs and Kevin Abourezk, March 4, 2020, Pawnee, Oklahoma.

277 **"Well, in the 1980s . . . my brother Walter Echo-Hawk had received some seeds";** (278) **"So it wasn't very long after we opened that people would come and find me"; and other O'Brien and D. Echo-Hawk quotes:** Interview with Deb Echo-Hawk and Ronnie O'Brien by Margaret Jacobs and Kevin Abourezk, December 6, 2019, Lincoln Indian Center, Lincoln, Nebraska.

280 **"we held onto that corn from that walk all the way from Nebraska down to Oklahoma":** Interview with Electa Hare-RedCorn, March 4, 2020.

281 **"The incremental grassroots approach achieves more than the grand gesture":** Interview with Peter Read by Margaret Jacobs, July 8, 2014, University of Queensland, Brisbane.

282 **"Saying Sorry isn't enough":** Pay the Rent campaign, https://paytherent.net.au/.

282 **"I pay Real Rent to the Duwamish Tribe monthly":** Real Rent Duwamish campaign, https://www.realrentduwamish.org/determine-rent.html#:~:text=%22I%20pay%20 Real%20Rent%20to,what%20our%20government%20has%20determined.

283 **now calls it "decolonized land" and "a liberated zone":** Terra Brockman, "A Church Returns Land to American Indians," *Christian Century*, March 3, 2020, https://www .christiancentury.org/article/features/church-returns-land-american-indians.

Conclusion

285 **"Let us be who we are—Aboriginal people in a modern world":** P. Galarrwuy Yunupingu, quoted in Mark McKenna, "Moment of Truth: History and Australia's Future," *Quarterly Essay* 69 (2018): frontispiece.

286 **"I feel like I lean toward the word reciprocity":** Interview with Electa Hare-RedCorn, March 4, 2020.

287 **The drafters assert that Aboriginal people have an "ancestral tie" to the land:** The Uluru Statement from the Heart, https://ulurustatement.org/the-statement.

288 **A group of Canadian scholars and activists have asserted that one of the most important gifts that Indigenous people have to share:** Michael Asch, John Borrows, and James Tully, eds., *Resurgence and Reconciliation: Indigenous-Settler Relations and Earth Teachings* (Toronto: University of Toronto Press, 2018).

289 **"Kind of the seed was planted there":** Tanderups and Wright interview, August 8, 2018.

290 **"I absolutely love that piece of ground":** Interview with Roger Welsch, August 26, 2018.

290 **"We hope again that we can grow more seed" and all subsequent quotes from Tanderup farm:** Land return ceremony, Tanderup family farm, June 10, 2018.

292 **"Difference must be not merely tolerated":** Audre Lorde, "The Master's Tools Will Never Dismantle the Master's House," in *Sister Outsider: Essays and Speeches*, reprint ed. (Berkeley, CA: Crossing Press, 2007), 111.

293 **"to honor this day, that we could all be together in unity" and all subsequent quotes from Tanderup farm:** Land return ceremony, Tanderup family farm, June 10, 2018.

FURTHER READING

Settler Colonialism

Belich, James. *Replenishing the Earth: The Settler Revolution and the Rise of the Anglo World.* Oxford: Oxford University Press, 2011.

Herbert, Xavier. "Australia Has the Black Pox." In *Xavier Herbert: Episodes from* Capricornia, Poor Fellow My Country, *and Other Fiction, Nonfiction, and Letters,* ed. Frances de Groen and Peter Pierce, 225–28. St. Lucia, Queensland: University of Queensland Press, 1992.

Lowman, Emma Battall, and Adam Barker. *Settler: Identity and Colonialism in 21st Century Canada.* Winnipeg: Fernwood Publishing, 2015.

Macoun, Alissa, and Elizabeth Strakosch. "The Ethical Demands of Settler Colonial Theory." *Settler Colonial Studies* 3, no. 3–4 (2013): 426–43.

Veracini, Lorenzo. *The Settler Colonial Present.* New York: Palgrave, 2015.

Wolfe, Patrick. "The Settler Complex." *American Indian Culture and Research Journal* 37, no. 2 (2013): 1–22.

Indigenous Theory, History, Law, and Activism

Borrows, John. *Recovering Canada: The Resurgence of Indigenous Law.* Toronto: University of Toronto Press, 2002.

Coulthard, Glen Sean. *Red Skin, White Masks: Rejecting the Colonial Politics of Recognition.* Minneapolis: University of Minnesota Press, 2014.

Deloria, Vine, Jr. *Custer Died for Your Sins: An Indian Manifesto.* New York: MacMillan, 1969.

Dunbar-Ortiz, Roxanne. *An Indigenous Peoples' History of the United States.* Boston: Beacon Press, 2015.

Echo-Hawk, Walter R. *In the Light of Justice: The Rise of Human Rights in Native America and the UN Declaration on the Rights of Indigenous Peoples.* Golden, CO: Fulcrum, 2013.

Estes, Nick. *Our History Is Our Future: Standing Rock versus the Dakota Access Pipeline, and the Long Tradition of Indigenous Resistance.* London: Verso, 2019.

Lightfoot, Sheryl. *Global Indigenous Politics: A Subtle Revolution.* New York: Routledge, 2018.

Richardson, Benjamin, Sin Imai, and Kent McNeil, eds. *Indigenous Peoples and the Law: Comparative and Critical Perspectives.* Oxford: Hart Publishing, 2009.

Simpson, Audra. *Mohawk Interruptus: Political Life across the Borders of Settler States*. Durham: Duke University Press, 2014.

Simpson, Leanne. *Dancing on Our Turtle's Back: Stories of Nishnaabeg Re-Creation, Resurgence and a New Emergence*. Winnipeg: Arbeiter Ring, 2011.

Treuer, David. *The Heartbeat of Wounded Knee: Native America from 1890 to the Present*. New York: Riverhead Books, 2019.

Yunupingu, Galarrwuy, ed. *Our Land Is Our Life: Land Rights—Past, Present and Future*. St. Lucia, Queensland: Queensland University Press, 1997.

Trauma and Memory

Atkinson, Judy. *Trauma Trails, Recreating Song Lines: The Transgenerational Effects of Trauma in Indigenous Australia*. North Melbourne: Spinifex Press, 2002.

van der Kolk, Bessel. *The Body Keeps the Score: Brain, Mind, and Body in the Healing of Trauma*. New York: Penguin, 2014.

Yellow Horse Brave Heart, Maria. "Historical Trauma among Indigenous Peoples of the Americas: Concepts, Research, and Clinical Considerations." *Journal of Psychoactive Drugs* 43 (2011): 282–90.

Truth and Reconciliation/Restorative Justice (General)

Bakiner, Onur. *Truth Commissions: Memory, Power, and Legitimacy*. Philadelphia: University of Pennsylvania Press, 2016.

Barkan, Elazar. *The Guilt of Nations: Restitution and Negotiating Historical Injustices*. New York: Norton, 2000.

Barkan, Elazar, and Alexander Karn, eds. *Taking Wrongs Seriously: Apologies and Reconciliation*. Stanford: Stanford University Press, 2006.

Blight, David. *Race and Reunion: The Civil War in American Memory*. Cambridge, MA: Harvard University Press, 2001.

Brooks, Roy, ed. *When Sorry Isn't Enough: The Controversy over Apologies and Reparations for Human Injustice*. New York: New York University Press, 1999.

Feinberg, Kenneth R. *What Is Life Worth? The Unprecedented Effort to Compensate the Victims of 9/11*. New York: Public Affairs, 2005.

Gobodo-Madikizela, Pumla. *A Human Being Died That Night: A South African Woman Confronts the Legacy of Apartheid*. New York: Houghton Mifflin, 2004.

Govier, Trudy. *Taking Wrongs Seriously: Acknowledgment, Reconciliation, and the Politics of Sustainable Peace*. New York: Humanity Books, 2006.

Hayner, Priscilla. *Unspeakable Truths: Confronting State Terror and Atrocity*. New York: Routledge, 2011.

Henderson, Jennifer, and Pauline Wakeham, eds. *Reconciling Canada: Critical Perspectives on the Culture of Redress*. Toronto: University of Toronto Press, 2013.

Hyde, Lewis. *A Primer for Forgetting: Getting Past the Past*. New York: Farrar, Straus and Giroux, 2019.

Ifill, Sherrilyn A. *On the Courthouse Lawn: Confronting the Legacy of Lynching in the Twenty-First Century*. Boston: Beacon Press, 2007.

Ignatieff, Michael. *The Warrior's Honour: Ethnic War and the Modern Conscience*. New York: Henry Holt, 1998.

Ladino, Jennifer K. *Memorials Matter: Emotions, Environment, and Public Memory at American Historical Sites*. Reno: University of Nevada Press, 2019.

Minow, Martha. *Between Vengeance and Forgiveness: Facing History after Genocide and Mass Violence*. Boston: Beacon Press, 1998.

Neiman, Susan. *Learning from the Germans: Race and the Memory of Evil*. New York: Farrar, Straus and Giroux, 2019.

Nussbaum, Martha. *Political Emotions: Why Love Matters for Justice*. Cambridge, MA: Belknap/ Harvard University Press, 2013.

Phelps, Teresa Godwin. *Shattered Voices: Language, Violence, and the Work of Truth Commissions*. Philadelphia: University of Pennsylvania Press, 2004.

Stauffer, Jill. *Ethical Loneliness: The Injustice of Not Being Heard*. New York: Columbia University Press, 2015.

Tavuchis, Nicholas. *Mea Culpa: A Sociology of Apology and Reconciliation*. Stanford: Stanford University Press, 1991.

Thompson, Janna. *Taking Responsibility for the Past: Reparation and Historical Injustice*. Cambridge: Polity, 2002.

Tutu, Desmond Mpilo. *No Future without Forgiveness*. New York: Random House, 1999.

Van Boven, Theo. "The United Nations Basic Principles and Guidelines on the Right to a Remedy and Reparation for Victims of Gross Violations of International Human Rights Law and Serious Violations of International Humanitarian Law." *United Nations Audiovisual Library of International Law* (New York: United Nations, 2005). https://legal.un.org /avl/ha/ga_60-147/ga_60-147.html. Incorporated into UN Resolution 60/147 of December 16, 2005, https://www.ohchr.org/EN/ProfessionalInterest/Pages/RemedyAndReparation .aspx.

Villa-Vicencio, Charles, and Wilhelm Verwoerd, eds. *Looking Back—Reaching Forward: Reflections on the Truth and Reconciliation Commission of South Africa*. Capetown: University of Capetown Press, 2000.

Truth and Reconciliation (Indigenous Peoples)

ABC News. "What America Owes Native Americans," September 23, 2020, part of "Turning Point," month-long ABC News series on "the racial reckoning sweeping the United States and exploring whether it can lead to lasting reconciliation." Part 1: "Native Americans Seek Reparations in Different Forms," https://abcn.ws/301cYmU. Part 2: "Native Communities Wait to See if their Fight for Atonement Gains Ground," https://abcn.ws/35Z8JMx.

Asch, Michael, John Borrows, and James Tully, eds. *Resurgence and Reconciliation: Indigenous-Settler Relations and Earth Teachings*. Toronto: University of Toronto Press, 2018.

Brantlinger, Patrick. "'Black Armband' versus 'White Blindfold' History in Australia." *Victorian Studies* 46, no. 4 (summer 2004): 655–74.

Buck, Christopher. "'Never Again': Kevin Gover's Apology for the Bureau of Indian Affairs." *Wicazo Sa Review* 21, no. 1 (spring 2006): 97–126.

Corntassel, Jeff, and Cindy Holder. "Who's Sorry Now? Government Apologies, Truth Commissions, and Indigenous Self-Determination in Australia, Canada, Guatemala, and Peru." *Human Rights Review* 9 (2008): 465–69.

Corntassel, Jeff, Chaw-win-is, and T'lakwadzi. "Indigenous Storytelling, Truth-telling, and Community Approaches to Reconciliation." *English Studies in Canada* 35, no. 1 (March 2009): 137–59.

Craft, Aimee, and Paulette Regan, eds. *Pathways of Reconciliation: Indigenous and Settler Approaches to Implementing the TRC's Calls to Action*. Winnipeg: University of Manitoba Press, 2020.

Davis, Lynne, ed. *Alliances: Re-Envisioning Indigenous–Non-Indigenous Relationships*. Toronto: University of Toronto Press, 2010.

Davis, Lynne, Jeff Denis, and Raven Sinclair. "Pathways of Settler Decolonization." *Settler Colonial Studies* (2016): 1–5.

Davis, Lynne, Chris Hiller, Cherylanne James, Kristen Lloyd, Tessa Nasca, and Sara Taylor. "Complicated Pathways: Settlers Learning to Re/frame Themselves and Their Relationships with Indigenous Peoples." *Settler Colonial Studies* (2016). DOI: 10.1080/2201473X.2016.1243086.

Epp, Roger. *We Are All Treaty People: Prairie Essays*. Edmonton: University of Alberta Press, 2008.

Graham, Lorie. "Reparations and the Indian Child Welfare Act." *Legal Studies Forum* 25 (2001): 619–40.

———. "Reparations, Self-Determination, and the Seventh Generation." *Harvard Human Rights Journal* 21 (2008): 47–104.

Grattan, Michelle, ed. *Reconciliation: Essays on Australian Reconciliation*. Melbourne: Bookman Press, 2000.

Grossman, Zoltán. *Unlikely Alliances: Native Nations and White Communities Join to Defend Rural Lands*. Seattle: University of Washington Press, 2017.

Grua, David W. *Surviving Wounded Knee: The Lakotas and the Politics of Memory*. New York: Oxford University Press, 2016.

Gunstone, Andrew. *Unfinished Business: The Australian Formal Reconciliation Process*. North Melbourne: Australian Scholarly Publishing, 2007.

Healey, Justin. *Stolen Generations: The Way Forward*. Vol. 289 in *Issues in Society*. Thirroul, New South Wales: Spinney Press, 2009.

"The Honor Tax Project." http://www.honortax.org/.

Human Rights and Equal Opportunity Commission. *Bringing Them Home: Report of the National Inquiry into the Separation of Aboriginal and Torres Strait Islander Children from Their Families*. Canberra: Commonwealth of Australia, 1997.

Johnson, Miranda. *The Land Is Our History: Indigeneity, Law, and the Settler State*. New York: Oxford University Press, 2016.

———. "Reconciliation, Indigeneity, and Postcolonial Nationhood in Settler States." *Journal of Postcolonial Studies* 14, no. 2 (2011): 187–201.

Jones, Carwyn. *New Treaty, New Tradition: Reconciling New Zealand and Maori Law*. Vancouver: University of British Columbia Press, 2016.

Little, Adrian. "The Politics of Makarrata: Understanding Indigenous-Settler Relations in Australia." *Political Theory* 48, no. 1 (2020): 30–56.

MacDonald, David B. *The Sleeping Giant Awakens: Genocide, Indian Residential Schools, and the Challenge of Reconciliation*. Toronto: University of Toronto Press, 2019.

Mackey, Eva. *Unsettled Expectations: Uncertainty, Land and Settler Decolonization*. Halifax: Fernwood Publishing, 2016.

Maddison, Sarah. *Beyond White Guilt: The Real Challenge for Black-White Relations in Australia*. Sydney: Allen & Unwin, 2011.

———. *The Colonial Fantasy: Why White Australia Can't Solve Black Problems*. Melbourne: Allen & Unwin, 2019.

Maddison, Sarah, Tom Clark, and Ravi de Costa, eds. *The Limits of Settler Colonial Reconciliation: Non-Indigenous People and the Responsibility to Engage*. Singapore: Springer, 2016.

Manuel, Arthur, and Grand Chief Ronald Derrickson, with preface by Naomi Klein. *The Reconciliation Manifesto: Recovering the Land, Rebuilding the Economy*. Toronto: Lorimer, 2017.

McKenna, Mark. "Moment of Truth: History and Australia's Future." *Quarterly Essay* 69 (2018): 1–86.

Miller, J. R. *Residential Schools and Reconciliation: Canada Confronts Its History*. Toronto: University of Toronto Press, 2017.

Niezen, Ronald. *Truth and Indignation: Canada's Truth and Reconciliation Commission on Indian Residential Schools*. Toronto: University of Toronto Press, 2013.

Nobles, Melissa. *The Politics of Official Apologies*. Cambridge: Cambridge University Press, 2008.

Palmer, Paula. "The Land Remembers: Connecting with Native Peoples through the Land." *Friends Journal* (February 2020): 21–25.

"Real Rent Duwamish." https://www.realrentduwamish.org/.

Regan, Paulette. *Unsettling the Settler Within: Indian Residential Schools, Truth Telling, and Reconciliation in Canada*. Vancouver: University of British Columbia Press, 2010.

Short, Damien. *Reconciliation and Colonial Power: Indigenous Rights in Australia*. Hampshire, England: Ashgate, 2008.

———. "Reconciliation and the Problem of Internal Colonialism." *Journal of Intercultural Studies* 26, no. 3 (2005): 267–82.

Singh, Maanvi. "Native American Land Taxes: A Step on the Roadmap to Reparations." *Guardian*, December 31, 2019, https://www.theguardian.com/us-news/2019/dec/31/native-american-land-taxes-reparations.

Smith, Andrea. "Boarding School Abuses, Human Rights, and Reparations." *Social Justice* 31, no. 4 (2004): 89–102.

Smith, Sherry. "Reconciliation and Restitution in the American West." *Western Historical Quarterly* 41, no. 1 (Spring 2010): 5–25.

Truth and Reconciliation Commission of Canada. *Final Report of the Truth and Reconciliation Commission of Canada: Honouring the Truth, Reconciling for the Future*. Toronto: Lorimer, 2015.

Wheen, Nicola R., and Janine Hayward, eds. *Treaty of Waitangi Settlements*. Wellington, New Zealand: Bridget Williams Books, 2012.

White Hawk, Sandra. "Generation after Generation We Are Coming Home." In *Outsiders Within: Writing on Transracial Adoption*, ed. Jane Jeong Trenka, Julia Chinyere Oparah, and Sun Yung Shin. Boston: South End Press, 2006.

Wilson, Shawn, Andrea V. Breen, and Lindsay Dupré. *Research & Reconciliation: Unsettling Ways of Knowing through Indigenous Relationships*. Toronto: Canadian Scholars, 2019.

Younging, Gregory, et al. *Response, Responsibility, and Renewal: Canada's Truth and Reconciliation Journey*. Ottawa: Aboriginal Healing Foundation, 2009.

The Poncas

Annual Reports of the Commissioner of Indian Affairs, Secretary of the Interior. Washington, DC: Government Printing Office, 1868, 1877, 1878, and 1879.

The Indian Question: Report of the Committee appointed by Hon. John D. Long, Governor of Massachusetts. Boston: Frank Wood, 1880.

Mathes, Valerie Sherer, and Richard Lowitt. *The Standing Bear Controversy: Prelude to Indian Reform*. Urbana: University of Illinois Press, 2003.

Ritter, Beth. "The Politics of Retribalization: The Northern Ponca Case." *Great Plains Research: A Journal of Natural and Social Sciences* 4 (August 1994): 237–55.

Standing Bear v. Crook. 25 F. Cas. 695 (D. Neb. 1879).

Starita, Joseph. *"I Am a Man": Chief Standing Bear's Journey for Justice*. New York: St. Martin's, 2008.

Tanderup, Art, Helen Tanderup, and Larry Wright Jr. Interview with Kevin Abourezk and Margaret Jacobs, August 8, 2018. Neligh, Nebraska. Edited audio version at https://soundcloud.com/indianz/a-farm-family-and-a-gift-to-two-tribes.

Tibbles, Thomas Henry. *Buckskin and Blanket Days: Memoirs of a Friend of the Indians*. 1905. Lincoln: University of Nebraska Press, 1957.

———. *Standing Bear and the Ponca Chiefs*. Edited and with an introduction by Kay Graber. 1880. Lincoln: University of Nebraska Press, 1972.

U.S. Senate. *Removal of the Ponca Indians*. 46th Cong., 2nd sess. Washington, DC: Government Printing Office, 1880.

———. *A Report of the commission appointed December 18, 1880 to ascertain the fact in regard to the removal of the Ponca Indians*. 46th Cong., 3rd sess. Washington, DC: Government Printing Office, 1881.

———. *Testimony Before the Select Committee on Removal of the Northern Cheyennes as to the Removal and Situation of the Ponca Indians*. 46th Cong., 3rd sess. Washington, DC: Government Printing Office, 1881.

Wilson, Dorothy Clarke. *Bright Eyes: The Story of Susette La Flesche, an Omaha Indian*. New York: McGraw-Hill, 1974.

Sand Creek and Other Massacres

Bensing, Tom. *Silas Soule: A Short, Eventful Life of Moral Courage*. Indianapolis: Dog Ear Publishing, 2012.

Bureau of Indian Affairs. *Annual Report of the Commissioner of Indian Affairs*. Washington, DC: Government Printing Office, 1860.

Cox-Paul, Lori. "Chivington." *Nebraska History* (winter 2007): 127–47.

Hyde, George E. *A Life of George Bent Written from His Letters.* Norman: University of Oklahoma Press, 1968.

Kelman, Ari. *A Misplaced Massacre: Struggling over the Memory of Sand Creek.* Cambridge, MA: Harvard University Press, 2013.

Madley, Benjamin. *An American Genocide; The United States and the California Indian Catastrophe.* New Haven: Yale University Press, 2016.

———. "Tactics of Nineteenth-Century Colonial Massacre: Tasmania, California, and Beyond." In *Theatres of Violence: Massacre, Mass Killing, and Atrocity throughout History,* ed. Phillip G. Dwyer and Lyndall Ryan, 110–25. New York: Berghahn Books, 2012.

Madsen, Brigham. *The Shoshoni Frontier and the Bear River Massacre.* Salt Lake City: University of Utah Press, 1985.

Northwestern University. *Report of the John Evans Study Group Committee* (May 2014), 69. Available at https://www.northwestern.edu/provost/committees/equity-and-inclusion/study-committee-report.pdf.

U.S. Congress. *Report of the Joint Committee on the Conduct of the War.* 38th Cong., 2nd sess. Washington, DC: Government Printing Office, 1865. https://www.kclonewolf.com/History/SandCreek/sc-documents/sc-1JCCW.html.

———. *Report of the Joint Special Committee to Inquire into the Conditions of Tribes.* Washington, DC: Government Printing Office, 1867.

U.S. Congress, Senate. *Report of the Secretary of War, Sand Creek Massacre.* 39th Cong., 2nd sess. Washington, DC: Government Printing Office, 1867. https://www.kclonewolf.com/History/SandCreek/sc-documents/sc-05hearing.html.

West, Elliott. *The Contested Plains: Indians, Goldseekers, & the Rush to Colorado.* Lawrence: University Press of Kansas, 1998.

The Pawnees

Echo-Hawk, Roger C. "Pawnee Mortuary Traditions." *American Indian Culture and Research Journal* 16, no. 2 (1992): 77–99.

Echo-Hawk, Roger C., and Walter R. Echo-Hawk. *Battlefields and Burial Grounds: The Indian Struggle to Protect Ancestral Graves in the United States.* Minneapolis: Lerner Publications, 1994.

Riding In, James. "Pawnee Removal: A Study of Pawnee-White Relations in Nebraska." MA thesis, University of California, Los Angeles, 1985.

———. "Repatriation: A Pawnee's Perspective." *American Indian Quarterly* 20, no. 2 (spring 1996): 238–50.

———. "Six Pawnee Crania: Historical and Contemporary Issues Associated with the Massacre and Decapitation of Pawnee Indians in 1869." *American Indian Culture and Research Journal* 16, no. 2 (1992): 101–19.

Svingen, Orlan J. "The Pawnee of Nebraska: Twice Removed." *American Indian Culture and Research Journal* 16, no. 2 (1992): 121–37.

Transcripts of Hearings on LB340. Nebraska State Legislature, 91st Legislature, First Session, March 1, 1889. https://www.nebraskalegislature.gov/transcripts/view_page.php?page=1&leg=91.

Wishart, David. *An Unspeakable Sadness: The Dispossession of the Nebraska Indians*. Lincoln: University of Nebraska Press, 1995.

Friends of the Indian

Hoxie, Frederick. *A Final Promise: The Campaign to Assimilate the Indians, 1880–1920*. New York: Cambridge University Press, 1984.

Jackson, Helen Hunt. *A Century of Dishonor: A Sketch of the United States Government's Dealings with Some of the Tribes*. Boston: Roberts, 1881.

Mathes, Valerie Sherer, ed. *Gender, Race, and Power in the Indian Reform Movement: Revisiting the History of the WNIA*. Albuquerque: University of New Mexico Press, 2020.

———, ed. *The Indian Reform Letters of Helen Hunt Jackson, 1879–1885*. Norman: University of Oklahoma Press, 1998.

———. *The Women's National Indian Association: A History*. Albuquerque: University of New Mexico Press, 2015.

Rhea, John. *A Field of Their Own: Women and American Indian History, 1830–1941*. Norman: University of Oklahoma Press, 2016.

Allotment

Fletcher, Alice C. *Lands in Severalty to Indians: Illustrated by Experiences with the Omaha Tribe*. Proceedings of the American Association for the Advancement of Science 33 (September 1884). Salem, MA: Salem Press, 1885.

———. *Life among the Indians: First Fieldwork among the Sioux and Omahas*. Edited and with an introduction by Joanna C. Scherer and Raymond DeMallie. Lincoln: University of Nebraska Press, 2013.

Genetin-Pilawa, C. Joseph. *Crooked Paths to Allotment: The Fight over Federal Indian Policy after the Civil War*. Chapel Hill: University of North Carolina Press, 2012.

Ruppel, Kristin T. *Unearthing Indian Land: Living with the Legacies of Allotment*. Tucson: University of Arizona Press, 2008.

Tonkovich, Nicole. *The Allotment Plot: Alice C. Fletcher, E. Jane Gay, and Nez Perce Survivance*. Lincoln: University of Nebraska Press, 2012.

Indian Boarding Schools

Adams, David Wallace. *Education for Extinction: American Indians and the Boarding School Experience, 1875–1928*. Lawrence: University Press of Kansas, 1995.

Brumley, Kim. *Chilocco: Memories of a Native American Boarding School*. Fairfax: Guardian Publishing House, 2010.

Child, Brenda. *Boarding School Seasons: American Indian Families, 1900–1940*. Lincoln: University of Nebraska Press, 1998.

Coleman, Michael C. *American Indian Children at School, 1850–1930*. Jackson: University Press of Mississippi, 1993.

Ellis, Clyde. *To Change Them Forever: Indian Education at the Rainy Mountain Boarding School, 1893–1920*. Norman: University of Oklahoma Press, 2008.

Fear-Segal, Jacqueline. *White Man's Club: Schools, Race, and the Struggle of Indian Acculturation*. Lincoln: University of Nebraska Press, 2007.

Fear-Segal, Jacqueline, and Susan D. Rose. *Carlisle Indian Industrial School: Indigenous Histories, Memories, and Reclamations*. Lincoln: University of Nebraska Press, 2016.

Fortunate Eagle, Adam. *Pipestone: My Life in an Indian Boarding School*. Norman: University of Oklahoma Press, 2010.

Gilbert, Matthew Sakiestewa. *Education beyond the Mesas: Hopi Students at Sherman Institute, 1902–1929*. Lincoln: University of Nebraska Press, 2010.

Gram, John R., and Theodore Jojola. *Education at the Edge of Empire: Negotiating Pueblo Identity in New Mexico's Indian Boarding Schools*. Seattle: University of Washington Press, 2015.

Griffith, Jane. *Words Have a Past: The English Language, Colonialism, and the Newspapers of Indian Boarding Schools*. Buffalo: University of Toronto Press, 2019.

Jacobs, Margaret. *White Mother to a Dark Race: Settler Colonialism, Maternalism, and the Removal of Indigenous Children in the American West and Australia, 1880–1940*. Lincoln: University of Nebraska Press, 2009.

Keller, Jean A. *Empty Beds: Indian Student Health at Sherman Institute, 1902–1922*. East Lansing: Michigan State University Press, 2002.

La Flesche, Francis. *The Middle Five: Indian Schoolboys of the Omaha Tribe*. With a foreword by David A. Baerreis. Lincoln: University of Nebraska Press, 1978.

Lajimodiere, Denise K. *Stringing Rosaries: The History, the Unforgivable, and the Healing of Northern Plains American Indian Boarding School Survivors*. Fargo: North Dakota State University Press, 2019.

Landrum, Cynthia Leanne. *The Dakota Sioux Experience at Flandreau and Pipestone Indian Schools*. Lincoln: University of Nebraska Press, 2019.

Lomawaima, K. Tsianina. *They Called It Prairie Light: The Story of Chilocco Indian School*. Lincoln: University of Nebraska Press, 1995.

Lomawaima, K. Tsianina, Brenda J. Child, and Margaret L. Archuleta. *Away from Home: American Indian Boarding School Experiences, 1879–2000*. Phoenix: Heard Museum, 2000.

Lomawaima, K. Tsianina, and Teresa L. McCarty. *"To Remain an Indian": Lessons in Democracy from a Century of Native American Education*. New York: Teachers College Press, 2006.

Meyers Bahr, Diana. *The Students of Sherman Indian School: Education and Native Identity since 1892*. Norman: University of Oklahoma Press, 2014.

Native American Rights Fund. *Trigger Points: Current State of Research on History, Impacts, and Healing Related to the United States' Indian Industrial/Boarding School Policy*. Boulder, CO: Native American Rights Fund, 2019.

Riney, Scott. *The Rapid City Indian School, 1898–1933*. Norman: University of Oklahoma Press, 2014.

Standing Bear, Luther. *My Indian Boyhood*. 1931. Reprint, Lincoln: Bison Books, 2006.

———. *My People the Sioux*. 1928. Reprint, Lincoln: University of Nebraska Press, 2006.

Trafzer, Clifford T., and Jean A. Keller. *Boarding School Blues: Revisiting American Indian Educational Experiences*. Lincoln: University of Nebraska Press, 2006.

Trafzer, Clifford E., Matthew Sakiestewa Gilbert, and Lorene Sisquoc. *The Indian School on Magnolia Avenue: Voices and Images from Sherman Institute*. Corvallis: Oregon State University Press, 2012.

Trennert, Robert A. *The Phoenix Indian School: Forced Assimilation in Arizona, 1891–1935*. Norman: University of Oklahoma Press, 1988.

Vuckovic, Myriam. *Voices from Haskell: Indian Students between Two Worlds, 1884–1928*. Lawrence: University Press of Kansas, 2008.

Whalen, Kevin. *Native Students at Work: American Indian Labor and Sherman Institute's Outing Program, 1900–1945*. Seattle: University of Washington Press, 2016.

Woolford, Andrew. *The Benevolent Experiment: Indigenous Boarding Schools, Genocide, and Redress in Canada and the United States*. Lincoln: University of Nebraska Press, 2015.

Zitkála-Šá. *American Indian Stories*. 1921. Reprint, New York: Penguin Classics, 2003.

Grave Desecration and Repatriation

Colwell, Chip. *Plundered Skulls and Stolen Spirits: Inside the Fight to Reclaim Native America's Culture*. Chicago: University of Chicago Press, 2017.

Fabian, Ann. *The Skull Collectors: Race, Science, and America's Unburied Dead*. Chicago: University of Chicago Press, 2010.

Fine-Dare, Kathleen S. *Grave Injustice: The American Indian Repatriation Movement and NAGPRA*. Lincoln: University of Nebraska Press, 2002.

Gould, Stephen Jay. *The Mismeasure of Man*. New York: Norton, 1981.

McKeown, Timothy. *In the Smaller Scope of Conscience: The Struggle for National Repatriation Legislation, 1986–1990*. Tucson: University of Arizona Press, 2012.

Mihesuah, Devon A. *Repatriation Reader: Who Owns American Indian Remains?* Lincoln: University of Nebraska Press, 2000.

Land Return

Brockman, Terra. "A Church Returns Lands to American Indians." *Christian Century*, March 3, 2020. https://www.christiancentury.org/article/features/church-returns-land-american -indians?reload=1583274807673&fbclid=IwAR3zlNZPrkPPs_OQzwTPVuYGDGY7rAPlg htWdvsoOvDQnCV2obr_rRXznUM.

Greenson, Thaddeus. "The Island's Return: The Unprecedented Repatriation of the Center of the Wiyot Universe." *North Coast Journal*, October 24, 2019. https://www.northcoastjournal .com/humboldt/the-islands-return/Content?oid=15494902.

Kaur, Harmeet. "Indigenous People across the US Want Their Land Back—and the Movement Is Gaining Momentum." CNN, November 26, 2020. https://www.cnn.com/2020/11/25/us /indigenous-people-reclaiming-their-lands-trnd/index.html.

Newsom, Gavin. Statement of Administration Policy on Native American Ancestral Lands, September 25, 2020. https://turtletalk.files.wordpress.com/2020/10/9.25.20-native-ancestral -lands-policy.pdf.

INDEX

abolitionists, 43, 89, 106, 120–22

Aboriginal people, 7, 163, 181–83, 192–200, 210–15, 285–87

Abourezk, Kevin, 66–67, 86, 157–58, 234, 242, 245, 251, 255, 259, 260, 266–68, 271–73, 275, 277–78, 280, 286, 290

Achumawis, 89

An Act Respecting First Nations, Inuit and Métis Children, Youth and Families, 225–26

Adopt Indian Métis program, 217

adoption, of Indian children, 179–83, 186, 207, 222

Adoptive Couple v. Baby Girl, 226

Adson, Herb, 242, 255

Advertiser (newspaper), 101, 105–6, 114

African Americans: anti-slavery efforts on behalf of, 43, 91, 115; boarding school for, 103; Civil War unit of, 120; demeaning views of, 122; enslaved, 8; Hampton Institute established for, 150; in Lincoln, Nebraska, 63; in post-slavery period, 89; reparations for, 218–21; as settlers, 8; treatment of American Indians compared to that of, 121–22; truth and reconciliation opportunity for, 110–11

agents. *See* government agents

Air Transportation Safety and System Stabilization Act, 222–23

Alaska Natives, 176, 178

Alcott, Louisa May, 101

Allen, Walter, 129

allies of American Indians: demeaning views of Indian peoples held by, 160–61;

Fletcher, 131–44; Friends of the Indian, 126–27, 129–30, 138–47; Jackson, 113–24; in nineteenth century, 109–47; Standing Bear's lecture tour as draw for, 88–89, 97; support for educational initiatives, 126, 149–51, 158; the Tanderups, 1–5, 10–15, 288–93; in truth and reconciliation efforts, 190; Welsch, 260–62, 268–77; white women as, 113, 121, 124, 130–31, 142–43, 158–59. *See also* reformers and reform efforts

allotment: as assimilation measure, 131, 139, 142, 146, 158; critique of, 144–47, 158; of land to Omahas, 135–43; of land to Poncas, 129, 144–45; as substitute for restitution, 126, 129–31

Altvater, Denise, 183, 186

American Antiquities Act, 250

American Friends Service Committee, 183

American Indian Magazine, 175

American Indians: citizenship for, 175; demeaning views of, 104, 114, 123, 134–35, 139, 160–61, 245–46, 258, 276; desecration of the dead of, 243–54, 256–65; dispossession of, as settler goal, 8, 71, 78, 127; fear, hostility, and violence directed at, 25–30, 37–39, 46, 58, 89, 95, 104–5, 127–28, 236–37, 239–40; intergenerational trauma of, 9, 57, 173, 187; legal standing/rights of, 92, 95–96, 102–3, 120, 122–24, 143, 159, 160; narratives told by, 10–11, 30, 37, 87–106; peace advocacy among, 26, 28–30, 42; protection of their lands and

American Indians (*continued*)
  lives by, 25–26; romantic notions of,
  100–102; settlers as allies of, 88–89, 97,
  109–47; shared history with settlers, 67;
  sovereignty of, 96, 226; studies of skulls
  of, 246–49; treatment of African Americans
  compared to that of, 121–22; venues for
  voices of, 88–89, 94, 105. *See also* assimilation; massacres of American Indians;
  plunder of American Indians
American Indians Against Desecration, 252
American Museum of Natural History,
  New York, 249
American Society for the Advancement of
  Science, 135
Ancestral Puebloans, 22
Anthony, Scott, 29–30, 40, 47–48
Apaches, 22
Apess, William, 89
apologies: in Australia, 192–200, 212; in
  Canada, 200–203; characteristics of
  inadequate, 202–5; characteristics of
  successful, 194, 201, 206–7; in New
  Zealand, 205–6; refusals to make, 195–96;
  role of, in truth and reconciliation process,
  208; skepticism about, 194, 199, 203–4;
  in United States, 204–8
Arapahos, 22–34, 46–51, 56–59, 61–62, 150,
  237. *See also* Northern Arapahos
Argentina, 209
Arikaras, 241
Armstrong, Samuel, 150, 152
Army Medical Museum, 246–49, 256
Arnzen, Isabella, 53
assimilation: of Aboriginal people in
  Australia, 163, 195; adoption and fostering
  as means of, 179–80; allotment as means of,
  131, 139, 142, 146, 158; as goal of boarding
  schools, 6, 149–54, 162–64, 174, 177; as
  goal of settler-initiated reform movement,
  102–3, 123, 134–35, 143, 147; harms to settler
  nation resulting from, 201; as human
  rights violation, 228; Indian peoples

failed by policies of, 158; of Indian prisoners, 150; of Indigenous peoples in Canada,
  162; "killing the Indian" strategies in, 150,
  154–55; land policies as means of, 131, 139,
  141–42, 146; of Pawnees, 159, 238; of
  Poncas, 69, 159; settlers' goals for, 150–52,
  159–60; twentieth-century efforts at,
  179–80; of Uighur population in China,
  163–64, 253–54
Association for the Advancement of
  Women (AAW), 131
Atkins, Allen, 250
Atlantic Monthly (magazine), 174
Australia: assimilation strategies in, 163, 195;
  child removal in, 15, 163, 181–83, 192–200,
  210–14, 223–25; "closing the gap" strategy
  in, 211, 214–15; and compensation, 210–15,
  282; plunder of Aboriginal people in, 7, 8;
  truth and reconciliation efforts in, 181–83,
  192–200, 210, 285–87
Australian Human Rights Commission, 181
Australian Reconciliation Convention, 195
Australians for Native Title (later Australians for Native Title and Reconciliation),
  197–98

Baack, Dennis, 263
Bacon, Charlotte, 185
Barkan, Elazar, 222
Bassiouni, Mahmoud Cherif, 193–94
Battle of Little Bighorn, 72, 89
Battle of the Infernal Caverns, 89
Battle of Washita, 51, 150
bearing witness: as component of truth and
  reconciliation process, 15, 87; as model of
  settlers', 42; motives for, 181–82; obstacles
  to, 87–88; to Ponca history, 88–106, 112;
  to Sand Creek Massacre, 40–42, 48, 55
Bear River Massacre, 36–39
Bear Shield, 84
Beckwourth, James, 21
Belford, James Burns, 118
Belich, James, 9

Bensing, Tom, 28

Bent, Charles, 22–23

Bent, George, 31–33, 40, 42

Bent, William, 22–25, 31

Bent's Fort, 23

Bethany Danish Lutheran Church,
    Denver, 283

Big Snake, 76–77, 128

Bilchik, Shay, 207–8

bison, 12, 23, 26, 67–68, 70, 71, 238–39

Black Elk, 80, 81

Blackfeet, 157

Black Kettle, 26, 28, 30, 32, 33, 42, 47, 51, 54,
    83, 150, 237

Blackstock, Cindy, 225

Blainey, Geoffrey, 195

Bland, Thomas, 143–44

Blight, David, 110–11

Blood Memory (documentary), 186

Boarding School Healing Symposium, 177

boarding schools, 148–64; assimilation as
    goal of, 6, 149–54, 162–64, 174, 177; in
    Canada, 162–63, 167–68, 193, 200, 210,
    215–16; children removed from families
    for enrollment in, 6, 149–50, 153, 157–58,
    162–64, 173–74; church-run, 149, 151,
    169; critique of, 158, 174, 176; cultural
    destruction enacted by, 6; deaths of
    children in, 156, 178–79; digital project
    about, 148, 157; establishment of, 151;
    forced labor in, 155, 162, 179; former
    students' memories of, 148–49, 154–56,
    168, 170, 172–73; Friends of the Indian's
    misguided support for, 126, 149–51;
    Indian opposition to, 152–53; legacy of,
    177; in the mid-twentieth century, 176,
    179; mission-run, 98, 133, 151, 155–56;
    mistreatment of children in, 153–56,
    162–64, 168–70, 172–73, 176; numbers
    of, 149; as reconciliation strategy, 126,
    149–50; truth and reconciliation efforts
    concerning, 126, 167–79. See also child
    removal

Board of Indian Commissioners, 152

Boas, Franz, 249

Bonnin, Raymond, 175

Bosnia, 194

Boston Conservatory of Music, 174

Boston Herald (newspaper), 143

Boston Indian Committee, 124, 127, 140

Brackeen case, 226

Branagh, Kenneth, 163

Brave Heart, Maria Yellow Horse, 172–73

Bringing Them Home report (Australia), 181,
    183, 194–96, 198, 202, 211

British settler colonial nations, 8

Bronson Alcott family, 101

Brookings Institution, 175

Brophy, Alfred, 220

Brownback, Sam, 204

Brown University, 219

Buffalo Chip, 85–86

Bureau of Indian Affairs, 179, 204

Bureau of Indian Education (BIE), 176–77

burial sites, of Indian peoples, 233–35,
    243–51, 254, 256–65

Burns, Penthea, 184

Butler, David, 240

Byers, William, 58, 95, 119

Byrd, Sidney, 154–55

Caddos, 248

Cahill, Cathleen, 126

California Indians, 39, 68, 205

Cambodia, 209

Camp-Horinek, Casey, 12–13, 290, 293

Canada: assimilation strategies in, 162; child
    removal in, 15, 181, 193, 200, 217, 224–25;
    and compensation, 210, 215–18; plunder
    of Indigenous peoples in, 8; residential
    schools in, 162–63, 167–68, 193, 200, 210,
    215–16; truth and reconciliation efforts
    in, 162, 167–71, 193, 200–203, 210, 228–29

Canadian Human Rights Tribunal, 225

Cannon, James, 47

Cannon, Katie, 9

Carlisle Indian Industrial School, 150–52, 156, 162, 171, 174, 178, 188; Standing Bear's visit to, 103

Carlson, Nancy, 148, 157

Cather, Willa, 64

Catholic Church, 169

Cayou, Orville, 157

Cellini, Richard, 219

Central Indian Committee of the Women's Home Mission Circle of the First Baptist Church of Philadelphia, 124

Chambers, Ernie, 262–63

Chauis, 235

Cherokee Advocate (newspaper), 143

Cherokees, 21, 83, 110, 120, 241

Cheyennes, 22–34, 46–51, 56–59, 61–62, 237–38, 248; Dog Soldiers, 28, 29. *See also* Northern Cheyennes; Southern Cheyennes

child removal: in Australia, 15, 163, 181–83, 192–200, 210–14, 223–25; in Canada, 15, 181, 192, 200, 217, 224–25; in United States, 179–84, 186, 207, 222, 226–27. *See also* boarding schools

Child Welfare League of America (CWLA), 207–8

China, oppression of Uighur population by, 163–64, 253–54

Chippewas, 156

Chivington, John, 28–34, 38, 44–54, 56–59, 61, 83, 119, 121, 240, 262

Christianity/Christians: conversion to, 75, 98, 113, 134, 150; hypocrisy of, 47, 53, 75; missionary activity of, 45, 74, 75, 77, 123; as sympathetic to Indian peoples, 91

Citizens to Save Nebraska's History, 258–59

Civil War, 25, 38, 43–45

Clark, Geoff, 200

Clemens, Samuel (aka Mark Twain), 100

Clinton, Bill, 59

Coalition of Anti-Racist Whites, 282

Coberly, Hersa, 51

Collier, John, 176

Colorado, 21–35, 46, 205

Colorado Historical Society, 58–59

Colorado Third Volunteers, 28–34, 40–41, 47

Colwell, Chip, 251, 252

Comanches, 22, 150, 237

Common Experience Payment (CEP) (Canada), 215

compensation: for African Americans, 218–20; in Australia, 210–15, 282; in Canada, 210, 215–18; controversies over, 210; critique of, 216–17; defined, 209; grassroots approaches to, 282–83; for Indian land loss, 129–31, 140, 144, 147, 158; refusals to make, 211–13, 220, 225; for Sand Creek Massacre, 50–51; in the United States, 218–23, 282–83. *See also* redress

Connor, Patrick, 38

Cook, Cecil, 163

Coons, Harry, 243

Corroborree 2000, 198

Costner, Kevin, 242

Council Fire (newspaper), 143

Council on Aboriginal Reconciliation (Australia), 196

COVID-19 pandemic, 180–81, 255

Cowcher, Trish, 197

Cox-Paul, Lori, 45

Cramer, Joseph, 40–44, 47–48, 50, 52, 54–55, 61

Crook, George, 85–86, 89–92, 95, 116, 129, 132, 144

Cross, Terry, 207

cultural theft, 6

Custer, George Armstrong, 51, 72, 89

Cuthbert, Denise, 203

Cut Nose, 246

Dakota Access Pipeline, 16

Dakotas, 246

Dances with Wolves (film), 242

Dannebrog, Nebraska, 234, 268, 276–77

Dawes, Henry Laurens, 124–25, 127, 129–30, 139–40, 142, 144, 159

Day of Apology (Australia), 192–93, 196–97

Day of Apology (Canada), 200–203

Dearly, Jerry, 187

Defense Appropriations Act, 204

dehumanization, 47

Delawares, 120

Deloria, Vine, Jr., 10

Department of Indian Affairs (Canada), 168

Dickson Mounds Museum, Illinois, 244

Diné people. See Navajos

disease, 5, 24, 26, 82, 83–84, 153, 163, 241–42, 291

Dodson, Mick, 181–82, 193, 199, 210, 212, 214, 227, 228

Dorsey, George, 249

Dorsey, James Owen, 129, 242

Doucette, Robert, 217, 224

Douglass, Frederick, 89

Dred Scott v. Sandford, 92

Duluwat Island, 283

Dunbar, John, 242–43

Dundy, Elmer, 92–93, 95–96, 102

Dunlap, Matthew, 186

Eagle Heart, Sarah, 188–89

Earlham College, 174

Echo-Hawk, Deb, 259, 260, 277–81

Echo-Hawk, Roger, 243, 248–50, 258; Battlefields and Burial Grounds, 244

Echo-Hawk, Walter, 227–28, 249–50, 252, 256, 258, 260, 263–64, 272–74, 277; Battlefields and Burial Grounds, 244; Sea of Grass, 238–39

education: government policies and funding for, 68, 70, 129, 157, 176; history curricula in, 7, 21–22, 60–61, 64–65, 177, 279; Indian administration of, 176–77. See also boarding schools

Elizabeth Institute, 113

Emerson, Ralph Waldo, 100, 114, 115–16

Episcopal Church, 90

Epp, Roger, 16

Equal Justice Initiative, 220

Ese-do-to-des, 240

Evans, John, 27–29, 33, 47, 49, 54, 57, 61

Fabian, Ann, 249

Farber, Bernie, 169

Farley, Ed, 132–33, 139

Farm and Ranch Heritage Museum, Las Cruces, New Mexico, 63

Feinberg, Kenneth, 223

Field Museum, Chicago, 249

First Alaskans Institute, 189

First Nations Orphan Association (now First Nations Repatriation Institute), 186

Fletcher, Alice Cunningham, 131–44, 146, 152, 155–57, 160–61; Indian Education and Civilization, 157

Floyd, George, 221

Fontaine, Phil, 201–2

Fort Laramie Treaty, 25, 26

Fort Lyon, 26, 28–31, 44, 47

Fort Omaha, 85, 89–90, 92, 95

Fort Wise, 26

fostering, of Indian children, 179–84, 222, 224

Four Winds American Indian Council, 283

Franklin, John Hope, 220

Friends of the Indian, 126–27, 129–30, 138–47, 149, 151–53, 158, 160, 164, 209

Fryer, B. E., 247–48

Fuller, Margaret, 116

Furnas, Robert, 240

Geliga, Susana, 98

General Allotment Act (Dawes Act), 139–41, 143

General Federation of Women's Clubs, 175

Genetin-Pilawa, C. Joseph, 143

Genoa Indian Boarding School, 148–50

Genoa U.S. Indian School Foundation, 148–49, 154, 157

genocide, 39, 61, 89, 111, 170, 173, 181, 185, 191

George, Caron, 216
Georgetown University, 219
Gilbert, Kevin, 199
Gilpin, Buddy, 261
gkisedtanamoogk, 186
Gobodo-Madikizela, Pumla, 269
Gonzalez, Angela, 189
Goodfox, Lawrence, Jr., 257, 260
Gordon School, 162
Gould, Corinna, 282
Gould, Stephen Jay, 246
Gover, Kevin, 204
government. *See* U.S. government
government agents, 69, 71
Graham, Billy, 272
Grant, Ulysses S., 113, 238
grassroots approaches to reconciliation,
    12–15, 66–67, 206–8, 268–74, 281–83,
    288–93
grave robbing, 243–54
Great Sioux Reserve, 70
Greeley, Horace, 116
Greensboro, North Carolina, 15
guarantees of non-repetition, 209, 210, 223–27

Haaland, Deb, 190–91
habeas corpus, 92
Haidas, 249
Hale, Edward Everett, 100
Hamilton, William, 74
Hamilton, Willie, 98
Hampton Institute, 103, 150, 152
Hanson, James, 257–59, 264
Hare-RedCorn, Electa, 275, 280, 286–87
Harper, Stephen, 200–201, 203
Harper's Monthly (magazine), 174
Hartford Courant (newspaper), 117
Harvard University, 219
Hawke, Grant, 206
Hayes, Rutherford, 83, 103, 125, 129
Hayt, E. A., 127–28
healing and healing ceremonies: purpose
    of, 57; Spiritual Healing Run, 56–57,

61–62; truth and reconciliation linked to,
    187, 189
Henry, Diana, 277
Herbert, Xavier, 7
Hickenlooper, John, 205
Hicksite Quakers, 238
Higginson, Thomas Wentworth, 120–21
Hill, Asa T., 244–45, 258
Hinton, Amos, 11
history: cooptation of Indian peoples'
    account of their own, 91–94; in school
    curricula, 7, 21–22, 60–61, 64–65, 177, 279;
    shared, by Indian peoples and settlers, 67,
    86; as told by Indian peoples, 10–11, 30,
    37, 87–106; as told by settlers, 5, 5–7, 9–10,
    16, 21–22, 30–31, 34, 58–61, 64–65, 88, 114,
    182, 254; venues for Indian peoples'
    telling of, 88–89, 94, 105
Holmes, Oliver Wendell, Sr., 100, 106, 114
Holocaust, 57, 61, 169, 173
Holt Joseph, 48–49
Horinek, Mekasi, 3–5, 10–11, 291, 293
Horse, 178
Houghton, Henry, 100–101
Howard, John, 195–96, 211
Howells, William Dean, 100
Hudayar, Salih, 253–54
Hungate, Ward, 26–27
Hunkpapas, 152
Hyde, George, 32–33
Hyde, Lewis, 62

IAP. *See* Independent Assessment Process
Ifill, Sherrilyn, 220–21, 229
Ignatieff, Michael, 16, 39
Independent Assessment Process (IAP)
    (Canada), 215–17
Indian Adoption Project, 179, 207
Indian Child Welfare Act (ICWA), 180,
    183–84, 210, 225–27
Indian Citizenship Act, 175
Indian Country Today (newspaper), 94
Indian New Deal, 176

Indian Peace Commission, 49–50

Indian policy: critique of, 104, 110, 134, 143, 175–76; demeaning views of, 287; Jackson's critique of, 114–15, 119–21; under Roosevelt, 176; Standing Bear's challenging of, 89–96. *See also* allotment; assimilation

Indian problem, 37–38, 105, 115, 125, 129, 140, 142, 151, 158, 180, 282

Indian Residential Schools Settlement Agreement (Canada), 202, 210, 215, 217

Indian Rights Association, 139, 143, 159, 188

Indian Self-Determination and Education Assistance Act, 176

Indian Territory, 4–5, 72–86, 95, 110, 127, 238, 240–43, 259–60

Indian Treaty-Keeping and Protective Association, 124, 130, 158–59

Indian Wars, 89

Indianz.com (website), 94

Indigenous Media Freedom Alliance, 94

Indigenous peoples: demeaning views of, 218; human rights of, 227–28; plunder of, 7–9; self-determination of, 200, 212, 228–29. *See also* Aboriginal people; Australia; Canada; Maori; Torres Strait Islanders

influenza, 241–42

Inouye, Daniel, 221

Institute for the Study of Human Rights, Columbia University, 193

intergenerational trauma, 9, 57, 62, 173, 187, 189

Inuit people, 215

Island, 23

Jackson, Helen Hunt, 79, 100, 113–24, 126, 127, 143, 144, 150, 162; *A Century of Dishonor*, 120, 122

Jackson, William Sharpless, 114, 115, 122

Jacobs, Ruthana, 59

James, Edwin, 245

Japanese American Citizens League, 221–22

Japanese Americans, internment of, 218, 221–22

Japanese Canadians, 218

Jefferson, Thomas, 251

Jefferson County School Board, 60–61

Jones, Carl Hugh, 250–51

Judéwin, 173

Kansa people, 248

Kansas-Nebraska Act, 43, 44, 67, 90, 236

Kaws, 73

Kellogg Foundation, 189

Kelman, Ari, 59

Kemble, E. C., 72–76, 79

Kennedy, Robert, 176

Kennedye, Boots, 66, 86, 234, 242, 255, 259, 266, 268, 286

Keystone XL pipeline, 2–3

Kiowa County Museum, 59

Kiowas, 22, 150, 237

Kitkahahkis, 235

Krakouer, Jacynta, 224

Ku Klux Klan, 15

Labor Party (Australia), 198, 212, 214

La Flesche, Francis (Frank), 98, 100, 102, 110, 130, 131, 136, 141, 146, 150, 155–56

La Flesche, Joseph, 84, 96, 98–100, 112, 132

La Flesche, Mary Gale, 132

La Flesche, Rosalie, 132–33, 139

La Flesche, Susan, 138

La Flesche, Susette, 88, 97–106, 109–10, 112–16, 120, 124–33, 139, 144, 149–51, 158, 160, 176

Lake Mohonk, New York, 126, 147

Lakotas, 11, 22, 67–72, 96, 152, 237–38, 272

Lambertson, Genio, 92

land: Aboriginal people's attachment to, 287; allotment of Omahas', 135–43; allotment of Poncas', 129, 144–45; of the Cheyennes and Arapahos, 23, 25–26; given as reparations, 50–51; government/settler theft of, 5–10, 17, 31, 34, 37–40, 46,

land (*continued*)
111, 122–23, 144–45, 235–36; Indian
peoples' attachment to, 56; inheritance
and transmission of, 145; of Maori in
New Zealand, 205–6; Omahas' attachment to, 134–35; of the Pawnees, 235–36,
240–41, 268–76; of the Poncas, 3–4, 9,
11–14, 67–79, 93–94, 96–97, 116–17,
124–30, 144–45, 289–93; repatriation
of, 12, 14, 186, 268–74, 283, 285, 289–93;
restitution of, 176; significance of, for
Indian culture and livelihood, 146
Lane, James Henry, 90
language, in boarding schools, 154–55,
162, 170
LaRose, Louis, 267
Leading Fox, Pat, 256, 267, 271, 275
lecture tours, on behalf of Poncas, 97–106,
110, 112–16, 126, 128
Left Hand, 29, 33, 42, 83
Lieth, Chris, 187
Little Bear, 33
Little Chief, 178
Littlechild, Wilton, 170
Little Plume, 178
Little Raven, 29, 83
Lone Bear, Lee, 56, 62
Long, Stephen H., 245
Longfellow, Henry Wadsworth, 100–101,
106, 114
Lorde, Audre, 292
Lowell, James Russell, 100
lynchings, 220–21

Madley, Benjamin, 38
Maine, truth and reconciliation efforts in,
183–86
Makarrata commission, 288
malaria, 5, 82, 83–84, 241–42, 291
Maliseet people, 183
Mandela, Nelson, 14
"man of his times" argument, 109, 252
Maori, 15, 205–6

Mark, Joan, 156–57
Marshall, Lyle, 204
Marston, Luke, 169
massacres of American Indians: Battle of the
Infernal Caverns, 89; Battle of Washita,
51, 150; Bear River, 36–39; Crook's leading
of, 89; dehumanization as key element in,
47; Duluwat Island, 283; Jackson's accounts
of, 120; Mulberry Creek, 239–40, 247,
256; numbers of, 39; Pawnee villages,
236; Pit River, 89; refusal of soldiers to
participate in, 40, 43, 47–48, 61; Sand
Creek, 29–34, 40–43, 47–54, 56–62, 83,
95, 117, 119, 246–48; settler ignorance/
forgetting/hiding of, 36, 39–40, 42, 50,
104–5; understanding and acknowledgment
of, 35–36; Wounded Knee, 35–36, 54.
See also plunder of American Indians
Mathes Valerie Sherer, 115
Mayo, William, 246
McCleave, Christine Diindiisi, 172, 178, 188
McGirt v. Oklahoma, 16
McGuinness, P. P., 195
Mead, Margaret, 145
Meeker Incident, 117–19
Meriam, Lewis, 175
Methodist Church, 44–45, 61–62
Métis people, 215, 217
Micmac people, 183
Miles, Nelson, 129
Miller, Joaquin, 115
Minik, 249
Minnesota Massacre, 246
Modocs, 89
Moonlight, Thomas, 48
Moran, Ry, 216–17, 223
Morgan, Thomas Jefferson, 157
Mormons, 37
Morris, Francis, 266–67, 270–71
Morrison, Scott, 215
Morton, Samuel George, 246, 249
Mulberry Creek Massacre, 239–40,
247, 256

Murie, James, 242–43
Muscogees (Creeks), 16, 241

NABS. *See* Native American Boarding
    School Healing Coalition
names, of children in boarding schools, 154,
    162
narratives. *See* history
National Centre for Truth and Reconcilia-
    tion (Canada), 216
National Council of American Indians, 175
National Indian Child Welfare Association
    (NICWA), 207–8
National Indian Defense Association, 143
National Museum of Natural History,
    Smithsonian, Washington, D.C., 251–52
National Native American Boarding School
    Healing Coalition (NABS), 156, 171–72,
    177–78, 186, 188, 190
National Park Service, 59, 61
Native American Apology Resolution, 204
Native American Graves Protection and
    Repatriation Act, 264
Native American Rights Fund (NARF), 177
Navajos, 176, 251
Nebraska City News (newspaper), 58
Nebraska Commission on Indian Affairs,
    256, 260, 272
Nebraska State Historical Society, 234–35,
    237, 245, 250, 254, 256–67
neo-Nazis, 15
Never Again principle. *See* guarantees of
    non-repetition
Neville, A. O., 163
Newsom, Gavin, 205
New York Herald (newspaper), 123
New York Times (newspaper), 143
New York Tribune (newspaper), 116, 117–19
New Zealand, 8, 9, 15, 205–6
Nez Perce, 120, 141
Nighthorse-Campbell, Ben, 59
9/11 terrorist attacks, 222–23
Niobrara Pioneer (newspaper), 76

Niobrara State Park, 3–4
Northern Arapahos, 56, 178
Northern Cheyennes, 26, 56
Nott, Josiah C., 245–46

Obama, Barack, 171, 204, 228
O'Brien, Rhonda (Ronnie), 278–80
Ochinee, 33, 42
Office of Indian Affairs, 25, 123, 139, 175
Ohlone people, 282
Oklahoma, reparations for African
    Americans in, 219–20
Omaha Herald (newspaper), 90–93, 97, 116
Omaha Republican (newspaper), 239
Omahas: allotment of land to, 135–43, 157;
    attachment to their land, 134–35; and
    burial sites, 256, 260; children taken to
    boarding school, 152; Fletcher's dealings
    with, 131–43, 146; Poncas and, 71–72, 74,
    85, 96–100; sufferings of, 113; and the
    Tanderups, 2; Tibbles and, 90; Welsch
    and, 261
Order of Indian Wars, 59
Osage people, 73, 248
Otis, George A., 247–48
Otoes, 74, 159
Owen, Amelia, 90
Owl Woman, 23, 31

Paiutes, 89
Palmer, Paula, 190
Parry, Darren, 36–39
Passamaquoddy people, 183
paternalism, 105, 141, 160, 169, 218, 229
Paul, Rand, 220
Pawnee Museum, Oklahoma, 255
Pawnees: assimilation attempts for, 159, 238;
    burial rituals of, 242–43, 248; desecration
    of the dead of, 243–51, 256–65, 267; land
    of, 235–36, 240–41, 268–76; massacre of,
    236; overview of, 235; peace initiatives of,
    237; Poncas and, 11, 73, 235; in present-
    day Nebraska, 255; preservation of corn

Pawnees (*continued*)
seed of, 259, 277–81, 286; pressures on settlement of, 236–41; recovery and reburial of the dead of, 233–35, 254, 256–72; relocation to Indian Territory, 238, 240–43, 259–60; service to U.S. Army, 237, 240, 256; theft of land from, 235–36; treaties signed by, 235–36
Pawnee Seed Preservation Project, 259, 277–81, 286
Pay the Rent, 282
Peace Policy, 238
Peary, Robert, 249
Pendleton blankets, 13, 270
Penobscot people, 104, 157, 183
Peregoy, Robert, 256–58
Peters, Emanual, 244
Phelps, Hattie, 52
Phillips, Wendell, 100–101, 106, 115, 124
Piatote, Beth, 9, 81
Pioneers of Colorado, 54
Pitahawiratas, 235
plunder of American Indians: allotment as means of, 144–45; America built on, 7, 17; in Colorado, 23–28; euphemisms for, 5, 39–40, 163; extent of, 5–6; need for reckoning with, 10, 14, 17, 30–31, 35, 172, 292–93; Ponca removal as exemplary of, 78; present-day, 6; psychological impacts of, 9; settlers' ignorance/forgetting/hiding/ justification of, 5–7, 39–40, 55, 109, 119, 170, 172, 284–85; settlers' opposition to, 24, 75–77, 109–25. *See also* land: government/ settler theft of; massacres of American Indians
Poe, Edgar Allan, 116
Point of Rocks Reserve, 26
Polis, Jared, 61
Ponca Relief Committee, 91, 96–99, 128
Ponca Reservation, 69–71
Poncas: allotment of land to, 129, 144–45; assimilation attempts for, 69, 159; bearing witness to history of, 88–106, 112; children

taken to boarding school, 150, 157; compensation for stolen land of, 125, 129–30; corn planting by, 1–3, 11–13, 288–89; government dealings with, 4–5, 67–79, 81–83, 85–86, 90–92, 99; history of, 3–5, 9, 66–86; in Indian Territory, 5, 81–84, 127–29; Jackson and, 120; Lakota attacks on, 67–71; land of, 3–4, 9, 11–14, 67–79, 93–94, 96–97, 116–17, 124–30, 144–45, 289–93; lectures tour on behalf of, 97–106, 110, 112–16, 126, 128; legal proceedings on behalf of, 92–96; refugees from Indian Territory, 84–86; removal to Indian Territory, 4–5, 72–86, 95; and the Tanderups, 2–3, 10–15, 66–67; termination and regaining of recognition, 145; Trail of Tears, 65, 79–81; truth and reconciliation effort involving, 12–15, 17
Ponca Treaty (1858), 4, 67–69
Ponca Treaty (1865), 69–70, 125
Poppleton, Andrew Jackson, 92, 112, 116
Prairie Flower, 80, 81
Pratt, Nora, 278
Pratt, Richard Henry, 141, 150–53, 155, 174
Pratt, Warren, 270
Prendergast, Terence, 169
Primavera, Diane, 62
Princeton Theological Seminary, 219
Princeton University, 219
The Problem of Administration (Meriam Report), 175–76
Putnam, Frederic, 131

Qisuk, 249
Quadrant (magazine), 195
Quakers, 173, 190, 238
Quapaws, 75, 81
Quinton, Amelia Stone, 142

Rabbit Proof Fence (film), 163
race theories, 245–46, 250
Read, Peter, 281
Real Rent Duwamish, 282–83

reconciliation: in Australia, 196–200; grassroots approaches to, 12–15, 66–67, 206–8,
268–74, 281–83; Indigenous attitudes
toward, 199–200; locally-based, 221, 229;
misguided attempts at, 188; skepticism
about, 188. See also truth and reconciliation
efforts
Reconciliation Rising (podcast), 157
Reconstruction, 89, 110
redress: for African Americans, 110; as
component of truth and reconciliation
process, 14–15, 110, 111, 117; for Indian
peoples, 112, 126; Jackson and, 123;
for Poncas, 129; principles of, 193–94;
Sand Creek Massacre as early instance
of, 50–51. See also compensation;
restitution
Red River War, 150
Reed, Matt, 255–56, 259
reformers and reform efforts: assimilation as
goal of, 102; betrayal of Indian's interests
by, 125, 142–43, 147, 158; boarding schools
as focus of, 149, 152; Indian behavior
as target of, 136–37, 147, 159–61; land as
focus of, 111, 124, 131, 140, 142, 146; lecture
tour aimed at, 97, 106; nineteenth-century,
109–10; social programs as focus of, 126,
131. See also allies of American Indians;
Fletcher, Alice Cunningham; Friends of
the Indian; Jackson, Helen Hunt; Tibbles,
Thomas
rehabilitation, 209–10, 212, 225
reparations. See compensation; redress
repatriation: of children removed from their
families, 186; of land, 12, 14, 268–74, 283,
285, 289–93; of sacred objects and burial
remains, 186, 234, 256–68
residential schools. See boarding schools
responsibility, of settlers for ancestors'
actions, 10, 13, 16–17, 171, 177, 195, 196,
199, 284
restitution: allotment as substitute for,
126, 129–31, 135, 140, 142; for Cheyennes

and Arapahos, 50–51; defined, 111, 209;
impossibility of, 210; of land in twenty-
first century, 273; nineteenth-century
opportunity for, 111, 125; opposition
to, 122, 126–27, 135; for Poncas, 111,
116–17, 124–27, 129–30, 140; under
Roosevelt administration, 176. See also
redress
restorative justice, 14, 116–17, 122, 193
Reynolds, Henry, 195, 211
Riding In, James, 236–37, 239–40, 245,
247–49, 251, 256
Riding In Hare, Dawna, 274
Rockefeller Foundation, 175
Rocky Mountain News (newspaper), 58,
95, 119
Rocky Mountain Synod, Evangelical
Lutheran Church in America, 283
Roe Cloud, Henry, 175
Roosevelt, Franklin, 176
Roosevelt, Theodore, 250
Roosevelt-Morris, Sky, 283
Rosebud Sioux, 133, 152
Ross, Daniel, 143
Rudd, Kevin, 192–93, 195, 198–99, 203, 212,
214, 223–24
Rwanda, 194

Sagwitch, 38
Sam, Bob, 156, 178
Sanborn, John, 50
Sand Creek Massacre, 29–34, 40–43, 47–54,
56–62, 83, 95, 117, 119, 246–48
Sand Creek Massacre National Historic
Site, 56, 59
Santa Fe Trail, 23
Santee Sioux, 2, 133, 157
satisfaction, from truth and reconciliation
efforts, 194, 217
Sawut, Nurgul, 254
scalping, 33–34, 40–41, 46, 48, 49, 104
schools. See boarding schools; education
Schurz, Carl, 119, 127, 143

Sea of Hands (Australia), 198

Second Great Awakening, 44

self-determination/self-government, Indigenous, 139, 176, 200, 212, 228–29

September 11th Victim Compensation Fund, 222–23

settler colonialism: aim of, 7–9, 96, 282; Indian allies' support of, 44, 123, 144, 147; narratives of, 37, 88, 239; need for reckoning with, 10, 17; of other nations, 8, 162; pressures on Indian peoples' from, 68, 98; truth and reconciliation efforts in context of, 123, 147, 193–94, 209–10, 229

settlers and settler mentality: as allies of Indian peoples, 88–89, 97, 109–47; in Colorado, 22–27; dispossession of Indian peoples as goal of, 8, 71, 78, 127; fear, hostility, and violence directed at Indian peoples, 25–30, 37–39, 46, 58, 89, 95, 104–5, 114, 127–28, 236–37, 239–40 (see also massacres of American Indians); identities of, 7–8; ignorance/forgetting/hiding/ justification of atrocities against Indigenous peoples, 5–7, 36, 39–40, 42, 55, 57–62, 109, 119, 147, 170, 172, 195–96, 203, 284–85; intergenerational effects on, 62, 196; Jackson's arguments in support of, 123; narratives told by, 5, 5–7, 9–10, 16, 21–22, 30–31, 34, 58–61, 64–65, 88, 114, 182, 254; need for reckoning with plunder of Indian peoples, 10, 14, 17, 30–31, 35, 169–72, 190, 292–93; opposition to plunder of Indian peoples, 75–77, 90–93, 109–25; our relationship to, 16–17; psychological case studies of, 43–48; shared history with Indian peoples, 67

Shapiro, Dan, 216–17

Sheridan, Philip, 63

Sherman, William Tecumseh, 70

Short-Colomb, Mélisande, 218–19

Shoshones, 36–39

Sinclair, Murray, 162, 167–70, 225, 228

Sioux, 120

Sioux City Journal (newspaper), 75, 76

Sitting Bull, 152

Sixties Scoop, 181, 193, 216–17

Skidis, 235

skulls, collection and study of American Indian, 246–49, 257–58

slavery, 8, 43–45, 121–22

Slough, John, 45

Smithsonian Institution, 247, 251, 252

Society of American Indians, 173, 175

Sogorea Te' Land Trust, 282

Soldierwolf, Yufna, 178

Sorosis, 131

Sorry Books (Australia), 197

Soule, Silas, 30, 40–48, 50–52, 54–55, 61, 262

South African Truth and Reconciliation Commission, 269

Southern Cheyennes, 26, 150

Special Subcommittee on Indian Education, 176

Spiritual Healing Run, 56–57, 61–62

Spotted Bear, Jodi Rave, 94

Spottedhorsechief, Adrian, 255, 258

Springer, Elizabeth, 155

Springer, John, 74–76

Squier, Charles, 51–52

Standing Bear, Chief: and allotment, 144; death of, 144; deaths of family members, 80, 82, 84, 103; on education, 144, 152; Indian policy challenged by, 89–96; lecture tour by, 88, 97–106, 109–10, 112–14, 120, 126, 131, 149, 158, 160, 176; life of, 69, 101; and removal to Indian Territory, 72–80, 82–86; and return of land, 93–94, 96–97, 116, 124–27, 133; visit to Carlisle boarding school, 150–51

Standing Buffalo, 130

Starita, Joe, 71, 84, 90, 95, 97

starvation: of Cheyennes and Arapahos, 24–25, 29, 31, 46; of Poncas, 5, 67, 68, 70–71, 76, 82; of Shoshones, 37; of Utes, 118–19

Stevenson, Bryan, 221

Stickney, William, 129

Stolen Generations, 181–83, 192–200, 210–12, 224, 281

Stott, Vicky, 189

Stowe, Harriet Beecher, 100, 151

St. Vrain, Ceran, 23

Svingen, Orlan, 243–44, 250

Tabor, Baby Doe, 21

Tanderup, Art, 1–5, 10–15, 17, 66–67, 80, 86, 288–93

Tanderup, Helen, 1–5, 10–15, 17, 66–67, 80, 86, 288–93

Tappan, Samuel, 48, 51–52

Teller, Henry, 118

termination, 145

Thayer, John, 237

theft. *See* plunder of American Indians

Thompson, Janna, 196, 208

Tibbles, Thomas, 90–106, 110, 112, 114–16, 120, 127–28, 131–34, 138–39, 144, 152, 160; *The Ponca Chiefs*, 124; *Standing Bear and the Ponca Chiefs*, 93–94

Torres Strait Islanders, 192, 197, 198

Toward Right Relationship with Native Peoples, 190

trauma: collective, 14; intergenerational, 9, 57, 62, 173, 187, 189; psychological effects of, 173; of survivors in truth and reconciliation process, 30, 87, 168, 210, 215–16

treaties: American Indians' use of, for challenging settlers' actions, 125; government violation of, 9, 68, 118, 123–24, 236; modern Indigenous demands for, 199–200; numbers of U.S. and British, 8

Treaty of Waitangi Tribunal, 205–6, 210

Trevorrow, Bruce, 212

Trimble, Chuck, 267, 270–72

Trope, Jack, 252

Trudeau, Justin, 225

Trump, Donald, 149

Truth, Racial Healing, and Transformation (TRHT), 189

Truth, Sojourner, 89

Truth and Healing Commission on Indian Boarding School Policy in the United States Act, 191

Truth and Reconciliation Commissions (TRCs), 14–15; Canada, 162, 167–71, 184–85, 202–3, 216–17, 228–29; Maine-Wabanaki, 184–86; South Africa, 269

truth and reconciliation efforts: application of van Boven/Bassiouni principles to, 193–94, 209–10, 228–29; in Australia, 181–83, 192–200, 210, 285–87; and boarding schools, 126, 167–79; bringing about change in, 261, 269, 281–82; in Canada, 162, 167–71, 193, 200–203, 210, 228–29; characteristics of successful, 283; and child removal policies, 179–87; compensatory social programs and, 126; components of, 15, 87, 110; Friends of the Indian and, 126–27, 129–30, 138–47; goals/outcomes of, 111, 285–93; grassroots approaches to, 288–93; growth in, 15; healing linked to, 187, 189; Indigenous peoples as leaders of, 188–90, 207; issues underlying, 14; lecture tour as early instance of, 110, 112, 158; misdirected, 126–27, 131, 142–43, 146–47, 158–61; in nineteenth century, 110–11, 125, 160–62; Pawnees and Welsch, 268–74, 281; for plunder of Indian peoples, 10–15, 30–31; Poncas and the Tanderups, 12–15, 66–67, 288–93; recommendations for, 227; retraumatization of survivors in, 30, 87, 168, 210, 215–16; role of apologies in, 208; Sand Creek Massacre investigations as early instance of, 48–51; skepticism about, 199, 203–4, 281; terminology concerning, 14; in twentieth century, 175; in the United States, 15–16, 87, 111, 171–72, 183, 188–89, 191, 204–8, 288–93. *See also* apologies; bearing witness; reconciliation; restitution tuberculosis, 153, 163

Tulsa Race Massacre, 220

Twain, Mark (Samuel Clemens), 100

Uighur population, 163–64, 253–54

Uluru Statement from the Heart, 287–88

Underground Railroad, 43

UNDRIP. *See* United Nations: Declaration on the Rights of Indigenous Peoples

Union Pacific Railroad, 238

United Nations: Convention on Genocide, 181; Declaration on the Rights of Indigenous Peoples (UNDRIP), 227–28; General Assembly, 193; Human Rights Commission, 193

University of Nebraska, 264, 270, 280

Unmarked Human Burial Sites and Skeletal Remains Protection Act, 263–64

U.S. Army: and Carlisle boarding school, 151, 171, 178; condemnation of Chivington by, 49, 52; indignities enacted on bodies of Indian peoples by, 178, 246–49, 252, 256; maltreatment of Indian peoples by, 113, 240; massacres conducted by, 38–39; Medical Museum, 246–49, 256; Pawnee service and betrayal, 237, 240, 256

U.S. Bill of Rights, 96

U.S. Congress: and child removal, 180; and Indian citizenship, 175; and investigation of Japanese American internment, 221–22; Joint Committee on the Conduct of War, 49; and land for Indian peoples, 135, 145; and 9/11 victims, 222–23

U.S. Constitution, 96

U.S. government: compensation from, 50, 222–23; failures and deceptions of, in dealing with Indian peoples, 25, 26, 29, 67–79, 81–83, 85–86, 90–92, 99, 104, 118–20, 122–23, 135, 144–45, 235–36

U.S. Senate, 103, 129; Select Committee, 124–25, 127

US War Department, 28

Utes, 22, 117–19

van Boven, Theo, 193–94

van Boven/Bassiouni principles, 193–94, 209, 212, 223–24, 227, 228–29

Virginia Theological Seminary, 219

Vision Maker Media, 94

Wabanaki federation, 183–86

Wabanaki REACH (Reconciliation, Engagement, Advocacy, Change, and Healing), 184–85

Wajapa, 133

Wallowing Bull, Dean, 57

War Bonnet, 41

Warren, Elizabeth, 190–91

Webster, John Lee, 92, 112

Weebach, Gail, 186

Welsch, Linda, 268–69, 272

Welsch, Roger, 234, 236, 241, 257, 260–62, 268–77, 279, 281, 289–90

Welsh, Herbert, 143

West, Elliott, 23

westward expansion, settler concept of, 5–7, 39, 58

Whipple, Henry, 121

White, Crawford, Sr., 178

White, Louellyn, 178–79

White Antelope, 33, 34, 41, 54

White Buffalo Girl, 80, 81

White Eagle, Chief, 5, 72, 75, 82, 112–13, 116, 124, 130

White Hawk, Sandy, 172, 186–89

White Shirt, Rebecca, 260

White's Manual Labor Institute, 173–74

white supremacy, 8, 15, 127, 160–62, 220

White Swan, 75

White Thunder, 23

White Thunder, Bobbie, 56, 57

white women: as advocates of assimilation, 152, 159; as allies of Indian peoples, 113, 121, 124, 130–31, 142–43, 158–59

Whittier, John Greenleaf, 100

Whose Settlement conference, 215–16, 224

Wichitas, 241, 248

Wilson, Dorothy Clarke, 98–99, 101, 115

Wilson, Ronald, 181, 193, 227

Windschuttle, Keith, 195

Winnebagos, 2, 120, 133, 141, 157, 256, 260

Wishart, David, 238

Wishcamper, Carol, 184–86

witness. *See* bearing witness

Wiyot people, 282–83

WNIA. *See* Women's National Indian Association

Wolf, Clifford, 157

Woman's Journal (newspaper), 102, 106

women. *See* white women

Women's National Indian Association (WNIA), 142–43, 159, 188

Works Progress Administration, 245

Wounded Knee Massacre, 35–36, 54

Wright, Larry, Jr., 9, 12–13, 66, 70, 86, 97, 157, 290

Wynkoop, Edward, 28–29, 40–42, 47–48, 50

Yale University, 219

Yellowhorse, Mose, 255

Yellow Woman, 23

Yothu Yindi, 199

Young, Brigham, 37

Yunupingu, Galarrwuy, 285–88

Zitkála-Šá (Gertrude Simmons), 154, 173–75; *American Indian Stories*, 174; *The Sun Dance Opera*, 175